PUBLIC SENTINELS

Public Sentinels

A Comparative Study of Australian Solicitors-General

Edited by

GABRIELLE APPLEBY
University of Adelaide, Australia

PATRICK KEYZER
Bond University, Australia

JOHN M. WILLIAMS
University of Adelaide, Australia

Routledge
Taylor & Francis Group
LONDON AND NEW YORK

First published 2014 by Ashgate Publishing

2 Park Square, Milton Park, Abingdon, Oxfordshire OX14 4RN
52 Vanderbilt Avenue, New York, NY 10017

Routledge is an imprint of the Taylor & Francis Group, an informa business

First issued in paperback 2020

British Library Cataloguing in Publication Data
A catalogue record for this book is available from the British Library

The Library of Congress has cataloged the printed edition as follows:
Public sentinels : a comparative study of Australian solicitors-general / by Gabrielle Appleby, Patrick Keyzer, John M. Williams.
pages cm
Includes bibliographical references and index.
ISBN 978-1-4094-5425-0 (hardback) 1. Attorneys general--Australia. 2. Attorneys general. I. Appleby, Gabrielle, editor of compilation. II. Keyzer, Patrick, 1966- editor of compilation. III. Williams, John (John Matthew), 1967- editor of compilation.
KU3428.P83 2014
345.94'01--dc23

2013023975

ISBN 978-1-4094-5425-0 (hbk)
ISBN 978-0-367-60093-8 (pbk)

Contents

PART III COMPARATIVE PERSPECTIVES

Notes on Contributors

Dr Gabrielle Appleby is a Senior Lecturer at the Adelaide Law School, University of Adelaide, South Australia. In 2012, she completed her PhD on 'The Constitutional Role of the Solicitor-General: An Historical, Legal and Lived Portrait', which was awarded the University Medal and the Bonython Prize. She received her LLM from the University of Melbourne in 2009 and her LLB (with first-class honours) from the University of Queensland in 2005. She researches in public and constitutional law, focussing on the accountability of the exercise of public power. She has published widely in these fields, including *Australian Public Law* (Oxford University Press, 2011) with Alexander Reilly, Laura Grenfell and Wendy Lacey, and *The Future of Australian Federalism: Comparative and Interdisciplinary Perspectives* (Cambridge University Press, 2012) with Nicholas Aroney and Thomas John.

Professor Harold Hastings Bruff is the Rosenbaum Professor of Law at the University of Colorado School of Law, where he was Dean from 1996 to 2003. He received his BA in American History from Williams College (Phi Beta Kappa) and his JD from Harvard Law School (magna cum laude). He has served in the Office of Legal Counsel in the United States Department of Justice, where he advised the Department of Justice, the White House and executive agencies on issues of constitutional and administrative law. He has testified before Congress many times, and has written several books and many articles on administrative law and separation of powers.

The Honourable Justice David Collins was appointed to the High Court of New Zealand on 16 March 2012. Prior to his appointment, he was Solicitor-General for New Zealand. In 1995 Dr Collins left the partnership now known as Rainey Collins to go to the Independent Bar. He appeared before the Privy Council and the Supreme Court of New Zealand on approximately 30 occasions and was appointed Queen's Counsel in 2000. Prior to his appointment as Solicitor-General Justice Collins was Chairman of the Accident Compensation Commission and Chairman of the Health Practitioners Disciplinary Tribunal. He was also an Executive Vice-President and member of the Board of Governors, World Association of Law and Medicine. Justice Collins has published a number of articles and was the author of *Medical Law in New Zealand* (Brooker and Friend, 1992). Justice Collins has been an honorary member of the Victoria University Law Faculty since 1992.

Dr Fiona Hanlon has worked in and around the Victorian public sector since the mid-1980s. She has worked in the office of the Victorian Government Solicitor and has held a number of senior management positions, including First Assistant Secretary of the Department of Premier and Cabinet and Deputy Secretary of the Department of Justice. She has extensive experience in the provision of high-level legal and policy advice and in representing government at a broad range of forums, including at the interstate and international intergovernmental level. She has worked as a bureaucrat for four Premiers, two Treasurers and three Attorneys-General. Since 2007, Dr Hanlon has been Principal of Serenus Thinking, an independent consultancy. She has B Juris and LLB degrees from Monash University and an LLM and PhD from the University of Melbourne. She was awarded her PhD for her thesis on the office of Attorney-General in Australia.

Martin Hinton QC is Solicitor-General of South Australia. He was appointed to that position in August 2008. Prior to that he was the Deputy Director of Public Prosecutions. He has undergraduate degrees from the University of Adelaide and has undertaken postgraduate study at the University of London. He is an Adjunct Professor of Law at the University of Adelaide.

Professor Patrick Keyzer is the Director of the Centre for Law, Governance and Public Policy at Bond University. A graduate in Arts and Law from the University of Sydney, Keyzer was Executive Associate to the Chief Justice of Australia, Sir Gerard Brennan, before completing a PhD on the topic of access to constitutional justice. Keyzer is a barrister who has appeared in a number of constitutional cases in the Australian High Court and has represented Australians in the United Nations Human Rights Committee. Keyzer co-wrote the Constitutional Law title for *Halsbury's Laws of Australia*, and his textbook and co-authored casebook on Australian constitutional law are prescribed or recommended in many Australian law schools.

Dr Klearchos A. Kyriakides is a Senior Lecturer in the School of Law of the University of Hertfordshire, a non-practising solicitor, a member of the Law Society of England and Wales and an executive committee member as well as past president of the West London Law Society. He has previously served as a Research Fellow of the Royal Air Force Staff College and as a tutor on strategic studies courses organised by the University of Cambridge for HM Forces. His publications include 'The Advisory Functions of the Attorney General' (2003. *Hertfordshire Law Journal*. Volume 1(1), 73–94), which was cited by Mr Justice Blake in *HM Treasury v The Information Commissioner & Anor* [2009] EWHC 1811 (Admin). He holds an LLB Hons (Law & Politics) degree from the University of Birmingham, together with MPhil (International Relations) and PhD (History) degrees from the University of Cambridge and a postgraduate diploma in Legal Practice from the University of Westminster.

The Honourable Sir Anthony Mason AC KBE QC was a Justice of the High Court of Australia from 1972 to 1987 and Chief Justice from 1987 to 1995. He was Commonwealth Solicitor-General from 1964 to 1969 and a judge of the New South Wales Court of Appeal from 1969 to 1972. Until recently, he was Chancellor of the University of New South Wales, National Fellow at the Research School of Social Sciences at the Australian National University (ANU), a judge of the Supreme Court of Fiji and President of the Solomon Islands Court of Appeal. In 1996–97 he was Arthur Goodhart Professor in Legal Science at Cambridge University. Since 2001 he has been Distinguished Visiting Fellow at the ANU College of Law. Sir Anthony has been a non-permanent judge of the Hong Kong Court of Final Appeal since 1997. Sir Anthony holds honorary doctorates from the Australian National University and Sydney, Melbourne, Monash, Griffith and Deakin Universities, the University of New South Wales and the Universities of Oxford and Hong Kong.

The Honourable Keith Mason AC QC holds undergraduate degrees from the University of Sydney (BA, LLB Hons I) and a Master of Laws from the University of London. In 2003 he was made a Companion of the Order of Australia, and in 2005 he received an honorary LLD from the University of Sydney. He was admitted to practice as a solicitor in 1970 and joined the Sydney Bar in 1972, where he practised in equity, commercial law and public law, with appearances before the High Court and Privy Council. In 1985 he was appointed Queen's Counsel. Between 1985 and 1987 he was the chairman of the New South Wales Law Reform Commission. In 1987 Mr Mason was appointed Solicitor-General for New South Wales, an office he held for 10 years. In 1997 he was appointed President of the New South Wales Court of Appeal, a position he retired from in 2008. Since 2008 he has been a Visiting Professorial Fellow at the University of New South Wales. He has published widely in the areas of judicial method, restitution, equity, succession, legal taxonomy and the rule of law.

M. Deborah MacNair is Corporate Counsel at the federal Department of Justice in Ottawa, Canada. Originally from the province of Nova Scotia, she is a graduate of Mount Allison University (BA Hons French Literature, 1974) and the University of New Brunswick (LLB, 1977). She was a member of the Nova Scotia Barristers' Society (December 1977 – June 2013) and is currently a member of the Law Society of Upper Canada (Ontario, 1997). Having received her diploma in Legislative Drafting in 1983, she then completed her masters in Law from the University of Ottawa in 2000. Deborah MacNair practised in the private sector in Nova Scotia and Alberta before joining the Privy Council Office in the federal government in 1983. Subsequently, she joined the federal Department of Justice in 1987. She has published numerous articles, mainly in relation to the ethical duties of government lawyers, and a book, *Conflicts of Interest: Principles for the Legal Profession* (Carswell, 2005).

Professor H.W. Perry, Jr (PhD, University of Michigan) has a joint appointment on the faculties of the School of Law and the Department of Government at the University of Texas at Austin. Prior to coming to Texas, he was on the faculty at Harvard University and at Washington University. He has held visiting lectureships abroad, including the Astor Visiting Lecturer, Centre for Socio-Legal Studies, Oxford University, and the Distinguished Visiting Professor at the Centre for Law, Governance and Public Policy, Bond University, Queensland. Perry's research interests focus on topics at the intersection of law and politics and on topics in constitutional law. His book *Deciding to Decide: Agenda Setting in the United States Supreme Court* (Harvard University Press, 1991) was awarded the Thomas J. Wilson Prize by Harvard University Press and the C. Herman Pritchett Award by the Law and Courts section of the American Political Science Association. He received the Wadsworth Publishing Award for a book 10 years old or older that has made a lasting impression on the field of law and courts. He is co-editor of *Civil Liberties and the Constitution: Cases and Commentaries* (Pearson, 9th edition, 2010). His articles appear in a variety of scholarly journals, law reviews and edited volumes.

Michael Sexton SC is a graduate of the law schools of the Universities of Melbourne and Virginia. He spent some years as an academic lawyer before taking up practice at the New South Wales Bar. Since 1998 he has been Solicitor-General for New South Wales. He is co-author of the Australian text on defamation law, *Defamation Law and Practice* (LexisNexis, looseleaf) and the author of several books on Australian politics and history. In the area of public administration he has been chairman of the New South Wales State Rail Authority and a board member of the New South Wales Public Transport Authority, the New South Wales State Library, the Sydney Writers' Festival and the University of Technology Council.

Professor John Williams is Dean of the Adelaide Law School at the University of Adelaide. His main research interest is public law and in particular Australian constitutional law, the High Court of Australia, comparative constitutional law, federalism and legal history.

Foreword

P.A. Keane[1]

From the time of Henry II, the 'royal justices were unashamedly the King's servants' (Turner 1985: 1–2); the close personal relationship between the justices and the King is attested by the fact that there are still extant the judges' notations on cases from about this time 'loquendum cum rege' (to be discussed with the King) (Turner 1985: 159). It seems likely that a similar personal relationship then existed between the King and office holders described as the King's Attorney and the King's Serjeant who had responsibility for representing the Crown's interests before the royal courts; and the post of King's Solicitor is also referred to in the early records. The office of Solicitor-General is first referred to by that description in 1515 (Edwards 1964: 3).

As the executive, legislative and judicial powers of government began to become identifiable as separate manifestations of sovereign authority within the structure of government in England and Wales, so the tensions implicit in an office which combined personal responsibility to advise and represent the Crown, political responsibilities as a Member of Parliament, and the professional duties of an officer of the Court emerged. These tensions were not merely theoretical; they were capable of entangling even the most brilliant lawyer. That this was so can be seen from the experiences of Sir Isaac Isaacs, when, as Solicitor-General for Victoria and a member of the State's Cabinet, his insistence on prosecuting individuals involved in the collapse of the Mercantile Bank led to his removal from the Cabinet.

In Australia, the Solicitors-General are now invariably not politicians but professional lawyers of some eminence and repute with many years of experience in the litigation of issues of public law. The most familiar of their roles is the argument, on behalf of the executive government of their respective polities, of the most important cases affecting the interests of the government and the governed and between the governments of the federation in the highest courts of the land. No less important, however, are the duties performed by these officers in ensuring the observance of the rule of law by advice given to the governments they serve on issues of constitutional, administrative and even commercial law. The importance of both these roles is neatly encapsulated in the title chosen for this volume: 'Public Sentinels'.

1 Justice of the High Court of Australia, former Chief Justice of the Federal Court of Australia, Justice of the Queensland Court of Appeal and Solicitor-General of Queensland.

As Dr Gabrielle Appleby and Professor John M. Williams explain in their introduction to the chapters, the most significant departure from the English model, in terms of the evolution in Australia of the office of the Solicitor-General as the second Law Officer, has been the depoliticisation of that office and the emergence of a predominant professional ethos in which the values of frank and fearless advice to governments and the barrister's duty as an officer of the court to the administration of justice have largely removed the office from the concerns of party politics.

The various countries of the tradition of the common law have approached the resolution of the tensions implicit in the office as it emerged in modern times in different ways. A comparative perspective on the modern evolution of the office in the countries of the common law inheritance is afforded by the chapters written by Justice David Collins, Professor H.W. Perry Jr, Professor Harold Bruff, Dr Klearchos A. Kyriakides and M. Deborah MacNair.

These chapters usefully serve to highlight the importance of the internal role of Solicitors-General to the rule of law in the modern anglophone democracies. I shall return to this aspect of the role of Australian Solicitors-General after first discussing their responsibilities for litigation on behalf of government.

The most public aspect of the work of the Solicitors-General in Australia is the representation of government in the superior courts, and especially in the High Court, where conflicts within the federal compact fall to be resolved. Section 78A of the *Judiciary Act 1903* (Cth) provides that the Attorneys-General of the Commonwealth, States and Territories may intervene in proceedings pending before the High Court or any other federal court or any court of a State or Territory that relate to a matter arising under the Constitution or involving its interpretation. This right is usually exercised on behalf of the Attorney-General of any given polity within the federation by the Solicitor-General of that polity. Further, it is usually on the advice of the Solicitor-General that the decision to intervene is made by the Attorney-General.

Section 78A creates an exception to the usual rule excluding non-parties from participating in litigation. It recognises that the litigation of issues which arise under the Constitution or involve its interpretation may have ramifications for the rights and obligations of the constituent parts of the federation and its citizens; and it ensures that the deliberations of the Court are informed by considerations of public interest rather than solely by arguments focused on the private interests of the parties.

Professor Patrick Keyzer's chapter provides an insightful, albeit controversial, examination of this aspect of the role of the Solicitors-General. In discussing public interest and interventions, he argues for an extension of the right of intervention to a broader range of advocates for the public interests, contending that 'after all, the courts are open to anyone who wants to participate'. This suggestion reveals, I think, a view of the courts as a forum for the discussion of matters of public interest by anyone with a point of view that he or she would like to share with the rest of the citizenry. That is not yet an accepted view of the role of the courts. Keyzer goes on to develop his point as to the desirability of expanding rights of intervention by reference to, among other things, the development by the High Court over the last 20 years of principles relating to freedom of political information and the institutional integrity of the courts.

Insofar as broader rights of intervention are said to be justified by the need to ensure that the broader public interest is considered, the representatives of elected governments might be thought to have a stronger claim to speak for the public interest than self-appointed guardians of the public interest. There is an internal contradiction in the proposition that those who advocate for an avowedly minority position speak for the public interest – unless, of course, the suggestion is that the public interest is in ensuring that minority voices are heard. That suggestion involves a view of the function of the judiciary in which the quelling of controversies is not of central importance. That view does not sit comfortably with the received view or, for that matter, with the separation of powers generally.

Further, while it may be that rights of those who seek to advocate minority views in constitutional cases would be advanced by the abolition of standing requirements, concerns about the costs and delays imposed on the parties by untrammelled rights of intervention, which have held sway until now, cannot be dismissed lightly.

And in any event, the history of the development of the implied freedom of political communication and of notions of the institutional integrity of courts hardly presents compelling evidence of the law being skewed against minorities in favour of elected governments and the majorities who elect them. The history of these developments may fairly be said to have been of a series of rebuffs to arguments presented by the representatives of elected governments.

Finally on this point, it may well be that the benefits expected from an expansion of the right to intervene will be obtainable by the further development by the High Court of its practice in relation to the grant of leave to amici curiae to make submissions in any given case (Walker 2011). The High Court's control of the development of its practice in relation to the grant of leave to amici enables it to limit the extent of non-party involvement to what is practically useful while avoiding the fiction that the amicus is representing the public, as opposed to a sectional, interest.

There can be no doubt that the most professionally satisfying part of the role of the Second Law Officers in Australia is representing the public interest (in its federal, State or Territory emanation) in cases in the High Court and the superior courts. If I might claim the indulgence of seeking to explain that comment, I would say immediately that I doubt that it has much to do with a Napoleonic ambition to shape the constitutional development of the nation.

In Australia's constitutional evolution, only Commonwealth Solicitor-General Sir Maurice Byers QC could truly be said to have earned the tribute paid to him by Sir Gerard Brennan on the occasion of Sir Gerard's retirement as Chief Justice of the High Court. Sir Gerard said of Sir Maurice: 'His participation in the work of this Court was perhaps no less on his side of the Bar table than it would have been on this' (Retirement of Chief Justice Sir Gerard Brennan (1998) 193 CLR v: vi).

Rather, the great satisfaction to be derived from advocacy as a Solicitor-General derives from being able to marshal one's professional skills in the service of the communities which comprise the federation. It is a great privilege for any advocate to be able to speak in court for one's client: the ancient Athenians, for example, did not allow professional advocates in their courts of law. It is a privilege for any advocate to be permitted to speak in court on behalf of another person, but it is quite an extraordinary privilege to be able to speak in the nation's highest courts to advance or defend the interests of millions of one's fellow citizens.

The sense of that responsibility has furnished the occasion and the motivation for some of the most memorable pieces of advocacy ever seen in the High Court. In *Capital Duplicators Pty Ltd v Australian Capital Territory (No 2)* (1993) 178 CLR 561, one of the last of the great cases concerning the much disputed limitation on State power in s 90 of the Constitution, John Doyle QC, Solicitor-General for the State of South Australia, presented a powerful argument in favour of the narrow view of that limitation. (Much of his argument may be found recorded at 569–74 of the Commonwealth Law Reports.) What the record of his argument does not reveal is the epic exchange between Mr Doyle QC and Deane J.

Sir William Deane was rightly feared by all counsel as the most deft of judges in exposing, by a few well-directed questions, the flaw in counsel's case. He would lure even the most wary of counsel out into the 'no-man's-land' of the case and then reduce him (and in those days it was usually 'him') to incoherent mumbling. On informal occasions, Wilson J used to provide kindly advice to young barristers: 'When my brother Deane asks you a question, always answer "No!"'.

During the course of the argument in *Capital Duplicators (No 2)*, over an extended period, Sir William challenged Mr Doyle again and again, but the responses Mr Doyle made to each question were so crisp, brisk and compelling that Sir William brought the exchange to a close, saying that he had pressed Mr Doyle so far only because of the strength of Mr Doyle's arguments, and that he did not intend to press him further. It was the only occasion in the experience of those at the Bar table that Sir William did not have the last word in an exchange with counsel.

I turn now to mention briefly the importance of the less public duties of the Solicitor-General. The evolution of the office in Australia as a professional, depoliticised office means that the office affords a level of non-judicial legal control of administrative action within the executive branch of government. This level of non-judicial legal control assists in ensuring integrity in governmental decision-making vis-à-vis the citizenry and coherence in government between governmental agencies where there are conflicting views as to the legal basis for governmental action (McMillan 2010). In this regard, the advisory role of the Solicitor-General can have an effect similar to, but even more direct and immediate than, the role performed by Ombudsmen and Integrity Commissioners.

The performance of this aspect of the duties of the office can entail, as the chapters by Sir Anthony Mason, M.G. Hinton QC, Michael Sexton SC and Dr

Gabrielle Appleby demonstrate, the exercise of a non-judicial responsibility to ensure legality in governmental decision-making.

These chapters afford a valuable corrective to the familiar focus on judicial review as virtually the sole guarantor of the legality and accountability of administrative action. Together, they make the important point that, in the age of the regulatory state, the integrity and quality of administrative decision-making is also supported by arrangements within the executive government which also include systems of internal merits reviews (as well as external merits reviews by other non-judicial agencies). And last, but not least, we should also keep it in mind that our communities are served by a professional civil service whose members are drawn from, and are (in a broad sense) representatives of, the communities it serves.

The focus of most judicial discussion, including extra-curial discussion in speeches and essays by judges, and the principal focus of academic discussion of legal control of administrative decision-making, is on judicial review, and the role of the courts as the third branch of government as guarantor of the rule of law and the integrity and quality of administrative decision-making.

The collection of essays in *Public Sentinels* performs an important service by providing an overdue examination of the contribution of the office of Solicitor-General to what former Chief Justice of the New South Wales Supreme Court James Spigelman has called the integrity branch of government (Spigelman 2004).

References

Edwards, J.Ll.J. 1964. *The Law Officers of the Crown: A Study of the Offices of the Attorney-General and Solicitor-General of England with an Account of the Office of the Director of Public Prosecutions of England.* London: Sweet & Maxwell.

McMillan, J. 2010. Re-Thinking the Separation of Powers. *Federal Law Review*. Volume 38(3), 423.

Spigelman, J.J. 2004. *The Integrity Branch of Government*. Australian Institute of Administrative Law (AIAL) Forum.

Turner, R.V. 1985. *The English Judiciary in the Age of Glanville and Bracton.* Cambridge: Cambridge University Press.

Walker, K. 2011. Amici Curiae and Access to Constitutional Justice: A Practical Perspective. *Bond Law Review*. Volume 22, 111.

Preface

This book is the germination of a seed that was planted separately in each of our minds that eventually brought us together: why is there no scholarship on the Australian Solicitor-General? Many of the themes and questions that the individual chapters address were raised at a Symposium on the role of the Solicitor-General held at Bond University in April 2011, hosted by the Centre for Law, Governance and Public Policy. The Symposium brought together many serving and former Solicitors-General from Australia and New Zealand and it was there, during an animated discussion over a boardroom table about what the Solicitor-General's role would be in the event of intragovernmental litigation, that the pressing need for this volume became apparent to us. As with all edited collections, this volume owes its breadth and depth to the contributors who very kindly agreed to sacrifice their time and thoughts to write a chapter for the collection. We thank them all.

In the various jurisdictions that are discussed in this volume, different norms have emerged for the hyphenation of the offices of Attorney-General and Solicitor-General. In Australia and New Zealand, the norm is to hyphenate. The *Law Officers Act 1964* (Cth), for example, states that '[t]here shall be a Solicitor-General of the Commonwealth'. However, this is not the case in the United Kingdom, the United States or Canada, where the established norm is no longer to hyphenate the names of these offices. This is a relatively recent development. For instance, when the office of US Attorney General was created in the *Judiciary Act of 1789* (US), it stated that 'there shall also be appointed a meet person, learned in the law, to act as attorney-general for the United States'. Today, the *US Code* provides that '[t]he President shall appoint … an Attorney General of the United States'. In deference to these historical anomalies, throughout this volume the editors have decided to maintain the different norms across the jurisdictions.

Gabrielle would like to thank Scott for gracefully, as ever, putting up with 'another project' that has occupied her time and mind.

Patrick would like to thank Sian Daniel and Mairead Courtney for co-ordinating the Symposium of Solicitors-General and Catherine Karcher for research and proofreading assistance.

John would like to thank his co-editors for their camaraderie and assistance throughout this project. He would also like to thank Wendy and Maaike for their ceaseless support.

Gabrielle Appleby, Patrick Keyzer, John M. Williams
December 2013

Introduction
Public Sentinels

Gabrielle Appleby and John M. Williams

Introduction

In Australia, the Solicitor-General is the chief legal adviser to government on constitutional and significant legal issues and the primary advocate for government interests in the High Court. Despite recent controversy around the role of top government lawyers in the United States and the United Kingdom, Australia's key 'public sentinels' have remained largely out of the public eye. This collection of chapters, written by current and former Australian Solicitors-General together with Australian and international scholars, will focus on this greatly understudied office. In doing so, it will address the question of the proper role of the office of Solicitor-General in the Australian constitutional system. The collection combines historical, theoretical, practical and comparative perspectives on this little known, but fundamentally important, office at a time when the transparency and accountability of government is a growing concern. As well as focussing on the office, this collection aims to deepen our understanding of constitutional norms and the role key actors play in their maintenance and development.

This chapter introduces the Australian office of Solicitor-General and equivalent offices in New Zealand, the United States, the United Kingdom and Canada. It will also provide an introduction to, and context for, the chapters that follow in the collection.

Evolution of the Modern Incidents of the Australian Solicitor-General

The first 'Law Officers' were appointed by the King in medieval England to represent his interests before the royal courts. These officers evolved into the modern Law Officers of England and Wales. Today in England, the Attorney-General and Solicitor-General are both parliamentary Ministers who advise but do not sit in the Cabinet.

The role of the Solicitor-General in Australia, after decades of remoulding and change, has stabilised. Despite its provenance in the English office, as with so many Australian institutions, the Australian office of Solicitor-General was modified to accommodate the unique Australian conditions. In Chapter 1 of the collection, former New South Wales Solicitor-General from 1987 to 1997 Keith Mason provides a brief history of Australian Solicitors-General and notes that the journey to what is now professional orthodoxy was not without the colour befitting colonial Australia.

It may have been intended – by the English Colonial Office and the colonists themselves – that the Australian offices of Attorney-General and Solicitor-General would mirror those found in the 'Mother Country'. However, adaptations were necessary to accommodate the exigencies of the local colonial circumstances and, more often, the sometimes erratic personalities of the early colonial Law Officers, Governors, judges, barristers and politicians. And personalities there were. Very few high legal offices can claim alumni that include megalomaniacs, criminals, murderers, duellers and one father of no less than *18* children amongst its ranks.

The origin of the Australian office of Attorney-General and deputy, the Solicitor-General, lies in a recommendation of Thomas Bigge (1823) in influential *Report of the Commissioner of Inquiry on the Judicial Establishments of New South Wales and Van Diemen's Land.* Bigge was scathing in his criticism of the role of the colonial Judge-Advocate – who at that time performed the role of judge, prosecutor and legal adviser to the Governor.

In Australia, one of the most significant departures from the English model of the Law Officers occurred when responsible government was brought to the colonies in the mid-1850s. This constitutional maturation meant that the colonial Law Officers were often ministerial officers in the new Parliaments, were often included in the Executive Council, and would later become members of the Cabinet. This politicisation of the Law Officers manifested itself dramatically in the Attorney-General, as the more senior of the Law Officers. This situation would, over the course of 50 years, eventually lead to the depoliticisation and professionalisation of the Solicitor-General. The non-political, professional Solicitor-General was able to assist the Attorney-General in his (and much later, her) legal services responsibilities.

By the late 1980s all Australian jurisdictions[1] had adopted the 'modern' model of the Solicitor-General. This model is defined by a number of critical incidents. The first is the statutory basis for the role – legislation now defines the term, tenure and functions of the Solicitor-General.[2]

The second incident is the specialised and professional nature of the role – free from the administrative burdens of running the Crown Law office and able to perform, predominantly, the role of counsel. The professionalisation of the role is a significant departure from the position adopted throughout the predominance of the twentieth century and now is a fundamental point of distinction between

---

1 With the exception of the Australian Capital Territory, which adopted a modified version of the model in 2011.

2 The various statutes that now establish and define these dimensions of the role are: *Law Officers Act 1964* (Cth); *Solicitor General Act 1985* (Qld); *Solicitor General Act 1969* (NSW); *Solicitor-General Act 1972* (SA); *Solicitor-General Act 1983* (Tas); *Attorney-General and Solicitor-General Act 1972* (Vic); *Solicitor-General Act 1969* (WA); *Law Officers Act 1978* (NT); *Law Officers Act 2011* (ACT).

the Australian offices and the New Zealand Solicitor-General. The only exception to this position is the Australian Capital Territory. In this smaller jurisdiction, the Solicitor-General may be directed by the Attorney-General to exercise the functions of the Chief Solicitor of the Australian Capital Territory, making the role more analogous to the New Zealand position.

The third incident is the constitutional and public law focus of the role. The creation of a statutory, independent office of Director of Public Prosecutions across the Australian jurisdictions in the 1980s and 1990s has meant that this specialist office now takes responsibility for the commencement and maintenance of criminal prosecutions – relieving the Solicitor-General from this increasingly specialist and often politically charged role. Freed of the prosecutorial function, the way was open for the Solicitor-General to develop a monopoly on constitutional and public law litigation.

The fourth incident is the withdrawal of the Solicitor-General's right to private practice, which was often controversial after it caused a number of embarrassing incidents for colonial Law Officers. In Queensland and Western Australia the right has been reintroduced (in Queensland in 1989, in Western Australia in 2012). In making this change, the government argued that the right was reintroduced to 'attract the most capable counsel' to the position (Queensland Parliamentary Debates 1985: 4098).

The Modern Role: 'Counsel for the Crown'

What, then, does the 'modern role' mean for the Solicitor-General's relationship with the Crown? As noted, the Australian Solicitor-General has evolved from the British tradition of parliamentary Law Officer to an independent statutory office charged with acting as 'counsel for the Crown'. The statutes that establish the Solicitor-General in each jurisdiction are remarkably similar – although, as already seen, there are unique dimensions in some jurisdictions. In this section, we introduce the statutory framework that establishes the functions, client and appointment conditions of the office.

Functions and Relationship with the Attorney-General

Undoubtedly, acting as counsel to government is the core function of the Solicitor-General, although there is no guarantee that the Solicitor-General will receive any particular *type* of legal work from the Crown – a position that stands in direct contrast to that which exists in the United States.

Some statutes (those in Queensland, South Australia and the Australian Capital Territory) require that the Solicitor-General act as counsel *at the request of the Attorney-General*, emphasising the Attorney-General's primary responsibility for government legal services and the relationship between the two Law Officers. Such an approach highlights the historic responsible government notions of accountability. At the Commonwealth level, the Solicitor-General acts as counsel for the Crown but may only 'furnish his or her opinion to the Attorney-General on questions of law referred to him or her by the Attorney-General'. The Commonwealth Act would therefore seem to separate the two functions – to act as an advocate (to the Crown at large) and to furnish advice (to the Attorney-General only) (*Law Officers Act 1964* (Cth): s 12).

Further, Solicitors-General across the jurisdictions may also perform other acts as counsel as the Attorney-General requests and can also have functions bestowed on the office through other pieces of legislation. At the Commonwealth level, for example, the Solicitor-General is vested with power to make an application for a declaration that a person is a vexatious litigant in the Industrial Relations Court (*Industrial Relations Court Rules* (Cth): O 21, Div 3, Rule 1) and in the High Court (*High Court Rules 2004* (Cth): rule 6.06). Under the Commonwealth, New South Wales, Tasmanian and Western Australian legislation, the Attorney-General can delegate certain powers to the Solicitor-General.

In New South Wales the relationship between the Solicitor-General and the Attorney-General is the most similar to that seen in colonial times. The Solicitor-General may 'exercise and discharge any powers, authorities, duties and functions conferred or imposed on the Attorney-General by or under any Act or incident by law to the office of the Attorney-General' in the event the senior Law Officer is absent or ill, or the office is vacant (*Solicitor-General Act 1969* (NSW): s 3(1)(b)).

Client

The Solicitor-General's 'client' is a matter that is expressed in a number of different ways in the statutes – although with little significance in practice. In most jurisdictions the legislation states that the Solicitor-General acts as counsel for the Crown. Many government entities and agencies fall within the often elusive concept of the Crown. However, the Attorney-General has been recognised as its only appropriate legal representative (*Kidman v Commonwealth* (1925) 37 CLR 233, 239–40 (Knox CJ); 243 (Isaacs J); Selway 1999: 115; New South Wales Law Reform Commission 1998: [3.17]). This means that while the client of the Solicitor-General may be the Crown (at least in theory), the proper instructor for the Solicitor-General remains the Attorney-General, emphasising the historical and ongoing relationship between the Law Officers. Further emphasising this relationship, some jurisdictions expressly state that the Solicitor-General acts only at the request of the Attorney-General.

By far the most prescriptive jurisdiction is the Commonwealth. Under the Commonwealth statute, the Solicitor-General can act as counsel for a long list of clients: the Crown in right of the Commonwealth, the Commonwealth, a person suing or being sued on behalf of the Commonwealth, a Minister, an officer of the Commonwealth, a person holding office under an Act or a law of a Territory, a body established by an Act or a law of a Territory, or any other person or body for whom the Attorney-General requests him or her to act. Unlike the States, this enumerated list, while it contains significant overlap, allows the Solicitor-General to receive instructions from a number of government entities, not just the Attorney-General as the traditional representative of the Crown. However, under the Commonwealth statute the Solicitor-General can only *furnish advice* to the Attorney-General. The statutory distinction between acting as counsel and furnishing advice is perplexing, as in practice it is a distinction without a difference.

The statutes leave largely unanswered a number of difficult questions surrounding the identity of the Solicitor-General's client and the potential for conflicts of interest to arise for an officeholder. While in theory the 'Crown' is indivisible (and therefore the Solicitor-General can, in theory, have *no* conflicts of interest), in practice the Crown is multi-faceted, increasingly divided and therefore, on occasion, will come into conflict with itself. A Solicitor-General can be confronted with the prospect of being requested to act for conflicting dimensions of the Crown. With increased competition in the provision of government legal services and rivalry between government departments and agencies, this remains one of the more challenging aspects of the office.

A notable example of this is when the Queen's representative (the Governor-General, Governor or Administrator) seeks the advice of the Solicitor-General on the exercise of the reserve powers – powers that, by their very nature, may be exercised against the interests of the incumbent ministry (and therefore the Attorney-General to whom the Solicitor-General maintains a direct line of responsibility). Other difficulties arise if the Solicitor-General is asked to advise an agency that has statutorily directed objectives that require it to act independently of the Crown and sometimes in direct conflict with the Crown's interests (for example, executive regulatory and accountability agencies).

In Chapter 4 of this collection, New South Wales Solicitor-General Michael Sexton considers the relationship between Solicitors-General and holders of a vice regal office. The relationship is generally extremely secretive – Sexton compares writing the chapter to 'working on an unauthorised history of the security services'. What his chapter reveals is that the legal position is unclear in many of the jurisdictions where the Solicitor-General is statutorily mandated to act for the 'Crown'. In practice, however, it would appear that, with some notable exceptions, the government facilitates, and even encourages, the vice regal representative to access the Solicitor-General.[3] Doing so achieves many objectives of the rule of law but also ensures from the government's perspective that the vice regal representative is not getting advice elsewhere.

3 The most notable of the exceptions was Prime Minister Gough Whitlam's refusal to allow the Governor-General, John Kerr, to access directly the Solicitor-General Maurice Byers in 1975 for advice on events that eventually led Kerr to dismiss the Prime Minister.

Appointment, Tenure and Remuneration

Turning to the office itself, the Solicitor-General's appointment, tenure and remuneration differ across the jurisdictions – providing differing levels of incentives to take the position and security (and therefore potentially protection of independence) in the position. The diversity in the statutory frameworks reflects the natural diversity consistent with a federal system. That said, the subtle distinctions could be seen as unusual given the relative uniformity in the statutory functions of the office.

Solicitors-General are appointed by the Executive – at the Commonwealth level by the Governor-General and in the States by the Governor. In the Commonwealth and Victoria, the more recent appointments have been preceded by a public advertisement of the position and a formal, merits-based process with a selection panel. The other jurisdictions continue to use a closed process that closely mirrors the system used in judicial appointments. Under the Commonwealth, New South Wales, Queensland, Western Australian and the Australian Capital Territory legislation, appointment is for a limited term of between five and 10 years, although individuals can be reappointed. In South Australia, Victoria, Tasmania and the Northern Territory, appointment can be for an unlimited term (although the practice in Victoria is for an individual to be appointed for a 10-year term).

To be qualified for appointment, most jurisdictions require an individual to be a legal practitioner of a number of years' standing – similar to qualifications for appointment to the bench. In Queensland the appointee *must* be a barrister and in Victoria the appointee *must* be Senior Counsel. The practice has been across the jurisdictions for appointees to be silks – the first Commonwealth Solicitor-General appointed under the *Law Officers Act 1964*, Anthony Mason, took silk in a special sitting prior to his appointment in 1964 (Appleby 2012: 265–6); and the same occurred for Mary Gaudron before she was appointed New South Wales Solicitor-General in 1981 (Burton 2010: 184).

Most of the statutes provide the Solicitor-General with security of tenure to a greater or lesser degree. Though, as will be noted, the formal security of tenure does not supplant the individual officeholder's view of their independence. In the Commonwealth and the Northern Territory the Governor-General or Administrator 'shall remove the Solicitor-General from office' in the event of incapacity (except by reason of temporary illness), misbehaviour or bankruptcy/insolvency. In South Australian and Western Australia the Governor *may* remove the Solicitor-General on similar grounds, implying a greater level of discretion. Queensland and the Australian Capital Territory combine the two mechanisms. In Queensland the Governor-in-Council *may* remove the Solicitor-General for misbehaviour or incapacity but *shall* remove the Solicitor-General if the Solicitor-General becomes bankrupt, is absent from duty or contravenes the conditions of the office's right to private practice. In Tasmania even stronger tenure is guaranteed, mirroring that afforded to the judiciary. The Governor can only remove the Solicitor-General after receiving resolutions requesting the removal from both Houses of Parliament.

New South Wales and Victoria provide for discretionary removal mechanisms, analogous to appointment at pleasure that defined the colonial office.

Solicitors-General are remunerated on a number of different bases. These combine facets of the remuneration of public servants, statutory officeholders, politicians and the judiciary. They demonstrate the difficulty in classifying the Solicitor-General: not a public servant; not a judge; no longer a politician. Under the Commonwealth, New South Wales, Western Australian and the Australian Capital Territory legislation, the salaries and pension or superannuation entitlements of the Solicitor-General are determined by an independent remuneration tribunal. In South Australia the remuneration is set by the Governor and in the Northern Territory by the Administrator. In Tasmania and Victoria the office is given the salary of a puisne judge of the Supreme Court. In New South Wales, South Australia, Victoria and the Northern Territory the Solicitor-General is entitled to a judicial pension. In Tasmania the public sector superannuation scheme applies to the position.

The anomalous jurisdiction in terms of remuneration is Queensland. In Queensland the position receives the salary of 80 per cent of a Supreme Court judge. This reflects the intention of the Queensland Parliament when establishing the office that the appointee would retain the right to private practice (the Queensland Solicitor-General continues to retain this right to this day). As such, the Queensland Solicitor-General would be expected to do less work than the 'full-time' Solicitors-General in other States. Queensland is not the only State to have contemplated private practice by the Solicitor-General. Only in Victoria is private practice completely prohibited, while only remunerated private practice is prohibited in New South Wales. In the other jurisdictions, as in Queensland, remunerated employment is allowed with the consent of the Attorney-General, Governor or Governor-in-Council. In Western Australia in 2012, this consent was given to entice a leading private barrister to accept the appointment.

History demonstrates that Solicitors-General are often appointed to the bench. Many of the statutes make provision for the appointment of a Solicitor-General to the bench by counting time served as Solicitor-General towards the period of service as a judge for pension entitlement purposes.

The Advisory Function

By far the most critical role of the Solicitor-General is as 'counsel for the Crown'. Absent a contrary judiciary ruling, the Solicitor-General's advice is often the final word on the legality of any policy or administrative action of government. The office is thus *central* to the regulation of public power in Australia, a theme this collection has sought to highlight. The Solicitor-General provides an important conduit between the federal judiciary and executive branches in a system where there is a strict separation of powers between the two. The office's role ensures that the Executive's interests and views are represented in all constitutional matters that fall for decision in a court. Thus the Solicitor-General performs a unique function, both ensuring the integrity of the exercise of government power and defending it before the Court. The centrality and uniqueness of the office emphasises the need for the study conducted in this volume.

The assurance that the Executive will act in accordance with law is fundamental to the proper working of our system. In accordance with this precept, the existence of a legal office that is beyond reproach is essential to the operation of government of the rule of law. In Australia, the High Court has held that the courts must be involved only in legal controversy: it is not their role to issue advisory opinions to assist governments in matters that have not yet, or may not, come before the courts (*In Re Judiciary and Navigation Acts* (1921) 29 CLR 257). Rather, the government relies on legal advisers to assist them in day-to-day governance and policy formation. The role of executive legal adviser is filled by a vast number of government legal professionals, at whose apex in each Australian jurisdiction sits the office of the Solicitor-General. It is in this context that the additional role of integrity agent is vested in the Solicitor-General.

In Chapter 3 of the collection, South Australian Solicitor-General M.G. Hinton explores the relationship between the Solicitor-General and the Executive through the prism of the relationship between the Solicitor-General and the Attorney-General. Hinton argues that, in a strict sense, the Australian Solicitor-General is not *secundarius attornatus* and does not stand in the place of the Attorney-General (perhaps with the exception of the position in New South Wales). However, he argues that the Solicitor-General is *secundarius attornatus* in ‘a very real sense’ deriving from the relationship between the Attorney-General and the Solicitor-General. The Solicitor-General is the principal legal adviser to the Attorney-General, who in the Australian system is solely responsible for legal advice to government and for all litigation in which the government is a party. The Solicitor-General must perform his or her function minded of the Attorney-General’s obligations to the law as well as to broader concepts such as the rule of law and a liberal democracy.

Ready access to lawyers and legal advice is fundamental to good government. As Mason and Wilson JJ said in *Waterford v Commonwealth* (1987) 163 CLR 54 (at 62):

> To our minds it is clearly in the public interest that those in government who bear the responsibility of making decisions should have free and ready confidential access to their legal advisers.

The importance of the Solicitor-General’s advisory function to the government is underscored by what is known as the ‘Law Officer’s Convention’. The Convention developed in the United Kingdom. It describes the practice whereby the government may resist calls from the Parliament for the production of the Law Officers’ opinions (Edwards 1964: 256–61). In Australia, there have been few instances that have required the government to invoke the Convention. One exception was in 2007, when Victorian Solicitor-General Pamela Tate was called to give evidence and produce documents (including her opinions) to a Select Committee of the Legislative Council. She responded robustly (Tate 2007), drawing on the Law Officers' Convention as well as on the government's claim of executive privilege over the documents:

> The integrity of my role as the second Law Officer of the Crown is dependent upon my capacity to maintain the confidentiality of the instructions and information given to me for the purpose of securing my advice. Unless the Crown is able to confide in me in a full and free manner, and, in turn, I am able to advise the Crown fully and freely on its legal rights and obligations, the performance of my functions as Solicitor-General would be compromised. I could not provide proper or adequate advice to the highest levels of government on matters of State if I could not discharge my obligation to maintain the confidentiality of all the instructions and information provided to me for the purpose of obtaining my advice. … Executive privilege has been asserted by the Crown over those documents. It is my obligation not to act inconsistently with the Crown's assertion of privilege.

Tate's position accorded with the position taken in an earlier episode in 1975 when Commonwealth Solicitor-General Maurice Byers had been called before the Bar of the Senate. It is this episode that former Commonwealth Solicitor-General and High Court Chief Justice Anthony Mason considers in Chapter 2 of this collection. The episode occurred in the context of the 'Loans Affair', a scandal that would contribute to the Governor-General, John Kerr dismissing the Commonwealth Labor government led by Prime Minister Gough Whitlam.

The Affair began when the government sought to obtain, eventually without success, financial loans from the Middle East without the consent of the Loans Council on the basis that the loans were 'for temporary purposes'. When details of the loan negotiations came to light, the Opposition used them, and other scandals plaguing the government, as the basis for refusing to pass the government's supply Bills. The government's financial position deteriorated and a constitutional crisis emerged. On 11 November 1975, the Governor-General dismissed the Prime Minister and his government because of his inability to guarantee supply (although not before Kerr had asked Whitlam for access to the Solicitor-General to be advised on the extent of his powers).

It was widely believed, and subsequently confirmed, that the government had consulted the Commonwealth Solicitor-General, Maurice Byers, at some point for his legal view on whether the loans would be 'for temporary purposes'. When the details of the loans negotiations were revealed by the government, the Senate resolved to call the Solicitor-General, Byers, and a number of other public servants, to the Bar of the Senate to answer questions and produce documents on the matter. The Solicitor-General refused. But on what basis? Mason dissects the arguments Byers put forward in 1975, which were largely mirrored in the reasons for Tate's refusal to appear before the Select Committee and produce documents over 30 years later.

Mason's chapter analyses the only relevant Australian authority on point: *Egan v Chadwick* (1999) 46 NSWLR 563. This case refutes the idea that, at least *legally*, the government can refuse a request from the Parliament to produce documents the subject of legal professional privilege or executive privilege, except in so far as the documents would be inconsistent with ministerial responsibility, such as Cabinet documents. Mason strongly challenges the logic of the judgments in drawing the exception. Where does this leave the Law Officers' Convention in Australia? Mason points out that the Convention is just that, 'a matter of convention, not of power'.

The Advocacy Function

By far the most visible role of the Solicitor-General is as chief advocate in defence of government interests before the High Court of Australia and other courts of appellate jurisdiction. It is in this role that the Solicitor-General has the capacity to make submissions as to the best interpretation of the constitutional documents and other legal norms and to provide the Court with advice on the government's policies and intentions. It is through the Solicitor-General that the Executive communicates with the judiciary and the judiciary are able to express their views to the Executive. The importance and influence of the analogous office of the Solicitor General in the United States in this advocacy role has been a matter of intense scrutiny. This was ignited initially by the controversial use by President Reagan of the Solicitor General to push what were viewed as political-agenda cases in the Supreme Court, particularly in the areas of abortion, civil rights and race relations. Unlike the American situation, there has been no political controversy surrounding the role of senior government lawyers in Australia. Perhaps due to this, the influence and proper role of Australian Solicitors-General in the jurisprudence of the judiciary has gone largely unstudied, despite the State and Commonwealth officers appearing as among the most frequent advocates in the High Court.

In Chapter 3, Hinton introduces the Australian Solicitor-General's relationship with the courts and the trend in more recent years for Solicitors-General to appear for their Attorneys-General in constitutional matters. He explains that, from the courts' point of view, the work done by the Solicitors-General plays a 'critical role in ensuring the rigour of judgments concerning the Constitution and the functioning of the federation'. Further, as one of the few counsel who appears regularly before the High Court, the Solicitor-General can act as a conduit between that apex court and the lower courts in the Solicitor-General's jurisdiction.

The role of the Solicitor-General in representing the interests of the Attorney-General in constitutional litigation is critically examined by Patrick Keyzer in Chapter 5. Since almost the inception of the High Court, State and Commonwealth Attorneys-General have been given leave to intervene in constitutional matters to represent the interests of their polity, and a broader, intangible and ill-defined concept of the public interest. Keyzer questions the capacity of the Attorney-General to put politics to one side and make, sometimes politically difficult, decisions about where the public interest lies. Keyzer critiques the current position, where standing rules and costs orders militate against non-government entities bringing public interest litigation or making interventions in the public interest.

In his foreword to this volume, Justice P.A. Keane of the High Court (and former Queensland Solicitor-General) provides a critique of Keyzer's primary position. He ripostes: 'the representatives of elected governments might be thought to have a stronger claim to speak for the public interest than self-appointed guardians of the public interest'.

The Solicitor-General in Context

As we have already discussed, understanding the office of the Australian Attorney-General is central to understanding the office of the Solicitor-General. The evolution in the role of Australia's Attorney-General towards the political and away from the British orthodoxy of an independent legal professional has driven the development of the modern Australian Solicitor-General. In Chapter 6 of the collection, Fiona Hanlon traces the divergent paths that the two offices have taken in Australia. She notes that this is not only a story of two offices in synchronised evolution but that it has also included a third: the Minister of Justice. Hanlon argues that, given the realities of the Australian Attorney-General as a highly politicised officer, no longer capable of acting independently in the public interest, there are dangers associated with continuing to call the office that of 'Attorney-General'. As such, she advocates for the adoption of a wholly political position of Attorney-General, called the 'Minister of Justice', which then emphasises the role of the Solicitor-General as the government's chief legal officer.

Hanlon's thesis is tellingly illustrated by the controversy engendered by the comments and actions of Commonwealth Attorney-General Daryl Williams, who held office from 1996 until 2003. When he was Shadow Attorney-General, Williams argued that any convention that the office of Attorney-General acted independently of the political Executive in Australia was 'erroneous or at least eroded' (Williams 1994: 192). He also doubted that the Attorney-General had a constitutional duty to defend the courts from political attacks (Williams 1994: 191–2; Williams 2002), a position that caused outcry among the judiciary and their supporters (Brennan 1997: 30; Mason 1997: 51).

The controversy drew academic and political interest in the role of the Australian Attorney-General. A number of academics highlighted the already vague definition of the role in Australia. For example, Ben Heraghty concluded that the nature of the office in Australia is 'left open to wide interpretation and is therefore interpreted by the particular officeholders themselves' (Heraghty 2002: 220). It is this observation that Hanlon responds to in her chapter. The 'Attorney-General' remains cloaked in the conventions and ideals of the ancient Law Officers but the officeholders themselves are often acting for base political objectives, akin to any other Minister.

The Australian Attorney-General is responsible for the provision of legal services to government departments and agencies. The question of the appropriate manner by which to provide legal services to the government is a complex one that permits of no ready answer. It is one that directly influences how Solicitors-General perform their functions. In Chapter 7 of the collection, Gabrielle Appleby examines the different ways this question has been answered in Australia across history, with a comparison to the English and Canadian positions. An overview of the New Zealand position is provided by David Collins later in the collection, and Harold H. Bruff and H.W. Perry, Jr provide an overview of the American position in their chapters.

Historically in Australia, legal services were provided centrally by the Law Officers' Department. This was initially headed by both the Law Officers – who were at that time both Ministers – until the Solicitor-General became a non-political office. The Attorney-General remains responsible for the provision of legal services, aided in large part by the Solicitor-General as well as the Crown Solicitor (or equivalent) and the Director of Public Prosecutions. However, the provision of legal services to government in Australia has more recently been dogged by controversy after the opening up of legal services to competition in many jurisdictions in the 1980s and 1990s and the increased use of in-house legal services. This has raised serious concerns over the ability of the Attorney-General to supervise and co-ordinate legal services properly across the whole of government. Appleby examines the current structure in the context of a number of concerns raised by two major Commonwealth-focussed reviews in 2009. She asserts that the Commonwealth's response to these reviews has been overly focussed on increasing cost-efficiency at the expense of considering reforms to ensure the quality and consistency of legal services provided to government.

International Perspectives: Government Lawyers across the World

The history and development of constitutional institutions cannot be studied as isolated islands. There is much to compare and contrast with other jurisdictions. In the last decade, the proper role of the government lawyer has come under immense scrutiny in a number of countries. International and domestic events demonstrate growing concern over the integrity of government lawyers and their role in events where government misconduct is alleged. The revelation of the 'Torture Memos' exhibited a culture within the government of the United States during the Bush administration of, at best, dubious legal reasoning, or, at worst, improper pressure placed on legal advisers to provide accommodating legal advice in times of crisis. The United Kingdom and the international community were rightly outraged by the revelations of pressure placed on Lord Goldsmith, the Attorney-General, to provide legal advice authorising the Iraq War to the Blair Labour government. The specific instances of the Torture Memos and the Iraq War advice highlight very public failings in high government legal office.

In contrast to the allegations of politicisation of the Law Officers in the United Kingdom and the United States, the New Zealand experience is perhaps the most non-political and 'departmental'. The New Zealand Solicitor-General may be considered an honorary Australian Solicitor-General – the officeholder has, from time to time, attended and hosted the regular meetings of Australian Solicitors-General (Commonwealth, State and Territory) known as the Special Committee of Solicitors-General (SCSG). The officeholder also occasionally attends the regular meetings of the Australian Crown Solicitors. This highlights the fundamental difference David Collins identifies in Chapter 8 of this collection between the Solicitors-General in Australia (with the exception of the Australian Capital Territory) and the Solicitor-General for New Zealand. The New Zealand office remains the most integrated of all. The office performs the role of Chief Executive of the Crown Law Office, legal counsel for and principal legal adviser to the Crown, Director of Public Prosecutions and Law Officer. The role reflects the broader role performed by the early Solicitors-General in Australia – who were often administrators of the Crown Law department as well as assisting in prosecutions – during a time the Australian jurisdictions were smaller and constitutional issues less complex.

In Australia the Solicitor-General's removal from involvement in criminal prosecutions and no Bills (terminating prosecutions) removed the office from a large degree of political controversy. The continued involvement in supervising prosecutions of indictable offences in New Zealand has been the subject of some criticism in New Zealand. Grant Huscroft (1999: 584–5) has argued that the New Zealand Solicitor-General is in fact *not* well suited to conducting public law litigation and that the politically accountable Attorney-General ought to reassert authority in this area. The current arrangements, Huscroft asserted (1999: 587–8), have been politically expedient for Attorneys-General eager to avoid contentious issues that often surround the criminal process.

However, in his chapter Collins vigorously defends the broad-ranging role of the New Zealand Solicitor-General. Collins describes the Crown Law Office in New Zealand as the 'undisputed focal point for almost all government legal work' after centralisation of government legal work was achieved in the 1950s. However, as in Australia, the regulation of legal services to government in New Zealand underwent significant change in the 1980s, loosening the Crown Law Office's 'vice-like grip' and presenting a risk to the cohesion of the government's legal position.

In Chapter 9 of the collection, Klearchos A. Kyriakides introduces the Law Officers of the Crown in the United Kingdom, focussing on the 'principal Law Officers': the Attorney General and his or her deputy, the Solicitor General (although, in many ways, these Law Officers need no introduction, being the blueprint for the Australian – and also the New Zealand, American and Canadian – Law Officers).

Kyriakides argues that in recent decades the increased complexity of law (both domestically and internationally) and the enhanced role of the courts as a check on executive power has highlighted the significance of the Law Officers in Britain. While often the Law Officers fulfil their functions discretely, like 'two submarines' below the surface (Garnier 2010), Kyriakides examines a number of events that have brought public attention and often controversy to the Law Officers' roles in Britain. As noted above, one of the most significant was the controversy around the Attorney-General's advice on the Iraq War in 2003. Kyriakides also examines the defence by the Attorney-General of a decision by the Serious Fraud Office to discontinue a criminal investigation into corruption allegations against BAE Systems, a leading arms manufacturer. These, and other examples that Kyriakides draws out in his chapter, highlight the very real tensions inherent in the continuation of the modern Law Officers as politicians as well as wearing the hats of chief legal advisers and guardians of the public interest. In these two functions, political interference is often improper and accountability is difficult.

Kyriakides explains that these controversies led to the release by the government of Prime Minister Gordon Brown in 2007 of a consultation paper: *The Governance of Britain: A Consultation on the Role of the Attorney General* (Scotland 2007). The consultation ultimately led to little in the way of actual reform and Kyriakides argues that the opportunity for strengthening the accountability of the Law Officers was lost.

One option canvassed at length in two inquiries – by Select Committees of both the House of Commons and the House of Lords (which ran concurrently with the 2007 government consultation) – was the possible creation of a legal adviser role to government, separate from the political government Minister. The proposal mirrors, in many respects, the framework in place in Australia: with a political Attorney-General acting predominantly as a Minister for Justice, assisted by a non-political Solicitor-General and Director of Public Prosecutions. The Constitutional Affairs Committee of the House of Commons recommended the United Kingdom adopt this model: 'to ensure clear lines of responsibility for particular decisions and to remove any credible allegation of political pressure' (House of Commons Constitutional Affairs Committee 2007: 4). The House of Lords Select Committee on the Constitution, while not expressing formal recommendations, raised concerns about how to ensure accountability if a non-ministerial Law Officer was introduced, whether political and non-political decisions could usefully be distinguished in practice, and whether only a *political* Attorney-General's opinions could carry sufficient weight among Cabinet Ministers (House of Lords Select Committee on the Constitution 2008). Thus while the Australian Law Officers have their provenance in England, the United Kingdom only today appears to be grappling with issues that Australia dealt with in the second half of the twentieth century.

Chapters 10 and 11 of the collection turn to the role of the Law Officers in the United States. The US Attorney General was, largely, modelled on the equivalent office in Britain (Fahy 1942; Lee 1988). Today the Attorney General performs a highly political role as a presidential appointee. The office has large administrative responsibilities and is assisted in the legal functions by the Office of Solicitor General (OSG) and Office of Legal Counsel (OLC) (Clayton 1992: 52–3). The OSG performs the primary function of prosecuting and conducting all suits in the Supreme Court on behalf of the government. The OLC assists the Attorney General by providing advice on the constitutionality of proposed legislation, advising on the legality of executive actions, reviewing executive orders and settling disputes among executive agencies. The division of responsibility for litigation and advising between the OSG and the OLC is unique to the United States.

While originally the OLC was created to alleviate the workload on the OSG, subsequently the division between the two offices has been relied upon to justify important differences in the ethical responsibilities of each office. After the scandal that followed the disclosure in 2004 of the 'Torture Memos', 19 former OLC lawyers, led by Dawn Johnsen,[4] issued a set of 'Principles to Guide the Office of Legal Counsel' (American Constitution Society for Law and Policy 2006). Principle 1 drew a distinction between the model of lawyering that was ethically appropriate for the OLC, as compared to that employed appropriately by advocates (such as those lawyers in the OSG):

> When providing legal advice to guide contemplated executive branch action, OLC should provide an accurate and honest appraisal of applicable law, even if that advice will constrain the administration's pursuit of desired policies. The advocacy model of lawyering, in which lawyers craft merely plausible legal arguments to support their clients' desired actions, inadequately promotes the President's constitutional obligation to ensure the legality of executive action.

The Principles acknowledged that sometimes the OLC would assist the OSG, and in such instances OLC lawyers may appropriately employ the advocacy model of lawyering. Principle 10, however, warned:

> OLC should be clear whenever it intends its advice to fall outside of OLC's typical role as the source of legal determinations that are binding within the executive branch. …
>
> Client agencies expect OLC to provide its best view of applicable legal constraints and if OLC acts otherwise without adequate warning, it risks prompting unlawful executive branch action.

The US institutional arrangements demonstrate that it is not imperative that the functions of adviser and advocate are combined in a single office – as still

4 President Barack Obama nominated Johnsen for the head of the OLC in March 2009, but she subsequently withdrew her nomination in April 2010 after lengthy delay and political opposition, possibly caused by her involvement in the Torture Memos scandal (Johnsen 2010).

occurs in Australia (with the exception of criminal litigation). The reference to the importance of the division of the two functions into separate offices after the revelations of the Torture Memos raises interesting comparative questions for the Australian office and invites further consideration of the implications of the fusion of the two functions under the Australian model.

Two chapters in this collection consider the US Attorney General's advisory and litigation functions separately. In Chapter 10, Harold H. Bruff considers the advisory function of the Attorney General of the United States. Bruff argues that the President's oath, to 'preserve, protect and defend the Constitution', and the oath of the President's lawyers, to 'support' the Constitution, give the President's lawyers the reference point from which they must try to hold the Executive to the law. This obligation exists in the context of a number of powerful incentives to provide compliant advice to the President that Bruff explores in the chapter. The Attorney General has often found himself one lawyer among many advising the President. Today, the OLC competes with the Office of White House Counsel for the President's ear. Structural competition between the President's legal advisers, Bruff argues, 'spurs compensatory aggressiveness in interpretation and argument (although at times they force a retreat from extreme positions)'. His conclusions have strong correlations with the concerns that Appleby argues have arisen in the Australian context with the introduction of *private* competition into the government legal services market. In the US, there have been times when the Attorney General's only method of drawing the attention of the President is through the threat of resignation. It is, Bruff warns, a weapon that may give the Attorney 'too much power', in light of the *President's* ultimate obligations to the Constitution.

While the history of the Attorney General that Bruff relates is one focussed on the quest for influence with the President, in Chapter 11 H.W. Perry, Jr examines the attempts of the Attorney General's Department to centralise the legal services provided across the US government (and particularly in the litigation area) in the Attorney General's Department, and specifically in the OSG. Bruff tells of the struggle of Attorneys General to gain influence with the President; Perry tells of the struggle of Attorneys General to gain influence and control over the other government attorneys.

Perry explains that with central control over the predominance of government litigation, the OSG has been able to ensure the protection of the *government's* interests – reducing the likelihood that departments and agencies will pursue their own narrow interests at the cost of the interests of the whole of government. With greater control concentrated in the OSG, the office has also been able to develop expertise and judgment so that the Supreme Court will rely heavily on the office both in the granting of writs of certiorari and in the substantive cases, giving rise to the enduring myth of the 'Tenth Justice' (Caplan 1987).

In Australia there is little evidence to support the idea that the Solicitor-General may operate as an influence on, or 'cue' to (Tanenhaus et al. 1963), the High Court. Former Commonwealth Solicitor-General Gavan Griffith (2007) wrote:

> It has been suggested that the American counterpart is the Tenth Justice of the United States Supreme Court. Similar influence cannot be claimed for the office in Australia, although as the senior counsel for each government in the federation, the Solicitors-General enhance the quality of practice in public law, and contribute to the depth and continuity of constitutional arguments presented for governments to the High Court.[5]

Many reasons for the difference can be proffered, and undoubtedly the truth lies in a combination of these. Australian Solicitors-General are relatively recent advocates in the High Court, developing a monopoly in constitutional advocacy before the High Court only in the 1970s (Appleby 2012: 76–7). Further, since the 1990s, in many Australian jurisdictions the government legal services provider has lost its monopoly on government legal work, opening the way for private firms to represent the government even in litigation. There is no requirement, for example, for litigants to have the permission of the Solicitor-General to appeal matters (although there are systems in place to ensure reporting of litigation matters and the ability for the Attorney-General to issue directions in the conduct of litigation).

Further, in Australia the Commonwealth Solicitor-General developed simultaneously with State Solicitors-General. Perry explains that in the United States the development of Solicitors General in the States is a relatively recent one, and one that has been, and continues to be, plagued with difficulties in establishing the appropriate authority and jurisdiction of the office. In contrast, when the Commonwealth Solicitor-General appears in constitutional matters in Australia, in the predominance of cases he or she appears alongside the Solicitors-General of the States.[6] The officeholders across the jurisdictions are all of exceptional calibre. Since the 1960s when the new model of a professional Solicitor-General was introduced, there have been two Commonwealth Solicitors-General appointed to the High Court and four State Solicitors-General (one from each of New South Wales, Queensland, Victoria and Western Australia).

In Chapter 12, the final chapter in the collection, M. Deborah MacNair examines the role of the public sector lawyer in Canada and the relevance of the public interest in both the civil and criminal context. Canada, unlike the other jurisdictions considered in this collection, replaced its Solicitor General with a Minister of Public Safety in 2004. This reflects the state of affairs that had existed in Canada where the Solicitor General had continued to perform a ministerial role

5 Although it is widely reported that Griffith's predecessor, Maurice Byers, enjoyed an exceptional success rate in High Court litigation when he was Commonwealth Solicitor-General.

6 This is particularly the case because in Australia the vast majority of constitutional cases that arise are federal ones. Further, under s 78A of the *Judiciary Act 1903* (Cth) all Attorneys-General have a right to intervene in matters that arise under the Constitution or involve its interpretation. Attorneys-General are, by and large, represented in these matters by their Solicitors-General.

with responsibility for a portfolio that spanned corrections and national security. The replacement of the office with a political Minister recognised the political character of the office, no longer acting in accordance with the conventions of the 'Law Officer' role.

In Canada, as in Australia, lawyers working for government have a nuanced relationship with the Crown by reference to the historical responsibilities of the Attorney General to the public interest. In her chapter, MacNair explores the extent to which public sector practitioners share ethical and professional obligations with those working in the private sector, the extent to which these obligations are in fact incongruent with the realities of public sector work, and the unique obligations that public sector lawyers may owe to the public interest.

MacNair emphasises that there is a healthy conversation and a burgeoning literature and regulatory framework around the obligations of the criminal prosecutor, which must commence with an understanding of the Attorney-General's traditional public interest obligations in bringing and superintending prosecutions. However, the obligations of public sector legal practitioners delivering *civil* services remain under-discussed. MacNair deals with the current regulation of these legal practitioners in the Canadian context, but her conclusions apply equally to the provision of legal services to government in Australia.

But who is best situated to expound and police the professional obligations of government lawyers? MacNair questions a recent Canadian Supreme Court decision that places the government lawyer under the jurisdiction of provincial law societies, wondering whether these law societies are well equipped to discuss the myriad challenges faced by government lawyers and provide them with rules that have relevance to their unique operational context. In Australia, the New South Wales Law Society (2010) has released a second edition of *A Guide to Ethical Issues for Government Lawyers* in response to the similar difficulty in New South Wales that MacNair identifies in Canada. Although the Guide does not create separate ethical or professional rules that apply to government lawyers, it attempts to apply the generic rules in the specific context of government lawyering. It is the only Australian jurisdiction to have introduced such a guide, although in many other jurisdictions the Law Society has established a separate public sector/government lawyers committee to offer support to this group. While there has been some progress, government lawyers still remain the 'orphans of legal ethics' (Hutchinson 2008: 106).

Conclusion

The Solicitors-General of Australia, like their counterparts elsewhere, are important integrity offices within government: 'public sentinels' guarding against illegality, and working at the heart of government in pursuit of the ideals of our constitutional system. The office's evolution to a professional, non-political officer underscores its importance in a system where the title of Attorney-General now describes an office that is often held by a highly political and senior Minister. However, the

Solicitor-General faces real challenges in ensuring the office's independence from politics while maintaining its relevance in an increasingly fragmented government legal services market. While there have developed statutory and institutional protections, it must ultimately come down to a human element. Like the Attorney-General or a member of the judiciary, the incumbent Solicitor-General has a significant degree of latitude to stamp the office with his or her own philosophy.

References

American Constitution Society for Law and Policy. 2006. Guidelines for the President's legal advisors. *Indiana Law Journal* [Online]. Volume 81, 1345. Available at: http://www.acslaw.org/files/Microsoft%20Word%20-%2011_Johnsen_OLC.pdf.

Appleby, G. 2012. *The Constitutional Role of the Solicitor-General: An Historical, Legal and Lived Portrait*. PhD thesis: University of Adelaide.

Bigge, J.T. 1823. *Report of the Commissioner of Inquiry on the Judicial Establishments of New South Wales and Van Dieman's Land*. London: House of Lords.

Brennan, G. 1997. *The State of the Judicature Address*. Paper presented at the 30th Australian Legal Convention: Melbourne, 19 September 1997.

Burton, P. 2010. *From Moree to Mabo: The Mary Gaudron Story*. Perth: UWA Publishing.

Caplan, L. 1987. *The Tenth Justice: The Solicitor General and the Rule of Law*. New York: Vintage Books.

Clayton, C.W. 1992. *The Politics of Justice: The Attorney General and the Making of Legal Policy*. Armonk, NY: M.E. Sharpe.

Edwards, J.Ll.J. 1964. *The Law Officers of the Crown: A Study of the Offices of the Attorney-General and Solicitor-General of England with an Account of the Office of the Director of Public Prosecutions of England*. London: Sweet & Maxwell.

Fahy, C. 1942. The Office of the Solicitor General. *American Bar Association Journal*. Volume 28, 20.

Garnier, E. 2010. *Speech to the Constitutional and Administrative Law Bar Association*. 17 July 2010 [Online]. Available at: www.attorneygeneral.gov.uk/News-Centre/Speeches/Pages/SolicitorGeneralspeechtotheALBAsummerconference.aspx [accessed 12 September 2012].

Griffith, G. 2007. Solicitors-General in *Oxford Companion to the High Court of Australia*, edited by M. Coper, T. Blackshield and G. Williams. Melbourne: Oxford University Press [Online]. Available at: http://www.oxfordreference.com.

Heraghty, B. 2002. Defender of the Faith? The Role of the Attorney-General in Defending the High Court. *Monash Law Review*. Volume 28(2), 209.

House of Commons Constitutional Affairs Committee. 2007. *The Constitutional Role of the Attorney General: Fifth Report of Session 2006–07*.

House of Lords Select Committee on the Constitution. 2008. Reform of the Office of Attorney General: Report with Evidence.

Huscroft, G. 1999. Politics and Principle in Public Law Advocacy: The Role of the Solicitor General. *New Zealand Universities Law Review*. Volume 18, 584.

Hutchinson, A.C. 2008. In the Public Interest: The Responsibilities and Rights of Government Lawyers. *Osgoode Hall Law Journal*. Volume 46, 105.

Johnsen, D. 2010. *Restoring Leadership and Integrity to the Office of Legal Counsel*. 11 June [Online]. Available at: http://www.washingtonpost.com/wp-dyn/content/article/2010/06/10/AR2010061004117.html [accessed 18 January 2013].

Lee, R.E. 1988. Lawyering in the Supreme Court: The Role of the Solicitor General. *Loyola of Los Angeles Law Review*. Volume 21, 1059.

Mason, A. 1997. No Place in a Modern Democratic Society for a Supine Judiciary. *Law Society Journal*. Volume 35(11), 51.

New South Wales Law Reform Commission. 1998. *Circulation of Legal Advice to Government, Report No 86*. [Online]. Available at: http://www.lawlink.nsw.gov.au/lrc.nsf/pages/R86TOC [accessed 27 March 2013].

New South Wales Law Society. 2010. *A Guide to Ethical Issues for Government Lawyers*. 2nd edition.

Queensland Parliamentary Debates. 1985. *Legislative Assembly*. 19 March 1985.

Scotland, Baroness. 2007. *The Governance of Britain: A Consultation on the Role of the Attorney General*. London: The Stationery Office.

Selway, B. 1999. The Duties of Lawyers Acting for Government. *Public Law Review*. Volume 10, 114.

Tanenhaus, J., Schick, M., Muraskin, M., Rosen, D. 1963. The Supreme Court's Certiorari Jurisdiction: Cue Theory, in *Judicial Decision Making*, edited by G. Schubert. Glencoe: The Free Press, 111–32.

Tate, P. 2007. Letter from the Solicitor-General to Mr Richard Willis, Secretary, Select Committee on Gaming. 11 April 2007. Extracted in Select Committee of the Legislative Council on Gaming Licensing. 2007. *First Interim Report Upon Gaming Licensing*. Melbourne: Legislative Council of Victoria.

Williams, D. 1994. Who Speaks for the Courts? *AIJA* 183.

Williams D. 2002. The Role of the Attorney-General. *Public Law Review*. Volume 13, 252.

PART I
The Australian Solicitor-General

Chapter 1
Aspects of the History of the Solicitor-General in Australia

Keith Mason

In offering this selective survey of the early history of the office of Solicitor-General in Australia, two general themes can be flagged. First, from the outset, there were adaptations to the English model, whatever the Colonial Office or the early colonists may have intended. Secondly, each jurisdiction did things its own way, moulding the office to local exigencies and local attitudes about the fusion of the profession, seeking to make the most of the capacities of the men who held the two related Law Officer positions as well as that of Crown Solicitor. (It was always men in the period of my survey.) This chapter shall briefly skim through the history of the office of the Solicitor-General across the various Australian jurisdictions before turning to address some general themes that arise in relation to the office's history.

New South Wales[1]

In the colony of New South Wales from its establishment in 1788 to the 1820s, the Judge-Advocate performed many of the Law Officers' roles as well as that of judge. Requiring the Judge-Advocate to be responsible for both initiating and hearing serious criminal charges was not a good look for avoiding bias. And having George Crossley (a former solicitor convicted of perjury) as principal legal adviser was similarly not a good look for a Governor. Yet it was not until 1824 that the first Attorney-General and Solicitor-General were appointed, the former as one of the recommendations of the Bigge Report into the judicial establishments of New South Wales and Van Diemen's Land (Bigge 1823: 34, 57).[2]

1 For other material about the office during the period in question, see Mason 1988; Sexton 2002.

2 Bigge recommended an English barrister be appointed as Attorney-General for New South Wales. The Vandemonians would be provided with 'one of the stipendiary solicitors practising at Sydney'. The Colonial Office nevertheless decided to send them an English barrister, Joseph Tice Gellibrand (see below).

Saxe Bannister, New South Wales' first Attorney-General, is described by John Bennett as 'an incompetent and unpleasant individual' (Bennett 1974: 33). Charles Currey (1966) explained:

> A succession of defeats in court lessened confidence in [Bannister's] professional competence … [Governor] Darling … had scant respect for his judgment and resented his unsolicited advice. [Chief Justice] Forbes deplored his 'irascibility', 'indecorous conduct' in court, and tendency to megalomania. With Brisbane and Darling, he thought that the attorney-general was at times mentally unbalanced.

Law Officers who get so far on the wrong side of both their principal client and the court before whom they urge that client's causes can always expect a hard time and bad press.

Our first Australian Solicitor-General, John Stephen, was a saint compared to Attorney-General Bannister. But comparisons are often odious and Stephen was in the job for only a year before he secured appointment as a puisne Supreme Court judge. He would be the first of four from the Stephen clan to progress to the Supreme Court of New South Wales. John Stephen was by no means the last Solicitor-General who should have avoided judicial promotion. 'Mr Stephen … poor man', Governor Darling informed the Colonial Secretary in 1828, 'is a tool in the hands of the Chief Justice, who works with him as best answers his immediate object' (Currey 1966). Stephen was admonished frequently by the Colonial Office for indiscretion. His own nephew, James Stephen (permanent counsel to the Colonial Office) prepared a despatch for Governor Darling in 1831 in which James recorded that 'if I have anything to reproach myself with, it is the forbearance I have shown in not reporting his unfitness for his office' (Mason 1988).

John Stephen's death in December 1833 offered him a more dignified departure from the colony than Bannister, whose parting shot before sailing to England was literally at the leading barrister Robert Wardell in a duel from which both men emerged uninjured (Currey 1966).

Like several of his successors as Solicitor-General, Stephen was appointed after lobbying and nepotism that would be scandalous today. The next appointee, James Holland, left behind in England the despatch from the Colonial Secretary, Lord Bathurst, nominating him for the office with the result that the Chief Justice refused to swear him in. This second Law Officer *manqué* was consoled by the fact that, like a number of early Solicitors-General, he was also a salaried Commissioner of the Courts of Request, which were small debts courts (Mason 1988). Several early incumbents also sat as magistrates or chairmen of Quarter Sessions concurrently with their position as second Law Officer. From time to time they also 'acted up' as temporary Supreme Court judges. And they invariably hoped that something good or bad would befall their Attorney-General so as to create a vacancy they expected to fill.

In the early years after 1824, the Attorney-General and Solicitor-General were usually members of the Executive Council and of the Legislative Council. After the legislative body became partly elective in 1842, the appointed Law Officers on it were expected all the more to perform as the 'Governor's men'. As was to occur in Van Diemen's Land, this sometimes put them in direct conflict with the judiciary, although they had the comfort of knowing that the judges themselves were dismissible by the Governor for misbehaviour, pursuant to *Burke's Act 1782*.[3] And, after the coming of responsible government in 1856, the Law Officers could get torn between loyalty to the Governor, who looked to England for instructions and advice from time to time, and the ministry of which they were usually members.

Before and after responsible government, the two Law Officers were often involved in drafting and promoting legislation. In the very early days, so too were the colonial judges who also sat in the Legislative Council.

There has been an Attorney-General for New South Wales continuously since 1824. But there were two periods without a Solicitor-General.

In 1836 Governor Bourke abolished the position and required John Hubert Plunkett (who had been Solicitor-General for the previous five years) to do double duty in the office of Attorney-General (Griffith 2007: 83). Plunkett was probably the most honourable man to have been a Law Officer in New South Wales. His career has been traced in two recent biographies, one of himself, the other of William Charles Wentworth who opposed him in many ways (Earls 2009; Tink 2009). Plunkett was assisted by Roger Therry, whose appointment to the Solicitor-General position was blocked for two reasons, one financial and the other because the Governor feared having two Roman Catholics as Law Officers so shortly after the abolition of the *Test Acts* (Mason 1988).

Eventually, William à Beckett (who later became the first Chief Justice of Victoria) was appointed acting Solicitor-General in 1841. From then until 1873 the office of Solicitor-General was held by a succession of worthies who were members of the Legislative Council or (after responsible government) the Legislative Assembly. The political instability of the early decades of responsible government saw frequent changes as Solicitors-General rose and fell with the governments of which they were members. During this time leading barristers were often Members of Parliament and Law Officers themselves were entitled to accept private briefs.

There was no Solicitor-General in New South Wales between 1873 and 1894. In this period, the law reform and managerial functions previously exercised by the Solicitor-General were performed by a Minister of Justice or were tacked

3 *Burke's Act 1782* (later named the *Colonial Leave of Absence Act 1782*) remained on the English statute book until 1964. There is a nice question as to whether it was capable of repeal by the colonial legislatures that, over the years, introduced judicial tenure by stages. Three judges were amoved in Australia (Algernon Montagu, John Willis and Benjamin Boothby), one of them, Willis, appealing successfully to the Privy Council on natural justice grounds. The last time that *Burke's Act* appears to have been resorted to involved the suspension of Chief Justice Alexander Onslow in Western Australia in the 1880s. See generally McLaren 2011.

onto the office of Attorney-General, which over the ensuing century edged closer to its modern embodiment. The weight of criminal law work left exclusively on the Attorney-General's shoulders undermined his capacity to attend to other responsibilities, and there were calls to revive the Solicitor-Generalship as a non-political appointment to assist in this area, for example, in the 1891 Public Service Inquiry (Public Service Inquiry Commission 1891).

Although it remained unfilled, in 1884 the post of Solicitor-General ceased to be one of the offices of profit under the Crown that did not disqualify the holder from membership of the Legislative Assembly. Constitutionally, this left four choices that were used from time to time in the following years: (1) absorb the non-advocacy functions of the office into a 'Ministry of Justice' in which the Minister in Parliament had a quiver-full of additional responsibilities; (2) appoint a senior public servant (who remained outside Parliament) to the office of Solicitor-General; (3) appoint a member of the *Upper* House to the office of Solicitor-General (sometimes concurrently with the Ministry of Justice); and (4) appoint a member of the Lower House to the office of Solicitor-General but provide no remuneration for that office.

This fourth technique was used from time to time in the 1890s when George Reid was Solicitor-General for shortish periods while holding the premiership. A motion to declare Reid's seat vacant because he had accepted an office of profit under the Crown not permitted by the Constitution was defeated on the ground, it appears, that no remuneration attached to the additional office (New South Wales Parliamentary Debates 1895: 3911, 3914). The exercise was repeated in 1915 with William Holman holding the premiership and the Solicitor-Generalship concurrently. One infers that these short-term appointments were to enable a lawyer effectively to deputise for the Attorney-General during his absence.[4]

Hugh Pollock held the office of Solicitor-General between 1901 and 1904. He had been Secretary and permanent head of the Attorney-General's Department for many years. One of the earliest activities of the New South Wales Bar Council, formed in 1902, was a complaint about Pollock's appointment as Solicitor-General. Leading silks were especially troubled with the *Law Almanac*'s statement that he had precedence next after the Attorney-General. The Bar Council resolved that:

> we are satisfied that Mr Pollock does not hold the office of Solicitor-General as known to the Constitution: that is, he is not, though called Solicitor-General in the Commission, entitled by virtue of his Commission to any precedence (Bennett 1969: 147).

---

4 For example, this occurred in 1893 when (concurrently with his office as Minister of Justice) Richard O'Connor was appointed Solicitor-General from July to September because Edmund Barton, the Attorney-General, was in Canada. As indicated below, there is a constitutional restraint in New South Wales upon the delegation of the Attorney-General's traditional functions to another Executive Councillor. It was obviously assumed that this did not apply to whatever arrangements were put in place as regards the Solicitor-General.

This resolution was forwarded to the Acting Chief Justice, with a request that he ask the Judges of the Supreme Court to determine Pollock's right to precedence. The judges ruled in favour of the Solicitor-General, considering themselves to be bound by the Letters Patent (Bennett 1969: 147). Pollock appeared before the Full Court as Solicitor-General to argue criminal matters during his term of office.

Reflecting the formal separation of the two branches of the profession that has been a hallmark of New South Wales for most of the time since 1834, the office of Solicitor-General seems always to have been held by a barrister, very often a silk. Alfred Lutwyche declined in 1856 to serve as Solicitor-General until the Attorney-General (James Martin, later Chief Justice) was admitted to the Bar. This principled stance was costly because the government fell only 21 days after Martin's delayed appointment. There had been a motion of no confidence that relied in part on the solecism of a non-barrister assuming the office of Attorney-General (Bennett 1969: 72–3).

Since 1880 the New South Wales Constitution has restricted the delegation to another Minister of the Attorney-General's powers as Law Officer (*Constitution Act 1902* (NSW): s 36; *Solicitor-General v Wylde* (1945) 46 SR (NSW) 83: 94; Twomey 2004: 692–3). Using a Solicitor-General to exercise the prerogative powers vested in the Attorney-General during his absence has not been regarded as a breach of this requirement.

Before the advent of the Director of Public Prosecutions in 1987 (*Director of Public Prosecutions Act 1986* (NSW)), the Attorney-General in New South Wales had the primary responsibility for criminal prosecutions and many Attorneys-General conducted them in person in the colonial period. Unlike in some of the smaller colonies, the split profession in New South Wales meant that the office of the Solicitor-General was always separate from that of Crown Solicitor and its responsibilities lay more on the civil side of government legal work in court. Each Law Officer was also involved in legislative drafting and enactment. The Solicitor-General also assisted the Attorney-General in the criminal work, sometimes complaining that the senior officer was not pulling his weight. As the Attorney-General post became increasingly that of a politician heading a large department, the Solicitor-General assumed the role of principal adviser to the Attorney-General on the commencement and maintenance of criminal prosecutions. This relatively behind the scenes role did not, of course, always shield the Solicitor-General from political controversy – as becomes clear from the recent biography of Mary Gaudron, who was Solicitor-General between 1981 and 1987 (Burton 2010). Throughout much of the twentieth century, the Solicitor-General for New South Wales also acted as the principal advocate for the Crown in the Court of Criminal Appeal. The deaf[5] and redoubtable criminal law expert Cecil Weigall was Solicitor-General between 1922 and 1953. Weigall's successor, Harold Snelling,

5 He is reputed once to have asked his instructing officer what it was that Jordan CJ had just said, only to reply to the officer in a loud voice: 'That is rubbish!' John Kinchela was another deaf Law Officer in New South Wales: see below.

who held office until 1974, did criminal matters while also arguing constitutional cases and reputedly keeping his eye open for stamp duty matters destined to go to the Privy Council (and the fees they carried).

A roll call of the memorable Solicitors-General of New South Wales for my period of study includes the names of John Hubert Plunkett, John Darvall, Julian Salomons, William Windeyer, Richard O'Connor, George Reid and Cecil Weigall.[6]

There are, however, some debit entries in the Honour Roll.

John Fletcher Hargrave was a judge both before and after he served several shortish terms as Solicitor-General. He resigned from the District Court in 1859 after 14 days in that office, to enter politics and become the Solicitor-General in the Cowper ministry. Six years later he left for the Supreme Court bench as a controversial reward for political services. The Attorney-General, John Darvall, opposed the appointment but was outvoted in Cabinet. Darvall resigned in protest and returned to England. The Bar boycotted the swearing-in.

Hargrave had a perverse streak as a judge, especially towards female suitors, not unconnected with his marital unhappiness and the inability to forgive his wife for having had him confined in a lunatic asylum in the 1850s. Notwithstanding, he became New South Wales' first judge in divorce. He drove Alfred Stephen, the Chief Justice, to distraction and eventual retirement (admittedly after a record innings of 34 years, 29 of them as Chief Justice). According to Stephen's unpublished lament (1894), called *A Trio of Judges*:

> [Hargrave] was simply incapable of seeing things … in any light but one which lunacy presented to his view. It is true that he has said many rude things to me, and that (so far as I know and believe) he rarely, if ever, failed to express a different opinion from my own, whatever the question.

How different from Stephen's own father, John, who, it will be remembered, was criticised for being 'a tool in the hands of the Chief justice'.

Joshua Josephson distinguished himself when, as a judge of the District Court of New South Wales from 1869 to 1884 (Holt 1976: 87–92), he became the subject of a complaint about his earlier conduct as Solicitor-General during the short-lived Robertson Ministry of 1868–69. Judge Cary's resignation from the bench on medical grounds created the vacancy that Josephson filled in August 1869. Coincidentally, Cary would die in Josephson's chambers the following year, but not before alleging that Cary's resignation from the bench had been procured by a secret payment (Holt 1976: 38). The matter was investigated by the Attorney-General, W.M. Manning. Manning reported that:

> [Josephson had] succeeded in mitigating but not in removing the charge of having, by a secret payment of £240, induced or precipitated Mr Cary's

6 Further information on the careers of these officeholders can be found in the *Australian Dictionary of Biography*.

resignation, in the expectation of becoming his immediate successor (extracted in Holt 1976: 90).

The Colonial Secretary, Cowper, issued a formal reprimand to Josephson for having been party to such negotiations while occupying the position of Solicitor-General and being at the same time a member of Cabinet. Josephson was instructed to resume his duties on the bench, which he did for a further 14 years.

By 1922 the office of Solicitor-General had reverted back to being remunerative, thus disqualifying officeholders from holding a seat in Parliament. This was fortunate because, had it not been for the Crown Solicitor's advice that he would forfeit his seat and put a fragile government majority at risk, Thomas Ley might also have become Solicitor-General. He had to settle for the Ministry of Justice. After his political career crashed in a flurry of litigation over fraud as a director of the ill-fated SOS Prickly Pear Poisons Ltd, Ley returned to his native England in 1928. In 1946 he arranged the murder of the man he wrongly suspected to be courting his ageing mistress. Upon conviction, Lord Chief Justice Goddard pronounced sentence of death, but to his extreme displeasure, the Home Secretary respited the sentence on the basis of medical evidence (first produced after the trial) that Ley was suffering from paranoia. Ley died of a stroke in Broadmoor Criminal Lunatic Asylum four months later. His biographer suggests that he had been responsible for two additional murders before he left Sydney (Morgan 1979).

Van Diemen's Land/Tasmania

As with New South Wales, the first Attorney-General for Van Diemen's Land was appointed from England in 1824. Alfred Stephen (who was the son of John Stephen) was appointed Solicitor-General the following year (under the colonial Great Seal) and he served in that role until 1833. There was a brief period when father and son held the Solicitor-General offices in the two colonies concurrently.

As often since in Tasmania, Stephen held a dual commission as Crown Solicitor. This was just as well for him because the Solicitor-General position was honorary. At times Stephen acted in the Attorney-General role as well. If time permitted, and even if it did not, he also took fee-paying work as an ordinary barrister. When taxed about neglect of government business he complained that his inadequate salary forced him to act this way (Bennett 2009: 35–6). (Similar claims and counterclaims dogged Australian colonial Law Officers throughout the nineteenth century, spiced up with instances when they took briefs against government parties; see below.)

The brash young Stephen never took a backward step, but he did have to put up with two extremely difficult Attorneys-General, Joseph Tice Gellibrand and Algernon Montagu (who was only one of three colonial judges amoved from the bench). Stephen went so far as to move the Supreme Court to have Gellibrand disbarred. Gellibrand had charged a fee for advice to a plaintiff who was suing a government party, only to turn round and charge the defendant for drawing the plea by way of defence.[7] Pedder CJ squibbed on the professional misconduct issue. Eventually Gellibrand was removed from office, but Stephen failed to get his job. He was mortally disappointed to be passed over in favour of Montagu, who was his junior by call to the Bar. The two men took an instant dislike to each other and hostilities continued after Montagu became a judge and Stephen, belatedly, the Attorney-General. Stephen for his part was often unpunctual in court and he ate at the Bar table.

Things erupted in a spectacular brawl in 1836. Montagu commenced hearing a case whose prosecution by information lay under the Law Officer's control. Stephen ambled into court to be greeted with a judicial tirade probably unequalled in Australian legal history. It culminated as follows:

> Sir, in your official capacity I shall always treat you with the courtesy and respect due to you. Were you elsewhere I should treat you after your conduct with even less courtesy than a dog or a cur as your conduct richly deserves. I say this, Sir, as an English gentleman, and only as such – perhaps in the capacity of a Judge I had better be silent (Bennett 2009: 85).

Perhaps indeed!

In this instance, the judicial anger was directed at the man himself. Of course, sometimes it is really aimed at the client sitting silently behind the barrister. With a Law Officer, the client will be a Minister who is usually absent, or an immanent Crown that cannot be seen at all. It has always been a Law Officer's function to be the public messenger between the government and the court, rather like an ambassador from Tudor times.[8]

Given the weight of his responsibilities and the ructions with his legal colleagues, it is little wonder that Stephen's health crumbled in Hobart Town. Few would have wagered that he would later serve a record term on the Supreme Court of New South Wales. He retired from the bench at the age of 71 only to re-enter politics and law reform as an active member of the Legislative Council.

His secret must have been a happy home life and two presumably contented wives. I hasten to point out that this pillar of the Church of England was no polygamist. His first wife, Virginia, died in 1837 two days after being delivered of her ninth child, which lived but predeceased her. Stephen described his domestic situation in a poem penned on the bench in 1859 while sitting at Bathurst during what he described as 'a very long reply in a Squatting action' (Bedford 1954: 188). It reminds all of us that we are people with families first and lawyers second – at least that's the theory. Stephen called his poem 'Twice nine, or Judicial Impartiality Exemplified' and he wrote:

7 Stephen himself ended up with the plaintiff's brief at trial.

8 See further discussion at page 44, below.

> Of children this Knight had no less than eighteen –
> Twice nine little heads, with a marriage between.
> He had nine when a barrister, nine when a judge,
> And of 'sex' – thus to Nature he owed not a grudge –
> Nine precisely were girls, the other half boys,
> An equal division 'twixt quiet and noise;
> While, if by marriage the number be reckoned,
> There were nine of the first and nine of the second.
> Nine in Tasmania, nine in New South Wales,
> Then, to show with what justice he still held the scales,
> Since nine it was clear he could not divide,
> (A third sex as yet never having been tried),
> Five sons and four daughters in Hobart were born,
> And four sons, five daughters might Sydney adorn.
> Twin daughters, twin sons, complete the strange story
> Of this patron of 'Wigs', though constant old Tory (extracted in Bedford 1954: 15).

In 1825 the Legislative and Executive Councils were separated in Van Diemen's Land, as in the northern colony of New South Wales, but continuing transportation on a large scale saw the withholding of the franchise until 1850.

The Law Officers in Van Diemen's Land were appointed members of the Legislative Council prior to representative government in 1856. As such, they were expected to act as the Governor wished, although one Solicitor-General, Francis Villeneuve Smith, made it a condition when he took office that he could exercise liberty of conscience on the transportation question (Fenton 1884: 241).[9] With responsible government in 1856 both the new House of Assembly and the revamped Legislative Council would (unlike the situation in New South Wales) each become elective.

Apart from shortish periods of vacancy, there appears to have been a Solicitor-General in Tasmania almost continuously since 1825. With responsible government the Solicitor-General initially became a member of the ministry, having a seat in one or other of the Houses of Parliament. However, in 1860 the position was made a permanent one in the civil service and it has remained so until the present time. According to a 1908 report into the possibility of making the office of *Attorney-General* non-political:

> The duties of the office [of Solicitor-General] have steadily increased, so that the branch of the service presided over by the Solicitor-General has become a separate Department. Whilst the Attorney-General is nominally a law officer, he really occupies a position similar to that of the Home Secretary in England.

9 In 1851, Smith and another appointee on the Legislative Council sided with the elected members in voting for an Address to the Queen praying the rescission of the Order-in-Council which made Van Diemen's Land a place for the reception of transported criminals.

> The administration of the criminal law has been placed entirely in the hands of the Solicitor-General. He advises the Crown and public departments, and has come to be regarded as the law officer upon whom successive governments rely for legal advice (Royal Commission on the Proposal to Make the Office of Attorney-General Permanent Non-Political 1908).

Solicitors-General for Tasmania who were notable (for a range of reasons) included Hugh Cokeley Ross, who acted in the position in 1832–33 when Stephen took leave of absence, was subsequently appointed Crown Solicitor and was later acquitted on a technicality when charged with embezzlement. He then set up practice in Wellington, New Zealand, where he mortally wounded a fellow lawyer in a duel after a legal dispute (Ross 1967). Thomas Horne was the Solicitor-General between 1841 and 1844. He went on to become a Supreme Court judge, to be passed over for the Chief Justiceship in favour of the Attorney-General Valentine Fleming. Horne consoled himself by gaining election in the Legislative Council and holding the offices of judge and President of the Legislative Council concurrently. Special legislation was rushed through to prevent him drawing two salaries. After a narrow squeak due to unfavourable findings about his conduct in a Victorian probate suit, he tried to borrow from a litigant who was appearing before him. He resigned to prevent his amoval from the bench (Nicholls 1972).

On the positive side of the Tasmanian ledger I mention Sir Stanley Burbury, who was Solicitor-General for four years in the 1950s before embarking on lengthy terms of office as Chief Justice and as Tasmania's first Australian-born Governor.

Victoria

Victoria has had a Solicitor-General since practically the establishment of the colony in 1851. One early occupant, Edward Eyre Williams, occupied a non-elective seat in the Legislative Council for a brief period.

Responsible government came to Victoria in 1856. As with Tasmania, both Houses were elective. Legislation in 1859 limited to nine the number of persons holding offices of profit under the Crown who could sit in either House and stipulated that the office of Solicitor-General was one of them. There were several very short-lived appointments in the political turmoil of the early period of responsible government.

For much of the first half of the twentieth century the office was held concurrently with the post of Attorney-General and sometimes additional portfolios as well, including Premier. The Solicitor-General administered part of the Victorian legal department. The office remained a political one until 1951. Notable Solicitors-General during my period of review include Alfred Deakin, Robert Molesworth, Isaac Isaacs, Frederick Eggleston and Robert Menzies.

Henry Winneke was the Victorian Solicitor-General between 1951 and 1964 (Coleman 1988). The legislation that defined the non-political nature of his office

(*Solicitor-General Act 1951* (Vic); *Solicitor-General Act 1958* (Vic)) stipulated that the Governor-in-Council could appoint and remove the officeholder, who was required to be senior counsel. The office was henceforth *not* to be held by a responsible Minister of the Crown. The 1951 Victorian Act became the model for the now almost standard formula about the primary role of the office, namely that the Solicitor-General is to 'act as counsel for [Her] Majesty and may perform such other duties of counsel as the Attorney-General directs'.

Victoria's Director of Public Prosecutions Act was passed in 1982, moving the responsibility of bringing and maintaining prosecutions from the shoulders of the Solicitor-General to the newly created statutory office of the DPP.

Queensland

Since its establishment as a separate colony from New South Wales in 1859, Queensland has always had an Attorney-General and a Crown Solicitor, but not always a Solicitor-General.

Overworked by ever-expanding duties as Attorney-General, Samuel Griffith introduced a Bill in 1876 providing for a Solicitor-General, but it was rejected in the Legislative Council (McPherson 1989: 113). Griffith would have to wait until 1890 to get the relief he desperately needed to be able to apply himself to the emerging Commonwealth.

Queensland's first Solicitor-General was Thomas Byrnes who (at the age of 29) was appointed by Griffith in 1890 to relieve him of some of his day-to-day burdens. Byrnes was in the Legislative Council at the time and he became a Minister with a seat in the Executive Council. He has been the only Queensland Solicitor-General who held the office as a Member of Parliament. He would become Attorney-General in 1893. The office of Solicitor-General would then go into abeyance for three decades. For the latter part of this hiatus period, Queensland was particularly well served by its energetic Attorney-General, T.J. Ryan, who (while also holding the Premier's portfolio) found time to appear in the High Court and Privy Council on several occasions, normally with ultimate success (McPherson 1989: 289).[10]

There was then no Solicitor-General in Queensland until the appointment of William Flood Webb in 1922. Webb's was a public service position, although he appeared in many civil and criminal cases, including the sensational Brennan bribery case in 1922 (Elvery 2009: 89, 91). Webb was subsequently appointed to the Supreme Court where he rose to become Chief Justice. He was appointed to the High Court in 1946.

Webb and his successors headed the Crown Law Office from then until the arrival of Geoffrey Davies, who was the first Solicitor-General appointed from the

10 According to McPherson, 'Ryan, as Attorney-General, himself appeared in every constitutional matter of any importance, even, while Premier, twice taking the long sea voyage to England to appear before the Privy Council in 1916 and 1919'.

private Bar. Building on the Victorian model, the duties of the office as 'counsel for the Crown' were spelt out in the *Solicitor-General Act 1985* (Qld), which did not commence operation until the eve of the appointment of Davies' successor. The Queensland Director of Public Prosecutions had been established in the mid-1980s, prior to the appointment of Davies.

The list of notable holders of the office of Solicitor-General for Queensland includes William Webb, Geoffrey Davies and Patrick Keane.

Western Australia

William Sayer was the first Solicitor-General for Western Australia, holding office between 1902 and 1930. The position was then abolished for five years to make way for separate offices of Crown Solicitor and Senior Parliamentary Draughtsman. The man appointed Crown Solicitor, J.L. Walker, later acquired a silk gown and was given the additional office of Solicitor-General in 1935.

Between 1935 and the present day it has been a matter of 'a few good men', with emphasis on both adjectives. There have been only five permanent occupants: Sydney Good, Ronald Wilson, Kevin Parker, Robert Meadows and Grant Donaldson.

The first two of these officers combined leadership of the Crown Law Department with advocacy roles, including at the highest appellate level. With the passing of the *Solicitor-General Act 1969* (WA), the office became tenured and open to 'an Australian lawyer [with] not less than 8 years' legal experience'. Western Australia has always had a fused legal profession and the emphasis on a *barristerial* appointment as had occurred in some of the larger colonies did not arise.

South Australia, the Northern Territory and the Australian Capital Territory

Until 1911 South Australia encompassed what we now know as the Northern Territory, when the area was transferred to the Commonwealth. The two areas have something else in common because each polity got along fine without a Solicitor-General during the period I am surveying.

Apart from 10 days in 1857, South Australia had no Solicitor-General until Andrew Wells was appointed in 1969, effectively the end of my period of interest.[11] Wells was Crown Solicitor at the time of his appointment and his title was simply changed to Solicitor-General. In 1970, when Brian Cox was appointed Solicitor-

11 The 10-day exception came to an end when it was pointed out that the South Australian Constitution did not treat the office of Solicitor-General as one of the exceptional group of offices of profit under the Crown that could be held by a sitting member (Finniss 1886: 470).

General, the position no longer had responsibility for the Crown Solicitor's Office. It was not until 1972 that it became a statutory position (*Solicitor-General Act 1972* (SA)). South Australia decided to manage its senior in-house legal affairs with an Advocate-General, later named the Attorney-General, who was assisted by the Crown Solicitor.

The Northern Territory got its first Solicitor-General in 1978 with Ian Barker (*Law Officers Act 1978* (NT)). Prior to then, the Northern Territory's legal services were predominantly provided by the Commonwealth.

The Australian Capital Territory has never had a Solicitor-General, until 2011, with the passage of the *Law Officers Act 2011* (ACT) and the appointment of the Chief Solicitor, Peter Garrisson, who now holds both positions.

Commonwealth

I mention the Commonwealth last to reflect the custom observed in the Special Committee of Solicitors-General (which meets periodically to discuss constitutional cases in the pipeline and other topics of mutual interest, often with the New Zealand Solicitor-General participating) in my time whereby the Commonwealth Solicitor-General would be invited to arrive late. This was to enable the State Solicitors-General (adopting Edmund Barton's catty remark about Isaac Isaacs) 'to colloque with our colleagues apart from' the Commonwealth Law Officer (Cowen 1967: 279).

There have been nine Solicitors-General for the Commonwealth, omitting one short acting appointment. Notable Commonwealth Solicitors-General of the past include Robert Garran, Anthony Mason, Robert Ellicott and Maurice Byers.

From its establishment in 1916 until 1964, the largely titular office was combined with that of Secretary of the Attorney-General's Department.

In 1916, it was given statutory recognition in a short enactment that specified no eligibility criteria and merely described the functions as those 'prescribed by or under any Act, or … delegated … by the Attorney-General'. Everyone knew that the first appointee, Robert Garran, would continue the work he was already performing as Secretary of the Attorney-General's Department, including exercising most of the Attorney-General's vast array of wartime powers. There was, however, debate about the open-ended delegating power coupled with concern about apparent lack of political accountability. The accountability concerns even provoked a suggestion that the Commonwealth Solicitor-General should become a member of the Senate, but this was not taken up.

Garran's successors, George Knowles and Kenneth Bailey, continued to hold the primary office of departmental secretary, although Bailey also appeared in the High Court to argue constitutional matters.

The *Law Officers Act 1964* (Cth) reconstituted the office of Solicitor-General with the intent, according to the debates, that it be kept free of departmental responsibility and administration so that the Solicitor-General could concentrate on his function as permanent counsel for the Crown. This was, in effect, the Victorian model. Part of this new Commonwealth package was security of tenure for a fixed term.

The office then moved into its modern phase.

Some Themes

Having completed my gallop across the jurisdictions I turn to develop eight general points, some of which have already been flagged.

1. A Non-statutory Office with 'English' Incidents

With the limited exception of the Commonwealth legislation of 1916 the office was non-statutory until 1951 when Victoria legislated to define and change its traditional incidents.

Apart from some very early appointments, which were by the monarch from England,[12] Solicitors-General seem always to have been appointed by the Governor or Governor-General. Those who were not members of a ministry were not liable to retire on political grounds (*Solicitor-General v Wylde* (1946) 46 SR (NSW) 83: 93) but would (on my understanding) have been dismissible at pleasure unless protected by civil service legislation. I think it unlikely that a nineteenth- or early twentieth-century court would have viewed things as the High Court now does, judging by cases such as *Annetts v McCann* (1990) 170 CLR 596 (at 598) and *Jarratt v Commissioner of Police* (2005) 224 CLR 44. In *Annetts*, it was stated (at [2]) that:

> It can now be taken as settled that, when a statute confers power upon a public official to destroy, defeat or prejudice a person's rights, interests or legitimate expectations, the rules of natural justice regulate the exercise of that power unless they are excluded by plain words of necessary intendment.

In 1946, the Full Court of the Supreme Court of New South Wales would confirm in the *Red Book Case* (*Solicitor-General v Wylde* (1946) 46 SR (NSW) 83) that at common law the Crown was free to appoint the Solicitor-General to deputise for the Attorney-General, generally or ad hoc. The case involved charitable trust proceedings in which laity in the Church of England sought to have the bishop of the diocese of Bathurst restrained from authorising a new form of communion service. The Court divided on a second issue, namely whether the mere appointment

12 Possibly the last was Mr J.W. Rogers, who arrived from England in 1855 with his appointment as Solicitor-General for what was about to be renamed Tasmania together with the despatch to the Governor announcing the Royal Assent to the legislation establishing responsible government.

of a Solicitor-General conferred upon the officeholder the authority traditionally exercised by the Solicitor-General in England, for example, when the Attorney-General was absent or the office vacant. Jordan CJ and Halse Rogers J (at 93–4) held that this was indeed so and that:

> the mere appointment to an office by name in a colony, generally carries with it the right and duty of doing all acts done by usage by an officer of the same name in the mother country.[13]

This reasoning explains why it was assumed without question in the nineteenth century that Law Officers could do whatever in the way of representing the Crown in court or in the exercise of prerogative powers that their counterparts in England could do. Local practices about the Solicitor-General having the right of private practice and to charge a brief fee for civil Crown briefs have similar derivation.

On the other hand, the practice of a Law Officer sitting as a member of Cabinet, with the increased risk of conflating the interests of the government with the interests of justice, was a distinctly Australian development. Before responsible government, Solicitors-General were members of the Executive and Legislative Councils and, as indicated already, they often sat in Cabinet afterwards. Australia has never had a Lord Chancellor and (before the changes that commenced in Victoria in 1951) both Law Officers here have always been given a lot more to do than act as counsel for the Crown.

2. Barrister/Solicitor Roles

Battles over the segregation or fusion of the two 'branches' of the profession have raged across the jurisdictions since 1824. That was the year when, immediately upon their admission as barristers, William Charles Wentworth and Robert Wardell coolly moved that 'the gentlemen at present practising as solicitors and acting as barristers' be henceforth denied audience in the Supreme Court of New South Wales (Bennett 1969: 34–5). In his work *The Divided Legal Profession*, J.R.S. Forbes (1979: 179) has observed that:

> it would be interesting to have a monograph comparing professional opposition to Torrens Title, the Judicature Acts, and fusion [of the two branches of the profession].

The powers that be in New South Wales and Victoria seem to have had a clear vision until at least the twentieth century that the Attorney-General should be a barrister or become one on appointment.[14] I suspect that the pull of the English precedent was

13 Citing *Attorney-General v Belson* (1867) 4 WW & a'B (E) 57: 63.

14 See also the stance taken by Alfred Lutwyche when he refused to serve as Solicitor-General under an Attorney-General so long as the latter remained a solicitor (discussed above).

the same as regards the Solicitor-General role at times when and in places where the division of the profession was a matter of faith, although I would need to check in relation to all Solicitors-General who were public servants heading a Crown Law office. Queensland's twentieth-century practice of preferring *not* to have a lawyer as Attorney-General[15] should theoretically have enhanced the standing of the Solicitor-General's legal opinions in that State. However, democracy's bumpy ride in Queensland during that century makes it difficult to draw any conclusion about the quality of Crown law advice at the highest levels or the extent to which it was followed in any event.[16]

Throughout the nineteenth century Solicitors-General exercised a variety of roles, some of them definitely solicitorial and/or managerial. Sometimes there was no Crown Solicitor or the one person held dual appointments as Solicitor-General and Crown Solicitor.

In all jurisdictions, the full rigours of professional regulation have always been relaxed somewhat in relation to those in Crown service. In addition, the smaller colonies and States have always been more comfortable with the fusion of the profession, and this has given them greater flexibility in moulding the incidents of the Solicitor-Generalship.

3. Nature of the Solicitor-General's Advocacy Practice

Until well into the twentieth century when Directors of Public Prosecutions were introduced, the focus of any advocacy work on the part of Solicitors-General was decidedly criminal. And much of their advice work for the Attorney-General related to his role in initiating and controlling criminal prosecutions.

Solicitors-General also exercised in their own name traditional or statutory rights to commence or discontinue prosecutions, sometimes with these powers supplemented by a general appointment as a Crown prosecutor with authority to file informations or indictments (Bennett 1974: 70; *R v Woolcott Forbes* (1944) 44 SR (NSW) 333: 338–9).[17] And they tended to spend their court time in prosecuting high-profile trials or representing the Crown in criminal appeals.

---

15 According to McPherson (1989: 291), after Ryan's departure in 1919 the office of Attorney-General in Queensland ceased for nearly 70 years, barring the interval in 1929–32, to be held by a lawyer of any kind.

16 See fn 21 below.

17 One aspect of Isaac Isaacs' misguided stance in the Davies matter (discussed below) was his assertion that s 338 of the *Crimes Act 1890* (Vic) – which declared it lawful for 'Her Majesty's Attorney-General or Solicitor-General for Victoria or for any prosecutor in the name of a law officer to make presentment … for any indictable offence' – both allowed him to institute proceedings (as it clearly did) and also did the double duty of allowing the second Law Officer to trump his Attorney-General's *nolle prosequi*.

The idea that the Solicitors-General would gain a virtual stranglehold on constitutional litigation, with expertise to match, was not in contemplation for most of my period of review.

For the seminal 1920 decision on constitutional interpretation and the relevance of federalism principles, the *Engineers' Case* (*Amalgamated Society of Engineers v Adelaide Steamship Co Ltd* (1920) 28 CLR 129), the Commonwealth was a defendant and there were interventions by New South Wales, Tasmania and Victoria. Leading counsel for those parties were Frank Leverrier, George Flannery and Edward Mitchell. Not a Law Officer in sight, let alone a Solicitor-General. Moving forward to the *Melbourne Corporation Case* in 1947 (*Melbourne v Commonwealth* (1947) 74 CLR 31), in which the High Court's approach to federalism was substantially redefined, it is a similar picture. Attorneys-General popped up as leaders from time to time, but, for Solicitors-General, things really only start to change, by stages, in the 1960s.

As Solicitor-General, Henry Winneke led for Victoria, and Kenneth Bailey and later Anthony Mason for the Commonwealth, in the constitutional battles of the 1960s. Solicitor-General Harold Snelling shared the New South Wales constitutional briefs with J.W. Smyth of the private Bar.[18] In Queensland during this time, Arnold Bennett and Harry Gibbs did the High Court constitutional work from the private Bar. The same situation prevailed in Western Australia with Ronald Wilson and in South Australia with Andrew Wells, although each of Wilson and Wells would later become Solicitor-General for their States.

4. Contested Conclusiveness and Monopoly of Advice to 'the Crown'?

Any expectation that a Solicitor-General's advice might be accepted as conclusive has often depended more on the exigencies of politics than the officeholder's nominal seniority at the Bar or a delicate investigation of the scope of the word 'Crown'.

In the modern era, the Crown (even within a single jurisdiction) is no longer one and indivisible. The removal by statute of the shield of the Crown can pit agency against agency. Government agencies also get prosecuted for pollution and occupational health and safety breaches and offences. These matters, coupled with the outsourcing of governmental legal services, may lead contending agencies to adopt aggressive and sometimes short-sighted stances one against each other. There are also delicate questions about the Solicitor-General's role in providing any (let alone definitive) advice for independent statutory authorities, such as the Auditor-General, the Independent Commission against Corruption, the Director of Public Prosecutions and the President of a hostile Upper House

18 Between Snelling's departure in 1974 and the arrival of Mary Gaudron in 1981, Malcolm McLelland and Michael McHugh (members of the private Bar) would enjoy what they probably saw as the best of both worlds, with full fee-paying briefs in important constitutional cases and freedom to take private work in other matters.

of Parliament,[19] not to mention a Governor or Governor-General contemplating the exercise of reserve powers.

There has probably always been a tension surrounding the authority of a Solicitor-General's legal advice, although the focus of uncertainty and dispute naturally differed in earlier times. Initially, the colonial Governor controlled executive and legislative powers as well as having his hands near the throats of the judges themselves. After the arrival of the Law Officers, he looked generally to them for advice. But sometimes he got conflicting opinions, especially if he or the Solicitor-General considered the Attorney-General to be out of his depth or simply wrong in the particular instance. Furthermore, Governors always thought for themselves and, in any event, had the option of dismissing an incompetent or disagreeable Law Officer (or judge for that matter). The Governor could also look to the Colonial Office and/or the English Law Officers if he wanted a second opinion.

The judges too were an alternative (and sometimes competing) source of confidential legal advice to Governors, especially since they also sat on the early Executive and Legislative Councils. Chief Justices continued to tender advice about the exercise of reserve powers until late in the twentieth century.

In the early nineteenth century, Chief Justices had additional roles in certifying the validity of local measures and their advice in this regard was, at times, not what the Governor wanted or what his Law Officers told him. A particularly late instance of a Governor referring a matter to the judges for their opinion occurred in 1853 when Australia's one and only Bill for the dissolution of a single marriage was sent to Parliament after the opinion of the New South Wales judges was obtained. It was also reserved for the Royal Assent which belatedly arrived (Bennett 1974: 144–5).

When, in 1847, Pedder CJ and Montagu J ruled in a criminal case against the validity of the local *Dog Act* that they had previously intimated was in order, Lieutenant-Governor Denison was so ropable that he proposed to the Colonial Office that both judges be dismissed under *Burke's Act*. Denison had the strong support of both Law Officers, one of whom (Attorney-General Thomas Horne) advised that the judges had exceeded their lawful authority in striking down a law they had previously certified to be in order. (One can speculate that the ambitious Law Officers also had something of a vested interest in booting the two judges off the bench.) The Colonial Office thought it a bad precedent to dismiss a judge for the good faith exercise of judicial power, so Pedder kept his job. Montagu

19 In 1855 a warrant was issued for the arrest of the Comptroller-General of Convicts, John Hampton, for his refusal to appear before the legislature of Van Diemen's Land. It was issued by the Speaker of the Legislative Council, Michael Fenton. The Solicitor-General ruled that the warrant was illegal. The Governor prorogued Parliament to avoid a riot. Hampton hurriedly departed from the colony. The Supreme Court and the Privy Council held that Parliament lacked the powers it purported to exercise: see *Fenton v Hampton* (1858) 11 Moo PC 347, 14 ER 727; Castles 2003: 206. Cf. *Egan v Willis* (1998) 195 CLR 424.

was dismissed for an alternative misdemeanour, namely that he (admittedly with the concurrence of his Chief Justice) had ruled that the Supreme Court lacked jurisdiction to entertain a creditor's claim against himself. There were a number of creditors lining up to do so (Castles 2003: 198–9). The insolvency of colonial judges was a recurring problem.

It took a while for acceptance of the idea that a judge's ruling in court (*ex cathedra* as it were) was the final word on any legal dispute (cf. *South Australia v Totani* (2010) 242 CLR 39, 20 [1] (French CJ)). For one thing, the Governor ran his own Court of Appeal for many years (until 1936, in South Australia). The Judge-Advocates in the infant colonies were always viewed as under the direction of the Governor. And until well into the nineteenth century the Supreme Court judges who followed them were 'amovable' by the Governor for 'misbehaviour', subject to a right of appeal to the Privy Council.

The Rum Rebellion,[20] which arose out of a court ruling that both sides disputed, would not be the last time that the solemn decisions of courts would be ignored deliberately by those holding executive power. There were spectacular incidents in 1865 and 1888 when the governments in Victoria and New South Wales simply defied their highest courts, presumably reliant in part on advice from their own Law Officers (*Stevenson v The Queen* (1865) 2 W W & a'B (L) 143; Parkinson 2001: 213; *Ex parte Lo Pak* (1888) NSWLR (L) 221; *Ex parte Leong Kum* (1888) 9 NSWLR (L) 25; *Ex parte Woo Tin* (1888) 9 NSWLR (L) 493).

After the coming of responsible government, a Solicitor-General in a ministry was bound to get into conflict with his Governor, especially if the latter had a mind of his own or if his reading of the Royal Instructions directed him to defy his Ministers.

Between 1859 and 1861 John Hargrave as Solicitor-General, later as Attorney-General, was involved in what became known as the 'Great Seal Case'. The Colonial Office directed Governor Denison to make a land grant under the great seal of the Colony. Charles Cowper, the Premier, refused to release the seal, which was in his custody, as his government disapproved of the purpose of the grant. Hargrave's advice backed his Premier. Denison pointed to his own commission, declaring that: 'Whatever may be Mr Hargrave's opinion, I have not the most distant intention of delegating the trust to others'. Hargrave later changed his mind and formally advised Cowper that 'unquestionably the power to keep and use the great seal was with his Excellency'. The government accordingly yielded to the Governor's demand to release the seal, but Cowper and his Ministers at once tendered their resignations. Denison used the seal in accordance with his instructions and then returned it to Cowper, whose resignation, with that of his colleagues, he simultaneously refused to accept (Holt 1976: 43).

When the two Houses of Parliament were deadlocked in Victoria over the ministry's practice of tacking unpalatable measures to Appropriation Bills, the

20 A coup which saw Governor Bligh deposed by officers of the New South Wales 'Rum Corps' in 1808.

colonial Law Officers (George Higinbotham and Archibald Michie) contended that the tack was in conformity with English precedents. The Upper House formed its own contrary view and stuck to its guns despite the government being returned in a snap election. The Governor himself asked the Colonial Office to get the advice of the English Law Officers, a step which led the local Law Officers to protest that their views had to be followed, in essence because of the principle of responsible government. Ultimately, the Colonial Office recalled the Governor, but for the separate sin of partisanship in that he borrowed funds from a bank to keep the government afloat during the blockage of supply (Parkinson 2001).

5. Relationships Between the Senior and Junior Law Officers

Before responsible government, the Solicitor-General always regarded himself as a barrister understudy to the Attorney-General. He had an expectation of promotion to the senior office if and when it fell vacant, and his salary was two-thirds that of the Attorney-General, in New South Wales at least. The Solicitor-General also exercised the traditional powers of the Attorney-General during the latter's illness or absence.

There were several big spats between the two Law Officers in the nineteenth century. Some were caused by overlapping functions, others by competing ambitions and disparate competencies.

When he was Solicitor-General, John Hubert Plunkett complained to the Governor that, although he conducted nearly 100 cases in the criminal sessions for the Attorney-General, John Kinchela, the latter gave him no assistance in civil matters. Kinchela's profound deafness also created problems in the Legislative Council, a problem that the Governor addressed by appointing him to the bench! Governor Darling also tried to differentiate the two offices by emphasising the Solicitor-General's primary role in civil litigation. The Colonial Office preferred to address this industrial dispute by reiterating the seniority of the Attorney-General's role while admonishing both officers to cooperate and share their several responsibilities as much as possible (Mason 1988).

The monumental brawls between Alfred Stephen and his Attorneys-General in Van Diemen's Land have already been mentioned.

In 1893 the Victorian Solicitor-General, Isaac Isaacs resigned his office and his seat in Parliament when the Attorney-General declined to prosecute Matthew Davies, chairman of the Mercantile Bank of Australia, and others, on charges of conspiring to issue false balance sheets. Isaacs claimed that as Solicitor-General he also had the right to institute proceedings and he announced in the press his intention to do so and to appear for the prosecution. The public loved it, but such a breach of Cabinet solidarity, not to mention overreaching of the powers of the junior Law Officer, has justly been criticised by Isaacs' biographer (Cowen 1967: 35–6) and others (Edwards 1984: 373–9).

A disagreement of a nobler sort will be involved in a test case in which competing positions on the law are thrashed out between the Law Officers in public and in court (as occurs to this day in High Court constitutional battles). In 1824 a dispute arose over the ability of the Court of Sessions to proceed by way of jury trial. Since the two Law Officers disagreed on the matter, it was decided to submit it to the Supreme Court for determination through a writ of mandamus filed by the Attorney-General. The Attorney-General represented himself and the Solicitor-General appeared for the magistrates (*R v Magistrates of Sydney* [1824] NSWLR 3).

6. Conflicts of Interest

The right of private practice at the Bar traditionally enjoyed by Law Officers who are not public servants has been a recurring source of temptation and controversy. Flare-ups often followed complaints by the Law Officers themselves that they were overworked or needed extra resources.

Queensland Attorney-General Samuel Griffith got a ticking off from the Full Court of the Supreme Court of Queensland in 1875 for appearing privately in a divorce matter. This was seen to conflict with his duty of intervention against collusion in the role of Queen's Proctor. He accepted the rebuke 'under protest' (McPherson 1989: 150).

While he was Attorney-General in Victoria Isaac Isaacs once accepted a brief to appear against the Fitzroy municipality. New South Wales Attorney-General Edmund Barton and his Minister of Justice, Richard O'Connor, almost caused the downfall of their government when, in 1893, they accepted briefs to appear for a plaintiff against the Railway Commissioners. Barton tried to brazen it out by relying on the cab-rank rule and the spurious argument that the Railway Commissioners were not really a department of government. The upshot was that the two men resigned their ministries after a motion was carried against them (Mason 2012: 137).

The Law Officers' right of remunerated private practice was abolished in New South Wales in 1894. It lives on, being reintroduced in Queensland in the 1980s[21] and in Western Australia in 2012 with the appointment of Grant Donaldson. As the first Queensland Solicitor-General to be appointed with a right to private practice, Geoff Davies' capacity to put on behalf of South Australia and the other States an argument he had prepared on behalf of Queensland, when the latter State pulled out of the *Incorporation Case* (*New South Wales v Commonwealth* (1990) 169 CLR 482: 483) at short notice, shows that it can produce unintended public benefits.

21 Former High Court Chief Justice Gerard Brennan has suggested to the writer that this was, in part, a reaction to a long period of Crown law advice that some observers viewed as tainted by partiality towards the government in power. A Solicitor-General with one foot rooted in the private Bar was seen to reinforce both the appearance and actuality of independence.

7. Towards an Independent, Non-political Office

In differing ways, the incidents already mentioned involving Higinbotham and Michie over tacking, Barton, O'Connor and Isaacs over accepting briefs to appear against the government, and Isaacs over disputing his Attorney-General and Cabinet over the Davies *nolle prosequi* all reveal a tension inherent in a Law Officer being a member of government. The British have tried to address that tension by placing the Law Officers in Parliament but outside Cabinet; but they have always been more adept at turning a blind eye to apparent conflicts of interest.

The early twentieth century saw the start of a definite trend in Australia towards the office of Attorney-General becoming more overtly political and that of Solicitor-General becoming non-political. Thus, we have seen that, in Tasmania and Western Australia, then New South Wales intermittently, then the Commonwealth, then Queensland, the Solicitor-General's office ceased to be ministerial. When or where it existed, it was that of a public servant with oversight of a government law department who was responsible to a Minister in Parliament. Victoria was the last to switch, but when it did so in 1951 it created a new and narrower role of in-house but independent senior counsel that has since become the model for most other Australian jurisdictions.

8. The Solicitor-General as Messenger

Sometimes the message conveyed to the court is the silent one that the case has wide ramifications; although undue coyness can backfire, as the interveners (the Attorneys-General for the Commonwealth and South Australia represented by their respective Solicitors-General) would learn to their cost in *Dietrich v The Queen* (1992) 177 CLR 292. The case involved a question of whether the court's inherent power to stay proceedings to prevent an abuse of process would extend to ordering a stay when a defendant in a criminal trial was unrepresented by counsel. In that case (at 312), Mason CJ and McHugh J surprised many observers by inferring from the interveners' silence about cost that the principle the court was about to usher into the common law would not be:

> likely to impose a substantial financial burden on governments and [that] it may require no more than a re-ordering of the priorities according to which legal aid funds are presently allocated.

The willingness of the High Court to permit intervention and to contemplate the relevance of such information in a non-constitutional appeal in a criminal matter is, with respect, to be applauded. It remains interesting to speculate as to the form of evidence that could have been led on the relevant point in criminal appellate proceedings before a court that cannot always function as a law reform agency.

Sometimes the Law Officer's role is to put on record a borderline submission close to the client's heart that a less experienced barrister will announce to be 'on instructions'. Sometimes the actual instructions do not bear repeating in polite company, with the advocate coming under a professional obligation to put it in his or her own words or merely submit to the order of an angry court.

Message-sending can be a two-way street. And sometimes the messenger gets shot at as the only available target. Think of the coded rebuke of the Victorian government directed by Dixon CJ at Sir Henry Winneke, both *arguendo* and in the High Court's final reasons in the *Tait* matter.[22] I have read the transcript of Winneke's submissions carefully (Burns 1962). In the finest tradition, he took the judicial flack without stepping back any further than his instructions allowed. Indeed, he assisted the Court in ensuring that injunctive relief was granted in wide enough terms to prevent the hangman from slipping through the judicial noose.

The tradition of a judicial shellacking directed at the government lives on. In 2002 Black CJ unloaded the following message to Commonwealth Solicitor-General David Bennett with reference to recent statements by his client, the Immigration Minister, Philip Ruddock, that the Federal Court was frustrating the intentions of Parliament:

> Despite these statements I have not previously responded to any of them publicly. The most recent statement however raises a new issue since it would appear that it could only refer to issues before the court in these appeals – appeals to which your client is a party. He is the respondent in four appeals, in which he was successful before the trial judge. The statement was made only a matter of days before the date fixed weeks ago for the hearing of the appeals. You would know of course Mr Solicitor that the court is not amenable to external pressures from Ministers or from anyone else whomsoever, but we are concerned that members of the public might see the Minister's statements as an attempt to bring pressure on the Court in relation to these appeals to which he is a party (Transcript *NAAV v Minister for Immigration and Multicultural and Indigenous Affairs* (2002) 123 FCR 298).

The following day, Bennett made a reply on behalf of his Minister.

History's mistakes are sometimes repeated, but its lessons are always valuable. Whether or not guided by them, the Solicitors-General of Australia will continue to occupy roles that are personally fulfilling and serve the interests of justice in a variety of ways.

---

22 *Tait v The Queen* (1962) 108 CLR 620. Tait was convicted of murder and sentenced to hang. After trial, and in the context of a campaign to abolish the death sentence, questions were raised as to his mental capacity and the lawfulness of carrying out the sentence in those circumstances. The Victorian government under the premiership of Henry Bolte was anxious to have the sentence carried out and bridled at the delays stemming from appellate intervention after the normal appeal processes touching the conviction itself had been exhausted.

References

Bedford, R. 1954. *Think of Stephen: A Family Chronicle*. Sydney: Angus and Robertson.

Bennett, J.M. 1969. *A History of the New South Wales Bar*. Sydney: Law Book Co.

Bennett, J.M. 1974. *A History of the Supreme Court of New South Wales*. Sydney: Law Book Co.

Bennett, J.M. 2009. *Sir Alfred Stephen: Third Chief Justice of New South Wales*. Annandale, NSW: Federation Press.

Bigge, J.T. 1823. *Report of the Commissioner of Inquiry on the Judicial Establishments of New South Wales and Van Dieman's Land*. London: House of Lords.

Burns, C. 1962. *The Tait Case*. Melbourne: Melbourne University Press.

Burton, P. 2010. *From Moree to Mabo: The Mary Gaudron Story*. Crawley, WA: UWA Publishing.

Castles, A.C. 2003. *Lawless Harvests or God Save the Judges*. North Melbourne: Australian Scholarly Publishing.

Cowen, Z. 1967. *Isaac Isaacs*. Melbourne: Oxford University Press.

Coleman, R. 1988. *Above Renown: The Biography of Sir Henry Winneke*. South Melbourne: Macmillan.

Currey, C.H. 1966. Bannister, Saxe (1790–1877) in *Australian Dictionary of Biography*. Melbourne: Melbourne University Press. Volume 1.

Earls, T. 2009. *Plunkett's Legacy: An Irishman's Contribution to the Rule of Law in New South Wales*. North Melbourne: Australian Scholarly Publishing.

Edwards, J.Ll.J. 1984. *The Attorney-General, Politics and the Public Interest*. London: Sweet & Maxwell.

Elvery, L. 2009. *In My Opinion: The History of Crown Law Queensland 1859–2009*. Brisbane: Crown Law Queensland.

Fenton, J. 1884. *A History of Tasmania*. Hobart: Melanie Publications.

Finniss, B.T. 1886. *The Constitutional History of South Australia: During 21 Years from the Foundation of the Settlement in 1836 to the Inauguration of Responsible Government in 1857*. Adelaide: R.V.C. Rigby.

Griffith, G. 2007. The Office of Attorney General in New South Wales. *Legal History*. Volume 11, 79.

Forbes, J.R.S. 1979. *The Divided Legal Profession*. Sydney: Law Book Co.

Holt, H.T.E. 1976. *A Court Rises: The Lives and Times of the Judges of the District Court of New South Wales (1859–1959)*. Sydney: Law Foundation of New South Wales.

Mason, K. 1988. The Office of Solicitor General for New South Wales. *Bar News*. Volume 22.

Mason K. 2012. *Lawyers Then and Now: An Australian Legal Miscellany*. Annandale, NSW: Federation Press.

McLaren, J. 2011. *Dewigged, Bothered, and Bewildered: British Colonial Judges on Trial, 1800–1900*. Toronto: Osgoode Society.

McPherson, B.H. 1989. *The Supreme Court of Queensland 1859–1960: History, Jurisdiction, Procedure*. Sydney: Butterworths.

Morgan, D. 1979. *The Minister for Murder*. Richmond, Vic: Hutchinson of Australia.

New South Wales Parliamentary Debates. 1895. Volume 75.

Nicholls, M. 1972. Horne, Thomas (1800–1870) in *Australian Dictionary of Biography*. Melbourne: Melbourne University Press. Volume 4.

Parkinson, C. 2001. George Higinbotham and Responsible Government in Colonial Victoria. *Melbourne University Law Review*. Volume 25, 181.

Public Service Inquiry Commission. 1891. *Report on the Attorney-General's Department*. Sydney.

Ross, H.D. 1967. Ross, Hugh Cokely (1795–1869) in *Australian Dictionary of Biography*. Melbourne: Melbourne University Press. Volume 2.

Royal Commission on the Proposal to Make the Office of Attorney-General Permanent Non-Political. 1908. *Report of the Commission*. Hobart: John Vale: Government Printer of Tasmania.

Sexton, M.G. 2002. The Role of the Solicitor General in *No Mere Mouthpiece: Servants of All, Yet of None*, edited by G. Lindsay. Chatswood, NSW: LexisNexis Butterworths, 86–93.

Stephen, A. 1894. *Stephen Papers (Fisher Library)*. ML MSS 777/2. 1 March 1894.

Tink, A. 2009. *William Charles Wentworth: Australia's Greatest Native Son*. Sydney: Allen & Unwin.

Twomey, A. 2004. *The Constitution of New South Wales*. Leichhardt, NSW: Federation Press.

Chapter 2

The Parliament, the Executive and the Solicitor-General

Anthony Mason

Introduction

In 1975, Commonwealth Solicitor-General Maurice Byers and 11 senior public servants refused to answer questions in the Senate relating to the notorious 1975 'Loans Agreement'. In the event, the Senate excused Byers from further attendance but referred the matter to the Committee of Privileges. The central thrust of this chapter will deal with the Byers claim and that of the 11 senior public servants.

At the outset, it is necessary to note the statutory functions of the Solicitor-General for the Commonwealth. An understanding of these functions is essential to any discussion of the relationship, if any, between the Solicitor-General, the Parliament and the Executive.

The *Law Officers Act 1964* (Cth)

The Solicitor-General is the second Law Officer of the Commonwealth (section 5). His or her functions, set out in section 12 of the *Law Officers Act 1964*, are:

a. to act as counsel for:
    i. the Crown in right of the Commonwealth
    ii. the Commonwealth
    iii. a person suing or being sued on behalf of the Commonwealth
    iv. a Minister
    v. an officer of the Commonwealth
    vi. a person holding office under an Act or a law of a Territory
    vii. a body established by an Act or a law of a Territory; or
    viii. any other person or body for whom the Attorney-General requests him or her to act;
b. to furnish his or her opinion to the Attorney-General on questions of law referred to him or her by the Attorney-General; and
c. to carry out such other functions ordinarily performed by counsel as the Attorney-General requests.

Except in the performance of the duties of his or her office, or with the consent of the Attorney-General, the Solicitor-General shall not engage in the practice of a barrister or solicitor or engage in paid employment (s 9(1)).

It is evident from these provisions that the primary role of the Solicitor-General is to act as counsel and principal professional legal adviser for the Commonwealth and its various emanations. In this capacity, the Solicitor-General is in receipt of highly confidential information on matters of the highest importance to the government and advises on these matters. The Solicitor-General has the status of second Law Officer of the Commonwealth. It is also clear that the Solicitor-General is an independent statutory officer who is not subject to control or direction by the government as to the way in which he or she will discharge his or her statutory responsibilities, though as counsel for the Commonwealth he or she will take account of the instructions given to him or her.

Two points should be made about the statutory provisions. The first is the obligation under section 12(b) to furnish an opinion on a question of law referred by the Attorney-General. It is not to be implied from this qualification that the Solicitor-General cannot furnish an opinion to the Commonwealth or its emanations without a request from the Attorney-General. As Solicitor-General I was instructed by the Crown Solicitor and the Attorney-General's Department to advise departments and other Commonwealth agencies without any express approval by the Attorney-General being communicated to me.

The second point relates to such other functions ordinarily performed by counsel as the Attorney-General requests (s 12(c)). They have been understood to include acting as a nominee or delegate of Australia in the United Nations and international bodies and assisting Parliamentary Committees on legal questions. I do not recall any specific request from the Attorney-General to advise a Parliamentary Committee; my instructions came from the Attorney-General's Department. It is possible that the Department had obtained the Attorney-General's assent to my so acting. Alternatively, it is possible that what I did was simply a continuation of long-standing practice, antedating the *Law Officers Act*, whereby the Solicitor-General/Secretary of the Department (because the one person held both offices) or an officer of the department assisted such committees on legal questions. In a particular case, a question of conflict might arise in circumstances where the Commonwealth had an interest. The existence of such a conflict might affect the Solicitor-General's willingness to assist a committee.

That the Solicitor-General is an independent actor and that he or she is not subject to the direction or control of the Attorney-General or the government as to how he or she will discharge his or her responsibilities was a point strongly made by Maurice Byers. It formed part of the foundation of his refusal to answer questions Senators wanted him to answer.

The Events Leading up to the Byers Thesis

Even in court, Byers' submissions at times verged on the mystical. Michael McHugh once said that his greatest difficulty as counsel was replying to a Byers argument because you were never sure what the argument was. Byers' appearance before the Senate in 1975 saw him at his mystical best. He certainly baffled his interlocutors, and 35 years later I am still bemused by what he had to say. In order to appreciate what that was, we need to understand what the Senators wanted from him and the 11 public servants who were summoned to appear.

On 9 July 1975 the Senate, then controlled by the Opposition, resolved that it was of the opinion:

> that the Government has failed to give the Parliament and the Australian people a proper, full and accurate account of the activities of its Ministers, servants and agents, relating to all dealings by them, both prior to and subsequent to the Executive Council Meeting of 13 December 1974 which authorised the Minister for Minerals and Energy to borrow a sum not exceeding [$4,000m] in the currency of the United States of America for temporary purposes … (Senate Standing Committee of Privileges 1975: 36)

The Senate went on to resolve that the Solicitor-General and the 11 public servants (including the Secretary to the Treasury) be called to the Bar of the Senate 'to answer questions upon these matters and to produce all documents, files or papers in their possession, custody or control relevant to these matters which have not been tabled in either House of the Parliament' (Senate Standing Committee of Privileges 1975: 3).

Summonses were duly served on the Solicitor-General and the 11 public servants.

The background to the Senate resolution was the Opposition case that the proposed borrowings were not 'for temporary purposes' and were illegal. The Opposition relied on an opinion of William Deane, which stated, 'It is clear that if the proposed borrowings had not been borrowings "for temporary purposes" they would have been in breach of the Financial Agreement and illegal' (Senate Standing Committee of Privileges 1975: 41).

It is understood that Robert Ellicott and Senator Ivor Greenwood gave opinions to the same effect.[1] The contrary view on which the government acted was understood to be supported by the opinion of Senator Lionel Murphy, the

1 On 20 November 1975, Danny Sankey, a private citizen, laid informations against Gough Whitlam and other Ministers including Senator Lionel Murphy, alleging (a) a conspiracy to effect a purpose that is unlawful under a law of the Commonwealth (*Crimes Act 1914* (Cth) section 86(1)(c)) and (b) a conspiracy at common law. In *Sankey v Whitlam* (1978) 142 CLR 1, the High Court held unanimously that the first conspiracy alleged was bad in law because neither the Financial Agreement nor section 105A of the Constitution was a law of the Commonwealth, and no law made unlawful a borrowing otherwise than in

then Attorney-General. It was believed at the time that the Solicitor-General considered the Attorney-General's view arguable,[2] though the Opposition may have thought otherwise.

On 15 July 1975, Prime Minister Gough Whitlam wrote to the President of the Senate saying that 'each officer will be instructed by his Minister to claim privilege in respect of all questions upon the matters contained in the Resolution of the Senate and in respect of the production of all documents, files and papers relevant to these matters' (Senate Standing Committee of Privileges 1975: 16).

The Prime Minister's letter concluded with this paragraph:

> I make plain the Government's view that what the Senate is seeking to do is to obtain through officers of the Public Service information and documents which should be sought from Ministers by the normal and proper procedures of the Parliament. In taking this course, the fundamental character of Ministerial responsibility is challenged. It is the Government – not the Public Service – that will answer in the Parliament any request, any challenge put to it. It is the Government – not the Public Service – that is responsible to the people. This is in accord with the principles on which our democracy is based. If these principles are successfully challenged, Government would become unworkable. (Senate Standing Committee of Privileges 1975: 17)

The letter quoted a statement by Robert Menzies, who had said that it would be:

> alarming if an anti-Government Senate could undermine the objectivity and non-political integrity of the Public Service by exposing its senior and most responsible officers to a Parliamentary inquisition from which they had a right to be immune and compelling their entry into a field of political debate.[3]

---

accordance with the Financial Agreement. Subsequently, Stipendiary Magistrate Darcy Leo dismissed the second charge in the Queanbeyan Court of Petty Sessions.

2 The transcript of evidence in *Sankey v Whitlam* before Stipendiary Magistrate Darcy Leo reveals that, whereas Senator Lionel Murphy considered that the loan was 'for temporary purposes', the Solicitor-General, while having reservations about that view, thought it was 'arguable'.

3 This statement made to Parliament in 1953 and a later opinion given by Kenneth Bailey, then Solicitor-General, tabled in Parliament in 1956, seem to have been strongly influenced by the House of Lords decision in *Duncan v Cammell Laird & Co Ltd* [1942] AC 624 (the high water mark of public interest immunity). The decision gave way to a much more restricted view: see *Conway v Rimmer* [1968] AC 610; *Sankey v Whitlam* (1978) 142 CLR 1; *Commonwealth v Northern Land Council* (1993) 176 CLR 604. See also Lindell 1995: 396–7, especially footnote 56.

The Byers Thesis

On the same day the Solicitor-General wrote to the President asserting that he (the Solicitor-General) stood in a constitutional relationship to the Crown 'in which under the Constitution the Executive power of the Commonwealth alone is vested'. The letter went on to state that 'the deliberations of the Crown are secret' and cited the well-known passage from the judgment of Justice Owen Dixon in *Australian Communist Party v Commonwealth* (*Communist Party Case*) (1951) 83 CLR 1 (at 179) and referred to the oath of confidentiality taken by members of the Federal Executive Council.

The letter went on to say that the Crown's claim of privilege extends to opinions of the Law Officers, whether written or oral, and that the privilege covering such opinions had been recognised by the House of Commons. The letter concluded with the statement that the author must object to answering any question relating to the resolution as otherwise the claim to privilege may be to that extent defeated.

In the course of responding to questions put to him by Senators, the Solicitor-General made the basis of his objection to answering any questions relating to the matters identified in the Senate resolution somewhat clearer than the case he presented in his letter to the President. First, he said that the government had made a claim of privilege covering these matters, a claim either made or evidenced by the Prime Minister's letter to the President. It was not a claim of privilege asserted by the Solicitor-General himself, though he considered the claim of privilege to have been validly made by the Crown and not waived.

Secondly, according to the Solicitor-General in his answer to a question put by Senator Reg Wright (Commonwealth Parliamentary Debates 1975: 2787–8):

> The privilege is the privilege of secrecy of Crown deliberations. That there was a Crown deliberation here seems to be indisputable. The question, therefore, is the extent to which the privilege extends. I should have thought that it extended to events prior and subsequent to those deliberations.

The Solicitor-General went on to say, 'The central constitutional notion is the secrecy of the deliberations. That is the central constitutional notion'.

Senator Wright then said, 'Yes, that is behind the privilege of confidentiality'.

And the Solicitor-General replied, 'That is right'.

The Prime Minister in his letter to the President made no mention of secrecy as such. His letter identified the principle of responsible government as the central constitutional principle at stake but focussed on the attempt to obtain information from the public service rather than from Ministers, thereby potentially undermining the integrity of the public service.

The third point made by the Solicitor-General was that it was his duty to abide by the government's claim of privilege based on secrecy. Even if the Committee or the Senate rejected that claim, he conceived it to be his duty to abide by the claim, though he did speak of it as a matter of conscience.

On the other hand, the Solicitor-General, in answer to questions put by Senator Greenwood, made it clear that, if the claim to Crown privilege was rejected by a court, the answers would have to be given and the documents produced. He did not explain the basis for the difference in outcome; nor was he asked to explain it.

The Senate, after excusing the witnesses, including the Solicitor-General, from further attendance, resolved that 'the action of the Government in directing public servants called to the Bar of the Senate not to answer any questions is a massive cover-up of the Government's involvement in the attempted raising of overseas loans' (Senate Standing Committee of Privileges 1975: 1).

The Senate went on to refer to the Committee of Privileges for report:

a. the direction of the Prime Minister and Ministers that public servants claim privilege;
b. the further direction of Ministers that notwithstanding any rejection by the Senate of the claim for privilege the public servants summoned were not to answer any questions; and
c. the further claim for privilege by the Solicitor-General.

The Committee of Privileges delivered a majority report, holding that there was no breach of parliamentary privilege on the part of anyone. The 7 October 1975 report stated, with reference to the Solicitor-General's claim of privilege:

> This is not a claim of Crown privilege. It is a claim which arises from the Solicitor-General's conception of his obligation as the Second Law Officer of the Crown in the situation where the Crown has claimed privilege. It is a claim entitled to the respect of the Senate and the Committee of Privileges and ancillary to the matters of 'Crown privilege' referred to above. (Senate Standing Committee of Privileges 1975: 13)

The minority (Senators Greenwood, Webster and Wright), in a comprehensive dissent, stated, so far as is relevant:

> 3. That the directions of the Australian Ministers to claim privilege in respect of investigations by the Senate were misconceived. Such a claim is a claim for a Senate not to require an answer or a document in appropriate cases.
>
> 4. That in practice the Senate would ordinarily refrain from requiring answers to questions as to confidential advisings by public servants.
>
> …
>
> 6. The ultimate decision as to whether a question must be answered or a document produced is for the Senate and not for the Executive.

> 7. That the Solicitor-General – not claiming any privilege on professional ground or self-incrimination – was wrong in claiming that he should join a claim for privilege to the Ministers' claim of privilege, simply because such a claim was made and he was an officer appointed by an Executive. He erred in not discharging his higher duty to give evidence before a House of Parliament when lawfully required – subject to all proper privilege in respect of any particular question or class of questions – e.g. questions which impaired the confidentiality on which his relationship with an Executive was based. (Senate Standing Committee of Privileges 1975: 56)

There are a number of puzzling features in the Byers thesis. First, there is the proposition that the Solicitor-General stands in a 'constitutional relationship' with the Crown (the Executive), a relationship that evidently rests on his status as second Law Officer of the Commonwealth. Why that status gives rise to a constitutional relationship and what that relationship entails was not explained. Perhaps the suggested relationship is tied to s 61 of the Constitution, but in what way remains a matter of surmise.[4] No doubt the Solicitor-General's status differentiates him from the 11 public servants, but it is not clear why it should make a difference between his obligation to answer questions put by Senators and the obligation of the 11 public servants to do so.

As will appear later, Law Officers' opinions and advices to the Crown have been traditionally privileged from production to a House of Parliament. While this privilege may distinguish opinions and advices of the Law Officers from other government advices, the privilege does not evidence a constitutional relationship apart from the existence of the privilege itself.

Quite apart from the Solicitor-General's status as a Law Officer of the Crown, Byers was right in maintaining to Senator Greenwood that he was an independent officer who was not amenable to instructions from government or the Attorney-General as to how he should discharge his statutory responsibilities or as a witness summoned to appear before the Senate.

Secondly, there is the proposition that the deliberations of the Crown are secret. So they are unless they are made public. Is the proposition any more than a statement of fact? The answer to this question depends upon Dixon's enigmatic comment in the *Communist Party Case* (at 179):

> The counsels of the Crown are secret and an inquiry into the grounds upon which the advice tendered proceeds may not be made for the purpose of invalidating the act formally done in the name of the Crown by the Governor-General in Council.

---

4 Section 61 of the Constitution provides: 'The executive power of the Commonwealth is vested in the Queen and is exercisable by the Governor-General as the Queen's representative, and extends to the execution and maintenance of this Constitution, and of the laws of the Commonwealth'.

If it was the obligation of the Solicitor-General to keep the relevant deliberations secret, it was also the obligation of the 11 public servants to keep the deliberations secret. A ministerial instruction was not necessary to bring this about. Indeed, the purpose of the ministerial instructions seems not to have been to trigger an obligation of secrecy but to reinforce the constitutional principle of responsible government, which was the central point of Prime Minister Whitlam's letter to the President of the Senate and the reason for instructing the public servants not to answer questions relating to the deliberations. The final element in the Byers thesis that is problematic is the distinction Byers made in answer to questions put by Senator Greenwood between the rejection of a claim to Crown privilege by a court and the rejection of such a claim by the Senate or one House of the Parliament.

Discussion of the Elements of the Byers Thesis

Significance of the Status of a Law Officer of the Crown

Professor J.LI.J. Edwards, the author of *The Law Officers of the Crown*, identifies 1461 as the first occasion on which the King's Attorney is described in the patent of appointment as 'Attorney-General' (1964: 27). Edwards notes that, in the same year, the 'King's Solicitor' was appointed and that this appointment has been universally regarded as the original precursor of the modern office of Solicitor-General (1964: 27–8).

Whether, from the beginning, the Solicitor-General was regarded as a deputy of the Attorney-General is a matter of some controversy. Certainly, from the beginning of the sixteenth century both the Attorney-General and the Solicitor-General occupied positions of prestige in the hierarchy of State officials. Later, in the United Kingdom it was recognised that the Solicitor-General was the deputy of the Attorney-General.

It has long been established, in both the United Kingdom and Australia, that the Law Officers are the principal legal advisers of the Crown and the leading representatives of the Crown in court. The Attorney-General is the titular head of the Bar, and the Solicitor-General ranks in precedence second only to him.

There was vested in the Attorney-General, as chief legal representative of the Crown in all court proceedings in which the Crown was a party, a number of wide common law powers (or prerogatives), including the filing of an *ex officio* information, the entering of a *nolle prosequi* in certain criminal prosecutions and the maintaining of relator actions in matters affecting the general public. Edwards (1964: 226), speaking of these powers, said:

> These powers, exercised by the granting of what is generally known as the Attorney-General's fiat, are of great antiquity, the Attorney-General being well nigh a matter unto himself as to whether or not, and in what precise circumstances, he will issue his certificate.

Others were added to these powers by statute. Thus, the institution of criminal proceedings in many instances has been conditioned on the Attorney-General's consent.

The exercise of these various powers, whether by the Attorney-General or the Solicitor-General (as his deputy), are unreviewable. But neither this circumstance nor the status of the Attorney-General or the Solicitor-General has any bearing on the question whether either of the Law Officers was amenable to the processes of either House of Parliament when it came to answering questions, whether concerning advice given to the Crown or otherwise. As we shall see, Parliament developed conventions by which it respected the confidentiality of legal advice tendered to the Crown by the Law Officers, but those conventions rest on practice and did not depend on the immunity of the Law Officers from the processes of Parliament.

The modern United Kingdom Solicitor-General is a Member of Parliament not a statutory officer, unlike his or her Australian counterpart. As a Member of Parliament, he or she may be said to stand in a constitutional relationship with the Parliament. But the Australian Solicitor-General stands in no comparable relationship. He or she is, in no sense, a deputy or a delegate of the Attorney-General, except in so far as particular functions may be specifically delegated to him or her.

The Secrecy of the Deliberations of the Crown

Dixon's comment in the *Communist Party Case* amounts to no more than a statement which recognises the secrecy of Crown deliberations. As Byers pointed out, the secrecy of Cabinet deliberations is protected or reinforced by the oath of confidentiality taken by members of the Federal Executive Council. Byers was not suggesting that Dixon's comment was a proposition of law or that it was itself the source of an obligation of secrecy. Byers was simply saying, as I understand him, that as the deliberations were confidential, he was under an obligation to maintain that confidentiality. As a matter of principle, it would seem to follow that public servants generally would be subject to a like obligation, with or without an instruction from the Minister to whom they were responsible. With respect to this point, there is no reason to distinguish their position from that of the Solicitor-General, except in so far as they are subject to instruction and he is not.

The Legal Effect of Confidentiality

The critical question is whether the confidentiality of Crown deliberations protects them from disclosure, either to a court in litigation or to a House of Parliament that seeks to inquire into them. Byers acknowledged to Senator Greenwood that, if a court rejected a claim to privilege, questions must be answered and documents produced. If this were so, why would the position be different if the Senate or a committee of the Senate, rather than a court, rejected the claim to confidentiality or privilege?

Ministerial Responsibility

The only basis for plausibly differentiating the two situations is the principle of ministerial responsibility invoked by Prime Minister Whitlam in his letter to the President of the Senate, which is supported by the statement of Menzies (set out above) and the majority judgments of Spigelman CJ and Meagher JA in *Egan v Chadwick* (1999) 46 NSWLR 563. This case was a sequel to *Egan v Willis* (1998) 195 CLR 224, in which Egan – who was a Minister of the Crown (Treasurer), a member of the Legislative Council of New South Wales ('the Council') and Leader of the Government in that House – had refused to table papers called for by a resolution of the House.[5] The House passed a resolution judging him guilty of contempt and suspending him from the service of the House for the remainder of the day's sittings. The High Court held that a House of the New South Wales Parliament had such power to suspend a member of the House who refuses to produce a non-privileged document called for by the House. In that case, Egan made no claim for privilege in relation to the documents called for.

Subsequently, he made a claim for privilege following resolutions of the Council passed on 13 October 1998 calling upon him to table 'all documents relating to the ongoing contamination of Sydney's water supply system' (New South Wales Parliamentary Debates 1998: 745).

The resolutions differentiated between documents that were the subject of a claim of legal professional privilege or public interest immunity and those that were not. In relation to the first category of documents, the resolutions provided that, in the event of a dispute as to the validity of a claim for privilege in relation to a document, the document was to be released to an independent legal arbiter appointed by the President of the Council for evaluation or report. The Council would then decide whether the document would be made public.

Egan refused to table any documents. At relevant times, he had in his possession two documents, production of which was called for by the resolutions. The documents were:

a. a letter of advice dated 26 August 1998 from the Crown Solicitor to the Director-General of the Cabinet Office; and
b. a submission to Cabinet from the Deputy Premier dated 21 September 1998.

Egan claimed that document (a) was the subject of legal professional privilege and that document (b) was the subject of public interest immunity.

5 See also *Egan v Willis* (1996) 40 NSWLR 650 (Court of Appeal).

On 20 October 1998, the Council resolved that Egan had failed to comply with its order for production and adjudged him guilty of contempt for that failure, suspending him from the service of the House for five sitting days.

On 24 November 1998, by a further resolution, the Council called on Egan to table previously identified documents as well as further documents, again involving an evaluation and report by an independent legal arbiter if there was a claim of legal professional privilege or public interest immunity. Egan delivered documents in his possession called for by the resolution of 24 November 1998, except the documents in respect of which he claimed legal professional privilege or public interest immunity. He refused to table these documents. Again, he was adjudged guilty of contempt of the House and suspended from the service of the House. He was escorted from the House by the Usher of the Black Rod, who was directed by Council's resolution on 27 November to remove Egan from the House.

Egan, in his statement of claim, alleged that his forcible removal from the House constituted an assault by the Usher of the Black Rod. In the proceedings that followed the filing of the statement of claim, two issues arose for determination:

1. did the power of the Council to require production of documents, upheld by the High Court in *Egan v Willis*, include power to require production of privileged documents of the two classes already mentioned; and, if not,
2. who was to decide whether the claim of privilege in relation to any class of document should be allowed?

The majority (Spigelman CJ and Meagher JA) held that the Council had power to require production of documents subject to either one of the two classes of privilege mentioned but that the Council had no power to require production of documents, production of which would be inconsistent with the doctrine of ministerial responsibility, such as Cabinet documents. Priestley JA dissented, holding that the power extended to such documents. The Court did not answer the second question.

The majority's reasoning The judgment of Spigelman CJ (with whom Meagher JA agreed) stated five propositions which are incontrovertible. They were:

1. each House exercises a constitutional function to make laws;
2. each House performs the function of parliamentary review of executive conduct, in accordance with the principle of responsible government;
3. the Council has such powers as are reasonably necessary for the proper exercise of its functions;
4. production of documents by Ministers is reasonably necessary for the proper exercise of both its functions; and
5. each House may impose sanctions on a member of the House for the purpose of inducing compliance by a member, but not for the purpose of punishing a member.

In New South Wales, unlike the other States, the powers, immunities and privileges of a House have not been declared or regulated by statute so that the common law rule in (3) above applies.

The central proposition of Spigelman CJ's judgment is that the power of the Council to require production of documents is derived 'in significant degree' from the doctrine of responsible government. Gleeson CJ described the concept of responsible government in *Egan v Willis* (1996) 40 NSWLR 650 (at 660) as 'a concept based upon a combination of law, convention and political practice. The way in which that concept manifests itself is not immutable'.[6]

The concept is fundamental to the Australian constitutional system of government. Indeed, along with representative government, it is the central theme in that system.

Ministerial responsibility to the Parliament is one of the elements of responsible government. This responsibility is owed by a Minister to both Houses of Parliament, but in particular to the House of which he or she is a member. The responsibility has individual and collective elements.

Spigelman CJ's conclusion that the Council's power to require a Minister to produce documents should not extend to documents the production of which would conflict with the doctrine of ministerial responsibility rested on two important paragraphs in his judgment (paragraphs 54 and 55, at 574):

> The high constitutional functions of the Legislative Council encompass both legislating, and the enforcement of the accountability of the Executive. Performance of these functions may require access to information the disclosure of which may harm the public interest. Access to such information may, accordingly, be 'reasonably necessary for the performance of the functions of the Legislative Council'.
>
> However, in my opinion, it is not reasonably necessary for the proper exercise of the functions of the Legislative Council to call for documents the production of which would conflict with the doctrine of ministerial responsibility, either in its individual or collective dimension. The power is itself, in significant degree, derived from that doctrine. The existence of an inconsistency or conflict constitutes a qualification on the power itself.

Spigelman CJ went on to note that, in the context of claims for public interest immunity in the course of litigation, the courts have always recognised the significance of Cabinet confidentiality as an application of the principle of collective responsibility. Applying the approach he thought had been adopted by the courts,[7] his Honour concluded that documents which disclose the actual deliberations of Cabinet, as distinct from those which are in the nature of reports

6 See also *Egan v Willis* (1998) 195 CLR 424, 451 (Gaudron, Gummow and Hayne JJ).

7 A view disputed by Priestley JA, whose view is set out below.

or submissions for the consideration of Cabinet, are inconsistent with the doctrine of ministerial responsibility. The conclusion was that the Council had no power to require their production.

His Honour reached a different conclusion in relation to documents that were the subject of a claim of legal professional privilege. In the performance of its accountability function, the Council may require access to the legal advice on the basis of which the Executive acted or purported to act. Access to such advice is reasonably necessary for the exercise by the Council of its functions.

The dissenting judgment of Priestley JA Priestley JA's specific ground for holding that the Council had power to compel production of documents subject to a public interest immunity claim was that the courts have such a power. He said:

> In the adversary situations where public interest immunity may attach to documents to prevent their production, there is no doubt that the decision whether the doctrine attaches or not is, finally, not for the Executive to make, but for a court, after the court has had the documents produced to it. The court may not require to see the documents itself. It may be satisfied by evidence about the nature of the documents or other circumstances in the particular case that it should refuse production to the parties because of public interest immunity: but it undoubtedly has the power to compel production to itself even of cabinet documents, even though the power will in regard to certain cabinet documents be used with the highest degree of circumspection: see *The Commonwealth v Northern Land Council* [1993] HCA 24; (1993) 176 CLR 604 at 617–19.

Priestley JA made the obvious point that the case for the existence of the power in the Council was stronger than the case for the existence of the power in the courts. When the constitutional role of the Council is regarded in reviewing executive action and holding the executive accountable, this must be so. Priestley JA noted that Senator Gareth Evans, as Leader of the Government in the Senate, said in his evidence to the Senate Standing Committee of Privileges (cited in Lindell 1995: 403–4):

> In the particular context that we are talking about here – a tussle about whether or not some document or some information should be revealed – the claim that an executive government may make of public interest immunity … is, I acknowledge, ultimately one for the House of Parliament to determine. That follows from first principles, if you accept that is the way the *Constitution* works on these matters.
>
> As a technical matter, that is the case. But we are arguing, as so often is the case when it comes to constitutional matters, that the technical power might

> be absolute but the way in which it should be exercised in practice should be regarded as subject to all sorts of conventions and limitations.[8]

The points of difference between the majority and minority judgments It will be apparent from the foregoing summary of the conflicting judgments that there are two points of difference between the majority and Priestley JA, namely:

1. the existence of power in the courts to compel production of documents relating to Cabinet deliberations; and, more importantly,
2. the significance of the doctrine of ministerial responsibility as an obstacle to the existence of the power.

The courts' power to order production of Cabinet documents That the courts possess this power is clearly established by the majority judgment of the High Court in *Commonwealth v Northern Land Council* (1993) 176 CLR 604. The majority pointed out that, though there are extremely strong considerations of public policy weighing against documents 'recording Cabinet deliberations upon current or controversial matters ... the immunity ... is not absolute' (at 617). The sole dissentient, Toohey J, who was in agreement with this proposition, pointed out (at 630–31) that a similar approach had been adopted in England, New Zealand, Ireland and the United States.

The majority went on to say (at 618):

> In the case of documents recording the actual deliberations of Cabinet, only considerations which are indeed exceptional would be sufficient to overcome the public interest in their immunity from disclosure, they being documents with a pre-eminent claim to confidentiality.

Later (at 618) the majority said:

> Indeed for our part we doubt whether the disclosure of the records of Cabinet deliberations upon matters which remain current or controversial would ever be warranted in civil proceedings. The public interest in avoiding serious damage to the proper working of government at the highest level must prevail over the interests of a litigant seeking to vindicate private rights. In criminal proceedings the position may be different.

These passages clearly acknowledge the existence of a power in the courts to order production of documents recording Cabinet deliberations, though they state that the power will be exercised only in exceptional circumstances.

---

8 This view is supported by various Senate Committees (Evans 1995: 484–96; Joint Select Committee on Parliamentary Privilege 1984: paragraphs 9.11–9.15; Campbell 1986: 10–19; Lindell 1995: 403).

The majority in *Egan v Chadwick* did not refer to the passages quoted above. The majority judgments proceeded as if these passages did not exist. On the other hand, Priestley JA relied on these passages in concluding that the courts have power to order production of Cabinet documents, even if the power will be exercised only in exceptional circumstances, if at all. He was right to do so. If claims for privilege for such documents are not treated as conclusive in the courts, why should they be treated differently in Parliament?

Ministerial responsibility The key to the majority conclusion that there is no such power is expressed in the last two sentences of paragraph 55 of the judgment in *Egan v Chadwick* (at 574). They present the proposition that because the power is 'in significant degree' derived from the doctrine of ministerial responsibility, the existence of an inconsistency between the power and the doctrine constitutes a qualification on the power itself.

Subject to the effect of s 49 of the Australian Constitution, a matter to be discussed later, it may be accepted that the power of a House to order production of documents is related to the doctrine of ministerial responsibility. A House has both a legislative function and a function of holding the Executive to account. In both roles, it may require information in order to achieve its purpose and, to that end, it may require information to be provided and documents to be produced on the basis that they are necessary for the House's performance of its functions. But it would seem that a House's power to require information to be provided and documents to be produced is associated with the doctrine of ministerial responsibility only in so far as the power is exercised in order to hold the executive to account. As far as the power exists for legislative purposes, its existence owes little, if anything, to the doctrine of ministerial responsibility.

In *Egan v Willis* (1998) 195 CLR 424 (at 451), Gaudron, Gummow and Hayne JJ said:

> A system of responsible government traditionally has been considered to encompass 'the means by which Parliament brings the Executive to account' so that 'the Executive's primary responsibility in its prosecution of government is owed to Parliament'. The point was made by Mill, writing in 1861, who spoke of the task of the legislature 'to watch and control the government: to throw the light of publicity on its acts'. It has been said of the contemporary position in Australia that, whilst 'the primary role of Parliament is to pass laws, it also has important functions to question and criticise government on behalf of the people' and that 'to secure accountability of government activity is the very essence of responsible government'.

Later (at 452), their Honours noted that the confidentiality of Cabinet deliberations reflects the principle of collective responsibility and that *Northern Land Council* stated that 'it remains an important element in our system of government'.

The statement that Cabinet confidentiality reflects the principle of collective responsibility means no more than that confidentiality is an important incident of, and conducive to, collective responsibility in promoting and maintaining full and frank deliberations in Cabinet. To say, as the majority in *Egan v Chadwick* did, that this element of ministerial responsibility is to prevail over the role of a House in securing accountability of government, inverts the true order of constitutional priorities and the right of the public to be fully informed about the activities of its government, and have those activities scrutinised by their elected representatives. Curiously enough, Spigelman CJ referred to the statement of Lord Chancellor Haldane on responsible government in which he said that the executive 'is almost the creature' of the legislature (*Egan v Chadwick*: 569). Today there are those who would say that the Executive dominates the Legislature, at least the Lower House if not the Senate in the Australian Parliament, though that domination is at odds with Parliament's historic purpose. To weaken the Parliament's oversight of the Executive by denying a House power to compel the production of documents recording Cabinet deliberations would be to subtract further from Parliament's historic role of oversight and holding the Executive to account.

The passage from the judgments of Gaudron, Gummow and Hayne JJ in *Egan v Willis* (at 451), quoted above, a passage not mentioned by the majority in *Egan v Chadwick*, makes it clear that securing the accountability of government activity is the 'very essence' of responsible government. If there is to be a collision between the attainment of this object and the preservation of Cabinet confidentiality, then the former must prevail over the latter.[9]

As the Executive is responsible and answerable to the Legislature, the confidentiality of Cabinet deliberations cannot stand as a reason for denying to the Council the existence of a power that is necessary for the purpose of achieving one of its constitutional functions when the Council considers that it needs access to Cabinet deliberations in order to review executive activity – and all the more so when there is no ground for denying the existence of the power when it is exercised for the purpose of enacting legislation. To deny the existence of the power would impair the Council's (and the Senate's) discharge of its high constitutional function of reviewing executive activity.

It is for the courts to determine the existence and the scope of the powers and privileges of a House of Parliament. In making this determination, it is appropriate that the courts, in deciding whether a House has a particular power, should proceed on the footing that the House will exercise the power responsibly, with all due regard to considerations which argue against an exercise of the power in the context of ministerial responsibility. As *Egan v Willis* makes clear, ministerial responsibility is a doctrine neither set in stone nor in law. It is a blend of law,

9 As an aside, it should be noted that the preservation of public service confidentiality designed to promote full and frank advice to Ministers, formerly regarded as supporting Crown privilege immunity of documents from production in court, has given way to inspections of the documents by a judge in appropriate cases.

convention, practice and understandings. Its development owes much to the political process, and its future development should be left to be shaped by that process. The question, which arose in *Egan v Chadwick* and for that matter in the Loans Agreement *imbroglio*, was in essence a political question, and it should have been resolved as a political question.

Section 49 of the Australian Constitution Section 49 provides:

> The powers, privileges and immunities of the Senate and the House of Representatives and of the members and committees of each House shall be such as are declared by the Parliament, and until declared shall be those of the Commons House of Parliament of the United Kingdom, and of its members and committees, at the establishment of the Commonwealth.

In 1901, the House of Commons had authority to act as 'the Grand Inquest of the Nation' (Lindell 1995: 385). The Commons were, in the words of Lord Coke, according to Coleridge J in *Howard v Gossett* (1845) 10 QBD 359 (at 379–80), 'the general inquisitors of the realm'. Commonwealth legislation relating to parliamentary privileges does not appear to have affected the powers of the Houses of the Australian Parliament to inquire (Lindell 1995: 385–6).

As Lindell points out, this inquisitorial function was developed before the evolution of the doctrine of responsible government (Lindell 1995: 385). Indeed, in *Commonwealth v Northern Land Council* (1991) 30 FCR 1 (at 16), the Full Court of the Federal Court noted that the 'concept of collective responsibility did not really emerge as an element of Cabinet government until the mid-nineteenth century'.

It cannot be persuasively argued that the subsequent acceptance of the doctrine at some unidentified point in time impliedly reduced the existing powers of the House to compel answers to questions and production of documents by reason of public interest community. The most that can be said of this argument is that in the United Kingdom Parliament it has always been accepted that, as a matter of convention, the opinions and advices of the Law Officers are kept confidential and are not laid before Parliament unless a Minister seeks to make an opinion or advice known (Edwards 1964: 258; Erskine May 2004: 433). The purpose of the convention is 'to enable the government to obtain frank and full legal advice in confidence' (Erskine May 2004: 433). But this is a matter of convention, not of power.

Conclusion

Although the confidentiality of Cabinet deliberations and Law Officers' opinions are protected by convention from disclosure in Parliament, a House of Parliament has power to compel disclosure or production, even if the power would be exercised only in exceptional circumstances.

References

Campbell, E. 1986. Parliamentary Inquiries and Executive Privilege. *Legislative Studies*. Volume 1(1), 10–19.

Commonwealth Parliamentary Debates. 1975. *Senate*. 16 July 1975.

Edwards, J.Ll.J. 1964. *The Law Officers of the Crown: A Study of the Offices of the Attorney-General and Solicitor-General of England with an Account of the Office of the Director of Public Prosecutions of England.* London: Sweet & Maxwell.

Evans, H. (ed.) 1995. *Odgers Australian Senate Practice*. 7th edition. Canberra: Australian Government Publishing Service for Department of the Senate.

Joint Select Committee on Parliamentary Privilege. 1984. *Exposure Report*. Parl Paper No 87.

Lindell, G. 1995. Parliamentary Inquiries and Government Witnesses. *Melbourne University Law Review*. Volume 20(2), 383–422.

May, T.E. 2004. *Erskine May's Treatise on the Law, Privileges, Procedures and Usages of Parliament*. 23rd edition. London: LexisNexis.

New South Wales Parliamentary Debates. 1998. *Legislative Assembly*. 13 October 1998.

Senate Standing Committee of Privileges. 1975. *Report on Matters Referred by Senate Resolution of 17 July 1975*. Parl Paper No 215.

Chapter 3
The Courts, the Executive and the Solicitor-General

M.G. Hinton

Introduction

On 27 February 1969, William Andrew Noye Wells, later the Honourable Justice Wells of the Supreme Court of South Australia, was appointed South Australia's second Solicitor-General. It is often thought that he was the first, but this is incorrect. South Australia's first Solicitor-General was John Tuthill Bagot. He was appointed to the position as part of the government formed by J. Baker in August 1858. That government lasted 10 days. Its demise was in no small part due to the appointment of Bagot. It occurred in the following circumstances (Hague 2005: 721). At the relevant time s 17 of South Australia's *Constitution Act 1855* provided:

> If any Member of the said Parliament shall accept of any office of profit or pension from the Crown, during pleasure, excepting those offices which are hereinafter required to be held by Members of the said Parliament, his seat shall thereupon and is hereby declared vacant.

Relying on this section Richard Hanson, later the Honourable Chief Justice Hanson of the Supreme Court of South Australia, raised with the House that there was a stranger on the floor. Hanson's contention was that by accepting the position of Solicitor-General, one for which there was no statutory provision and thus, he assumed, had been made in accordance with the custom established in England, Bagot had accepted an office of profit from the Crown during pleasure. Bagot's seat was, therefore, vacant and he was a stranger. Hague (2005: 271) explained:

> Bagot replied that he would not receive a sixpence from his appointment, and a somewhat acrimonious debate followed, which was still in progress when the House adjourned. Next day a motion of want of confidence in Mr Baker's administration was carried by a majority of twenty-four to seven. The ministry resigned, having held office for ten days …

Over 100 years passed before South Australia again broached the subject of creating the office of Solicitor-General. As I have indicated, this occurred with the appointment of Wells in 1969. Even then the creation of the position was the product of nothing more than changing the title of the permanent head of the Crown Law Department from Crown Solicitor to Solicitor-General.[1]

It was not until 1972 and the enactment of the *Solicitor-General Act 1972* (SA) that the position as it is known today was created.[2] The then Attorney-General, subsequently Chief Justice of South Australia, L.J. King, explained that the office of Solicitor-General was an ancient one, that whilst in England he was the Second Law Officer of the Crown and a member of Parliament, in Australia he was usually a senior barrister, outside Parliament, in the employment of the government as the senior legal adviser to the Crown (South Australian Parliamentary Debates 1972a: 3563). As such it was:

> desirable that the Solicitor-General should be free of any responsibility for the everyday affairs of a department, so that he may devote the whole of his time to the more important legal matters, including court cases, in which the government is concerned, and be free for any special duties in which his services might be required.

Consequently the Act removed the office of Solicitor-General from the public service and restored to the Crown Solicitor his department. The intention was that South Australia be brought into line with the Commonwealth and the other States. Hence the provisions of the Act were based upon its equivalents in New South Wales, Victoria, Western Australia and at the Commonwealth level.

The terms and conditions of the Solicitor-General for South Australia – an appointment of the Crown[3] who can be removed from office only if incapable of performing the duties of the office for some reason other than temporary illness, or if found guilty of misconduct[4] – were:

---

1 This was effected under the *Public Service Act 1967* (SA). See the South Australian Government Gazette 1969: 577.

2 As at this date Brian Cox was Solicitor-General, having succeeded Wells to the office upon the appointment of the latter to the Supreme Court of South Australia. Cox, later the Honourable Justice Cox of the Supreme Court of South Australia, was Solicitor-General from 30 July 1970 until 21 December 1978.

3 *Solicitor-General Act 1972* (SA) s 4. In the other jurisdictions see *Law Officers Act 1964* (Cth) s 6; *Solicitor-General Act 1969* (WA) s 3; *Solicitor-General Act 1985* (Qld) s 5; *Attorney-General and Solicitor-General Act 1972* (Vic) s 4; *Solicitor-General Act 1983* (Tas) s 4; *Law Officers Act 1978* (NT) s 13; *Solicitor-General Act 1969* (NSW) s 2; *Law Officers Act 2011* (ACT) s 16.

4 *Solicitor-General Act 1972* (SA) s 7. In the other jurisdictions see *Law Officers Act 1964* (Cth) s 10; Solicitor-General Act 1969 (WA) s 7; *Solicitor-General Act 1985* (Qld) s 17; *Attorney-General and Solicitor-General Act 1972* (Vic) s 4; *Solicitor-General Act 1983* (Tas) s 6; *Law Officers Act 1978* (NT) s 15; *Solicitor-General Act 1969* (NSW) s 2; *Law Officers Act 2011* (ACT) s 21.

> designed to give the office some measure of formal status and practical independence which appears desirable, and also make the position attractive, in the event of a vacancy, to suitably qualified lawyers in private practice as well as to those in the Public Service (South Australian Parliamentary Debates 1972a: 3563).

As to the duties of the Solicitor-General, these were set out in s 6 of the Act, which provided:

> The Solicitor-General:
>
> (a) shall at the request of the Attorney-General –
> (i) act as Her Majesty's counsel; and
> (ii) perform such other duties as are ordinarily performed by counsel; and
> (b) shall not, except with the consent of the Attorney-General, engage in any other remunerative employment.

This remains the position. With the exception of New South Wales, the duties of each of the Solicitors-General of the Commonwealth, the States and the Territories, as statutorily prescribed, are broadly similar.[5] In New South Wales the difference lies in the capacity of the Solicitor-General to perform some of the functions of the Attorney-General in certain circumstances. Those circumstances aside, the function of the New South Wales Solicitor-General is generally the same as in the other jurisdictions.

Clearly as the principal legal advisers to the governments of the federation, the Solicitors-General play an important role in the practice and development of public law. As will be seen, in practice the Solicitors-General have a similar responsibility for the Constitution and its application, born not only of their role as principal legal adviser to the governments of the federation, but facilitated in no small part by s 78A of the *Judiciary Act 1903* (Cth).[6] Beyond this, the day-to-

---

5 See *Law Officers Act 1964* (Cth) s 12; *Solicitor-General Act 1969* (WA) s 9; *Solicitor-General Act 1985* (Qld) s 8; *Attorney-General and Solicitor-General Act 1972* (Vic) s 5; *Solicitor-General Act 1983* (Tas) s 7; *Law Officers Act 1978* (NT) s 14; *Solicitor-General Act 1969* (NSW) s 3; *Law Officers Act 2011* (ACT) s 17. It should be noted that the Solicitors-General of Queensland and Western Australia are not as constrained as their colleagues in the other jurisdictions in their ability to accept briefs from the private profession: see *Solicitor-General Act 1985* (Qld) s 16; *Solicitor-General Act 1969* (WA) s 6. See also Appleby 2012: 3.4.

6 Section 78A of the *Judiciary Act 1903* (Cth) grants to the Attorneys-General of each of the Commonwealth, the States and Territories the right to intervene in proceedings before the High Court, or any other federal court, or any court of a State or Territory, where those proceedings relate to a matter arising under, or involving the interpretation of, the Constitution. Pursuant to s 78B of the *Judiciary Act 1903* (Cth), where in a matter in any of the said courts a question arises under, or involves the interpretation of, the Constitution, the

day duties of the Solicitor-General vary depending upon the requirements of the particular jurisdiction. That said, there is an overarching approach brought to each and every matter presented to the Solicitors-General. It is a responsibility to the rule of law, acutely felt and religiously discharged in the service of the Executive and in acceptance of the Executive's subservience to the rule of law.

In what follows I deal with the relationship between the Solicitor-General and the Executive and the Solicitor-General and the courts through the prism of the office of the Solicitor-General for South Australia. My understanding is that the position is not materially different in the other jurisdictions of the federation.

The Solicitor-General and the Attorney-General

In his speech on the motion that the Solicitor-General Bill be read a second time, the Attorney-General for South Australia did not refer to the Solicitor-General as the Second Law Officer of the State. Rather he described the position as that of senior legal adviser to the Crown. This was deliberate, minded of the origins of the position in South Australia and that, unlike the Solicitor-General in England, the Solicitor-General in South Australia was not expected to act in the place of the Attorney-General when he was unable. Thus, the Solicitor-General did not draw authority to act in such circumstances 'from the prerogative powers inherent in the office of the Attorney-General' (*R v John Wilkes* (1770) 4 Burr 2527: 2555; 98 ER 327: 343).[7] In this regard the role of the Solicitor-General in England as including the power to act in the place of the Attorney-General when he was unable was confirmed in *R v John Wilkes*. In that case the question was whether or not the Solicitor-General could lay an *ex officio* information for criminal libel during the vacancy of the office of the Attorney-General. In the House of Lords the Chief Justice of the Court of Common Pleas, Wilmot CJ, stated:

> the Solicitor-General is the *secundarius attornatus*; and as the Courts take notice judicially of the Attorney-General, when there is one, they take notice of the Solicitor-General, as standing in his place, when there is none. He is a known and sworn officer of the Crown, as much as the Attorney; and, in the vacancy of that office, does every act, and executes every branch of it. But, whether it be the one or the other, they only echo the King's complaint, and his application to the Court to act upon it (*R v John Wilkes* (1768) Wilm 322: 330; 97 ER 123: 126).[8]

court is obliged to halt proceedings unless and until the court is satisfied that the Attorneys-General of each of the Commonwealth, the States and Territories have received notice of the cause, such notice specifying the nature of the matter, and reasonable time in which to consider the question of intervening in the cause. See also the discussion below at pp. 86–7.

7 As to the history of the office of Solicitor-General in Australia, see Mason 1988. See also Appleby 2012: chapter 3.

8 See also *Solicitor-General v Wylde* (1945) 46 SR (NSW) 83.

Of course by this time it was also the position that the Solicitor-General in England was a member of the House of Commons.[9]

It may be contended, as it was in *Solicitor-General v Wylde* (1945) 46 SR (NSW) 83, that in creating an office bearing the title 'Solicitor-General', knowing that an office by the same name existed in the mother country, the intention was that the office created have similar powers. Putting the position at the Commonwealth level and in New South Wales to one side momentarily, such argument is unlikely to succeed as a matter of construction of the various statutes creating the office in the States and the Territories.[10]

In New South Wales s 3(1)(b) of the *Solicitor-General Act 1969* (NSW) provides that the Solicitor-General may:

> when the office of Attorney General is vacant, or the Attorney General is absent from the State or is by reason of illness unable to exercise and discharge his or her powers, authorities, duties and functions, exercise and discharge any powers, authorities, duties and functions conferred or imposed on the Attorney General by or under any Act or incident by law to the office of Attorney General.[11]

At the Commonwealth level s 5 of the *Law Officers Act 1964* (Cth) does expressly style the Solicitor-General the 'second Law Officer of the Commonwealth'. However, the power vested by s 17 of that Act in the Attorney-General to delegate all or any of his or her powers and functions under all or any laws of the Commonwealth or a Territory to the Solicitor-General suggests that s 5 does not itself confer any power. What it does is establish the status of the office within the ranks of the Commonwealth legal service and, coupled with s 12,[12] gives content to the relationship between Solicitor-General and Attorney-General.

For the purposes of this contribution the point is that with the exception of s 3(1)(b) of the *Solicitor-General Act 1969* (NSW) and the circumstances in which it is operative, and any lawful delegation of power by an Attorney-General to a Solicitor-General,[13] the Solicitors-General are not *secundarius attornatus* in the sense that that expression was used by Wilmot CJ. Nonetheless, in another very

9 As to the historical origins of the position of Solicitor-General, see Edwards 1964.

10 This appeared to be the view of the Full Court of the Supreme Court of South Australia in relation to the *Solicitor-General Act 1972* (SA) in *Question of Law (No 3 of 1995)* (1996) 66 SASR 450: 456.

11 See further discussion in Sexton 2002.

12 It is s 12 of the *Law Officers Act 1964* (Cth) that prescribes the functions of the Solicitor-General of the Commonwealth. In particular ss 12(a)(viii),12(b) and 12(c) give content to the relationship shared by the First and Second Law Officers of the Commonwealth.

13 Express power to delegate the powers of the Attorney-General to the Solicitor-General similar to that in the *Law Officers Act 1964* (Cth) s 17 is to be found in the *Solicitor-General Act 1983* (Tas) s 8; *Solicitor-General Act 1969* (NSW) s 4; *Solicitor-General Act 1969* (WA) s 13.

real sense the Solicitors-General are *secundarius attornatus*. In this regard the status of Solicitors-General as Second Law Officer of the State derives from the special relationship that they have with the Attorney-General and the responsibility inherent in that role for the maintenance and the observance of the rule of law by the Executive. Section 5 of the *Law Officers Act 1964* (Cth) can be considered as contemplating the same.

Returning to the South Australian *Solicitor-General Act 1972*, s 6 makes clear that the Solicitor-General in South Australia receives his or her instructions from the Attorney-General and no one else.[14] It follows that the Solicitor-General is answerable to the Attorney-General. In my view this reflects the role of the Attorney-General as First Law Officer in that in South Australia, as in many if not all of the other States and Territories,[15] he or she is the Minister responsible for legal advice to the government and for the conduct of all litigation in which the government is a party. That is, if responsibility for legal advice to the government and the conduct of litigation involving the government is reposed in the one Minister, namely the Attorney-General, and is not spread among a number of Ministers and departments,[16] then it stands to reason that the Solicitor-General's functions should be framed in terms of the Solicitor-General taking his or her instructions from the Attorney-General and being answerable to the Attorney-General. In my opinion this is what Attorney-General King had in mind when during the debate on the Solicitor-General Bill he said:

> I think it must be recognized, as it is recognized in other places, that the relationship between the Government and the Solicitor-General, or between the Attorney-General and the Solicitor-General, is a special relationship, and this is one reason why it is desirable that the Solicitor-General should not form part of the Public Service (South Australian Parliamentary Debates 1972b: 3651).

---

14 See also the broadly corresponding provisions in the *Solicitor-General Act 1969* (NSW) s 3; *Law Officers Act 1978* (NT) s 14; *Solicitor-General Act 1985* (Qld) s 8; *Solicitor-General Act 1983* (Tas) s 7; *Attorney-General and Solicitor-General Act 1972* (Vic) s 5; *Solicitor-General Act 1969* (WA) s 9; *Law Officers Act 2011* (ACT) s 17.

15 I have excluded the Commonwealth for the sole reason that Bradley Selway (2002: 269) has suggested that legislative changes to the role and function of the Australian Government Solicitor may have affected the characterisation of the role of the Commonwealth Attorney-General. I have not considered whether or not this is the case; but see *Law Officers Act 1964* (Cth) s 12.

16 Whilst it may be accepted that at common law the Attorney-General remains responsible for the legal representation of the Crown in civil proceedings, the reality of modern-day executive governance is that decisions concerning major litigation will generally be made collectively by the Cabinet, and in lesser matters the Attorney-General will consult with the Minister or agency with portfolio responsibility for the legislation or area of government to which the litigation pertains.

As to the nature of the special relationship, as I have flagged, I am of the view that its form and content is derived from the common law functions and duties of the First Law Officer.[17] It stands to reason that if the First Law Officer of the State is responsible for, and has control of, the legal services provided to and on behalf of government departments and the litigation in which they become involved, then the work of the Solicitor-General, who acts only upon the instructions of the Attorney-General and may not accept other work without the permission of the Attorney-General, will be reflective in no small part of the role of the Attorney-General as First Law Officer of the State. It is important then for a Solicitor-General to understand the role of the First Law Officer of the State.

As explained by a former South Australian Solicitor-General, Bradley Selway,[18] in Australia the Attorneys-General of the States in particular, unlike the Attorneys-General of England, are not just legal advisers to the Crown in the narrow sense, but are generally responsible for the provision of legal advice to all government departments and the conduct of all government litigation. Selway (2002: 266–7) explained:

> The enhanced role of the Attorney-General in the Australian colonies pre-dated the commencement of responsible government. …
>
> However, the enhanced role became significantly more marked with responsible government. In contrast with the position in England, the move to responsible government in the Australian colonies did result in the centralisation of legal services under the control of the respective colonial Attorneys-General. There were probably a number of reasons for this – these included that governments were smaller and centralisation was easier; that colonial Attorneys-General were adequately paid; and that colonial Attorneys-General usually had the support of competent professional lawyers in the Solicitor-General (at least in some jurisdictions) and Crown Solicitor. In the colonies it was accepted that the role of Attorney-General as legal adviser to the Crown necessarily had the result that the Attorney-General provided legal services to the whole of government. In the Canadian, Australian and New Zealand colonies the Attorney-General was responsible for, and had control of, the legal services not only to the monarch, but to all government departments. Even 'in-house' lawyers engaged by a department not directly answerable to the Attorney-General are deemed to be ultimately responsible to the Attorney-General, and to act on his or her

17 The desirability referred to by the Attorney-General that the office should not form part of the public service derives in turn from the fact that the Solicitor-General's responsibilities for the legal representation of the Crown, the provision of legal advice to government and the provision of legal advice to the Parliament call for independence of office, release from onerous administrative burdens and freedom from partisan political influence.

18 Appointed Solicitor-General for South Australia on 31 August 1995.

> instructions, simply on the basis that the Attorney-General has sole responsibility for the legal services of government. The role of the Attorney-General can be seen as being the 'ultimate instructor' of legal work for government.

This broad conception of the role of the Attorney-General is enhanced by s 78A of the *Judiciary Act 1903* (Cth)[19] and s 9 of the *Crown Proceedings Act 1992* (SA).[20] It also is enhanced by the power of the Attorney-General that goes with his or her membership of Cabinet[21] and convention, which dictates that the Attorney-General be informed about all proceedings concerning the government.[22]

That at common law this is the role expected of Attorneys-General is reflected in the attitude of the courts toward any attempt by the Crown in right of any jurisdiction appearing in more than one emanation. Hence the comments made in passing by members of the High Court in the *Momcilovic* litigation regarding the appearance at the Bar table of counsel for the Victorian Director of Public Prosecutions and separate counsel for the Attorney-General for Victoria not necessarily singing from the same hymn sheet.[23] Those passing references echoed the interchange recorded by Selway (2002: 267–7) as having taken place during the application to remove the matter to the High Court in *Northern Territory v Fejo* (21 May 1998).[24]

Selway notes a number of consequences that flow from the role of the Attorney-General. First, by virtue of his or her membership of Cabinet, he or she is arguably less independent of the government in the exercise of their responsibilities as

19 See fn 6 above.

20 Section 9 of the *Crown Proceedings Act 1992* (SA) grants to the Attorneys-General of each of the Commonwealth, the States and the Territories the right to intervene in any civil proceedings in the courts of South Australia where the interpretation or validity of a law of the particular polity is in question, or the legislative, executive or judicial powers of the polity or any of its agencies are in question, or with permission of the court on the grounds that the proceedings raise a question of public importance. See also *Court Procedures Act 2004* (ACT) s 27; *Crown Proceedings Act 1988* (NSW) s 9; *Crown Proceedings Act* (NT) s 16; *Crown Proceedings Act 1993* (Tas) ss 16–17; *Crown Proceedings Act 1958* (Vic) s 10; *Crown Suits Act 1947* (WA) ss 7–8. And see below at pp. 85–6.

21 Remembering that historically the Attorney-General of England was not accorded membership of the Cabinet save for a short period between 1912 and 1928: see Edwards 1964: 169–70, 174. Of course, the increase in political influence that comes with membership of Cabinet is attended by a diminution in the detachment of the office of Attorney-General.

22 In some jurisdictions positive arrangements have been put in place; see, for example, at the Commonwealth level, Direction 3 of the *Legal Services Directions 2005* (Cth). Those directions are issued by the Attorney-General of the Commonwealth pursuant to the power vested by s 55ZF of the *Judiciary Act 1903* (Cth).

23 *Momcilovic v The Queen* (2010) HCA Trans 227: 2 (French CJ); *Momcilovic v The Queen* (2011) HCA Trans 015: 102–3 (Gummow J).

24 But note the approach taken by the Supreme Court of South Australia in *Campbell v Employers Mutual Ltd* (2011) 110 SASR 57: [119–24] (Gray and Sulan JJ).

First Law Officer of the State than their English equivalent.[25] Second, unlike their English equivalent, he or she has far greater capacity to protect the rule of law within government and by the government in the course of litigation. Third, his or her responsibility across government serves to prevent litigation between departments or agencies of the Crown. Fourth, as a member of Cabinet he or she bears responsibility for advising Cabinet colleagues of the consequences for the rule of law of any decision made. As will be seen, each of these aspects of the role of the Attorney-General gives content to the role of the Solicitor-General.

With respect to the rule of law, the Attorney-General's responsibility flows from the fact that it is an assumption underpinning the Constitution.[26] More particularly, the Executive is subject to the rule of law. Accepting this, as Selway has also explained, it falls to those providing advice to government, for whom and for what the Attorney-General is responsible, to identify what the law is and, where appropriate, to enforce it (Selway 1999). Often this will involve the formulation of an opinion as to what the law is and how it is lawfully to be enforced in the absence of any judicial consideration of the issue. Further, it is suggested that the notion of the rule of law for which the Attorney-General is responsible has a content somewhat broader than the constitutional assumption, in that it extends beyond questions as to the limits of power as interpreted and declared by courts, to the manner in which compliance must be undertaken and to matters of ethics, practice and procedure (Selway 1999: 120–21; Finn 1995: 5–21).

Former Chief Justice of New South Wales J.J. Spigelman (2003: 201) would agree that the source of the principles that guide the practice of government is to be found in the broader conception of the rule of law. For him:

> The rule of law is not inconsistent with the exercise of authority. It is, however, inconsistent with the exercise of authority in an arbitrary manner. Indeed, government authority is essential to a system of rule by law. The administration of justice is a core function of government, developed precisely in order to prevent violence or the exercise of any form of coercion by the strong, the powerful or the wealthy against others, less powerful or less well off or less well-organised. The proper exercise of government authority is, I repeat, an essential aspect of the rule of law.

Selway (2002: 271) considered:

---

25 As to the independence of the Attorney-General, see, for example, King 2000; Carney 1997; Jones 1969; Silkin 1978; Plehwe 1980; Bennett 2002; McColl 2003.

26 See statements to this effect in *Australian Communist Party v Commonwealth* (1951) 83 CLR 1: 193 (Dixon J); *Miller v TCN Nine* (1986) 11 CLR 556: 581 (Murphy J); *Kartinyeri v Commonwealth* (1998) 195 CLR 337: 381 (Gummow and Hayne JJ); *Abebe v Commonwealth* (1999) 197 CLR 510: 560 (Gummow and Hayne JJ); *Kruger v Commonwealth* (1997) 190 CLR 1: 66–8 (Dawson J); 112–14 (Gaudron J). See also Mason 1995.

> Yet another difference relates to the power and capacity of the Attorney-General in the Australian States, as a member of his or her Cabinet, to provide advice on and warn his or her Cabinet colleagues of broad issues relating to the rule of law, such as human rights issues. There are basic ethical principles that underlie any liberal democratic government; principles such as honesty and integrity, care and diligence, legality, respect and courtesy, selflessness and confidentiality. Under the Australian constitutional system these basic ethical principles are not enforced by the courts through judicial review – they are left to the Parliament and the executive to protect and enforce. The Attorney-General has a particular responsibility to alert government to these basic ethical principles.

For Selway the responsibility of the Attorney-General for ensuring adherence by the Executive to the ethical principles he identifies is derived from our system of liberal democracy. That system is, like the rule of law, an assumption upon which the Constitution is based. But reference to the constitutional anchor provides no real assistance in determining the content of the ethical principles that underlie liberal democratic government. Former Commonwealth Solicitor-General and later Chief Justice of the High Court, Anthony Mason, once described the concept of modern democracy in Australia in the following terms:

> That concept goes beyond simple majoritarian government and parliamentary sovereignty. It extends to a new notion of responsible government which respects the fundamental rights and dignity of the individual and calls for the protection of the individual's rights against undue interference and intrusion by authority.[27]

Paul Finn (1995) has suggested that the answer lies in the notion of government as being a matter of public trust. That is, it exists to serve the interests of the people and what is in the public interest operates as a limiting principle upon the exercise of executive power. Finn also contemplates a link between the notion of public trust and popular sovereignty. Whatever the answer, at a minimum the ethical principles that underlie a liberal democracy are the stuff of convention, and that convention is one which the public have come to expect the Executive to observe. Generally Attorneys-General have accepted the convention, although perhaps with varying degrees of enthusiasm, and have discharged their responsibility as to its enforcement.

I return to the role of the Solicitor-General. As the principal legal adviser to the Minister who is solely responsible for legal advice to government and for all litigation in which the government is a party, he or she will have occasion to give advice or make submissions against the understanding of the role of the Attorney-General as First Law Officer of the State. In fact, the Solicitor-General is expected to do so and, minded of the many other duties of an Attorney-General, who will

---

27 Opening Address, New South Wales Supreme Court Judges Conference, 30 April 1993, as quoted in Finn 1995: 7.

in some cases hold a number of diverse portfolios, it is often essential that the Solicitor-General do so.

It is by no means a stretch in describing the importance of the role to state that in many areas the opinion of the Solicitor-General will constitute the Executive's understanding of the law and of what is required in its enforcement. Further, it is by no means an overstatement to observe that disputes between departments, or departments and employees, are often resolved by the opinion of the Solicitor-General. Further again, it is not an overstatement to indicate that the attitude of an Attorney-General toward a particular issue in proceedings in which he or she has decided to intervene will often reflect the views, attitude or advice of the Solicitor-General.

It is for these reasons that in my view the role of the Solicitor-General in Australia is that of *secundarius attornatus* in a very real and practical sense, even in the absence of an express statutory authority to exercise powers during a vacancy in the office of the Attorney-General.

I do not overlook the divisible nature of the Crown in right of a particular polity and the consequent creation of agencies and instrumentalities, variously distanced from the Executive. I also do not overlook the power of governments to arrange for the conduct of their legal business by independent lawyers taking their instructions from Ministers other than the Attorney-General or from heads of department or some such. Arrangements such as these compromise the ability of the Attorney-General to superintend the legal service provided. Three things flow from this: first, the Attorney-General's ability to protect and maintain the rule of law is impaired. Second, Parliament's ability to monitor the exercise of power, ostensibly for the State, is compromised. Third, the provision of advice and the conduct of matters in accordance with the broader notion of the rule of law become diluted.[28] None of these consequences relieve those acting for the Executive from the responsibilities of the Crown in right of the polity, hence the High Court's response in *Momcilovic* and *Fejo* to the Crown appearing with two heads.[29] If this is right then it also follows that whilst the Attorney-General's responsibilities are made more difficult to fulfil, the burden of their discharge remains. The question is one of how this is to be achieved. In South Australia one means is to be found in s 9 of the *Crown Proceedings Act 1992* (SA).[30] This, however, is limited to empowering the Attorney-General to intervene in proceedings. The more difficult issue is the superintendence of advice given by independent lawyers to emanations of the Crown distant from the departments of Ministers and action then taken that does not result in proceedings being instituted. One possible antidote is to be

28 See, for example, *Thompson v Duffin* (2009) 105 SASR 181; *ASIC v Hellicar* (2012) 86 ALJR 522; *LVR (WA) Pty Ltd v AAT* (2012) 289 ALR 244.

29 See above fns 6 and 20 and also the authorities referred to at fn 28.

30 See fn 20 above and the treatment below at pp. 85–6. Further, see *Campbell v Employers Mutual Limited* (2011) SASR 57: [119–24] (Gray and Sulan JJ).

found in the power to give a legal services direction as contained in s 10 of the *Law Officers Act 2011* (ACT) and s 55ZF of the *Judiciary Act 1903* (Cth).[31]

The Solicitor-General and Advice Provided to the Executive Government

I put to one side issues concerning advice given to the vice regal officer. That is the subject of Michael Sexton's chapter in this volume. It may be of some utility to record, however, that in South Australia it is customary for the Solicitor-General to call upon a newly appointed Governor and to explain to them the vice regal role generally, in Executive Council and in the exercise of the reserve powers. Likewise, if a new Solicitor-General is appointed during a Governor's term in office it is customary for the Governor to request that the Solicitor-General call upon him or her in order that the Governor may acquaint himself or herself with whoever is the Solicitor-General.

The question arises as to the principles that guide the Solicitor-General in the provision of advice to the Executive. By that I do not mean to refer to the legal principles that govern a particular matter. Rather I refer to the principles that govern advice as to the conduct of the Executive in its relations with other governments, other arms of government and the people of the polity. That is, advice as to the practice of governing or which involves an element of how government is practised. That returns us to the broader notion of the rule of law and to those ethical principles that underlie the concept of a liberal democracy referred to above. Selway (1999: 120–23) identified them as:

- honesty and integrity;
- care and diligence;
- legality;
- respect and courtesy;
- selflessness; and
- confidentiality.

Against the touchstone of our system of government being decided upon as the preferred means of advancing the interests of the people, Finn (1995) identifies five core principles that serve as criteria that guide how the exercise of government is practised. They are:

- *The democratic principle:* here it is notions of the public's interest derived

31 Such powers permit the Attorney-General to issue directions to those undertaking legal work on behalf of the polity that must be complied with. For example, at the Commonwealth level the *Legal Services Directions 2005* include in Appendix B specific reference to the obligation of the Commonwealth and its agencies to act as model litigants in the conduct of litigation in addition to giving content to that obligation.

from the democratic process that limit or direct government practice. Representative democracy is a means of channelling the power of the people into a workable system. It is then to be viewed as a means to an end, the end being the interest of the people.

- *The public servant principle:* officials act for and on behalf of the public.
- *The integrity principle:* requires integrity in the practices and processes of government.
- *The open government principle.*
- *The accountability principle:* that is, accountability to the people.

I doubt that these principles come as any surprise. Equally I doubt that their relevance to advising government departments, officials, agencies and instrumentalities of the Crown would be disputed. These principles may be refined; they may be added to. As Anthony Mason has indicated, our conception of democracy is evolving (as quoted in Finn 1995).

Clearly these principles or derivations of them apply to all lawyers acting for government and not just the Solicitor-General. They are, however, of particular importance to the Solicitor-General for the obvious reason that the weight that will attach in government circles to an opinion of the Solicitor-General requires that he or she applies the principles and values that inform how government should be practised. And, of course, providing the best possible advice to the First Law Officer demands as much.

Here a further point on the role of the Attorney-General falls to be made. It is not purely reactive. This being so, it is open to, and in my view incumbent on, the Solicitor-General to advise the Attorney-General of any errant practice of which he or she becomes aware that should be remedied. This is not a matter of the subjective appraisal of performance or any attempt to impose one's own value system. As demonstrated by Selway and Finn, one looks for objective criteria discernible in history, convention, the Constitution, notions of representative and responsible government, the rule of law and the common law.

Quite obviously there is potential for advice to be given that is unpalatable to a department or particular official – perhaps even a member of Cabinet. Equally obviously, any temptation to avoid the unpalatable at the expense of providing the best advice or in sacrifice of the principles identified above is to be resisted. In this connection I should note that the Solicitor-General has a degree of independence from the elected government in that he or she can only be removed from office by the Governor if, by reason other than temporary illness, he or she is incapable of performing his or her duties, or has been guilty of misconduct.[32] Thus governments may come and go; Attorneys-General may come and go, but the Solicitor-General remains.[33]

---

32 See fn 4 above.

33 I note that in some jurisdictions the Solicitor-General is appointed for a fixed term. In South Australia, provided the Solicitor-General is not removed from office under s 7, he

When the Solicitor-General Bill was debated in Parliament what amounted to misconduct was queried (South Australian Parliamentary Debates 1972b: 3651–2). The fact that the Solicitor-General could be removed without his guilt being established by any independent body was thought troubling. Nevertheless, the House of Assembly appears to have been satisfied by the assurance of the Attorney-General that:

> it would be a serious step for any Government to remove the incumbent of the office of Solicitor-General from that office, and one which it is certainly very unlikely that any Government accountable to the Parliament and the people would be likely to take unless there were very grave and compelling reasons for it to do so (South Australian Parliamentary Debates 1972b: 3652).

Where independence is not protected by the terms and conditions of appointment, the status accorded the office generally has the same effect. That is, underpinning that status is the implicit acceptance that a Solicitor-General, generally an experienced and highly regarded legal practitioner, acts in accordance with principles such as I have identified. Thus, irrespective of whether a Solicitor-General's terms and conditions guarantee him or her independence, it is a serious step for any government to ignore the advice of its Solicitor-General or to remove its Solicitor-General if their advice does not accord with the government's wishes, or to risk the Solicitor-General's resignation. Consequently the status accorded the Solicitor-General's office provides, in effect, independence.

The Attorney-General looks to the Solicitor-General for his or her best advice, not necessarily the advice that the government would like to hear. The independence given to the office of the Solicitor-General offers fortification if he or she is ever tempted or pressured to appease the government, as opposed to providing what in his or her view is the appropriate response.

Things are more complex when it comes to the interpretation of the Constitution, if for no other reason than that the advice may require a consideration of the position of one polity's powers, rights and duties in the context of the federal structure. Here a State's interests may not readily align with those of the Commonwealth or the other States and Territories. Advice given must respect the nature of the federation and the position of the particular polity within it. The principles identified above remain applicable but the change in context must be firmly understood.

I accept that the ethical principles that guide the Solicitor-General and may shape his or her advice as to government practice may not be embraced with equal commitment by an Attorney-General or Cabinet. There is nothing to compel a government to adopt or adhere as rigidly as a Solicitor-General may to such

---

or she may occupy the position until age 65; *Solicitor-General Act 1972* (SA) s 8. Clearly independence of the position is all the stronger if an appointment is made until an identified retirement age or for a fixed term without the possibility of reappointment and provided that dismissal for no good reason cannot occur.

principles. There is nothing save the implicit understanding that a Solicitor-General may resign if his or her integrity and the integrity of the position is compromised by government action to serve as a check on government in matters legal in which the Solicitor-General becomes involved. The resignation of a Solicitor-General may be expected to carry a political consequence that would cause a government to at least pause before continuing on its course.

From the above it is clear that, in my view, whilst the Solicitor-General's immediate client is the Attorney-General, like the First Law Officer, he or she also serves that abstraction, the Crown, in the broadest sense. Here I do not equate the Crown with a 'piece of jewelled head gear under guard in the Tower of London' (*Town Investments v Department of Environment* [1978] AC 359: 397 (Lord Diplock)), the government or the Executive. To my way of thinking, having regard to the rule of law that is an assumption upon which the Constitution is constructed, and to the developing conception of liberal democracy that the Constitution advances, the abstraction, 'the Crown', better captures those aspirational aspects of a conception of government, a corporation aggregate perhaps (*Town Investments v Department of Environment* [1978] AC 359: 400 (Lord Simon)), that governs for the peace, order and good government of people.

Such approach sees the Law Officers as servants of something greater than the government of the day. In my view this broad notion is what gives rise to the tendency for conflict in the role of the First Law Officer to arise due to their political allegiance to the particular government of which they are a member. But no such tension exists in the role of the Second Law Officer, making it all the more important that he or she applies those principles drawn from the broad notion of the rule of law and those ethical principles that underlie the concept of a liberal democracy.

There is a further point here – perhaps a note of warning for Solicitors-General. Solicitors-General must take care in the provision of advice not to be dogmatic and closed to the possibility of contrary views. The convention that underpins the Solicitor-General's role and function can be eroded by intransigence. There is an important balance to be struck, one that contributes to the legitimacy of the position and all it carries with it.

I turn to the formulation of matters of policy. Generally speaking, matters of policy are not for the Solicitor-General to advise upon or to suggest. That said, I note that Keith Mason (1988: 26), then Solicitor-General for New South Wales, and later the President of the New South Wales Court of Appeal, said:

> The position does provide opportunities for the tendering of advice on policy matters. The Solicitor General may be consulted on proposals for law reform and there may be opportunities flowing from constant involvement in litigation on the Crown side to suggest changes in practice or the law.

I agree. An example can be seen in the involvement of the Solicitors-General in the genesis and formulation of the *Australia Acts 1986* (Twomey 2010). A second example may be seen in those areas where the State is contemplating whether or not to address a particular issue by referring power to the Commonwealth, enacting uniform legislation or going it alone. Here policy is sometimes caught up in the method of implementation, and the advice of the Solicitor-General may be expected to lay bare all aspects of the issue for consideration by the Attorney-General and Cabinet. A third example lies in intergovernmental relations, particularly where there arises the possibility of dispute and a number of means of addressing the issue; the River Murray and water come to mind. A fourth example may be that rare situation where the Solicitor-General's advice is sought on what is ultimately a political decision. These are rare, but an example may be advice sought as to whether or not the Executive Council, which is entrusted with the responsibility of determining when a prisoner sentenced to life imprisonment should be released on parole, should release him. A further example in this category is the resolution of native title claims. When he was South Australian Solicitor-General, Selway was instrumental in devising a State-wide approach in South Australia to settling native title claims and, in particular, the employment of Indigenous Land Use Agreements.

In all of these circumstances the Solicitor-General does not consider what the electorate may or may not think, or advise in accordance with his or her own values. Rather, he or she is properly guided by the sort of ethical principles alluded to above, with the public interest being paramount.

At a lower and less rarefied level there is often opportunity to influence the way in which a particular policy or policy decision is implemented. The Solicitor-General is regularly called upon to advise on draft Bills, the content of government discussion papers, submissions to the Commonwealth, inquiries and other bodies, codes of practice and similar documents or initiatives.

The Solicitor-General and the Courts

The relative freedom that the Solicitor-General has in advising the Executive as to the practice of government is constrained when he or she appears in court. In court the Solicitor-General must, subject to the usual ethical and professional constraints, act in accordance with instructions. This does not mean that the principles that guide the Solicitor-General in the discharge of his or her duties to the Executive as identified above have no application when he or she acts on instructions appearing in court representing the Crown. The Crown must conduct itself as the model litigant. This is an expectation that can be considered as an expression of the principles identified above. Those principles no doubt informed the observations of Griffith CJ (*Melbourne Steamship Co Ltd v Moorehead* (1912) 15 CLR 333: 342) when he described the Crown's approach to litigation as:

> the old fashioned traditional, and almost instinctive, standard of fair play to be observed by the Crown in dealing with subjects, which I learned a very long time ago to regard as elementary …

More recently the Full Federal Court (*LVR (WA) Pty Ltd v AAT* (2012) 289 ALR 244: 251, [42]) reminded the Crown in right of the Commonwealth, and those who act on its behalf, of its obligations:

> Speaking generally and without reflecting on counsel who appeared before us, being a model litigant requires the Commonwealth and its agencies, as parties to litigation, to act with complete propriety, fairly and in accordance with the highest professional standards. This obligation may require more than merely acting honestly and in accordance with the law and court rules. It also goes beyond the requirement for lawyers to act in accordance with their ethical obligations: see notes 2 and 3 to clause 2 of Appendix B to the *Legal Services Directions 2005* made under section 55ZF of the *Judiciary Act 1903* (Cth). That statutory instrument reflects an expectation the courts in our system of justice have of the executive government and its emanations but this is no new subject owing its origin just to that statutory instrument. Instead, as *Melbourne Steamship Limited v Moorehead* reveals, that expectation, even a century ago, was of long standing. To bring the matter up to the present we note that in *Australian Securities and Investments Commission v Hellicar*, Heydon J said ASIC accepted that there was, in the words of Griffith CJ in *Moorehead*, an 'old-fashioned traditional, and almost instinctive, standard of fair play to be observed by the Crown in dealing with subjects'. Its powers are exercised for the public good. It has no legitimate private interest in the performance of its functions. And often it is larger and has access to greater resources than private litigants. Hence it must act as a moral exemplar: see [239] per Heydon J. ASIC accepted what was said on these points in *P & C Cantarella Pty Ltd v Egg Marketing Board for New South Wales*; *Hughes Aircraft Systems International v Airservices Australia*; and *Scott v Handley*. In our opinion, counsel representing the executive government must pay scrupulous attention to what the discharge of that obligation requires, especially where legal representatives who are independent of the agency are not involved in the litigation.[34]

It goes without saying that these obligations apply equally to the States and Territories. Significantly, the court expresses the model litigant principle in terms of a judicial demand, a standard to be met, not merely one to which the Crown is to aspire. Insistence upon the Crown meeting the standard 'is a recurrent theme in judicial decisions in this country' (*Scott v Handley* (1999) 58 ALD 373: [44–5] (The Court)).

As toward the judiciary, being the model litigant demands of the Crown 'conscientious compliance with the procedures designed to minimise cost and delay and to make the maximum use of the resources committed to the Court' (*Kenny v South Australia* (1987) 45 SASR 268: 273 (King CJ)).

---

34 Citations omitted.

It is arguable that the expectation that the Crown act as the model litigant is also an aspect of the rule of law. If it is accepted that a polity does not operate under the rule of law unless it has in place laws and a system for their enforcement that operate 'fairly, rationally, predictably, consistently and impartially' (Spigelman 2003: 205), then any abuse of those laws or that system corrupts it. That would be to act contrary to the rule of law, contrary to the Executive's responsibility to maintain the rule of law, contrary to the notion that the Crown is the fountain of justice, and contrary to the role and responsibilities of the First Law Officer of the State.

The requirement that the Crown act as model litigant must without fail manifest itself in the conduct of the Solicitor-General in court, appearing as he or she does on the instructions of the First Law Officer and as the Crown's legal representative. Thus the Solicitor-General's conduct of matters before the various courts must be beyond reproach. Rightly, the courts expect no less.

As to the courts' expectations of the Solicitors-General: with the advent of s 78A of the *Judiciary Act 1903* (Cth) the Solicitors-General have become constitutional specialists who play an important role in the development of constitutional jurisprudence. In no small part has this reinforced the legitimacy of the status of Solicitor-General when advice is given on the proper exercise of power and constraints on power. From the courts' point of view, the written and oral submissions of the Solicitors-General play a critical role in ensuring the rigour of judgments concerning the Constitution and the functioning of the federation.[35] Generally it can be expected that if the outcome of a matter that raises a question of constitutional law is important to the functioning of any of the three arms of government of a polity in the federation, or to the federation, the First Law Officer will intervene and the Solicitor-General will appear. The mere fact of the intervention, particularly in the High Court, signals the significance of the matter to the polity. In my view this is not lost on the courts.[36]

I consider more generally that the courts of the nation expect the highest standard of advocacy from the Solicitor-General. In particular the Solicitor-General is looked to by the intermediate appellate courts as providing a link to what is expected by the High Court and therein performs an important function as a conduit that assists in the maintenance of the required grade of justice administered by the integrated Australian judicial system.

It should be noted that the independence enjoyed by counsel is not diminished by the fact that the Solicitor-General holds an appointment from the Crown. The Solicitor-General must have the same degree of freedom as is normally afforded

35 In this regard an example of the expectations of the High Court is to be found in the judgment of Mason CJ and McHugh J in *Dietrich v The Queen* (1992) 177 CLR 292: 312.

36 In this connection it is interesting to ruminate on the implicit statement made by the Solicitors-General in *Momcilovic v The Queen* (2011) 245 CLR 1, who in answer to questions asked by the High Court took the unprecedented course of all joining in the one written submission.

counsel in the presentation of a client's case. I would have thought that the courts expect no less. In this regard I note that Keith Mason (1988: 26) said:

> just as can happen to counsel who appears regularly for the one client, judges or fellow practitioners may take the opportunity of your presence in a specific case as the occasion for some direct or indirect remonstrance against your client generally. I hope, nevertheless, that it is generally perceived that the Solicitor-General appears in court as counsel making submissions of the Crown, and not as an agent making speeches or submission on behalf of the government of the day. Furthermore, the adversary system and the friendly critical jibes of one's fellow barristers are hopefully the best antidote against the risks of developing an excessively genign [sic] attitude towards ministers and bureaucrats.

Interventions

In what follows I deal more specifically with the powers to intervene in proceedings vested in the First Law Officer. The exercise of those powers plays a very important role in the administration of the law and functioning of the State and the federation generally. As I have attempted to describe above, the Solicitors-General play a pivotal role in the practical discharge by the First Law Officers of their responsibilities for the superintendence of the rule of law by the Executive. The power to intervene in proceedings, however, transcends that purpose. It provides the First Law Officer with the very important opportunity to have input into the question of the limits of power of the various arms of government, where raised in proceedings, of the limits of the powers of the various polities and the effective implementation of the laws of the relevant polities. In all this the Solicitors-General are rarely far away, for often it is their advice that will dictate whether the First Law Officer intervenes and the content of submissions to be made if he or she does so. Further it is often the Solicitor-General who is despatched to put the First Law Officer and the relevant polity's position.

Once again I deal with intervention through the prism of the position in South Australia.

I have referred above to the two statutory powers of intervention given to the Attorney-General of South Australia. Leaving constitutional matters to one side momentarily, s 9 of the *Crown Proceedings Act 1992* (SA) relevantly provides:

> **9—Right of Attorney-General to appear in proceedings**
>
> …
>
> (2) The Attorney-General may intervene, on behalf of the Crown, in any proceedings—

> (a) in which the interpretation or validity of a law of the State or Commonwealth is in question; or
> (b) in which—
> (i) legislative or executive powers of the State or Commonwealth, or of an instrumentality or agency of the State or Commonwealth are in question; or
> (ii) judicial powers of a court or tribunal established under the law of the State or Commonwealth are in question; or
> (c) in which the Court grants permission to intervene on the ground that the proceedings raise issues of public importance,
> for the purpose of submitting argument on issues of public importance.
> ...
> (5) In this section references to the Attorney-General extend not only to the Attorney-General for this State but also to the Attorney-General for any other State or the Commonwealth and references to the Crown have a correspondingly extended meaning.

A similar facility exists in the Territories, Western Australia, Tasmania and New South Wales.[37]

Returning to s 9 of the South Australian Act, the first observation is that the right of intervention is extended to the Attorney-General, consistent with his or her role as First Law Officer. Second, the right is extended to the Attorneys-General of the other States and the Commonwealth. Third, the ambit of the right again reflects the Attorney-General's role as First Law Officer. A fourth observation is the absence of a notice requirement similar to s 78B of the *Judiciary Act 1903* (Cth).[38]

In my experience the power contained in s 9 is exercised commonly but sparingly. In most instances the essential criteria is necessity in terms of the relative need for the Attorney-General to appear and make submissions in order that the understanding and administration of the law in South Australia is advanced. Here the Attorney-General does not intervene for the purpose of supporting one party or another. Of course there will be cases where the Crown has a real interest in the outcome and so the position of the Attorney-General may align with one or other of the parties. The Attorney-General must always be conscious of not intervening unnecessarily because of the impact it may have in terms of time and cost to the parties, and the efficient conduct of the court's business.

Turning to s 78A of the *Judiciary Act 1903* (Cth) and the right to intervene in matters arising under the Constitution or involving its interpretation, it is very tempting to treat the opportunity to intervene in constitutional matters as the chance to open up a new front in that never-ending 'turf war' with the Commonwealth or to re-engage in that other great 'turf war' between judiciary and executive or the judiciary and the legislature. But to succumb too readily to these temptations is to

---

37 See fn 20 above

38 See fn 6 above.

deny the nature of the federation and its operation. That does not mean that there is not fertile ground for intervening Attorneys-General to advance arguments as to the operation of the federation that do not also serve the parochial interests of the State. There is, and the challenge is to identify and develop these arguments on legally and constitutionally rational grounds. That, of course, is a multi-staged process.

First, an assessment must be undertaken as to whether or not to intervene. The approach in South Australia has been for the Attorney-General to delegate to the Crown Solicitor the authority to determine *not* to intervene in matters in a federal court other than the High Court, in the courts of the other States and in the inferior courts of South Australia. The Attorney-General has delegated to the Solicitor-General the authority to determine *not* to intervene in all other matters. Those delegations are subject to the Attorney-General's overarching power to determine that a different course be taken in any particular case. In practice, the Crown Solicitor acts as a first filter and the Solicitor-General as a second. Where it is considered advisable to intervene, the decision is made by the Attorney-General on the advice of the Solicitor-General. Further, anything that falls into the 'borderline' category is forwarded to the Attorney-General for consideration, accompanied by an explanatory minute either prepared by the Solicitor-General or bearing an endorsement as to his or her view. I understand that similar arrangements exist in the other States and in the Territories and at the Commonwealth level.

The Solicitor-General for Tasmania has said that the delegation of responsibility for determining whether or not to intervene under s 78A *Judiciary Act 1903* (Cth) 'might be thought to be unsatisfactory in that it reposes in the Solicitor-General a very broad (some would say, political) discretion to determine which questions of constitutional interpretation are referred to the government of the day and those which are not' (Solicitor-General of Tasmania 2008). I do not disagree. His response was to develop a protocol that would provide a greater degree of transparency and guidance as to what should and should not be forwarded to the Attorney-General.

As to the content of such protocol, former Commonwealth Solicitor-General David Bennett identified the following six factors (2009: 104), depending upon their relevance to the particular case, as considerations relevant to the decision of the Commonwealth Attorney-General to intervene in a case arising under the Constitution or involving its interpretation:

- whether the matter involves an attack on the validity of a Commonwealth law;
- whether the constitutional principles involved are well established by decisions of the High Court or are the subject of a reserved judgment of the High Court;
- the level of the court;
- whether there is likely to be an appeal from the judgment of the court;
- whether a Commonwealth party is already involved in the matter; and

- whether the applicant is represented, and whether the applicant's constitutional argument is well conceived.

Adjusting the first and fifth factor for the particular polity, these factors are equally applicable to all polities of the federation. To them must be added the anticipated consequences of the matter for the polity. It is true that the decision to intervene and what to put by way of submissions may be influenced by partisan political considerations (Campbell 1998). But those considerations must be informed by a contemporary and rational appreciation of the federal structure. In these determinations, a Solicitor-General has a real opportunity to play a leading role in the development of his or her body politic's theory of the Constitution and how it works, and to make submissions consistent with that theory. This requires that a Solicitor-General develop a coherent construct as to the interrelationship of the powers of the Legislature, Judiciary and Executive under the Constitution and the respective limits of Commonwealth and State power. That is an evolutionary process.

Conclusion

In Australia, in a practical sense, the Solicitors-General are the Second Law Officers of the polities which they serve irrespective of whether those polities expressly designate them as such. The content of the role and function of the Solicitors-General is drawn in no small part from the relationship of the office with that of the Attorneys-General and the duties and responsibilities of the First Law Officer. The Solicitors-General discharge their duties having regard to fundamental ethical principles which underpin the rule of law and the Australian system of liberal democracy. So doing so, they play an important role in the maintenance of a form of government that 'respects the fundamental rights and dignity of the individual'.

References

Appleby, G. 2012. *The Constitutional Role of the Solicitor-General: An Historical, Legal and Lived Portrait*. PhD thesis: University of Adelaide.

Bennett, D. 2002. The Roles and Functions of the Attorney-General of the Commonwealth. *Australian Bar Review*. Volume 23, 61.

Bennett, D. 2009. Constitutional Litigation and the Commonwealth, in *Critical Reflections on Australian Public Policy: Selected Essays*, edited by J. Wanna. Canberra: ANU E Press, 104.

Campbell, E. 1998. Intervention in Constitutional Cases. *Public Law Review*. Volume 4, 255.

Carney, G. 1997. The Role of the Attorney General. *Bond Law Review*. Volume 9, 1.

Edwards, J.Ll.J. 1964. *The Law Officers of the Crown: A Study of the Offices of the Attorney-General and Solicitor-General of England with an Account of the Office of the Director of Public Prosecutions of England.* London: Sweet & Maxwell.

Finn, P. 1995. A Sovereign People, A Public Trust, in *Essays on Law and Government*, edited by P. Finn. North Ryde, NSW: Lawbook. Volume 1, 1.

Hague, R.M. 2005. *Hague's History of the Law in South Australia 1837–1867.* Adelaide: Barr Smith Press.

Jones, E. 1969. The Office of the Attorney-General. *Commonwealth Law Journal.* Volume 27, 43.

King, L.J. 2000. The Attorney-General, Politics and the Judiciary. *Australian Law Journal.* Volume 74, 44.

Mason, K. 1995. The Rule of Law, in *Essays on Law and Government*, edited by P. Finn. North Ryde, NSW: Lawbook. Volume 1, 114.

Mason, K. 1988. The Office of Solicitor General for New South Wales. *Bar News.* Autumn Issue, 22.

McColl, R. 2003. Reflections on the Role of the Attorney-General. *Public Law Review.* Volume 14, 20.

Plehwe, R. 1980. The Attorney General and Cabinet: Some Australian Precedents. *Federal Law Review.* Volume 11, 1.

Selway, B.M. 1999. The Duties of Lawyers Acting for Government. *Public Law Review.* Volume 10, 114.

Selway, B. 2002. The Different Role of an Australian Attorney-General. *Public Law Review.* Volume 13, 263.

Sexton, M.G. 2002. The Role of the Solicitor General, in *No Mere Mouthpiece: Servants of All, Yet of None*, edited by G. Lindsay. Chatswood, NSW: LexisNexis, Butterworths, 86.

Silkin, S. 1978. The Functions and Position of the Attorney-General in the United Kingdom. *The Parliamentarian.* Volume 59, 19.

Solicitor-General of Tasmania. 2008. *Annual Report 2007–8.*

South Australian Government Gazette. 1969. 27 February 1969.

South Australian Parliamentary Debates. 1972a. *House of Assembly.* 1 March 1972.

South Australian Parliamentary Debates, 1972b. *House of Assembly*, 7 March 1972.

Spigelman, J.J. 2003. The Rule of Law and Enforcement. *University of New South Wales Law Journal.* Volume 26, 200.

Twomey, A. 2010. *The Australia Acts 1986.* Annandale, NSW: Federation Press.

Chapter 4

The Role of Solicitors-General in Advising the Holders of Vice Regal Offices

Michael Sexton

In many ways writing this chapter is somewhat akin to working on an unauthorised history of the security services. As might be expected, the contents of any advice by a Solicitor-General to the Governor-General, to a State Governor or to the Administrator of the Northern Territory will only very rarely, if ever, be made public. Similarly, it will be very unusual for even the fact that such advice has been provided to appear anywhere on the public record. Nevertheless, the provision of advice to the holders of vice regal offices has often been one of the roles of Solicitors-General and various aspects of this role are discussed in this chapter. Although this role may not be exercised as frequently as some of the Solicitor-General's other functions, it is an important one as it usually involves sensitive questions at the highest level of government including in relation to issues arising between the legislative and executive branches. There is, of course, little tangible evidence of how often such advice is given in particular jurisdictions but my own inquiries suggest in some States and Territories it is relatively common practice.

In this chapter, I will normally refer to the provision of advice in the context of a State Governor, although the same considerations largely apply in the case of advice to the Governor-General or the Administrator of the Northern Territory. The Australian Capital Territory has, of course, no Administrator. The Governor-General and the Governors of the States are the Sovereign's representatives in these respective jurisdictions. Their powers are discussed below but they have their origins in the powers that the Sovereign would have been entitled to exercise if he or she did not have what is effectively an Australian deputy with the same role to play.

It may be useful at the outset to outline briefly the normal powers of holders of vice regal offices, given that any request for advice by the holder of that office will ultimately relate to the exercise of one of those powers.

Powers of Vice Regal Representatives

At one time the powers of a Governor were outlined in Letters Patent that were delivered to the Governor on his or her appointment. Those powers, now, however, find their source in s 7 of the *Australia Act 1986* (Cth) which relevantly provides that 'all powers and functions of Her Majesty in respect of a State are exercisable only by the Governor of the State'.[1] The powers exercisable under s 7 can be divided into three broad categories:

i. powers exercised under a statute;
ii. prerogative powers; and
iii. reserve powers.

In relation to statutory powers, it is common for interpretation legislation (such as the *Interpretation Act 1987* (NSW)) to provide that a reference to the Governor is a reference to the Governor with the advice of the Executive Council (*Interpretation Act 1987* (NSW): s 14). Such a provision is, of course, subject to a contrary intention expressed in any particular statute. The exercise of prerogative powers, such as the prerogative of mercy, would also be exercised on the advice of the Executive Council.

The exercise of the so-called reserve powers, however, may on occasions be exercised without ministerial advice or even contrary to ministerial advice. These powers largely relate to the formation and – occasionally the termination – of governments. There has always been some debate on their full ambit and they have generally defied attempts at definition and codification. In a situation where, for example, following an election, no party has an absolute majority in the Lower House of Parliament, the question for the Governor is who should be asked initially to form a government. There is, in these circumstances, of course, still an existing government and it is open to the Governor to ask the advice of the Premier or the Attorney-General. But the Governor may well consider that their obvious interests in who is commissioned to form a government means that the Governor needs to consult more widely.[2]

---

1 In addition, s 9F of the *Constitution Act 1902* (NSW) specifically provides that the Letters Patent – originally dated 29 October 1900 – and all instructions to the Governor ceased to have effect on the commencement of the *Constitution (Amendment) Act 1987* (NSW).

2 Section 35A of the *Constitution Act 1902* (NSW) expressly provides that this statute does not affect any law or established constitutional convention relating to the exercise or performance of the functions of the Governor 'otherwise than on the advice of the Executive Council', in other words, the so-called reserve powers.

Is Government Approval Required for a Solicitor-General's Advice to a Governor?

One question that arises initially in the case of a request by a Governor for advice from a Solicitor-General is whether the approval of the relevant government is required – or at least desirable – before the advice might be given.

At one level, this might be considered as a question of statutory construction. The *Solicitor General Act 1969* (NSW) relevantly provides in s 3(1)(a) that the Solicitor-General may 'act as Counsel for Her Majesty and may perform such other duties and functions of Counsel as the Attorney General directs'. This provision is essentially mirrored in the relevant Victorian, Western Australian, Tasmanian and Northern Territory legislation (*Attorney-General and Solicitor-General Act 1972* (Vic): s 5(a); *Solicitor-General Act 1969* (WA): s 9(a); *Solicitor-General Act 1983* (Tas): s 7(a)). One of the functions of the Commonwealth Solicitor-General under the *Law Officers Act 1964* (Cth) (s 12(a)(i)) is 'to act as counsel for the Crown in right of the Commonwealth'. It might be argued that acting as counsel for the Sovereign in these State statutes includes advising the holder of a vice regal office and so does not require the direction of the Attorney-General on the basis that the Governor is the Sovereign's representative in the State in question. The Commonwealth legislation (*Law Officers Act 1964* (Cth)) refers to acting as counsel for the Crown, although it also provides in s 12(b) that one function of the Solicitor-General is to furnish advice to the Attorney-General on questions of law referred by the Attorney-General. This might suggest that the consent of the Attorney-General is required before the Solicitor General can provide advice to the Governor-General.

The relevant Queensland and South Australian provisions essentially state that the Solicitor-General is to carry out certain functions, including acting as counsel to the Crown, at the request of the Attorney-General (*Solicitor-General Act 1985* (Qld) s 8(a); *Solicitor-General Act 1972* (SA) s 6(a)).

It might be noted that the New South Wales legislation appears to provide a right of unremunerated private practice to the Solicitor General (*Solicitor General Act 1969* (NSW) s 2(5)(f)) and there is provision in the Queensland, South Australia, Tasmanian, Western Australian, Australian Capital Territory, Northern Territory and Commonwealth legislation for remunerated private practice on the part of the Solicitor General to be approved by the Governor-in-Council or the Attorney-General (*Solicitor General Act 1985* (Qld): s 16(1); *Solicitor-General Act 1972* (SA): s 6(b); *Solicitor-General Act 1983* (Tas): s 10(2)(b); *Solicitor-General Act 1969* (WA): s 6; *Law Officers Act 2011* (ACT): s 19; *Law Officers Act 1978* (NT): s 14(c); *Law Officers Act 1964* (Cth): s 9)). On one view, a right of private practice might allow the provision of advice to the Governor by a Solicitor-General, whatever requirements of direction by the Attorney-General might otherwise be imposed by the relevant statute.

In the case of the reserve powers, it seems to be accepted that the government of the day is not the only appropriate source of advice for a Governor but there is still a question as to whether a Solicitor-General should provide advice without the approval of the Premier or the Attorney-General.

Various views have been expressed on this question. Maurice Byers was Commonwealth Solicitor-General in November 1975, when the Whitlam government was dismissed from office by the Governor-General after a period of a month during which the Senate had refused to pass the government's budget Bills. Byers has said that the Governor-General, John Kerr, asked the Prime Minister, Gough Whitlam, whether Kerr could approach the Solicitor-General for legal advice on the powers of the Governor-General when supply is blocked by the Senate but the Prime Minister had insisted that such advice could only go through him as head of the government who, normally through the Executive Council, advised the Governor-General as to his available courses of action (National Library of Australia 1997: 55). In the event, an opinion in the name of the Solicitor-General and the Attorney-General, Kep Enderby, was provided to the Governor-General by Enderby but as an unsigned draft (indicating Enderby's view that the advice was not finalised in some respects) (Sexton 1979: 226).

This might be compared with events in early 1917 when the Prime Minister, William Hughes, raised with the Governor-General, Munro Ferguson, the question of a dissolution of the Parliament. The Prime Minister agreed that the Governor General was entitled to an independent legal opinion – other than from the Attorney-General (who was also Hughes) – and the Governor-General nominated a number of persons, including the Solicitor-General, Robert Garran, as possible sources of advice, to which the Prime Minister agreed (Markwell 1999: 288).

It later became public knowledge that in December 2009 the New South Wales Governor, Marie Bashir, sought advice from the Solicitor-General, in this case myself, in the wake of several calls in the media for the government to be dismissed (Hall and Robins 2010). The *Constitution Act 1902* (NSW) (ss 24 and 24B) provides the circumstances in which the Governor may dissolve the Legislative Assembly earlier than the date provided for every four years.

Subject to the comments made earlier about individual statutes governing the office of Solicitor-General, it might be argued that a Governor is entitled to the advice of a Solicitor-General in relation to the exercise of reserve powers without the request for advice and the advice itself going through the government of the day on the basis that the Governor may ultimately have to take a course of action that is contrary to the political interest of that government. This would certainly be so if the Governor sought advice from the Chief Justice (who is not part of the Executive like the Solicitor General but head of the judiciary), although there is now considerable agreement – reflected in the view of High Court Chief Justice French (French 2009) – that this is an unsatisfactory source of advice, not least because any exercise of the Governor's powers might be the subject of litigation before the courts.

The argument that the Governor is entitled to the advice of a Solicitor-General has perhaps less force in relation to advice sought concerning the exercise of statutory or prerogative powers by a Governor, although it remains true that a

Governor may not necessarily wish the Premier or the Attorney-General to know that he or she is effectively questioning their advice and seeking another opinion. Alpheus Todd (1894: 59) considered that a Governor was entitled to go beyond the advice of Ministers because of their political role:

> Upon the nice question as to the discretion of a governor who applies for legal advice to law officers who are also cabinet ministers, and has reason to believe that their legal judgment has been unconsciously biased by political considerations, so that he cannot accept their interpretation of the law, it should be remembered that a governor is not bound by opinions given under such circumstances, but is free to ask further assistance from elsewhere to aid him in his judgment …

Herbert Vere Evatt (1967: 191) was, however, dismissive of this view and quoted Herman Merivale – Permanent Under Secretary of the State for the Colonies over the period 1847–59 – that the Governor should avoid the temptation to surround himself with 'a camarilla of special advisors, distinct from [his] Ministers'.

Anne Twomey (2004: 635) has written that in New South Wales 'the Governor is given access … to the Solicitor General to give independent legal advice to the Governor if this is requested'. Bradley Selway (1999: 127 n 36) wrote in relation to the same question:

> It is likely that the consent of the Attorney-General will need to be obtained before the Solicitor-General could so advise but the practice in some jurisdictions is now so longstanding that such consent would seem to be implied.

Both Twomey and Selway, therefore, seem to suggest that in some jurisdictions there is a standing general approval on the part of the Premier or Attorney-General for the Solicitor-General to provide advice to the Governor.

In the absence of such an approval, however, the issue remains of whether approval should be sought for particular requests for advice. This depends to some extent on how the role of the Solicitor-General is perceived. In one sense, he or she is broadly responsible to the Attorney-General and takes instructions for the conduct of litigation. In another sense, however, he or she is the Second Law Officer *of the Crown* and historically in a different position from civil servants and even other statutory officers.

In one Australian jurisdiction, according to one of my colleagues, the Solicitor-General commonly provides advice to the Governor on the direct request of the Governor or the Governor's Official Secretary and, where the advice is given in writing, sends a copy to the Attorney-General. There would seem no convention in this jurisdiction that the Governor advises the Premier or the Attorney-General of his or her intention to request the advice of the Solicitor-General before doing so.

In another jurisdiction the vice regal representative has on occasions sought the advice of the Solicitor-General on parliamentary and other questions. In this case the Solicitor-General has not sought the approval of the executive government before providing advice, although none of the advices in question appear to involve any conflict between the interests of the vice regal representative and the executive government. In this same jurisdiction the vice regal representative is provided – with the approval of the executive government – of a copy of any opinion given by the Solicitor-General to the executive government in relation to the powers and duties of the vice regal representative.

George Winterton (2004: 44) proposed a protocol for the seeking of advice by a Governor in relation to the legality of executive action:

> It is suggested that the appropriate role of a governor-general or governor in ensuring the legality of executive action falling outside the reserve powers is as follows: if the matter is clearly justiciable, doubts as to its lawfulness should not be pressed beyond seeking the advice of the solicitor-general. If doubts persist notwithstanding such advice, the appropriate course would be to record them in the Executive Council minutes but nevertheless follow ministerial advice. A vice-regal representative would be justified in seeking further advice from reputable independent counsel where the matter is unlikely to be justiciable. If such advice contradicts that of the solicitor-general, the latter's response should be sought. However, if the solicitor-general maintains his or her opinion notwithstanding the contrary legal advice, the governor-general or governor should again note his or her reservations but ultimately follow ministerial advice.

It is hard to quarrel with this protocol, which allows a Governor to effectively question the legality of a government action but requires him or her to accept the advice of the relevant ministers if it is ultimately pressed.

Commissioning a New Government Following an Inconclusive Election Result

The issue of who should be called on to form a new government following an inconclusive election result is, as already observed, one in which a Governor may particularly want advice beyond that of the existing Premier and Attorney-General. There have been a number of occasions in modern Australian political history where this problem has arisen and, in a number of those cases, Solicitors-General have played an important role in advising the Governor in question.

South Australian Election of March 1968

Although the Solicitor-General appears not to have been involved in the aftermath of this election, it provides a good example of the kind of problem that can arise after a close result. In the election held in South Australia on 3 March 1968 each of the major parties won nineteen seats in the House of Assembly with the remaining seat held by an independent member (Harris and Crawford 1969). The Leader of the Opposition wrote to the Governor, stating that he had the support of the independent member on vital issues and asking that he be entrusted with the formation of a government. The Premier and the Attorney-General on the other hand – both offices being held by Don Dunstan advised the Governor that existing Ministers should retain their commissions and take their positions as Ministers in Parliament when it assembled. The Governor accepted this advice but, when the House of Assembly met, the government lost an adjournment motion and the Premier then resigned. The Leader of the Opposition was then commissioned to form a government.

Tasmanian Election of May 1989

At the election held in Tasmania on 13 May 1989 the existing Liberal government won 17 seats in the House of Assembly and the Labor Opposition 13 so that the balance of power was held by five Green independent members (Comment 1991). The Leader of the Opposition wrote to the Governor proposing that a Labor government be commissioned on the basis of its support by the five Green members. The Premier advised the Governor that, in the absence of a formal coalition arrangement between Labor and the Greens, the existing government should remain in office. The Governor accepted this advice and maintained this position, despite receiving a copy of an agreement signed by the Leader of the Opposition and the apparent leader of the Greens. When the House of Assembly met, an effective motion of no-confidence in the government was passed by the House. The Governor then summoned the Premier and secured his agreement to explore the capacity of the Leader of the Opposition to form a minority government. The Governor sought written assurances from the Leader of the Opposition and each of the five Greens in relation to a number of issues and consulted separately with each of the five Greens. After the Governor informed the Premier of the results of these discussions, the Premier resigned and the Leader of the Opposition was commissioned as Premier.

Over the period 29 May 1989, when the election result was officially declared, until 3 July 1989, when the new government was sworn into office, the Governor took extensive advice from the then Solicitor-General, William Bale, who was described by the Premier as the principal independent legal adviser to the Governor (Comment 1991). Twomey (2011) has noted, however, that the Attorney-General complained that he had not approved the provision of this advice. The Governor then returned the Solicitor-General's opinions to the Attorney-General but the Attorney-General sent them back to the Governor, conceding that there may be a convention that the Solicitor-General can advise the Governor directly on constitutional matters.

The role of the Attorney-General in this situation had been raised by the Secretary of the Tasmanian Department of Justice, John Ramsay, in a letter to the Attorney-General of 14 June 1989 (Royal Commission into an Attempt to Bribe a Member of the House of Assembly and other matters 1991: Annexure JAR1). Ramsay referred to 'the difficult role [of] your loyalty to Cabinet and the Premier on political matters as a Minister, and the special position that the Attorney-General has traditionally held in giving advice to Cabinet and, in some circumstances, the Governor as first law officer of the Crown, on constitutional issues'. Ramsay then noted that the Premier had been reported as consulting a variety of constitutional sources and added:

> [Y]ou may need to carefully consider your position if the Premier is obtaining advice from outside constitutional law experts, and in particular whether you need to be aware of any advice tendered and the propriety of accepting this advice without reference to your second law officer, the Solicitor-General.
>
> There is a strong tradition of the Government taking the Solicitor-General's advice on constitutional issues, and where outside advice is sought, that advice is ordinarily sought with the full knowledge of the Solicitor-General, and the Solicitor-General being able to comment on that advice to you.

In addition to the advice of the Solicitor-General, the Governor obtained opinions from Harry Gibbs, a former Chief Justice of the High Court of Australia, and Colin Howard, a former professor of constitutional law at the University of Melbourne, on the question of whether the Governor might refuse advice from the Premier to dissolve the Parliament (Winterton 1992: 310–11). The existing government sought a number of legal opinions on the constitutional alternatives available to the Governor and supplied them to him. These were from Thomas Hughes, a former Commonwealth Attorney-General; Robert Ellicott, a former Commonwealth Solicitor-General, Attorney-General and judge of the Federal Court; Maurice Byers, a former Commonwealth Solicitor-General; Professor Patrick Lane of the University of Sydney Law School; and Professor Darrell Lumb of the University of Queensland Law School. The Greens obtained a legal opinion from Professor James Crawford of the University of Sydney Law School, which was sent to the Governor.

Tasmanian Election of March 2010

At the election of 20 March 2010 the existing Labor government and the Liberal opposition each won ten seats in the House of Assembly with the Greens winning the remaining five seats (Stokes 2010). The Premier advised the Governor to invite the leader of the Liberal Party to indicate whether he was willing and able to accept a commission to form a government. The leader of the Liberal Party told the Governor that he could form a government that would enjoy the confidence of the House of Assembly because the Premier had earlier stated that his party would not vote against legislation appropriating supply nor support a no confidence motion. The Premier, however, wrote to the Governor refusing to give such commitments.

The Governor then commissioned the Premier to form a government and published his reasons for doing so. When the House of Assembly met, the Greens supported the Labor government, with their leader becoming a member of the Cabinet. It became publicly known over this period that the Solicitor-General, Leigh Sealy, provided advice to the Governor in relation to the alternatives available to him following the election result.

Federal Election of August 2010

At the election of 21 August 2010 the existing Labor government and Liberal Opposition each won 73 seats in the House of Representatives with three seats being held by independent members and one seat by a Green member. As it happened, these four members gave their support to the existing government and there does not appear to have been any involvement by the Governor-General in the negotiations that led to this support being provided.

In the immediate aftermath of the election, however, the question of the Governor-General's role in the commissioning of the new government was raised in the light of the fact that her son-in-law was a Parliamentary Secretary in the existing government and was widely considered a likely appointment as a Minister in any new Labor government. The Commonwealth Solicitor-General then provided advice to the Governor-General – at her request – on this issue. The advice, dated 26 August 2010, was subsequently made public by the Governor-General.

The advice referred to the possibility that there may be circumstances in which the Governor-General would act otherwise than on the advice of the Prime Minister and then went on to say:

> The notion that the Governor-General might in such circumstances be constitutionally inhibited in the performance of her functions by reason of a perception of bias or of a conflict of interest is one that, in my opinion, finds no foothold in the structure or text of the Constitution.

The advice concluded that the existence of relationships between the Governor-General and other persons in public life did not affect in a legal sense the exercise of vice regal powers:

> There has in the history of the Commonwealth of Australia been a number of Governors-General who have had significant prior political careers and a number of Governors-General who have had continuing personal relationships with senators and members of the House of Representatives. In my opinion, the existence of connections and relationships of that kind can give rise to no disqualification from holding the office nor to any legal impediment to the performance of the functions of the office. Where they exist, connections

> and relationships of that kind must be recognised as realities. They fall to be managed as a matter of prudence, not of legal obligation or legal impediment.

It is perhaps difficult to draw in any firm conclusions about the role of a Solicitor General in the aftermath of a close election result. The Tasmanian cases suggest that the Solicitor General is likely to be a major – possibly the chief – source of legal advice to the Governor but do not resolve the question of whether such advice should occur with the knowledge and/or consent of the existing Premier or Attorney General.

Certification of Legislation Prior to Assent

One long-term and on-going example of advice by a Solicitor-General to a Governor is the practice in New South Wales where both the Attorney-General and Solicitor-General are required to express the formal opinion – prior to legislation receiving the Governor's assent – that there is no objection – presumably on any question on form or substance – to the Governor giving that assent (see Figure 1). Each Bill that goes to the Governor for assent has a covering minute in the following terms set out in Figure 2.

In other jurisdictions – Victoria, for example – this certification to the Governor is done by the Attorney-General alone (Taylor 2006: 100).

Conclusion

There could be little doubt that the various texts and articles considering the role of Solicitors-General in advising the holders of vice regal offices raise almost as many questions as they answer. This is a difficult and still largely unexplored area for those who carry out the role of Second Law Officer of the Crown. Much may depend, of course, on the personal interaction between the vice regal representative, the Attorney-General, the Chief Minister and the Solicitor-General in the particular jurisdiction. Nevertheless, it is worth considering whether some basic principles at least might not be established in relation to this intriguing aspect of the modern day functions of the Solicitor-General.

Leaving aside, for these purposes, questions of the statutory capacity of a Solicitor-General to advise a Governor without the direction of the Attorney-General, the source of any such principles can really only lie in the Westminster system of representative and responsible government. On this basis it should be open to a vice regal officer holder to seek the advice of the Solicitor-General on questions of his or her statutory or prerogative powers but only with the knowledge and consent of the government expressed by the Chief Minister or Attorney-General. This knowledge and consent could, however, be the subject of a general approval that did not require notification to the government by the Solicitor-General of particular requests for advice by the Governor or the submission of any such advice to the government. In relation to the reserve powers, it is more difficult to suggest any generally applicable principles because the survival of the existing government may be in issue so that both the Premier and Attorney-General have a personal interest in any advice that might be provided to the Governor. It is arguable that in this situation the Governor is entitled to consult the Solicitor-General without the Solicitor-General being required to obtain the approval of the Premier or the Attorney-General to provide advice to Governor. It may be, however, in these circumstances that the Solicitor-General should inform the Premier or the Attorney-General that the Governor has requested advice and that it will be provided, albeit without being submitted to the government as well.

Figure 1 Certification of Legislation Prior to Assent

TITLE: [SHORT TITLE]

THE DIRECTOR GENERAL

SUBMITTED for favour of the Solicitor General's opinion, and subject to the Solicitor General indicating that he has no objection to Her Excellency the Governor giving her assent to this measure.

SUBMITTED for the Attorney General's approval of advice being given to Her Excellency the Governor accordingly.

[SIGNED]
for Director General

THE SOLICITOR GENERAL

In my opinion there is not any objection to Her Excellency the Governor giving her assent to this measure.

[SIGNED]
Solicitor General

THE ATTORNEY GENERAL

I concur with the Solicitor General's opinion.

[SIGNED]
Attorney General

Figure 2 Minute to Her Excellency the Governor

The Attorney General has received a communication dated [ ] transmitting, by command of Her Excellency the Governor, copy of a Bill passed by the Legislative Council and Legislative Assembly, and presented to Her Excellency for the Royal Assent, intituled

[LONG TITLE OF BILL]
The Attorney General has the honour to report that, in his opinion, there is no objection to Her Excellency the Governor giving her assent to the Bill.

[SIGNED]
Attorney General.

Department of Attorney General and Justice
Sydney

References

Comment. 1991. Documents Concerning the Constitutional Events which Surrounded the Tasmanian General Election in 1989. *Public Law Review*. Volume 2, 4.

Evatt, H.V. 1967. *The King and his Dominion Governors*. 2nd edition. Melbourne: Cheshire.

French, R. 2009. *The Chief Justice and the Governor-General*. Address to Melbourne University Law Review Annual Dinner, 29 October 2009.

Hall, L. and Robins, B. 2010. Bashir Sought Advice on Sacking Government. *Sydney Morning Herald*, 11 June 2010.

Harris, M.C. and Crawford, J.R. 1969. 'The Powers and Authorities Vested in Him': The Discretionary Authority of State Governors and the Power of Dissolution. *Adelaide Law Review*. Volume 3(3), 303.

Markwell, D. 1999. Griffith, Barton and the Early Governors-General: Aspects of Australia's Constitutional Development. *Public Law Review*. Volume 10, 280.

National Library of Australia. 1997. *Oral History: An Interview with Sir Maurice Byers (by Daniel Connell)*. Law in Australian Society Oral History Project. Oral TRC 3554.

Royal Commission into an Attempt to Bribe a Member of the House of Assembly and Other Matters. 1991. *Report of the Royal Commission*. Hobart: Government Printer.

Selway, B. 1999. The Duties of Lawyers Acting for Government. *Public Law Review*. Volume 10, 114.

Sexton, M. 1979. *Illusions of Power*. Sydney: Allen & Unwin.

Stokes, M.D. 2010. The Role of the Governor when there is a Hung Parliament: The 2010 Tasmanian Experience. *Public Law Review*. Volume 21, 223.

Taylor, G. 2006. *The Constitution of Victoria*. Annandale, NSW: Federation Press.

Todd, A. 1894. *Parliamentary Government in the British Colonies*. 2nd edition. London: Longmans, Green & Co.

Twomey, A. 2004. *The Constitution of New South Wales*. Annandale, NSW: Federation Press.

Twomey, A. 2011. The Governor-General's Role in the Formation of Government in a Hung Parliament. *Public Law Review*. Volume 22, 1.

Winterton, G. 1992. The Constitutional Position of Australian State Governors, in *Australian Constitutional Perspectives*, edited by H.P Lee and G. Winterton. Sydney: Law Book Company.

Winterton, G. 2004. The Evolving Role of the Governor-General. *Quadrant*. March.

Chapter 5

Attorneys-General, Solicitors-General and 'the Public Interest' in Australian Constitutional Cases: A Case for Citizen Input into the Development of Constitutional Policy

Patrick Keyzer

Introduction

This chapter explores the power enjoyed by Attorneys-General and their Solicitors-General to intervene in Australian constitutional cases and develops an argument that the public should have the opportunity to provide input into the development of constitutional policy that informs interventions. I use the expression 'constitutional policy' in this chapter to describe decisions about whether particular laws should be defended or opposed in constitutional proceedings. At present constitutional policy is resolved by Attorneys-General and Solicitors-General (and probably also Crown Solicitors and staff) without any direct public input. In this chapter I argue that because contemporary Australian constitutional cases raise significant civil liberty issues, and access to constitutional justice by conventional means is fraught with difficulty and risks, a consultation process should be developed to provide public input on the resolution of questions of constitutional policy.

In the first part of the chapter I outline the historical development of interventions in constitutional cases. In its early decisions the High Court developed a practice of granting leave to the Attorneys-General of the Commonwealth and the States to intervene to represent the public interest in these cases. Initially the rationale for granting leave was to enable the Commonwealth and the States to protect their 'legal territory' from trespass in federal disputes. Interventions made on this ground have declined in significance given the High Court's strongly centralist constitutional jurisprudence.

However, two developments have significantly increased the potential influence of Attorneys-General and Solicitors-General in constitutional interventions. First, in 1976 the Commonwealth amended the *Judiciary Act 1903* (Cth) to provide the Commonwealth and State Solicitors-General (and the Territories, in 1983) with a right to intervene in constitutional cases. This has dramatically increased the volume and intensity of interventions. Second, over the last two decades or so, the Australian High Court has developed a new, civil liberties jurisprudence: new constitutional doctrines that protect freedom of political communication and the integrity of courts. In this Chapter I build on the arguments I developed in *Open Constitutional Courts* (Keyzer 2010a) and argue that this jurisprudence has disclosed a significant defect in the way that constitutional litigation is organised. At present, Attorneys-General and their Solicitors-General have guaranteed access to make submissions to the High Court in these new cases. But their submissions often advocate the limitation of these new civil liberties rather than their expansion. People and associations with a serious constitutional argument to raise may want to participate in constitutional litigation to offer a different perspective than the polities in these cases, but they are confronted by serious procedural obstacles that can preclude them from being heard. I argue that this highlights the need for a new process for accommodating public input.

The orthodox account of the relationship between an Attorney-General and a Solicitor-General contrasts the politician from the public servant and the client from the lawyer. According to this account, Solicitors-General take instructions from the government of the day (typically the Attorney-General), and then act on those instructions. Support for this account can be traced to a number of sources. For example, the New South Wales Law Reform Commission has observed that in that State, 'the Solicitor-General functions within the administrative structure of the Attorney-General's Department, *and is under the direction of the Attorney-General*' (emphasis added, New South Wales Law Reform Commission 1997: [2.25]; see also Mason 1988: 22; Selway 2002: 267). If Solicitors-General are under the direction of Attorneys-General, then one could describe their role in the development of constitutional policy as merely 'advisory'.

On the other hand, it is very likely that many Attorneys-General, perhaps particularly those Attorneys-General who are not legally qualified or who have minimal legal experience, are strongly influenced, perhaps even guided, by their Solicitors-General (and perhaps their Crown Solicitors) when they adopt particular positions on issues of constitutional policy (Appleby 2012: 6.3). Furthermore, in constitutional litigation in Australian courts, Solicitors-General enjoy a very considerable degree of practical autonomy, particularly during hearings (for example, when positions shift, when concessions are made and the like). During hearings, Solicitors-General make submissions and craft tactics about matters of constitutional policy that can have significant ramifications.

Historically there has only been a limited Australian scholarship that explores the relationship between Solicitors-General and Attorneys-General in a detailed way (Appleby 2012: 2.1). Furthermore every relationship is different and relationships change over time. For the purposes of this chapter I am glossing over the distinct functions and roles of the respective personnel. I am also proceeding on the assumption that Solicitors-General who intervene in constitutional cases are doing so on the basis of instructions that are, at least to some degree, politically motivated, and these instructions are informed by their own advice regarding what is or may be possible (Selway 2002). The relationship, though murky, is both 'political' and 'legal'.

The Rationale for Interventions in the Early Years

The early constitutional jurisprudence of the Australian High Court was largely concerned with the division of power between the Commonwealth national government and the States. From 1904 to 1920 the High Court held that the Commonwealth and the States were, in general, immune from each other's legislation. For example, in *D'Emden v Pedder* (1904) 1 CLR 91, the Court held that the *Stamp Duties Amendment Act 1902* (Tas) could not oblige a Commonwealth public servant to pay a State tax on his salary. The Court held (at 111):

> When a State attempts to give to its legislative or executive authority an operation which, if valid, would fetter, control, or interfere with the free exercise of the legislative or executive power of the Commonwealth, the attempt, unless expressly authorised by the Constitution, is to that extent invalid and inoperative.

Likewise, in *Federated Amalgamated Government Railway & Tramway Service Association v New South Wales Railway Traffic Employees Association (Railway Servants' Case)* (1906) 4 CLR 488, the High Court held that a New South Wales government instrumentality could not be subjected, as an employer, to the *Conciliation and Arbitration Act 1904* (Cth). Griffith CJ, Barton and O'Connor JJ said that to subject the State railways to Commonwealth legislation regulating the rights of employers and employees would interfere with the control of those railways. This interference would be inconsistent with a principle of intergovernmental immunity that was reciprocal and not limited to taxation. Nor, in the Court's view (at 538–9), was the State's immunity confined to those functions which could be described as governmental because no activity undertaken by a State could be regarded as anything other than governmental.

Before Federation, the English courts had established that Attorneys-General had the right to intervene wherever the prerogatives of the Crown were contested (*Adams v Adams* [1971] P 188: 197–8; Selway 2002). The emergence of a High Court practice of granting leave to Attorneys-General to intervene to protect the public interest in constitutional cases mirrored the federal preoccupations of the early Court. The High Court merely adapted the English rule to the Australian federal system, and allowed the polities to intervene when their interests were affected.

The first case in which an Attorney-General's role was explored in detail was *Attorney-General (NSW); Ex rel Tooth & Co Ltd v Brewery Employés Union of New South Wales (the Union Label Case)* (1908) 6 CLR 469 (at 492–4, 541–2). In this case, the defendants, a union of brewery employees, sought registration of a 'union label' or 'workers' mark' under Part VII of the federal *Trade Marks Act*

1905 (Cth). The Act provided workers and their industrial associations with the right to register 'Workers' Trade Marks' to signify that goods to which the marks were attached were made in Australian factories by Australian workers and/or members of Australian trade unions. A 'union label' would signify that the goods to which it was attached had been made in factories staffed by union labour and, correlatively, having proper working conditions.

Anticipating an objection to their standing, a brewery sought to prevent registration and successfully lobbied the Attorney-General for New South Wales who, standing on their behalf, sought an injunction restraining registration of the mark and a declaration that the federal legislation authorising the registration of the mark was constitutionally invalid (*Union Label Case*: 471–3). The brewery opposed registration on the basis that it would interfere with their business (*Union Label Case*: 473–4). The union opposed the application by the brewery on several grounds, including, as anticipated, that it lacked standing. A majority of the Court held that the English requirement of a direct, material interest in the dispute was required to warrant standing to sue (*Union Label Case*: 491, 510 and 549). Isaacs J (at 557) took the opportunity to reflect on the right of Attorneys-General to have standing in constitutional cases generally:

> I next consider the position of the Attorney-General for New South Wales. The fact that he acts on the relation of another is not material. If a public right is infringed, and the whole community is thereby affected, the Attorney-General may protect the public interests by appropriate action. If the public interests involved are State interests, the State Attorney-General may sue; if Commonwealth interests are involved, then the Commonwealth Attorney-General, representing the larger community, may sue.

Importantly, the position taken by the Attorney-General was assumed to be co-extensive with the interests of the people. But was it? Even in this early case it was evident that the decision of an Attorney-General to intervene was a *political* decision. Was the 'public interest' really reflected by the State Attorney-General's intervention in support of the breweries in the *Union Label* Case? Or would the 'public interest' have been better served by the endorsement of the workers' mark, which would signify that the beer had been produced in safe working conditions? It is certainly arguable – perhaps even strongly arguable – that some or even many people in New South Wales would have welcomed the registration of the workers' mark (and other workers' marks).

The early federal doctrines of State reserved powers and implied immunity noted above were rejected in the *Engineers' Case* (*Amalgamated Society of Engineers v Adelaide Steamship Co Ltd* (1920) 28 CLR 129). However the High Court's practice of allowing Attorneys-General and their Solicitors-General to intervene in constitutional cases became a regular feature of constitutional litigation during the twentieth century (see, for example, *New South Wales v Commonwealth (No 1)* (1932) 46 CLR 155: 160–63; *R v Burgess; Ex parte Henry* (1936) 55 CLR 608; *R v*

Commonwealth Conciliation and Arbitration Commission; Ex parte Professional Engineers' Association (1959) 107 CLR 208; *Gosford Meats Pty Ltd v New South Wales* (1985) 155 CLR 368). So, for example, in *Australian Railways Union v Victorian Railways Commissioners* (1930) 44 CLR 319, a case concerning the applicability of federal law to State railways, Isaacs CJ, developing his earlier reasoning in the *Union Label Case*, said (at 330):

> [I]t seems to me that any State has a right to come into this Court and defend its own personal legal territory, and also any legal territory that it thinks will conduce to its welfare.

The potential for the Attorneys-General and their Solicitors-General to influence the High Court in constitutional cases was expanded considerably in 1976, when the Commonwealth amended the *Judiciary Act* to accord the Commonwealth and the States a statutory right of intervention in constitutional cases. This right to intervene was extended to the Territories in 1983. Since these changes, constitutional interventions have taken place more frequently and with greater intensity; more Solicitors-General appear for their Attorneys-General in more constitutional cases more often (Keyzer 2010a: 91).

Ultimately, though, the *Engineers* principle, that the legislative power of the Commonwealth should be construed without reference to the doctrines of implied immunity and State reserved powers, has realised its logical trajectory. The Commonwealth can now use its powers over corporations (s 51(xx) of the Constitution) and the external affairs power (s 51(xxix) of the Constitution, which has been interpreted to include the power to make laws for the purpose of implementing Australia's treaty obligations) to expand its statute book, resulting in a corresponding reduction in State legislative competence. A good example of this was in the *Work Choices Case* (*New South Wales v Commonwealth* (2006) 229 CLR 1). In that case the High Court upheld federal legislation that used s 51(xx) to authorise the regulation of the industrial relations activities of corporations, overriding a significant portion of the industrial relations of the States (via the federal supremacy clause, s 109 of the Constitution). *All* of the States and Territories intervened in the High Court to oppose the legislation, advancing arguments that sought to qualify and limit the broad and centralist approach to the construction of the Constitution that was enunciated in the *Engineers' Case*. But the High Court rejected the constitutional change.

The result of the *Engineers' Case* and the many cases that have applied the interpretative principles set out in that case is that the Commonwealth enjoys legislative and fiscal dominance over the States. Barring a seismic shift in the approach of the High Court to the interpretation of the Commonwealth's legislative powers, the impact of interventions by the Attorneys-General (of the States) in traditional federal disputes is, in this author's opinion, likely to be quite limited. This is significant because the principal justification for interventions was to prevent federal trespass by the Commonwealth on the States, and vice versa.

Now that justification for interventions has been eclipsed by the Court's centralist federal jurisprudence, this leaves only the second rationale identified by Isaacs CJ in the *Australian Railways Union Case*: the protection of 'legal territory that it thinks will conduce to its welfare'.

This statement contemplates an exceptionally wide discretion.

The Wide (and Secret) Discretion of Attorneys-General and Solicitors-General to Protect the Welfare of their Citizens in the Development of Constitutional Policy

How is it exercised? When it comes to the Solicitors-General, we do not really know, and this should not be surprising. Executive privilege and legal professional privilege would apply in many if not all of the conversations between Attorneys-General and their Solicitors-General. As Gabrielle Appleby has pointed out, until recently there has been a dearth of research relating to the Australian Solicitors-General (Appleby 2012: 2.3).

However, when it comes to the Attorneys-General, there is a wider literature. The most prominent observation made in this literature is that the role of the modern Attorney-General has become politicised (Carney 1997; Leigh 1999; King 2000; Bennett 2002; Appleby 2012: 2.3, and references there cited). As recently as 1974, in *Attorney-General (UK) v Times Newspapers* [1974] AC 273 (at 311), the House of Lords said:

> The Attorney-General … is the appropriate public officer to represent the public interest in the administration of justice. In doing so he acts in constitutional theory on behalf of the Crown, as do Her Majesty's judges themselves; but he acts on behalf of the Crown as 'the fountain of justice' *and not in the exercise of its executive functions*. (emphasis added)

Today, however, the notion that Attorneys-General act 'above politics' and might adopt a position at odds with their government is regarded by many as ironic (Walker 2002). The editor of the (Australian) *Public Law Review*, in a special volume of that journal in 2002 dedicated to the topic of the Australian Attorneys-General, commented:

> There is undoubted difficulty … [in] balancing the vague notions of independence against the pressures of party politics in Australia's highly adversarial political culture. The evidence … is … that this view of the nature of the office is inconsistent with widely held expectations of it.

For these reasons, the expression 'public interest intervention' is now more likely to be used to refer to an intervention by a person or association that is *at odds with* the position taken by the polities (Kenny 1998).

The upshot of all of this is that, with the exception of those circumstances in which an Attorney-General, the Government or Opposition make constitutionality a political issue (perhaps by referring to advice they have received from their Solicitor-General about a particular constitutional issue, which can provoke a public debate), questions of constitutional policy are being resolved for a mixture of political and legal reasons that are almost completely shielded from public scrutiny and input.

Limitations on the Capacity of People to Participate in the Development of Constitutional Policy via Litigation

Before considering what might be done about this, it is pertinent to ask whether Attorneys-General and Solicitors-General *should* consult with the public about issues of constitutional policy. Other remedies may be available. After all, the courts are open to anyone who wants to participate. Should a member of the public have a serious constitutional argument to raise, they could commence constitutional litigation, or seek leave to intervene in constitutional litigation that is on foot. They could seek to participate as amicus curiae, or even seek the 'fiat' (consent) of the Attorney-General to bring their own action by way of a relator.

Perhaps. But access to constitutional justice in Australia can be very complicated and prohibitively expensive. Ordinarily a person must demonstrate they have standing to sue, and this ordinarily requires a special interest in the litigation (Evans and Donaghue 2002). This test is not always satisfied by every would-be litigant, and governments do object to standing relatively frequently. For example, standing rules have been invoked in a number of Australian constitutional cases to chill the ardour of people and associations representing minority groups seeking to advance non-pecuniary 'identity' claims such as freedom from homophobic discrimination (*Croome v Tasmania* (1997) 191 CLR 119), the right to protest the dispossession of Aboriginal people (*Davis v Commonwealth* (1986) 68 ALR 18), or the right to oppose environmental development (*Australian Conservation Foundation v Commonwealth* (1980) 146 CLR 493) (see further Keyzer 2010a). It may be noted that these matters all raised serious constitutional arguments and were advanced by experienced counsel (A H Goldberg QC [later Justice Goldberg] represented Croome; Duncan Colquhoun-Kerr represented Davis [Justice Kerr is now President of the Administrative Appeals Tribunal] and M R Wilcox QC [later appointed Chief Justice of the Industrial Court of Australia] and Gavan Griffith [later appointed Commonwealth Solicitor-General] represented the Australian Conservation Foundation).

Importantly, if a person fails to convince a court that they have standing, or if they commence a constitutional case and lose, then they will ordinarily be ordered to pay the costs of their failed application, including the costs incurred by their opponent (the 'winner'). This can be a crippling amount of money, calculated in the millions of dollars. With the notable exception that an Attorney-

General intervening is not liable to pay (or entitled to receive) costs (*Attorney-General (Queensland) v Holland* (1912) 15 CLR 46), the High Court has almost invariably applied the indemnity rule. An analysis of the High Court's decisions where the indemnity rule has not been applied demonstrates that exceptions are few and unpredictable (Keyzer 2010a). Even the prospect of an adverse costs order can have a chilling effect on the ardour of the would-be constitutional litigant (Keyzer 2010b).

If access is refused on standing grounds, then a would-be litigant could petition an Attorney-General for his or her fiat to bring a 'relator action'. The relator action allows an Attorney-General to lend standing to a person without standing to seek a declaration of constitutional invalidity (Mantziaris 2004: 214–15). However the relator device has many limitations and, unsurprisingly, has fallen into disuse (there have only been 12 such actions in constitutional cases in the High Court since Federation). The most obvious defect of the relator device is that the Attorney-General is under no obligation to consent to a request to lend standing to a person without it (*London County Council v Attorney-General* [1902] AC 165). No reasons for refusal need be given (except in Queensland, where the Attorney-General must table a report in Parliament providing reasons: see *Attorney-General Act 1999* (Qld): s 10). The decision to withhold the fiat to a relator action is non-justiciable (*London County Council v Attorney-General* [1902] AC 165: 169). Even if the Attorney-General grants the fiat to a relator action, the Attorney-General remains *dominus litus* throughout the proceedings (*Gouriet v Union of Post Office Workers* [1977] 3 WLR 300: 311), can withhold approval to the amendment of court documents, veto the relator's choice of counsel and even discontinue proceedings, notwithstanding the opposition of the relator (*Attorney-General (NSW); Ex rel Wentworth v Woollahra Municipal Council* [1980] 41 LGRA 376). Finally, in a relator action it is the relator, not the Attorney-General, who will generally be ordered to pay the costs of the case if it is lost.

What about participation as an amicus curiae? The High Court has traditionally adopted a negative posture when people or associations make applications to participate in constitutional cases as amici curiae (Willheim 2010). In *Wurridjal v Commonwealth* (2009) 237 CLR 309 (at 312–13) French CJ, for the Court, said:

> The Court may be assisted where a prospective amicus curiae can present arguments on aspects of a matter before the Court which are otherwise unlikely to receive full or adequate treatment by the parties because (a) it is not in the interests of the parties to present argument on those aspects or (b) one or other of the parties lacks the resources to present full argument to the Court on them. In some cases it may be in the interests of the administration of justice that the Court have the benefit of a larger view of the matter before it than the parties are able or willing to offer.

This approach recognises that amici curiae can play a role in expanding the normative horizon of the Court. However in practice the current approach to the admission of amici curiae is far short of ideal. At present, applications for amicus curiae status must be made orally on the morning of the substantive hearing. This puts applicants to unnecessary inconvenience and expense (Willheim 2010).

For the reasons above, the development of a mechanism to accommodate input on questions of constitutional policy remains needed.

Freedom of Political Communication, the Institutional Integrity of Courts, and Interventions

Interventions by Attorneys-General and Solicitors-General in constitutional cases have become all the more important in the last two decades for another very significant reason: the emergence and rise of a constitutional jurisprudence of civil liberties. Over the last 20 years, the High Court held that even though the Australian Constitution does not expressly protect freedom of political communication, it is implied by the Constitution, which provides for a system of representative government in which members of the Houses of Parliament are 'directly chosen by the people' (Constitution: ss 7 and 24). The current test of whether a law infringes freedom of communication is taken from *Lange v Australian Broadcasting Corporation* (1997) 189 CLR 520, as modified in *Coleman v Power* (2004) 220 CLR 1 (at 51, 77–8, 82):

> First, does the law effectively burden freedom of communication about government or political matters either in its terms, operation or effect? Second, if the law effectively burdens that freedom, is the law reasonably appropriate and adapted to serve a legitimate end in a manner which is compatible with the maintenance of the constitutionally prescribed system of representative government and the procedure prescribed by s 128 for submitting a proposed amendment of the Constitution to the informed decision of the people.

This test applies to all laws, whether made by the Commonwealth, State or Territory legislatures (*Lange v Australian Broadcasting Corporation* (1997) 189 CLR 520: 564). The freedom has been successfully invoked to protect the political speech of anti-government protestors (*Coleman v Power* (2004) 220 CLR 1).

The second significant doctrine that has emerged in the last two decades is the *Kable* doctrine. In a series of cases commencing in 1996, the High Court recognised that, while there is no strict separation of powers that applies to State courts as it applies to federal courts, the institutional integrity of *all* Australian courts is protected from legislative or executive intrusion (*Kable v Director of Public Prosecutions (NSW)* (1996) 189 CLR 51). Kable, a minority of one, challenged the constitutional validity of a law enacted by the elected representatives in the Parliament of New South Wales authorising his preventive detention on the ground that he was a danger to the community if released. A majority of the High Court in that case developed a constitutional principle, drawn from the separation of powers effected by the

Constitution, that upheld his (counsel's) argument that the institutional integrity of the Supreme Court of NSW would be compromised if it exercised the jurisdiction conferred by the legislation (Keyzer 2008). The institutional integrity principle applies throughout the Australian court hierarchy because the Constitution does not permit of different grades or qualities of justice between federal and State courts (*Kable v Director of Public Prosecutions (NSW)* (1996) 189 CLR 51: 103; *Fardon v Attorney-General (Qld)* (2004) 223 CLR 575: 617–18; *South Australia v Totani* (2010) 242 CLR 1: 37–9). Repugnancy to or incompatibility with the institutional integrity of the courts may be manifested by State and Territory, as well as federal, legislation (*North Australian Aboriginal Legal Aid Service Inc v Bradley* (2004) 218 CLR 146: 163; *South Australia v Totani* (2010) 242 CLR 1: 37–9; *Wainohu v New South Wales* (2011) 243 CLR 181: 229).

The *Lange* doctrine has been applied to invalidate legislation that made it an offence to criticise the decisions of a government agency (*Nationwide News Pty Ltd v Wills* (1992) 177 CLR 1) and legislation that banned paid political advertising during an election period (*Australian Capital Television Pty Ltd v Commonwealth* (1992) 177 CLR 106). The *Kable* doctrine has been applied to invalidate legislation that required a court to make a forfeiture order upon the application of a State government agency, an order that could be made on an *ex parte* basis (*International Trust Finance Company Ltd v New South Wales Crime Commission* (2009) 240 CLR 319) and legislation that required a magistrates court, upon application by the Attorney-General, to make a control order against a member of a declared organisation (*South Australia v Totani* (2010) 242 CLR 1). These new principles limit the legislative power of all of the polities, and although they are formulated as limits on legislative power, they operate effectively to protect the freedoms and rights of people in Australia. In the political communication and institutional integrity cases, the polities have often opposed the expansion of these doctrines (Keyzer 2010a). In the 689 interventions that took place in the 292 constitutional cases decided in the 30 years following the amendments to the *Judiciary Act*, only two interventions were made in support of the expansion of civil rights and freedoms (Keyzer 2010a: 94).

This gives rise to the question whether the polities, when they join to oppose the expansion of these doctrines, are *indeed* representing the general welfare of their citizens, as Isaacs CJ hypothesised in the *Australian Railways Union* case in 1930. After all, while some of the citizens of the Commonwealth, States and/or Territories might not welcome the expansion of these doctrines, there may be many others who would welcome such a development.

Conclusion

How might people react if they knew that their governments were taking the approach that they do in these cases? What if they found out that the policies their governments were enacting in legislation and supporting in interventions were in breach of international human rights instruments? Would people in the Australian Capital Territory or Victoria, who have elected governments that have enacted statutory protection of human rights (including freedom of speech and the right to a fair trial), become anxious if they learned that their governments were intervening in constitutional cases to advance arguments that similar rights should be restricted? Should the people of the Commonwealth, States and Territories have some *role* in the process of devising the constitutional policies that are acted on by Attorneys-General?

In 1994, Jürgen Habermas observed (at 148):

> In a democratic constitutional state, in which all political power is ultimately founded on the will of the people (there must be) ... a factual connection between the arguments brought forth by the constitutional court and by the citizens, and this connection also has to be made in institutionalized discourses in which the citizens' democratically formed will is expressed.

In this chapter I have argued that there is a case for a public consultation process to be developed to inform Attorneys-General and their Solicitors-General when they are resolving questions of constitutional policy. Contemporary Australian constitutional cases often raise significant civil liberty issues, and Attorneys-General and their Solicitors-General are assumed to represent the public interest in these cases, when they may not. Steps should be taken to ensure that they do.

References

Appleby, G. 2012. *The Constitutional Role of the Solicitor-General: An Historical, Legal and Lived Portrait*. PhD Thesis: The University of Adelaide.

Bennett, D. 2002. The Roles and Functions of the Attorney-General of the Commonwealth. *Australian Bar Review*. Volume 23, 61.

Carney, G. 1997. The Role of the Attorney General. *Bond Law Review*. Volume 9, 1.

Editorial. 2002. *Public Law Review*. Volume 13, 239.

Evans, S. and Donaghue, S. 2002. Standing to Raise Constitutional Issues in Australia, in *The Convergence of Legal Systems in the 21st Century: An Australian Approach* edited by G. Moens and R. Biffor. Brisbane: Copyright Publishing.

Habermas, J. 1994. Struggles for Recognition in the Democratic Constitutional State, in *Multiculturalism*, edited by A. Gutman. Princeton: Princeton University Press.

Kenny, S. 1998. Interveners and Amici Curiae in the High Court. *Adelaide Law Review*. Volume 20, 159.

Keyzer, P. 2008. Preserving Due Process or Warehousing the Undesirables: To What End the Separation of Judicial Power of the Commonwealth? *Sydney Law Review*. Volume 30, 101.

Keyzer, P. 2010a. *Open Constitutional Courts*. Annandale, NSW: Federation Press.

Keyzer, P. 2010b. A Battle and a Gamble: The Spectre of an Adverse Costs Order in Constitutional Cases. *Bond Law Review*. Volume 22, 82.

King, L.J. 2000. The Attorney-General, Politics and the Judiciary. *Australian Law Journal*. Volume 74, 44.

Leigh, A. 1999. The Successful Attorney General – An Oxymoron? *Australian Law Journal*. Volume 73(2), 91.

Mantziaris, C. 2004. The Federal Division of Public Interest Suits by an Attorney-General. *Adelaide Law Review*. Volume 25, 211.

Mason, K. 1988. The Office of Solicitor General for New South Wales. *Bar News*, 22.

NSW Law Reform Commission. 1997. *Circulation of Legal Advice to Government: Issues Paper No 13* [Online]. Available at: http://www.lawlink.nsw.gov.au/lrc.nsf/pages/IP13TOC [accessed 18 April 2013].

Selway, B. 2002. The Different Role of an Australian Attorney-General. *Public Law Review*. Volume 13, 263.

Walker, K. 2002. The Bishops, the Doctor, His Patient and the Attorney-General: The Conclusion of the *McBain* Litigation. *Federal Law Review*. Volume 30, 507.

Willheim, E. 2010. Amici Curiae and Access to Constitutional Justice in the High Court of Australia. *Bond Law Review*. Volume 22, 126–47.

PART II
The Solicitor-General in Context

Chapter 6

The Modern First Law Officer in Australia

Fiona Hanlon

Introduction

Australia derives the titles of its two principal Law Officers from British tradition. Under that tradition the Solicitor-General is the Second Law Officer and junior to the First Law Officer, the Attorney-General. The titles and the ranking – First and Second – acknowledge the British origins of the titles. The modern relationship between the two officers, however, is a product of the evolution of Australia's legal and political systems.

This chapter tells the story of how the office of First Law Officer has evolved in Australia. It does so by reflecting on how that evolution has altered the relationship between the First and Second Law Officers. It asks the question whether, in modern Australia, it is the Attorney-General or the Solicitor-General who is in fact the First Law Officer.

The chapter also reflects on a third office, that of Minister of Justice. Its history in Australia is not as long as that of either the Attorney-General or the Solicitor-General but its future may prove to be more enduring than that of Attorney-General. The Minister of Justice is an unambiguously political ministerial office. The Solicitor-General is an ongoing non-political office. The clear distinction between those two offices necessarily raises the issue of how to characterise the nature of the Attorney-General in the political context of modern Australian: as Law Officer or as Minister of Justice by another name.

The Law Officers in Australia: The Attorney-General, Solicitor-General and Minister of Justice

The modern office of Attorney-General exists as a ministerial office in each of the six Australian States, at the Commonwealth level and in each of the self-governing territories of the Northern Territory and the Australian Capital Territory. It is not possible to detail the history of the office in each of those nine jurisdictions in full over the course of this chapter. It is possible, however, to tell the story of the relationship between the First and Second Law Officers and the Minister of Justice through some of the milestones in Australia's political development and the experience of some of the individuals who have occupied the office of Attorney-General at significant moments in time.

One of those significant moments occurred on Wednesday 31 October 1951, when Thomas Mitchell, MLA for Benambra, rose to his feet to deliver the Second Reading speech to the Legislative Assembly of the Parliament of the State of Victoria on the Solicitor-General Bill. That Bill created a statutory office of Solicitor-General that would be available at all times to give advice to the Crown and to represent it as counsel in court. Mitchell told the Victorian Legislative Assembly that over the years administrative and parliamentary duties had increased so as to preclude the Attorney-General from appearing in courts, even should the holder of that office possess the 'requisite skills' (Victorian Parliamentary Debates 1951a: 5683). The Solicitor-General Bill specified that the Solicitor-General must be drawn from the ranks of 'His Majesty's Counsel'. Mitchell told the Legislative Assembly that this would ensure that the Solicitor-General had the 'necessary academic and professional skills' for the role (Victorian Parliamentary Debates 1951a: 5684).

The introduction of the Solicitor-General Bill into the Victorian Parliament by Attorney-General Mitchell is an appropriate place to begin this story because at the time he rose to give his Second Reading speech Thomas Mitchell was both Attorney-General and Solicitor-General. Both were political ministerial offices held by a member of Cabinet within the executive government of the day. The office of Solicitor-General had earlier been a ministerial office in the Australian jurisdictions of Tasmania, Queensland and New South Wales but had lost that status by 1863, 1893 and 1922, respectively. By 1951 Victoria was the only Australian jurisdiction where the office of Solicitor-General retained the status of a political ministerial office.

The story of how the Attorney-General and the Solicitor-General each became political offices and then diverged – one continuing as a political office and one becoming a non-political office – illustrates how the relationship between the First and the Second Law Officer had evolved in Australia to that point in time.

The History of the Australian Attorney-General

Colonial Attorneys-General

The story begins in 1823 when, acting on the recommendations of John Thomas Bigge in his report on the *Judicial Administration of New South Wales and Van Diemen's Land* (1823), the Colonial Office appointed separate Attorneys-General for each colony. The Attorneys-General were to act as legal advisers to their respective colonial Governors, prepare criminal indictments, conduct prosecutions and draft the colonial Governor's legal documents and legislation.

The Attorney-General for New South Wales was also the Attorney-General for the Port Phillip District until its separation as the Colony of Victoria in 1851. On separation, Lieutenant Governor La Trobe drew on the membership of the local Port Phillip Bar to appoint the first Attorney-General for the Colony of Victoria.

The Attorney-General for New South Wales was the Attorney-General for the Moreton Bay District until its separation from New South Wales as the Colony of Queensland in 1859. Legal advisers to the local colonial administration were appointed for the Swan River Settlement, later the Colony of Western Australia, and for South Australia in 1829 and 1836 respectively. In both jurisdictions the title 'Advocate General' was initially adopted but was eventually replaced with the title Attorney-General for the senior legal adviser to the executive administration (Hanlon 2007: 42).

A Solicitor-General was appointed in January 1824 to assist the newly appointed Attorney-General for New South Wales. Initially, as accorded with British conventions, no distinction was made between the respective roles of Attorney-General and Solicitor-General as Law Officers. The Colonial Office resisted attempts by the New South Wales incumbents in 1828 to specify and divide duties between them. The only distinction that the Secretary of State for the Colonies, George Murray, was prepared to accept between the holders of the two offices in Australia was that in the event of a disagreement the Attorney-General should have the right to dictate to the Solicitor-General (Historical Records of Australia 1922: 10).

As other legal officers were appointed for the various Australian colonies, the title of Solicitor-General was adopted for those legal officers who were immediately subordinate to the Attorney-General. Neither the Attorneys-General nor the other appointed legal advisers had any special status as compared with other officials appointed to advise and assist a Governor. A colonial Governor could both disregard the advice of his officials, including advice tendered at meetings of Executive Council, and expect obedience from those officials, including the Law Officers. This was not simply an artefact of autocratic behaviour on the part of colonial Governors. It was a consequence of the locus of accountability for the actions of colonial executive administrations. It was the local colonial Governor that the Colonial Office held to account. There was no protection to be had in the Governor claiming reliance on the advice of his local advisers.

Representative and Responsible Government and the Politicisation of the Office of Attorney-General

Between 1855 and 1860 a form of representative and responsible government was introduced into each of the Australian colonies of New South Wales, Tasmania, Victoria, South Australia and Queensland. Western Australia followed in 1890. Bi-cameral Parliaments were established for each colony. Officials selected from the membership of those Parliaments formed Westminster-style ministries that held office while they had the confidence of the Lower House. Initially the titles allocated to the new ministerial portfolios mirrored the titles of appointed advisers to the colonial Governor immediately prior to the establishment of the new Parliaments. As the Attorney-General had been such an adviser, that title became the title of a ministerial portfolio. The Solicitor-General made a similar transition in Victoria, Tasmania, Queensland and New South Wales. In those colonies the offices of Attorney-General and Solicitor-General thus changed in character from appointed professional advisers to the colonial Governor to Ministers selected from amongst the membership of the elected Parliament and liable to retire from office 'on political grounds', namely the loss of support and confidence of their parliamentary colleagues and liable also to go in and out of office as the executive government of which they were a member went in and out of political power.

With the change to representative and responsible government came a shift in accountability. The colonial Governor ceased to be responsible for the day-to-day executive administration. That accountability shifted to the newly formed executive ministries for as long as they maintained the confidence of their Parliament. Some colonial Governors found the change of status that accompanied the transition to representative and responsible government under the Westminster model difficult and attempted to exert influence over individual Ministers. To protect against this and ensure consistency of advice to the Governor early colonial ministries quickly developed a culture of collective decision-making through the processes of Cabinet. In such a culture there was little room for individual or independent action on the part of the ministerial Attorney-General. New South Wales Attorney-General James Martin believed that each member of a ministry should be individually responsible to the Legislative Assembly. This view so alienated his ministerial colleagues that he was forced to resign from the Cowper ministry in 1858 (Loveday and Martin 1966: 112–13). The view commonly held by colonial Premiers was that differences of opinion within a ministry constituted a grave disadvantage to the government of the day (Loveday and Martin 1966: 117).

In the second half of the nineteenth century some individual New South Wales Attorneys-General sought to remain outside this collective culture by only accepting appointment on the understanding that they would not join Cabinet. However, some Premiers found this option unacceptable as they wanted to be sure of the active political support as well as the legal support of their Attorney-General (Loveday and Martin 1966: 117). For a period of five years, commencing in 1873, New South Wales Premier Henry Parkes replaced the Attorney-General in Cabinet with a Minister of Justice and Public Education in an attempt to free the Attorney-General from responsibility for the administration of a government department and give the incumbent time to fulfil the legal professional tasks associated with the office. Parkes brought the practice of excluding the Attorney-General from Cabinet to an end in 1878 by including both the Attorney-General and the Minister for Justice in the Cabinet (Hawker 1971: 50).

In each Australian colony the change in the status of the Attorney-General from an appointed Law Officer to a Minister liable to retire on political grounds meant that the legal skill and legal professional standing of the individual ceased to be the only factor relevant to the choice of an Attorney-General. Once representative and responsible government was introduced, the political standing and influence of a candidate for office as Attorney-General became equally relevant. Writing to a political colleague in 1872 about the considerations that exercised his mind in the selection of an Attorney-General, New South Wales Premier Parkes described his chosen candidate, Edward Butler, as representing the best: 'concurrence of political opinion, Parliamentary standing and popular sympathies' (Loveday and Martin 1966: 81).

The title Minister of Justice began to appear amongst colonial ministerial portfolio titles. The range of policy and administrative responsibilities assigned to that portfolio resembled those assigned to a ministerial Attorney-General or Solicitor-General. There were only two clear differences. The title Minister of Justice was preferred usage when the holder of the ministerial portfolio either lacked any legal qualifications or was not a member of the local Bar. The second difference was that any functions requiring the exercise of professional legal skills were allocated to either the ministerial Attorney-General or the ministerial Solicitor-General and not to the Minister of Justice.

The lack of a clear distinction between the roles of a ministerial Attorney-General and a ministerial Solicitor-General could result in clashes between the incumbents. In 1893 the Victorian Attorney-General Bryan O'Loghlen declined to prosecute a number of prominent Victorians on charges connected with the collapse of the Mercantile Bank of Australia Limited. The Solicitor-General, Isaac Isaacs, disagreed with Attorney-General O'Loghlen's decision and claimed that as Solicitor-General he possessed the same range of powers as the Attorney-General and intended to use them to commence a prosecution against the individuals concerned. Attorney-General O'Loghlen, with the support of the Premier, instructed the Crown Law Officers to ignore Isaacs' instructions and Isaacs resigned from the ministry (Plehwe 1980: 3–7).

The subordinate nature of the ministerial office of Solicitor-General sometimes made recruitment to that office difficult. This could result in the office ceasing to be included amongst ministerial portfolios. Alternatively, it could result, as became common practice in Victoria, in one individual being appointed to the combined ministerial portfolio of Attorney-General and Solicitor-General. This combining of the two offices eroded the status of the office of Solicitor-General as a distinct ministerial office.

Immediately following the transition to responsible government ministerial Attorneys-General continued to perform the same types of legal professional tasks performed by appointed Attorneys-General prior to the transition. However, the pressures of parliamentary and ministerial work restricted their capacity to personally provide legal advice and appear in court. Increasing reliance was placed on appointed legal officers and dedicated parliamentary draftsmen for the actual performance of professional duties associated with the office of Attorney-General.

Parliamentary and ministerial work pressures also restricted the ability of Attorneys-General to maintain private legal practices. Those who managed to do so were often criticised for not devoting sufficient attention to their public duties or for placing themselves in a position of conflict between their public and private roles. It was alleged against Queensland Attorney-General Thomas Byrnes that he failed to fulfil the requirements the office of Attorney-General during the late

1890s. Byrnes was concurrently Premier, Chief Secretary and Attorney-General while also maintaining a private legal practice (Gill 1978: 186). In 1867 James Boucaut resigned as South Australian Attorney-General in order to act for private claimants seeking to invalidate certain mining leases that had been issued by the South Australian government. Boucaut believed that to appear in court to impugn the actions of the government would be untenable for him while he held office as Attorney-General (Combe 1957: 99). In 1893 New South Wales Attorney-General Edmund Barton and Minister of Justice Richard O'Connor resigned from Parliament. Their resignations were in response to criticism of their each accepting a brief to appear for private litigants in an action against the New South Wales Railway Commissioners and against the interests of the New South Wales government (Bennett 1969: 115).

Ministerial Attorneys-General also began to acquire additional ministerial portfolios with subject matter that was unrelated to the exercise of professional legal skills. Minister for Education was a portfolio commonly assigned to Attorneys-General. However, ministerial Attorneys-General could be assigned portfolio areas that raised potential areas of conflict with their duties as Attorney-General. In Tasmania in 1887 Attorneys-General began to be assigned ministerial responsibility for police and gaols. As a consequence, responsibility for criminal prosecutions was transferred from the Tasmanian Attorney-General to the Solicitor-General, which had become a non-political permanent office in that colony in 1863. The additional workload associated with ministerial responsibility for police and gaols also resulted in Tasmanian Attorneys-General choosing to relinquish private legal practice from that date (Wettenhall 1968: 94–5).

The acquisition of additional ministerial responsibilities indicated that the holder of the office of Attorney-General was included within the ministry for their political skills. It marks their ceasing to act as a professional legal adviser to ministerial colleagues or the executive administration generally. Over time, because of the lack of opportunity to personally exercise legal skills, a lack of confidence manifested on the part of individual Attorneys-General themselves and on the part of the executive government and of the legal profession as to the capacity of some Attorneys-General to personally provide high-level and reliable legal advice and services.

As early as 1856 some members of the New South Wales Parliament argued that if the Attorney-General was to act as a professional legal adviser they should become a permanent officer in the public service. Similar suggestions were made over the course of the next 40 years in that colony (Hawker 1971: 50). In 1905 the Legislative Council of the Tasmanian Parliament sought the advice of Solicitor-General Edward Dobbie as to whether, given the designation of the office as a Law Officer, the Attorney-General should be a practising member of the legal profession. Solicitor-General Dobbie advised that while it was not contrary to law to appoint a person not of the legal profession, that person would be Attorney-General 'only in name'. Dobbie (1905) observed that the consequence of this would be that the 'business and authority' of the Attorney-General would devolve upon the Solicitor-General.

In 1906 concerns about the ongoing capacity of ministerial Attorneys-General to perform the legal functions associated with the office led the Tasmanian Parliament establish a Royal Commission to consider whether the office of Attorney-General in that State should be made a non-political permanent office. In 1908 two of the three Royal Commissioners handed down a report recommending that the office of Attorney-General be abolished, the legal duties associated with it transferred to the Solicitor-General and that the departments then administered by the Attorney-General be transferred to another Minister who might be styled the Minister of Justice. Commissioners W.O. Davis and C.E. Wise stated that while the Attorney-General was 'nominally' a Law Officer, in reality the Attorney-General occupied a position similar to that of the Home Secretary in the United Kingdom (Royal Commission on the Proposal to Make the Office of Attorney-General Permanent Non-Political 1908: iv). Evidence was given to the Royal Commission suggesting that the accumulation by the Attorney-General of ministerial responsibilities capable of being performed by any other Minister at the expense of the professional legal functions made the continued use of the title 'Attorney-General' inappropriate.

Federation and the Commonwealth Attorney-General

Upon Federation of the Australian colonies in 1901, the Australian Constitution made no special reference to the office of Attorney-General. The appointment of Ministers was governed by s 64 of the Constitution, which provided for the Governor-General to appoint officers to administer such departments of State of the Commonwealth as the Governor-General in Council may establish. Section 64 specified that no Minister could hold office for longer than three months unless he or she was or became a Senator or Member of the House of Representatives. In so doing it excluded the option of appointing a ministerial Attorney-General from outside the Parliament. The office of Attorney-General was included as one of the seven Ministers constituting the first Commonwealth ministry and Cabinet.

In the first quarter of the twentieth century, Commonwealth Attorneys-General personally provided legal advice, appeared in court and were involved in the preparation of draft legislation. However, as had occurred in the colonies, and continued to occur with State Attorneys-General, Commonwealth Attorneys-General began taking on broader ministerial responsibilities. Coinciding with the First World War but continuing to the present day, Attorneys-General acquired ministerial responsibilities for national and State security and public safety. These responsibilities were akin to those allocated to the Home Secretary in the United Kingdom, a political ministerial office never associated with any role as a Law Officer.

During the first half of the twentieth century a number of Commonwealth Attorneys-General maintained some form of private legal practice. From 1901 until 1927 the Victorian-based Commonwealth Attorneys-General were assisted in maintaining their practices by the location of the Commonwealth Parliament in Melbourne. Isaac Isaacs had maintained an active private practice at the Melbourne Bar while Victorian Attorney-General in the 1890s and continued this while Commonwealth Attorney-General between 1905 and 1906. However, Isaacs was criticised for it (Fricke 1986: 42).

Frustration at not being able to maintain his practice at the Queensland Bar contributed to Commonwealth Attorney-General James Drake's decision not to seek re-election at the 1906 general election (Johnston 1979: 184). Drake had successfully represented the Commonwealth as Attorney-General in the first major constitutional case heard by the High Court of Australia (*D'Emden v Pedder* (1904) 1 CLR 91). Littleton Ernest Groom, who served as Commonwealth Attorney-General between 1906 and 1908 and again between 1921 and 1925, found it impossible to maintain his practice at the Queensland Bar because of the distance from Canberra (Rydon 1987: 26).

The move of the national Parliament to Canberra in 1927 extended these difficulties to all legally qualified Ministers and Members of Parliament generally. However, a number of Commonwealth Attorneys-General continued to practise privately in conjunction with their ministerial responsibilities. Robert Menzies maintained a private practice while Commonwealth Attorney-General in the 1930s (Fricke 1986: 16); as did John Latham, who did opinion work and held a number of retainers from private clients during his two terms as Commonwealth Attorney-General in the 1920s and 1930s (Lloyd 1987: 177). However, physical distance was not the only issue faced by lawyer Members of Parliament. Over the course of the twentieth century both occupations, the practice of the law and the role of a Member of Parliament, were becoming more specialised and more demanding of time and effort (Johnston 1979: 184).

General Themes

It is a general theme of this chapter that despite having a common beginning the First and Second Law Officers have developed differently within Australia's legal and political system. The Second Law Officer has formalised into a permanent, unambiguously legal, ongoing and non-political office. This has occurred in response to the growing need of governments for ready access to high-level legal advice and advocacy and the decline in the ability of Attorneys-General to fill that need due to increased ministerial responsibilities and reduced professional capacity.

A number of characteristics can be taken together to make an assessment of the level of the legal professional profile of any individual holding office as Attorney-General. These include the number of years spent in legal practice prior to appointment as Attorney-General, membership of the Bar, status as a senior counsel and appointment to judicial office following service as Attorney-General. As the First Law Officer evolved the legal professional profile of the individuals appointed to the office tended to decline. That profile also came to lack any uniformity or predictability across jurisdictions. As the Second Law Officer evolved the legal professional profile of the individuals appointed to the office increased. That profile also became uniform across all Australian jurisdictions.

The characteristics that can be taken together to make an assessment of the depth of the political professional profile of any individual holding office as Attorney-General include the number of years spent in Parliament prior to appointment to ministerial office, the number and topic range of portfolios held and membership of Cabinet. As the First Law Officer evolved the political professional profile of the individuals appointed to the office increased while the legal professional profile declined.

The Decline of the Legal Professional Profiles of Australian Attorneys-General

Over the course of the twentieth century the legal professional profiles of Australian Attorneys-General declined across Australian jurisdictions overall. As the century progressed it became less likely that any individual Attorney-General would be a barrister or have attained the status of Senior Counsel prior to their appointment as Attorney-General. It became more common that despite possessing legal qualifications an Attorney-General may never have been admitted to practise or may have practised only briefly prior to concentrating on a political career. It also became more likely at the State level that the Attorney-General would be without legal qualifications entirely. In Queensland from 1932 until 1986, none of those appointed to the office of Attorney-General had any legal qualifications; the office was held variously by an accountant, a railway worker, a miner, a butcher and a tramway union official (Hanlon 2007: 137). The practice of not appointing lawyers to the office of Attorney-General in Queensland was a deliberate one and not the result of there being no qualified lawyers amongst the ranks of the government parties willing to accept appointment. For example, in 1976 Bill Lickiss, a valuer by profession, was appointed Attorney-General; and John Greenwood, a member of the Queensland Bar and the only barrister in the Cabinet at that time, was appointed Minister for Survey and Valuation (Hughes 1980: 162).

Although some individual Attorneys-General sought to make the claim, there was no generally accepted right for serving Attorneys-General to be appointed to judicial office in Australia either before or after Federation. There were individual serving and former Attorneys-General whose legal skill and standing qualified them for high judicial office, and a number were appointed to State Supreme Courts and to the High Court. However, as the depth of experience of legal practice possessed by Attorneys-General on average declined, so did the number of Attorneys-General appointed to judicial office.

Over the period from 1901 to 2000 the percentage of Australian Attorneys-General overall who lacked legal qualifications rose from 6 per cent to 19 per cent. The percentage of Attorneys-General who were barristers dropped from 58 per cent to 23 per cent and the percentage of serving Attorneys-General who were appointed to judicial office dropped from 11 per cent to nil (Hanlon 2007: 236).

The Rise of the Professional Political Profiles of Australian Attorneys-General

From the early twentieth century onward parliamentary politics ceased to be based on loose factions and personal alliances and began to be dominated by formal political parties. This carried with it the requirement that to be considered for appointment to ministerial office an individual Member of Parliament had to have developed standing and credibility within a political party and a preparedness to respect and defend party platforms and policies. Moreover a range of factors unconnected with the personal or professional qualities of an individual Member of Parliament – such as the need to maintain a balance between regional and factional elements within the party and between the Upper and Lower Houses, and, where relevant, between coalition members – influenced whether an individual would be considered for appointment to the ministry. In Queensland from the late 1950s to the 1980s the Country/National/Liberal coalition governments adopted the practice of selecting the Attorney-General only from the ranks of the Liberal members of the coalition (Hughes 1980: 159). This practice, combined with that of not appointing lawyers to that office, resulted in a situation where it could be predicted with absolute certainty that the Queensland Attorney-General of the day would be a non-lawyer Liberal Member of Parliament.

As their professional legal profiles declined, the professional political profiles of Attorneys-General began to rise. The average period that an individual spent as a Member of Parliament before appointment as a ministerial Attorney-General increased. This indicated a consolidation of their status as professional politicians rather than individuals recruited to the ranks of a parliamentary party for their professional expertise and appointed quickly to ministerial office when the occasion arose. It also became less likely that a person would be appointed Attorney-General without having first held some ministerial office unrelated to law or the administration of justice.

As discussed, it also became common for the individual who was appointed Attorney-General to also hold other ministerial offices, unconnected with law or justice, concurrently with the office of Attorney-General. Commonwealth Attorneys-General John Latham and Herbert Vere Evatt held the Attorney-General's portfolio concurrently with that of External Affairs in the 1920s and the 1940s respectively. Evatt was also Deputy Prime Minister while Attorney-General and Minister for External Affairs. William Morris Hughes was Commonwealth Attorney-General on four occasions between 1908 and 1941 and variously was Prime Minister, Minister for External Affairs, Minister for Industry and Minister for the Navy while Attorney-General. In Tasmania, solicitor Henry Baker was Attorney-General and Minister for Education concurrently in the 1920s and 1930s, as was George Baker in the 1920s. Baker had no legal qualifications of any kind. In Victoria in the 1920s through the 1940s there were many examples. John Allan was Victorian Premier, Minister for Water Supply, Minister for Railways, Attorney-General and Solicitor-General concurrently. Ian Macfarlan was Victorian Premier, Treasurer, Minister for Health, Attorney-General and Solicitor-General concurrently. Albert Bussau was Victorian Attorney-General, Solicitor-General and Minister for Transport concurrently. Bussau had no legal qualifications. These are just a few of the examples that can be found at both the Commonwealth and State levels.

Over the period from 1901 to 2000 the percentage of Australian Attorneys-General overall who held ministerial portfolios not related to the administration of justice while Attorney-General rose from 49 per cent to 74 per cent. The percentage whose first ministerial appointment was as Attorney-General as a standalone portfolio fell from 43 per cent to 14 per cent. The percentage of Attorneys-General who held that portfolio concurrently with the office of Minister of Justice rose from 21 per cent to 44 per cent. Across the period the percentage of Attorneys-General who were members of Cabinet never fell below 83 per cent, averaging 93 per cent (Hanlon 2007: 237).

As the twentieth century progressed, although the political profile of the ministerial office of Attorney-General increased in comparison with its legal professional profile, the political standing and influence of the office weakened in an institutional sense due to the lack of any basis upon which to distinguish the office from other ministerial offices. The conventions of collective decision-making associated with membership of Cabinet necessarily restricted the independence of the individual Ministers, Attorneys-General included. The breadth and complexity of responsibilities associated with executive government and the number of Ministers doubled, tripled, quadrupled and more over the century. The increased size of ministries created a more complex system in which an Attorney-General might seek to exercise influence. It also allowed for a gradual strengthening of the offices of Prime Minister and Premier by allowing them to become full-time and distinct ministerial positions.

The capacity of an individual Attorney-General to influence their ministerial colleagues came to depend upon their political standing and their capacity to resist domination by a strong Premier or Prime Minister. In many ways this is illustrated by the role played by Frank Brennan in the Commonwealth Scullin ministry between 1929 and 1932. Brennan had no particular standing or reputation within the legal profession. He was not regarded as a skilled lawyer. He also lacked 'political clout' among his ministerial and party colleagues. He, therefore, had no basis from which to exert influence over his Cabinet colleagues either in terms of pragmatic politics or in the furtherance of respect for legal principles and the rule of law. Because of this he was regarded as a weak Attorney-General (Ryan 1977; Ryan 1978: 182).

State Attorneys-General are members of Cabinet and vulnerable to the dominance of the collective decision-making processes of Cabinet that are part of Australian political culture. At the Commonwealth level all Attorneys-General were automatically members of Cabinet until 1956, when Prime Minister Menzies adopted the practice of selecting a sub-set of the ministry for membership of Cabinet, leaving the remaining Ministers to form an outer ministry. This practice meant that membership of Cabinet depended on the political standing of the individual Minister rather than the portfolio held. Membership of the Cabinet, therefore, became dependent on personal associations, political loyalties, influence and seniority. In the case of Attorneys-General, this served only to increase the importance of an individual's political characteristics at the expense of their legal professional characteristics. This model of selective membership of Cabinet was rejected by the Whitlam Labor government but has been adopted by other Coalition and Labor Prime Ministers since. Under this model the presence of the Attorney-General within Cabinet confirms the holder of the office as a senior member of the ministry who can be trusted to abide by the collective nature of the Cabinet process.

The Independence of the Attorney-General in Government

It has been rare in Australia for an Attorney-General to take a public stand against his or her Cabinet colleagues. When this has occurred, it has been the collective decision of the Cabinet that has prevailed and not the individual stance of the Attorney-General.

At the State level this is illustrated by the circumstances surrounding the resignation in August 1972 of Tasmanian Attorney-General Mervyn Everett from the government led by Premier Reece. Attorney-General Everett formed the view that he should grant a fiat requested by the Save Lake Pedder Action Committee to commence an action in the Supreme Court of Tasmania to challenge the proposed flooding of Lake Pedder by the Tasmanian Hydro-Electric Commission on the basis that the flooding was not authorised by the legislation governing the activities of the Commission.

However, rather than simply granting the fiat, Attorney-General Everett put the matter before Cabinet, where he was outvoted by his colleagues. Cabinet's decision having been made, Everett resigned without issuing the fiat. Everett deferred to the collective decision of the Cabinet of which he was a member. By resigning without granting the fiat, Everett gave precedence to the principle of Cabinet solidarity and the importance of collective responsibility and denied the office of Attorney-General any independent power or authority. Following Everett's resignation Premier Reece, who had no legal qualifications, allocated himself the Attorney-General's portfolio and formally refused the fiat in that capacity. Shortly thereafter the Tasmanian Parliament enacted retrospective legislation validating the provisions of the Hydro-Electric Commission legislation sought to be challenged. At a special caucus meeting held just 55 minutes after Parliament had passed the validating legislation Everett was re-elected to the ministry as Deputy Leader of the Parliamentary Labor Party. Shortly thereafter he was reappointed as Attorney-General (Lowe 1984: 41–2; The Mercury 1972).

At the Commonwealth level, the trend is illustrated by Attorney-General Robert Ellicott's resignation from the Fraser ministry on 6 September 1977. Ellicott had received a request to assume conduct of a private prosecution launched against former Prime Minister Whitlam and three of his former Ministers over actions connected with the 'loans affair'. In order to make a decision on that request Ellicott believed that he needed access to Cabinet papers of the Whitlam government. As Attorney-General in the Fraser ministry Ellicott was not a member of Cabinet. His request for access to the material was denied by the Fraser Cabinet and Ellicott resigned as Attorney-General, alleging interference with the discretion of the Attorney-General in relation to criminal prosecutions (Bennett 2002: 68–9).

Prime Minister Malcolm Fraser viewed the pursuit of criminal charges against the former government as a contravention of undertakings he had given to Governor-General John Kerr when assuming the Prime Ministership after the dismissal of the Whitlam government. Fraser told Ellicott to take over the prosecution and terminate it (Hocking 2012: 409–10). The prosecution was eventually concluded when the High Court of Australia (*Sankey v Whitlam* (1978) 142 CLR 1) found that the charge set out in the information was bad in law (Blackshield 2012).

Disputes about criminal prosecutions had taken place between Prime Ministers and Attorneys-General in earlier cases, notably between Prime Minister Bruce and Attorney-General Latham in 1929 (Hanlon 2007: 149). However, the issue has been resolved in Australia. Starting in 1982, every Australian jurisdiction has created a statutory office of a professional Director of Public Prosecutions to assume all effective responsibility for criminal prosecutions (Johns 2001). The purpose behind this was to remove decisions related to the institution or withdrawal of criminal prosecutions from the possibility of inappropriate political influence through the exercise of pressure by a ministerial Attorney-General acting either on their own initiative or under pressure from political colleagues.

The Rise of the Professional Solicitor-General

By the time Attorney-General Mitchell presented the Solicitor-General Bill to the Victorian Parliament in October 1951, the decline in the depth of legal professional expertise on the part of the average Australian Attorney-General was acknowledged. John Cain Snr observed in the course of debate on that Bill in the Victorian Legislative Assembly:

> [T]he average Attorney-General has restricted qualifications because he is a member of Parliament. Any professional man who devotes most of his time to his duties as a member of Parliament does not have opportunities to practise the same as have outside members of the legal profession … The Government is entitled to receive the best advice available. (Victorian Parliamentary Debates 1951b: 224)

In his Second Reading speech on the Solicitor-General Bill Attorney-General Mitchell spoke of the importance of the State having ready access to legal advice, citing 'the extremely acute and complex questions connected with the constitutional interrelations between the Commonwealth and the States' as one of the matters requiring attention from a full-time Solicitor-General (Victorian

Parliamentary Debates 1951a: 5682–3). In so commenting he was responding to the manner in which Commonwealth governments had moved quickly from Federation to test the scope of Commonwealth legislative powers.

The First World War, in particular, provided an opportunity for the extent of those powers to be tested in a number of areas. Commonwealth Attorneys-General approached the task of advising their Cabinet colleagues in ways that took a broad view of Commonwealth power. In so doing, Commonwealth Attorneys-General were not acting to ensure the government complied with existing understandings of the constitutional limits of the power of the Commonwealth because there were no such settled understandings. Instead it was a case of the Attorney-General, both in the formulation of legislation and the conduct of and oversight litigation before the High Court, urging the Commonwealth to assume all of its constitutional authority.

Attorney-General Mitchell cited the issue of the financial relationship between the States and the Commonwealth as one that had given the Victorian government 'headaches' that year and was anticipated to produce more headaches for the State government in the future. The Attorney-General expressed the fear that without 'careful Constitutional guidance' the State of Victoria would suffer during the then forthcoming decade to the 1960s (Victorian Parliamentary Debates 1951a: 5683). Significantly, Attorney-General Mitchell foreshadowed the increasing dominance of the Commonwealth executive over the States that would mark the second half of the twentieth century.

With the enactment of the *Solicitor-General Act 1951* (Vic) the office of Solicitor-General in Victoria became a full-time non-political office. The office of Attorney-General remained a ministerial office. Mitchell ceased to be Solicitor-General but remained Attorney-General until the end of the McDonald government in December 1952. He remained a backbencher and an active member of a number of Parliamentary committees for the next 24 years until his retirement from Parliament. Henry Winneke of the Victorian Bar was appointed to the newly established statutory office of Solicitor-General. Winneke was appointed Chief Justice of the Supreme Court of Victoria in 1964.

The career paths of Mitchell and Winneke, career politician and distinguished jurist, respectively, illustrate the different ways in which the First and Second Law Officers Attorney-General and Solicitor-General had evolved. The years from 1951 to the present have served only to consolidate those two separate paths and deepen the differences between the professional characteristics of each office in the Australian context, one political and one legal.

In each Australian jurisdiction the office of Solicitor-General is an ongoing non-political office. It is regarded as a significant legal office suitable only for senior members of the Bar with proven legal and advocacy capacity and demonstrated competence. An individual Solicitor-General may carry out the duties of his or her office for a number of governments. The office of Attorney-General in Australia has developed into a political office which is part of, not independent of, the executive government. An Attorney-General remains in office only so long as they have the support of their parliamentary colleagues and of their Premier or Prime Minister, and only so long as the government led by that Premier or Prime Minister remains in office.

In practice the legal professional tasks associated with the First Law Officer have devolved to the Second Law Officer either through specific delegation or through machinery of government arrangements for the provision of high-level legal services adopted by the executive government in each Australian jurisdiction.

The Attorney-General and the Minister of Justice

Over the course of the twentieth century the title Minister of Justice comes and goes from ministerial titles, and for much of the time its use follows no fixed pattern. In New South Wales, the Minister of Justice was sometimes a separate ministry junior to that of the ministerial office of Attorney-General. At other times in that State it was a ministerial office that was held jointly with that of Attorney-General. In Western Australia the practice developed of allocating the title of Attorney-General to the ministerial portfolio with responsibility for law and justice only if the Minister assigned that portfolio had been admitted to legal practice. If the Minister had not been admitted or lacked legal qualifications, the title 'Minister of Justice' was given to the portfolio. The portfolio responsibilities were not altered.

The Western Australian *Supreme Court Act* was amended in 1899 to formalise this distinction. That the distinction meant little in practice is illustrated by the allocation of the portfolio titles to Thomas Walker in the Scaddan government in 1911. When he was appointed to that ministry in October 1911, as Minister of Justice Walker was yet to complete the legal studies he had been undertaking part-time while a Member of Parliament. By November 1911 he had completed his studies and been admitted to practise as a barrister and solicitor of the Supreme Court of Western Australia. On 22 November 1911, the day he was admitted, he shed the title Minister of Justice and was sworn in as Attorney-General, his ministerial responsibilities unchanged (Bolton and Byrne 2005: 131–2).

In Queensland 'Attorney-General and Minister of Justice' were bracketed together from 1957 to 1989 as a combined portfolio title. In 1989, Commissioner Fitzgerald in the Report of the Commission of Inquiry into Possible Illegal Activities and Associated Police Misconduct recommended that the office of Attorney-General be separated from that of Minister of Justice. The Commissioner was concerned to preserve a distinct identity for the role of Chief Law Officer in the person of the ministerial Attorney-General that otherwise risked being made dependent on Justice Department officials and vulnerable to influence from Cabinet control (Commission of Inquiry into Possible Illegal Activities and Associated Police Misconduct 1989: 138).

Queensland governments accepted Fitzgerald's recommendation briefly before once again combining the offices of Attorney-General and Minister of Justice in 1992. The issue was considered again in 1993 by the Queensland Electoral and

Administration Review Commission (1993) and by the Parliamentary Committee for Electoral and Administrative Review of the Legislative Assembly of the Queensland Parliament (1993). Each recommended the enactment of legislation to set out the role of the Attorney-General.

In 1999, in response to those recommendations, the Beattie government introduced the *Attorney-General Act 1999* (Qld). Section 3 of that Act specified that there was to be an 'Attorney-General for the State of Queensland', which it defined as either the Minister designated as 'Attorney-General' or 'Minister for Justice and Attorney-General', or, if no such Minister was designated, whichever Minister was allocated responsibility for the administration of the *Attorney-General Act*. Section 4 specified that the Attorney-General of Queensland was the First Law Officer of that State, but did not otherwise change the basis for appointment as Attorney-General or specify any legal professional qualifications for holding that office.

Over the latter part of the twentieth century and continuing to the present the combined ministerial title 'Attorney-General and Minister of Justice' has become increasingly common at State and Territory level. There has been a gradual alignment in both the legal professional and political professional profiles of Attorneys-General and Ministers of Justice. It is no longer possible to point to any clear distinction between the two. Even in Western Australia the combined title has become common usage even when the holder of the office has legal qualifications. The Attorney-General and Minister of Justice can no longer be distinguished on the basis of one having legal qualifications and the other not.

The ministerial council formed in the early 1960s to provide a forum for Attorneys-General for the various Australian jurisdictions to discuss and progress matters of mutual interest was called the Standing Committee of Attorneys-General (SCAG). In 2011 the Committee's title was changed to the Standing Council on Law and Justice (SCLJ). The change reflected the fact that a wide range of Ministers had responsibility for matters that might once have been regarded as falling clearly and solely within the Attorney-General's portfolio.

The Attorney-General and the Crown

The Attorney-General is the First Law Officer of 'the Crown'. The modern Australian conception of the term 'Crown' equates it with the 'government', being the executive government of the day of which the Attorney-General is a member (*Sue v Hill* (1999) 199 CLR 462: 497, 499). Even if the office had evolved differently and a modern Australian Attorney-General still acted as a Law Officer in practice, as legal adviser to the government of which he or she is a member, should an Attorney-General be expected to act independently of the interests of that client government or do other than exercise loyalty to that government?

The ability to exercise partiality in favour of the executive government of the day has been presented as an argument in favour of the Australian office of Attorney-General retaining its status as a political ministerial office since the second half of the nineteenth century. For example, New South Wales Premier Henry Parkes rejected the option of the Attorney-General becoming a permanent non-political office selected only on the grounds of technical legal competence because of a fear that such an Attorney-General would come to be 'out of tune with the times' and hold up the passage of government legislation (Hawker 1971: 50).

In 1908 the Tasmanian *Royal Commission on the Proposal to Make the Office of Attorney-General Permanent Non-Political* (1908: 35, [708]) heard evidence from Norman Kirkwood Ewing. Ewing was a member of the Tasmanian Bar. He was variously a Member of the Parliaments of Western Australia, Tasmania and the Australian Senate. He was appointed a Judge of the Supreme Court of Tasmania in 1915. Ewing told the Commission:

> My reason for believing in the retention of the office of Attorney-General as a political office is that, if possible, a Government chooses a lawyer of the same political colour as itself. He therefore becomes competent to advise the Government from its point of view and to advance the ends that the Government really has in view.

At the Commonwealth level, in 1904 – when the then only recently admitted William Morris Hughes declined the offer, and with no other legally qualified member of Caucus – the first Labor Prime Minister, Chris Watson, turned to independent member Henry Bournes Higgins as Attorney-General. As Attorney-General Higgins was a member of Cabinet but not of the Labor caucus. Although publicly defended by Prime Minister Watson, Higgins was criticised for being insufficiently active on behalf of the government in securing the passage of its legislation and for frequent absences from the House of Representatives to attend to private business. *The Bulletin* (extracted in McMullin 2004: 98–101) attacked Higgins for insufficient partiality, claiming:

> Higgins is far from being the cantilever bridge of strength to the Federal Government that he ought to be. … The duty of an Attorney-General is to defend his Ministry at all times.

In 1965 Commonwealth Attorney-General Billy Snedden was singled out for criticism over the government's actions in making the *Customs (Prohibited Imports) Regulations 1965* (Cth), which were designed specifically and intentionally at rendering ineffective a pending Privy Council appeal by IPEC in litigation against the Commonwealth government (*R v Anderson; Ex parte Ipec-Air Pty Ltd* (1965) 113 CLR 177). Snedden responded, 'I regarded it as a decision of government and I was just the Attorney-General doing what I was instructed to do' (Schedvin 1983–87: 7:10; Snedden and Schedvin 1990: 56–9). Snedden was Attorney-General in the Menzies and Holt governments between 1963 and 1966, and was appointed a Queen's Counsel in 1964 while serving as Attorney-General. Snedden regarded the Attorney-General as the legal representative of the executive government and claimed no independent role for the Attorney-General as First Law Officer.

Summary: The Evolution of the Three Offices

Three titles – Attorney-General, Solicitor-General and Minister of Justice – have survived since the establishment of representative and responsible government in the Australian colonies in the second half of the nineteenth century. But survival has involved change. The nature of the office associated with each title has evolved as Australia's political and legal institutions have evolved. As various responsibilities have been associated now with one and then with another title it is that of Solicitor-General that has become the most clearly defined and consistent in each Australian jurisdiction. 'Attorney-General' has undergone the greatest change to the extent that few, if any, of the original duties associated with the role of First Law Officer survive, despite the retention of the title.

In modern Australia the office of Attorney-General is likely to be held by a lawyer, but one who has engaged predominately in a political career and not one who has been engaged in the active practice of the law, at least not at any time recent to their appointment as Attorney-General. Such legal professional functions as continue to be associated with the office are performed by a combination of the Solicitor-General, a government solicitor, public service legal officers and private sector lawyers. It is common for the office of Attorney-General to be held concurrently with other unrelated ministerial portfolios.

In each Australian jurisdiction the Attorney-General is a member of the executive branch of government. He or she is a member of the Executive Council, participates in parliamentary debates, is a member of a political party with a particular political philosophy or ideology and is involved in the development and implementation of that party political policy. In all Australian States the Attorney-General is a member of Cabinet. At the Commonwealth level the Attorney-General is included in Cabinet unless lacking sufficient political seniority and standing with the Prime Minister and other senior ministerial colleagues to justify membership. The Australian office of Attorney-General retains the designation of First Law Officer either by custom and convention or because of legislation that preserves that characterisation so as to retain for the executive such powers as may continue to be associated with the designation Attorney-General at common law. However, there is nothing in either the constitutional provisions and conventions or in the legislation of the various jurisdictions to ensure that all those who hold the office that bears the title 'Attorney-General' will act in the same way when confronted by an issue of principle associated with the defence of the rule of law, the independence of the judiciary or in the exercise of common law functions.

The manner in which an individual Attorney-General will carry out the responsibilities associated with the office will depend on the skill, integrity, values, and personal and political beliefs of that individual and not on any fixed institutional character of the office itself. Although an individual Attorney-General may choose personally to exercise legal skills in the conduct of the office of Attorney-General, it would not be correct to characterise the role of Attorney-General in Australia in an institutional sense as a practising Law Officer in the way it is possible to so characterise the Attorney-General in the United Kingdom. The breadth of ministerial responsibilities allocated to the Attorney-General and their presence in Cabinet prevent that.

The Future of the Law Officers

When Victorian Attorney-General Mitchell presented the Solicitor-General Bill in 1951 he told the Victorian Parliament that it was important that the government have ready access to dedicated legal advice because of the 'various legal problems which nowadays are continually cropping up' (Victorian Parliamentary Debates 1951a: 5682). While it was true in 1951 that Australian governments used law and legislation as a means of implementing government policy and regulation, the years following 1951 have seen an exponential increase in the way governments use legislation to advance a range of political policy-based initiatives. Matters associated with law cannot be confined to the Attorney-General's portfolio but are inherent in the responsibilities of all Ministers.

When Victorian Attorney-General Mitchell presented the Solicitor-General Bill to the Victorian Legislative Assembly in 1951 he stressed that the Solicitor-General would have 'no political functions or responsibilities' and that all duties of such a nature were to be attached only to the Attorney-General who would be politically responsible (Victorian Parliamentary Debates 1951a: 5684). However, despite its long-held status as a political office, the ministerial office of Attorney-General in Australia continues to be referred to as First Law Officer. That designation can carry the implication that the person appointed holds two offices – the political office of Attorney-General and the separate legal office of First Law Officer that is capable of being distinguished from the political office.

The danger in maintaining this dual characterisation is that it works to confuse and reduce accountability for both the Attorney-General and the executive government. By focussing on the First Law Officer as actor, the government of which the Attorney-General is a member and in whose political interests they act can attempt to depoliticise an issue and escape scrutiny by deflecting responsibility from other ministers or from the government as a whole in relation to its respect for the rule of law and the legal system and the use of legislation as a political tool. Moreover, the dominance of collective over individual ministerial responsibility in Australia's political culture will, in turn, protect the Attorney-General from being held to account individually. Both the Attorney-General and the executive government of which they are a member should be accountable through all the mechanisms of Parliament and the democratic, legal and judicial process for actions taken in the exercise of ministerial responsibilities and the collective decisions of Cabinet.

Any distinction between the Attorney-General and the First Law Officer is based on the First Law Officer having a distinct function related to the exercise of legal professional skill and judgment. It would be unrealistic at this point in the evolution of the office of Attorney-General within the Australian political context to attempt to reconstitute that office in an institutional sense as a genuine First Law Officer engaged full-time in professional legal practice as the senior legal adviser and counsel to the executive government. That is the role into which the office of Solicitor-General has evolved in every Australian jurisdiction. Removing the quasi-judicial virtual robe of First Law Officer from an Australian Attorney-General reveals a member of the executive government administering a ministerial portfolio who could appropriately carry the title of Minister of Justice. In many Australian States it already does.

Earlier in this chapter I observed that while the history of the office of Minister of Justice in Australia is not as long as that of either the Attorney-General or the Solicitor-General, its future as a ministerial office might prove to be more enduring than that of Attorney-General and its existence serve to reinforce the characterisation of the office of Solicitor-General as a non-political office. It may be that the final evolution of the three offices will involve the ultimate atrophy of the title 'Attorney-General' and the recognition going forward of two distinct offices: the political ministerial office of Minister of Justice accountable through the democratic and legal processes and the ongoing non-political legal office of Solicitor-General as First Law Officer in its own right and accountable as an officer of the court subject to professional standards of ethical legal conduct.

References

Bennett, D. 2002. The Roles and Functions of the Attorney General of the Commonwealth. *Australian Bar Review*. Volume 23(1), 61.

Bennett, J.M. 1969. *A History of the New South Wales Bar*. Sydney: Law Book Co.

Bigge, J.T. 1823. *Report of the Commissioner of Inquiry on the Judicial Establishments of New South Wales and Van Dieman's Land.* London: House of Lords.

Blackshield, T. 2012. Sankey v Whitlam, in *The Oxford Companion to the High Court of Australia*, edited by M. Coper, T. Blackshield and G. Williams. Melbourne: Oxford University Press [Online]. Available at: http://www.oxfordreference.com/view/10.1093/acref/9780195540222.001.0001/acref-9780195540222-e-361?rskey=m1PACS&result=362&q= [accessed 27 March 2013].

Bolton, G. and Byrne, G. 2005. *May It Please Your Honour: A History of the Supreme Court of Western Australia 1861–2005*. Perth: Supreme Court of Western Australia.

Combe, G.D. 1957. *Responsible Government in South Australia*. Adelaide: W.L. Hawes, Government Printer.

Commission of Inquiry into Possible Illegal Activities and Associated Police Misconduct (Queensland). 1989. *Report of a Commission of Inquiry Pursuant to Orders in Council, dated 26 May 1987, 24 June 1987, 25 August 1988, 29 June 1989*. Brisbane (Fitzgerald Report).

Dobbie, E.D. 1905. Attorney-General: Whether it is Necessary, Under the Constitution Act, that He Should be a Member of the Legal Profession – Opinion of the Solicitor-General. *Parliamentary Paper No. 30*, Legislative Council, Parliament of Tasmania, Ordered by the Legislative Council to be printed, 26 August 1905.

Electoral and Administrative Review Commission. 1993. *Report on Review of Independence of the Attorney-General*. Brisbane: V.R. Ward, Government Printer.

Fricke, G. 1986. *Judges of the High Court*. Melbourne: Hutchinson of Australia.

Gill, R. 1978. Thomas Joseph Byrnes: The Man and the Legend, in *Queensland Political Portraits 1859–1952,* edited by D.J. Murphy and R.B. Joyce. St Lucia: University of Queensland Press.

Hanlon, F. 2007. *An Analysis of the Office of Attorney-General in Australia and Directions for the Future*. PhD thesis: University of Melbourne.

Hawker, G.N. 1971. *The Parliament of New South Wales 1856–1965*. Ultimo, NSW: Government Printer.

Historical Records of Australia. 1922. *Series I: Governors' Despatches to and from England, Vol. XV July 1829-December 1830*. The Library Committee of the Commonwealth Parliament.

Hocking, J. 2012. *Gough Whitlam: His Time*. Carlton, Victoria: Miegunyah Press.

Hughes, C.A. 1980. *The Government of Queensland*. St Lucia: University of Queensland Press.

Johns, R. 2001. *Independence and Accountability of the Director of Public Prosecutions: A Comparative Survey*. Sydney: Parliament of New South Wales.

Johnston, R. 1979, *History of the Queensland Bar*. Brisbane: Bar Association of Queensland.

Lloyd, C. 1987. Not Peace But a Sword! – The High Court Under J.G. Latham. *Adelaide Law Review*. Volume 11, 175.

Loveday, P. and Martin, A.W. 1966. *Parliament Factions and Parties: The First Thirty Years of Responsible Government in New South Wales, 1856–1889*. Melbourne: Melbourne University Press.

Lowe, D. 1984. *The Price of Power: The Politics Behind the Tasmanian Dams Case*. South Melbourne: Macmillan.

McMullin, R. 2004. *So Monstrous a Travesty*. Carlton North, Victoria: Scribe Publications.

Parliamentary Committee for Electoral and Administrative Review. 1993. *Report on Review of the Independence of the Attorney-General*. Legislative Assembly of Queensland.

Plehwe, R. 1980. The Attorney General and Cabinet: Some Australian Precedents. *Federal Law Review*. Volume 11, 1.

Royal Commission on the Proposal to Make the Office of Attorney-General Permanent Non-Political. 1908. *Report of the Commissioners*. Hobart: John Vale, Government Printer.

Ryan, K. 1977. *Kevin Ryan Papers*. National Library of Australia, Manuscripts Collection, MS 1736, note of interview with John Michael Brennan, Chief Judge of the District Court of NSW in Chambers, Sydney 19 February 1977.

Ryan, K. 1978. *Frank Brennan: A Political Biography*. MA thesis: La Trobe University.

Rydon, J. 1987. Lawyers in the Australian Commonwealth Parliament. *Australian Journal of Politics and History*. Volume 33(2), 23.

Schedvin, B. 1983–87. Interview with Sir Billy Mackie Snedden. National Library of Australia Oral History Project. TRC 4900/57.

Snedden, B.M. and Schedvin, M.B. 1990. *Billy Snedden: An Unlikely Liberal*. South Melbourne: Macmillan Australia.

The Mercury, 31 July 1972; 17 August 1972.

Victorian Parliamentary Debates. 1951a. Legislative Assembly. 31 October 1951.

Victorian Parliamentary Debates. 1951b. Legislative Assembly. 27 November 1951.

Wettenhall, R.L. 1968. *A Guide to Tasmanian Government Administration*. Hobart: Platypus Publications.

Chapter 7
The Challenges of Providing Legal Services to Government

Gabrielle Appleby[1]

Introduction

Ready and frequent access to lawyers is essential to the proper functioning of a government operating under the rule of law. That much is clear (although always bears repeating). Lawyers are, or ought to be, consulted by government when it drafts laws, interprets them prior to taking action, enters into commercial transactions, takes action to defend its interests or action is taken against it, takes action on behalf of the community (such as through the conduct of prosecutions) and even when it formulates policy. Drewry has observed that 'the public importance of lawyers and their discipline is guaranteed by the legalistic basis of the modern state' (Drewry 1981: 18).

Across the world governments have struggled with a fundamental question: what is the best manner of providing legal services to government? Should government departments and agencies employ lawyers in-house? Should departments and agencies have access to private legal services, and, if so, should this be restricted or regulated? Should there be a single centralised provider of legal services to all government departments and agencies?

Proponents of greater centralisation highlight its flexibility, its reduction of duplication, its capacity to attract greater resourcing, to foster specialist legal expertise, to ensure consistency in and oversight of the overall government legal position, to attract and retain lawyers of high calibre and, most fundamentally, the protection it affords to the professional independence of the individual lawyer. Proponents of greater use of in-house legal practices have targeted the delay experienced with the centralisation of legal services providers and the general failure of such providers to be responsive to, or understand, the objectives of the department or agency. Reformists arguing for government access to private firms are driven by the economic rationalism that underpinned many of the neo-liberal reforms in the 1980s and 1990s.

In this chapter I consider how these different positions have manifested in the provision of government legal services in Australia. I start with a brief comparative

1 I would like to thank my colleague Dr Suzanne Le Mire for her comments on an earlier version of this chapter.

exploration of the frameworks adopted for the delivery of government legal services in the United Kingdom and Canada. I then chronicle the history of the provision of legal services to government in Australia and analyse some recent reforms that have been implemented at the Commonwealth level.

What my research reveals is that in the last 20 years, the Commonwealth regulatory framework for providing legal services to government has been dominated by the goals of efficiency and cost-effectiveness. I argue that the focus on these principles has come at the cost of meeting the Attorney-General's responsibility to ensure all legal services provided to government are conducted with an eye to whole-of-government considerations and the public interest.

Contrasting Models: England and Canada

As at the time English law was received in Australia, the English Law Officers (the Attorney-General and Solicitor-General)[2] were Ministers of the Crown, holding seats in Parliament. However, a Law Officers' Department was not created in England until 1893 (Edwards 1964: 141) and today the Law Officers are still supported by a relatively small department: a Director-General, about 15 civil and criminal lawyers, and policy and administrative staff (Government Legal Service: 4).

The English Law Officers are often described as the chief legal advisers to government but as government has become increasingly complex and diverse, they provide advice only on significant, sensitive or particularly difficult legal issues (Shawcross 1953: 6). They will also deal with questions that arise in the Parliament about government Bills and government legal policy. Much of the government's legal business was historically not dealt with by the Law Officers but by the Lord Chancellor (who, for example, made appointments to courts and tribunals) and the Home Office (which is responsible for prisons and police). The Lord Chancellor, by virtue of the officeholder's usually prestigious legal qualifications and experience, would also advise the Prime Minister and Cabinet from time to time (Edwards 1964: 2; 1984: 193 n 58).[3]

The majority of legal services are provided to the English government by other legal officers, most notably the Treasury Solicitor. While not providing the majority of legal services to government, the Attorney-General is now responsible for the Treasury Solicitor and oversight of the Government Legal Service (GLS). The Attorney-General is also responsible for superintending the prosecuting authorities in England and Wales.

2 Until 1872 there was a third English Law Officer, the Advocate-General, who advised on international, maritime and ecclesiastical law. This officer's functions are now performed by the Legal Adviser to the Foreign Office (Edwards 1964: 2).

3 Although constitutional reforms in 2006–07 substantially altered the Lord Chancellor's traditional responsibilities.

In England, the Treasury Solicitor is a very important office. First established in the mid-seventeenth century to negotiate and look after the affairs of the Treasury, the nineteenth century saw the Treasury Solicitor take responsibility for the predominance of government legal work. As government departments grew, the Treasury Solicitor was asked to act for many of the new departments, although some preferred to hire their own legal advisers. In 1842, the Treasury Solicitor handled the legal work of 13 of the 23 departments (Treasury Solicitor). For much of the second half of the nineteenth century, the Treasury Solicitor also held the office of Director of Public Prosecutions (Edwards 1964: 373–4).

In 1875, a report by the Jessel Committee on the Legal Business of Government recommended not that there be a single provider of legal services to government, but that a common head (the Treasury Solicitor) be appointed to 'act as a referee in all matters of practise, and would be adviser to the Government in all that concerned the organisation of the legal departments of its offices' (extracted in Drewry 1981: 20). The *Treasury Solicitor Act 1876* (UK) transferred more responsibilities to the office's jurisdiction. This led to Treasury Solicitor Augustus Stephenson declaring 'sovereignty' over almost all of government legal business, including prosecutions. As government expanded and more responsibilities were bestowed on the Treasury Solicitor it became apparent that perhaps the legal services of government were too large to be supervised by just 'one man' (Edwards 1964: 387). In 1908, the criminal law division was spun off as the Director of Public Prosecutions (Edwards 1964: 388).

In the 1960s and 1970s a number of important inquiries into the provision of government legal services were conducted. In each of them, the Treasury Solicitor consistently argued that greater centralisation would ensure professional detachment, improve flexibility, be a better use of manpower and improve career management of government lawyers (thus attracting better-quality lawyers to government service) (Drewry 1981: 24, 27).

In the 1960s, the Fulton Report rejected the Treasury's request for centralisation but agreed that the Treasury Solicitor should be the head of the 'Government Legal Service' – thus trying to seek the elusive balance between centralisation and departmental autonomy (Drewry 1981: 24).

In 1971, the Compton Report recommended that government litigation and conveyancing be run by the Treasury Solicitor, transferring some more responsibility to the office. However, the report also recommended that for those departments that needed continuous legal advice, legal services ought to be provided in-house; whereas in those departments that did not, legal services ought to be provided by the Treasury Solicitor. The report went further and said that in those departments where law and policy questions were highly intermingled 'it is essential that the departmental lawyer regard himself, and be viewed as such, as a fully integrated member of the departmental team' (Edwards 1984: 184–5; Drewry 1981: 27). The model recommended by the Compton Report is, by and large, how the Treasury Solicitor operates today. In 2012, the Treasury Solicitor provided legal services to over 180 departments, agencies, research councils and even non-governmental bodies such as museums (Treasury Solicitor).

Today, those who provide legal services to the English government have all been brought under the umbrella of the GLS. The Treasury Solicitor heads the GLS, which also includes all of those lawyers working *within* government departments (although it excludes some specialist legal service providers, including the Crown Prosecution Service, the Foreign and Commonwealth Office and the Office of the Parliamentary Counsel). The GLS is used for recruitment purposes, offers training and support and facilitates a degree of institutional knowledge sharing. While the Treasury Solicitor heads the GLS, ultimately the Attorney-General sits at its apex. The Treasury Solicitor may have responsibility for recruitment and staffing across the GLS, but it is the Attorney-General or Solicitor-General who acts as the final referee on legal questions (Edwards 1984: 194–5).

In the late 1980s and early 1990s, a growing trend in government was the use of private sector legal providers for government legal work. The Attorney-General responded by issuing the 'Guidelines on the Use of the Private Sector for Government Legal Work'.[4] The Guidelines indicate that legal work should be contracted out only where the necessary expertise does not exist in the GLS and there is no long-term value in growing it (for example in commercial areas), the GLS does not have the resources to do the work without undue delay or it is more cost-effective for the work to be done in the private sector (Guidelines 2.1).

The Guidelines indicate that for certain 'core government work'[5] it is in the government's interests that the work remains within government (Guidelines 2.25). An additional concern that the Guidelines express is that work should not be contracted out if doing so would impact on the ability of the GLS to continue to provide high-quality legal services, such as by reducing its critical mass (Guidelines 2.26).

Compliance with the Guidelines is left to the in-house lawyers within departments and agencies. The Treasury Solicitor has no role in relation to the oversight of work contracted out to private service providers (Fish 2013).

The history of the provision of legal services in England is characterised by three major themes. First, while it is littered with calls for greater centralisation of legal services, these have always been resisted. Drewry commented that departmentalism of the legal service remains its most 'obvious and enduring characteristic' (Drewry 1981: 28). Amalgamation of the Law Officers' Department with the Treasury Solicitor (and thereby achieving greater, albeit far from complete,

4 These are available as an annexure to Government Legal Service and Government Procurement Service 2013: Annex 3, cited as Guidelines.

5 Defined to include work with national security or other specially sensitive implications; work relating to major policy or constitutional issues, government to government and other international non-commercial work; work affecting the long-term interests of more than one department, e.g., claims of public interest immunity; and work where Cabinet Office co-ordination is necessary (Guidelines 3.2).

centralisation) has been consistently rejected. In 1949, Attorney-General Hartley Shawcross rejected a request from the Treasury Solicitor for amalgamation on the grounds that 'integrity and independence' required the Law Officers' Department to be preserved separately.

The UK position is in direct contrast with Canada. Canada implemented a major reorganisation of its legal service following the recommendations of the 1960s Glassco Royal Commission. The Commission explained its preference for a centralised body of lawyers at least notionally detached, and therefore independent, from government departments and agencies (Glassco 1962–63: 412–12):

> Among the more important tasks of the lawyer in public service, the initial framing of bills and regulations and advising on their application in individual cases, demand a special degree of independence for the lawyer, setting him somewhat apart from the 'line' activities of his department. Lawyers often find themselves drawn into the policy-making machinery of their departments, thereby becoming so closely identified with departmental management that their capacity to provide impartial advice becomes impaired. At the other end of the scale, some lawyers perform duties of such routine nature that they could be performed adequately and more economically by clerical employees. When this happens, professional skill tends to deteriorate. Isolated from members of his own profession, the sole lawyer in a department is usually further handicapped by lack of access to that indispensable tool of a lawyer – a good legal library. The integration of isolated departmental lawyers into a common legal service, revolving around the Department of Justice, appears to Commissioners to offer the most practicable remedy – if not the sovereign solution – for many of the present afflictions.

In Canada, almost full centralisation has been achieved. The Attorney-General (and Minister of Justice) is directly responsible for almost all of the legal services provided to the federal government (Edwards 1984: 191). The Department of Justice is responsible for providing in-house legal services to departments and agencies, although some lawyers in private practice may be appointed as 'Legal Agents' to handle routine litigation cases (Logan et al. 1997: 110–11; Blunn and Krieger 2009: 85).

In contrast to the position taken by the Glassco Commission, in England, Edwards (1984: 185) argued that:

> The professional detachment of the trained lawyer should be capable of being maintained alongside his readiness to share in the common goal of implementing the department's objectives.

One of the possible repercussions caused by the decentralisation of government legal services in England and the embedded nature of many government lawyers within departments and agencies is that their professional and ethical obligations are associated more with the essential character of their appointment as lawyers, rather than any relationship with, or delegation from, the Law Officers (Edwards 1984: 185). Thus, the departmental lawyer is perceived as a professional in a bureaucracy, with obligations both to the profession and to the government. The Law Officers have some relationship to the government lawyer – they operate as a sort of 'final Court of Appeal' on legal questions. Edwards (1984: 185–6) has also suggested that departmental legal advisers may turn to the Attorney-General as a:

> refuge and tower of strength in time of need, as where a major confrontation erupts between departments or the adviser's legal opinion is rejected by his own minister and the feeling is entertained that serious consequences will follow if the department refuses to heed the legal opinion placed before it.

The second theme that characterises the English history of government legal services is the difficulty in recruiting legal staff (Drewry 1981: 22). Responsible factors included rates of remuneration and conditions of service, with concerns that the best lawyers are recruited into private practice.

Finally, the English system has struggled with the question of the extent to which the government departments and agencies may engage private sector legal providers. The Guidelines that have been issued demonstrate the difficulty in allowing the use of private providers where necessary and beneficial, without undermining the ability of the GLS to provide high-quality, whole-of-government legal services.

The Australian Law Officers and the Provision of Legal Services to Government

Compared to the position in England the provision of legal services to government in Australia has been different *from the start*. As in England, colonial Attorneys-General were responsible for representing the Crown. But they were also responsible for providing *all* legal services to the government (Logan et al. 1997: 2 and 39; Selway 1999: 118; Beale 2009: 1). Bradley Selway surmised the reasons for the divergence. He recalled that in England, historically, advice was provided to departments by non-Law Officers – including the Treasury Solicitor – which meant there was a distinction between the Crown (for whom the Attorney-General acted) and public offices under the Crown. In the mid-nineteenth century, with the introduction of Cabinet government and responsibility of Ministers across government, the separate status of public offices was subsumed into the Crown proper. While in Canada and Australia the Attorney-General thereby subsumed responsibility for all of the Crown's legal work – including those formerly distinct public offices – the English structure managed to continue and defied attempts at centralisation. Selway also surmised that the English Attorney-General's weaker position (not being a member of Cabinet) may also have been a factor (Selway 1999: 119).

Also relevant was that when the Australian colonies were established, and at the introduction of responsible government, the administration of legal services was a relatively small task capable of being overseen by the Law Officers personally. Australian Colonial Law Officers were also 'adequately paid' and 'usually had the support of competent professional lawyers in the Solicitor-General … and Crown Solicitor' (Selway 2002: 266–7).

When the Commonwealth was created in 1901, it adopted a model that was substantially similar to the centralised one known in the colonies. The Attorney-General's Department was headed by the Secretary (and later the first Solicitor-General), Robert Garran. Garran was assisted by a Crown Solicitor from 1903, Charles Powers.[6] The Crown Solicitor was transformed in 1984 into the Australian Government Solicitor (AGS), although all of its employees remained public servants and its budget continued to come directly from the government (Blunn and Krieger 2009: 63).

In direct contrast to England then, in Australia history has entrenched centralisation of legal services rather than decentralisation and the prioritisation of departmental expertise and autonomy.

That is not to say that the centralisation of government legal services has gone unquestioned. It has had to be defended. In a submission to the 1975 Royal Commission on Australian Government Administration, the Attorney-General's Department argued that centralisation allowed lawyers to be 'objective, impartial and consistent' in the provision of professional advice (Hawker 1978: 379). It also contended:

> [T]he concentration of legal services in the one department, as is done in the Australian Attorney-General's Department, has the advantage that the lawyers in that Department are better able to resist pressures to subordinate law to administrative convenience. They ought to be in a position of greater professional independence than if they were serving officers of the departments being advised (extracted in Sexton and Maher 1982: 103).

The Attorney-General's Department emphasised that its role as a centralised and relatively separate source of legal advice combats many of the claims made against government lawyers. It allows for flexibility to meet the intermittent legal need of some departments; ensures appropriate resources, experience and expertise are maintained; reduces duplication and delay in rendering opinions (although often the argument *against* centralisation is based on claims of delay: see Australian Government Solicitor 2001: 25); ensures consistency of constitutional approach; and ensures the existence of constitutional problems is perceived and, where there

6 Prior to that date, the Attorney-General's Department used private firms (Meiklejohn 2001: 5). Almost a century later, the department would return to the practice.

is a constitutional problem proceeding along one course, other ways and means of proceeding within the Constitution are expertly explored (Sexton and Maher 1982: 103; see also Australian Government Solicitor 2001: 25–6).

Geoffrey Hawker considered views to the contrary, including that departments want (perhaps even need) lawyers who will fight interdepartmental battles with commitment, and that central advice can be slow (Hawker 1978: 379–80). Ultimately, however, Hawker asserted that if the monopoly of the Attorney-General's Department were to break it would make lawyers, 'in short, be less like professionals than bureaucrats' (Hawker 1978: 380).

Michael Sexton and Laurence Maher have also explored the claim that the bureaucratic pressures operating on government lawyers necessarily diminish their ability to fulfil their ethical responsibilities to the court and the profession. They claimed that the antimony between these two loyalties has been over-emphasised, pointing to similar bureaucratic pressures operating on private practitioners because of the culture of the private law firm (Sexton and Maher 1982: 100–101).

Consequences of Australia's Centralised Position

The Attorney-General and the Government Lawyer

Australian Attorneys-General have responsibility for providing legal services not just to the Cabinet but across the 'whole of government'. Thus, the Attorney-General has historically been responsible for ensuring the quality of all of the legal services provided to government. As such, most government lawyers in Australia have had a direct line of accountability to the Attorney-General. This has changed with reforms in the last two decades that have allowed for extensive outsourcing and development of in-house legal practices. I address these later in the chapter.

The special relationship between government lawyers and the Attorney-General means that when government lawyers advise the government on the legal position they are not only balancing being professionals and bureaucrats, like in England. They must also be cognisant of the Attorney-General's important *public interest obligations*.

The Attorney-General and the Public Interest

It is not necessary for me to canvass in depth the history and content of the Attorney-General's obligations to the public interest in Australia. This is done by others in this volume. For the purposes of this chapter I simply need to briefly outline the existence, content and importance of these obligations.

In Australia, even with the politicisation of the Attorney-General's position, the office's role in protecting the public interest has been considered broadly the same as that in Britain (Selway 1999: 270; Griffith 2007: 95). The obligation to act in the public interest manifests itself in a number of ways: in bringing litigation 'in the public interest'; in the fair and objective conduct of litigation (now recognised in Australia in the model litigant principle); and in the advisory function.

This last point requires further comment. In a primary sense, providing objective legal advice itself contributes to the rule of law and the public interest. The Law Officers also have an obligation to ensure government complies with the law because of the Crown's obligations to the rule of law (*Eastern Trust Co v McKenzie, Mann & Co* [1915] AC 750: 759). In this sense, the Law Officer's duty as a legal adviser to the Crown is distinct from other lawyers because private lawyers must not assist the client to commit illegal acts but do not have a positive obligation to prevent them from doing so (Dodek 2010: 24).

The Law Officers' advisory function can have a further impact on the public interest by fostering government action and policy in accordance with those principles that underpin its existence.[7] I will refer to these principles as the 'Core Government Principles'. In Britain Lord Goldsmith (2001), during his tenure as Attorney-General, said:

> It is very important that new proposals, from early on in the policy making process, are worked up and developed with the aim of ensuring that they achieve proper respect for the rule of law, for human rights and for our domestic and international legal obligations.[8]

In addition to the public interest at large informing the role of the Attorney-General in his or her advisory capacity in Australia, the office has responsibility for the provision of legal services to the 'whole of government'. This means the Attorney-General must ensure that 'whole of government' issues are taken into account by the emanations of the Crown, rather than the sometimes narrower interests of an individual department or agency captured, as they may be, by narrow bureaucratic concerns. While this is not analogous to the 'public interest', it produces a number of public interest-related benefits. It ensures the Crown takes a unified legal position in respect of issues, giving consistency to the actions of government across departments and agencies. It ensures government resources are not wasted pursuing litigation between government departments and agencies, and it ensures the broader impact of government policies are considered by individual departments and agencies.

The Government Lawyer and the Public Interest

The public interest's relevance to the government lawyer lies in the transposition of the Attorney-General's obligations to the public interest to those legal professionals

7 Some have even argued that lawyers acting for private clients hold an obligation to draw the client's attention to underlying principles within the legal system (Greenwood 1991; Dunphy 2008).

8 See also Omergee 1997: 102; Edwards 1984: 189.

who assist him or her in fulfilling the legal services functions. From the historical, highly centralised position, it is still relatively easy to identify the relationship between the Attorney-General and the government lawyer when one considers the lawyers within the Attorney-General's departments or the centralised legal services provider such as the AGS, as they remain responsible to the Attorney-General.[9]

The transposition of traditional public interest duties of the Law Officers to the government lawyer must be approached with caution. Any obligation to act in the public interest must be reconciled with the professional duties of the government lawyer and the necessity of maintaining accountability within the government system. The most satisfactory manner of doing so is to conclude that while government lawyers may have an obligation to the public interest because of their relationship with the Attorney-General, this must be limited by the strict delineation of the functions of the government lawyer. The government lawyer cannot continue to have any obligation to *act* independently in the furtherance of the public interest unless this is conferred by statute.

The transposition of the Attorney-General's public interest obligations therefore reflects the type of work the government lawyer performs. So the lawyers in the Director of Public Prosecutions office who assist the Attorney-General in fulfilling the public interest function of bringing prosecutions now have an independent statutory mandate to consider questions of the public interest and bring prosecutions accordingly (subject to any overriding direction). The lawyers who conduct litigation on behalf of the Crown must advise the Crown to act in accordance with the model litigant principles. At the Commonwealth level, this is now mandated by the *Legal Services Directions 2005* (Cth) (clause 4.2). The lawyers who assist the Attorney-General to provide legal advice to government must take on the Attorney-General's responsibility to the public interest in considering not just the legal position but also broader government principles.

In relation to this last obligation, when the government lawyer gives advice on the Core Government Principles, it is not strictly legal advice. As such, three important things must be remembered. First is that this advice is supplementary to and does not form the dominant purpose of the advice. If it were to go beyond supplementary advice there would be questions as to whether the advice would attract legal professional privilege.

---

9 There are some questions regarding the continued relationship between the AGS and the Attorney-General with the creation of the AGS as a fully commercial legal firm owned by the government. However, I would argue that when you look at the full extent of the changes and the mechanisms put in place by the amendments which introduced the AGS to ensure the continued responsibility of the Attorney-General for the oversight of government legal services (and particularly the functions of the Office of Legal Services Coordination), the better view is that this relationship continues, even if there have been some difficulties in practice.

Secondly, the government lawyer must be very careful to ensure that in giving advice on these questions they are not providing advice on substantive policy questions. Such advice is both beyond the expertise of the lawyer and risks alienating the client. But where is the line between advising on Core Government Principles and substantive policy? Allan Hutchinson (2008: 120–21) has explained:

> [G]overnment lawyers have a significant contribution to make in debates within government about how to determine what the public interest demands; they often have the training, experience, and knowledge to help develop a nuanced and sophisticated approach to identifying the public interest and crafting a range of practical strategies for its realization in practical circumstances. Indeed, being relatively independent of political pressures and partisan agendas, government lawyers are well placed to act as trusted advisors to their political superiors.[10]

Hutchinson (2008: 121) also emphasised that it was 'incumbent on government lawyers to leave the final decision on what government policy and legal strategy should be adopted and implemented to elected officials'.

This leads to the final point. In providing advice on non-legal public interest questions, the government lawyer should always be very careful to distinguish legal advice from non-legal advice. Selway explained that where the government lawyer provides advice on non-legal principles, the lawyer must make a clear distinction in the advice between 'the matters where the client is bound to comply and what parts relate to matters where the client's policy opinion is the ultimate determinant' (Selway 1999: 121–2).[11]

The responsibility of government lawyers to advise the government upon the congruence between proposed policies and actions and Core Government Principles should not be dismissed lightly. The government lawyer is in a unique position to provide an independent, fresh and informed assessment of those principles against any new policy or action to assist the elected government in the exercise of public power. The government lawyer's expertise in the law and institutional knowledge of the government's broader legal position provides them with superior qualifications to provide advice to the government on the impact of actions and policies on legal institutions and principles.

Decentralisation: Competition and In-house Legal Practices

While centralisation has been the predominant trend in Australia, Attorney-General's Departments have not been able to resist decentralisation of legal services. Two factors leading to decentralisation can be identified. First, all jurisdictions have been affected by the increased use of in-house legal practices

10 See also Tait 1997: 65–6.

11 Referring to Curtis and Kolts 1975: 338–9, 342.

by departments and agencies. Secondly, under the guise of competition reform at the end of the twentieth century, outsourcing of services to the private sector was introduced in some jurisdictions. The jurisdictions affected by outsourcing reforms are the Commonwealth, New South Wales, Victoria and Queensland, and, to a lesser extent, Western Australia and the Northern Territory.[12] As a case study, this chapter will focus on the changes to the framework and regulation of provision of legal services to the Commonwealth.[13] The 2001 centenary publication of the Attorney-General's Department described these changes as the 'most far-reaching change to the Department's role' since its establishment (Meiklejohn 2001: 118).

Competition Reforms

In the early 1990s, the Commonwealth government moved towards a user-pays system for legal services. The AGS was expected to charge other government departments and agencies for its services (together with a number of other parts of the Attorney-General's Department, including the Chief General Counsel, legislative drafting and some policy divisions; these, combined, were known as the 'Attorney-General's Legal Practice'). This created a direct financial relationship between the lawyer and client (Australian Government Solicitor 2001: 12; Meiklejohn 2001: 100, 119). The changes were implemented because it was thought that the budget-funded model of legal services provision did not reflect the actual demand for those services, leading to a lack of responsiveness in service delivery.

In 1994 the user-pays system was reviewed, and in 1995 *some* work was opened to full competition with private sector law firms (Meiklejohn 2001: 100). 'Tied work' remained with the Attorney-General's Legal Practice and included all litigation at that time (although the Attorney-General's Legal Practice had to conduct this at no charge to departments and agencies).

The biggest reforms happened in the late 1990s following the *Report of the Review of the Attorney-General's Legal Practice* (Logan et al. 1997). Against the background of the principle of competitive neutrality, best practice and the privatisation principles, the Logan Report concluded that the government

12 The Australian Capital Territory experimented with the outsourcing model but has reverted to a more centralised system since 2005 (ACT Government Solicitor 2012). In the Australian Capital Territory today outsourcing of legal services can only be undertaken in consultation with the ACT Government Solicitor and with the agreement of the Solicitor-General. In South Australia, government agencies cannot generally seek legal services from private providers except with the permission of the Crown Solicitor's Office or the Cabinet (Crown Solicitor's Office (SA) 2012).

13 An overview of the various reviews and reforms implemented in Queensland in these areas is available in Crown Law 2009: 258–92. In New South Wales, see Byers and Gill 1993; New South Wales Government 1993. In Victoria, see Beaton Consulting 2008; Department of Justice (Victoria) 2003. In the Northern Territory, see the Department of Justice (NT) 2012.

should only provide legal services if it were in the clear public interest to do so. These reforms were part of a larger trend across government. There was always recognition that legal services were slightly different from other services provided to government (such as engineering, accounting or architecture: Beale 2009: viii) on the basis that, as the primary legal services provider to government, the Attorney-General had particular obligations to the public interest and the law.

The Logan Report found that there was a need to maintain government-operated legal services in order for the particular needs of the Commonwealth government to be met, specifically in public law services (constitutional and national security areas); to ensure a whole-of-government approach was adopted in key areas; and to ensure the Attorney-General was appropriately supported in his role as First Law Officer. Keeping these considerations in mind, the Logan Report recommended that greater contestability for legal services be introduced; the legal services elements of the Attorney-General's Legal Practice (the AGS) be separated and established as a statutory authority with a Chief Executive Officer responsible and accountable to the Attorney-General; the establishment of the Office of Legal Services Coordination (OLSC) to support the Attorney-General and oversee compliance with the Legal Services Directions (these are explained in greater detail below); and departments and agencies be required to use the AGS for legal services that relate to a core executive activity, but otherwise should be free to manage their own legal services.

These recommendations were all implemented. At this stage it is worth commenting on the notable difference between the moves in Australia towards outsourcing and the response to the outsourcing that was occurring in England. The Australian government was pushing for *greater* outsourcing, or outsourcing as a *first* resort, while the phenomenon was viewed in England as an approach of *last* resort, if the GLS was unable to or incapable of providing the service.

Today, legal services are provided to the Commonwealth government and its agencies by: the Attorney-General; the Solicitor-General; the AGS;[14] the Attorney-General's Department (which includes the Office of International Law, the Office of Legislative Drafting and Publishing, and the OLSC); the Department of Foreign Affairs and Trade; in-house legal providers within government departments, agencies and Government Business Enterprises (GBEs); private law firms; private counsel (barristers) from the independent Bar; the Office of Parliamentary Counsel; and the Director of Public Prosecutions (Australian Government Solicitor 2001: 10–11; Blunn and Krieger 2009: Appendix C, 73 ff).

By allowing governments to access private law firms, the reforms have raised questions about the quality and independence of advice provided, the ability of

---

14 The AGS was established as a statutory agency by an amendment to the *Judiciary Act 1903* (Cth) by the *Judiciary Amendment Act 1999* (Cth). It is now a Government Business Enterprise with the Minister for Finance and Deregulation and the Attorney-General as joint shareholders. It is headed by a Chief Executive Officer assisted by an Advisory Board.

private firms to understand and advise departments and agencies about any whole-of-government implications and the consistency of advice provided to departments and agencies (and therefore the consistency of their legal position over time).

Some legal work has remained 'tied', although the work included in these areas was reduced after the Logan Report.[15]

The OLSC was also created. The OLSC supports the Attorney-General in relation to his or her responsibilities by overseeing the implementation of the *Legal Services Directions*. The *Legal Services Directions* are issued by the Attorney-General and apply to all Commonwealth legal work, including that performed by private law firms (*Judiciary Act 1903* (Cth): s 55ZF). The Directions cover matters such as the type of work that is tied to government legal services providers, sharing of advice across government, notification of the Attorney-General in relation to significant litigation and compliance with the model litigant principles. In introducing the OLSC and the *Legal Services Directions*, the government has sought to achieve a structure that acknowledges the unity of the Crown and the obligations of the Crown to the public interest but balances that against the reality of the multi-faceted, fragmented nature of government.

The nature of the Directions makes them difficult to enforce. There are no sanctions that automatically attach to non-compliance; s 55ZG(2) of the *Judiciary Act 1903* (Cth) provides that 'Compliance with a Legal Services Direction is not enforceable except by, or upon the application of, the Attorney-General'. It is not clear how this is achieved. *Legal Services Direction* 14.1 simply states that 'the Attorney-General may impose sanctions for non-compliance with the Directions'. Compliance relies upon self-regulation, certification and reporting of alleged breaches to the OLSC (see *Legal Services Direction* 11.1(d) and 11.2; Office of Legal Services 2013). Compliance has been found to be variable (Blunn and Krieger 2009: 39).

In-house Legal Service Growth

While in England decentralisation of legal services throughout government and in-house legal practices has been the norm for centuries, it is a recent phenomenon in Australia.

At the Commonwealth level, GBEs and independent statutory agencies had been able to choose their legal services providers since the 1970s. Together with the major competition reforms that saw substantial outsourcing of government legal services, the 1990s also saw an increase in the use of in-house legal services (Australian Government Solicitor 2001: 12). The Logan Report noted that in the private sector 'centralised, in-house, legal groups [are regarded] as a valuable management resource' (Logan et al. 1997: 115). In 2009, the Blunn Krieger Report noted that the development of large in-house legal practices has been driven by

---

15 The categories of 'tied work' are now set out in the *Legal Services Directions 2005* (Cth), Appendix A.

the increased demand for legal services across government (Blunn and Krieger 2009: 34).

A relatively recent phenomenon, the growth of in-house legal practices in government has led to a fragmentation of the formerly highly centralised legal services delivery system. It raises similar questions to the outsourcing of legal services – particularly over quality and independence of advice and the ability of in-house practices to understand and advise departments and agencies of any whole-of-government implications.

In England, debates over centralisation, or at least central co-ordination, have defined debates about the structure of government legal services since the nineteenth century. This rich debate has led to the Treasury Solicitor taking a co-ordinating and mentoring role across the entire GLS. Such a framework has not yet been developed, or had time to develop, in Australia (Blunn and Krieger 2009: 49).

Consequences of Decentralisation

The reform of Commonwealth legal services has been the subject of many reviews subsequent to the Logan Report. Two major concerns have arisen: the cost-efficiency of the reforms and use of private law firms; and the decrease in the ability of the Attorney-General (and the Attorney-General's Department and the Solicitor-General) to effectively monitor the provision of legal services across government, and thereby meet the Law Officer's public interest and legal service obligations.

In 2005, the Australian National Audit Office released a report, *Legal Services Arrangements in the Australian Public Service*, which generally concluded that greater guidance to government agencies was required to ensure that the most cost-effective legal services were being used. The Audit Office subsequently released the *Legal Services Arrangements in Australian Government Agencies: Better Practice* (2006) to achieve these goals.

In 2009, two reviews of the Attorney-General's Department reported. The first, the *Organisational Audit of the Attorney-General's Department*, was undertaken by the Allen Consulting Group (Beale 2009). The report noted the changes implemented as a result of the Logan Report and a number of positive implications from these, including increased responsiveness to departmental priorities because of the greater flexibility and choice offered to departments regarding their choice of legal services and an increase in the competitiveness of the AGS while maintaining the Commonwealth's capacity to be effective in constitutional and national security litigation because of the retention of the tied-work scheme (Beale 2009: ix).

However, a number of 'costs' of the increased outsourcing as well as the increased use of in-house practices were identified (Beale 2009: ix, 2). These included:

- the [Attorney-General's Department's] legal capacity has been substantially diminished;
- support for the Solicitor-General, and the intimacy and flexibility of his engagement in the Commonwealth's advice and litigation has deteriorated;
- the Department's ability to advise the Attorney in relation to Cabinet matters is constrained both because of skill levels and the absence of the 'early warning' that comes from a more intimate advisory relationship with departments as they develop proposals;
- the Department's ability to be an active player in constitutional policy issues has diminished and it does not have sufficient capacity to make a significant contribution to policy development in relation to the Government's constitutional reform election commitments and federalism policy;
- its ability to monitor the appropriateness of strategies pursued in non-constitutional and security litigation is handicapped both because of the lack of in-house litigation experience and because it is not directly connected with the case load;
- overall Commonwealth expenditure on legal services has probably increased.

The report concluded that the *critical disadvantage* of the reforms has been the weakening of the support for the First Law Officer, the Attorney-General, and the Solicitor-General as the Second Law Officer because the Attorney-General's Department can no longer provide the necessary 'first rate professional legal support' (Beale 2009: x). The report considered the competitive model under which the AGS now operates to be the cause of this. Competition has encouraged the AGS to be overly client-centred, with the client identified as the relevant department or agency providing instructions and paying the legal fees. This detracts from the focus of the 'whole of government' as a client (Beale 2009: x, 2).

Ultimately, however, the report concluded whether the advantages of a decentralised, competitive service model outweigh the disadvantages was 'a policy judgement' and it made no recommendation as to any change (Beale 2009: 2). It did, however, recommend that the *Legal Services Directions* be tightened to increase reporting to the Attorney-General's Department of legal matters (including decisions and litigation), even where advice has been provided by an in-house lawyer (Beale 2009: Recommendation 1).[16] The report also recommended the establishment of a centralised liaison group composed of representatives from the Attorney-General's Department and senior lawyers within government departments and agencies (Beale 2009: Recommendation 2, xxiii). The purpose of the group would be to:

- reduce duplication of advice;
- reinforce the independence of professional advice;

16 It must be noted that this recommendation is offered in the report as an alternative, but the initial alternative has not been released and the government has claimed Cabinet confidentiality over it.

- ensure a whole of government approach to legal services;
- strengthen agency-wide knowledge and understanding of the *Legal Services Directions*;
- advise on quality control measures to foster high-quality services across the Commonwealth; and
- monitor benchmarking and costing of in-house services across agencies to underpin effective decision-making by agencies about the level of resources appropriate to meet agency needs.[17]

One of the other findings of the Beale Report was that the current provision of legal advice on foreign affairs is 'dysfunctional' (Beale 2009: xiii; see also 21–2). This area provides a telling illustration of some of the disadvantages of decentralised and fragmented government legal services. Currently, the Office of International Law (located within the Attorney-General's Department), the Department of Foreign Affairs and the AGS can *all* provide advice to government on public international law issues. As a tied area of work (*Legal Services Directions 2005* (Cth): Appendix A, cl 2), this effectively means that three government departments or agencies are competing *against each other* for work (certain types of which can attract fees). This has led to refusals to share advice, and therefore concerns have arisen about consistency and quality of advice provided.

The Beale Report's findings about the provision of legal services to government are concerning on many levels. They raise serious concerns not only about the professional independence and appropriate detachment from the client of in-house legal practices and private law firms but also about the government legal services provider: AGS. There is also a significant impact on the Law Officers' obligations to the public interest in their advocacy and advisory roles. The reduced awareness of the Attorney-General's Department of litigation strategies pursued in the courts by government departments and agencies raises questions about whether the government is always adhering to its model litigant obligations. The Rule of Law Institute of Australia (an independent, not-for-profit body) has recently released a report alleging that breaches of the model litigant principles are on the rise (Rule of Law Institute of Australia 2012).

If the Attorney-General and his deputy, the Solicitor-General, are losing the intimacy of their involvement in the Commonwealth's legal position, this means the Law Officers, and legal officers within the Attorney-General's Department, are no longer receiving information on proposals *as they develop*. This reduces their ability to identify potential legal and ethical issues early in the continuum of decision-making (Rosen 2001: 204) and actively influence government to behave

17 The Beale Report's recommendations here are based on a submission from the AGS to implement a co-ordinating body like that seen in the Government Legal Service in the UK, chaired by the Treasury Solicitor (Beale Report 2009: Appendix 2, 2.22).

in ways more congruent with the constitutional structure.[18] Robert Eli Rosen has argued that the later in the continuum of decision-making the government lawyer is involved, the more difficult it is for lawyers to have any influence as organisations are already committed to a particular course of action (Rosen 2001: 205–6).

The other review that reported in 2009 was the *Report of the Commonwealth Legal Services Procurement* (Blunn and Krieger 2009). The report is predominantly concerned with the streamlining and co-ordination of the procurement of legal services by government agencies. (The report described as 'key' to the review 'the desire of Government to achieve further efficiencies and to maximise value for taxpayers' money in the procurement of legal services' (Blunn and Krieger 2009: 15)). The report also considered other consequences of competition reforms and the increase of in-house legal services beyond implications on cost and efficiency. In regard to the increase in in-house legal practices, it found:

> The independence and uncoordinated development of in-house legal practices has been a major factor in the erosion of the role of the Attorney-General as the First Law Officer, and as such, responsible to Cabinet for ensuring the provision of appropriate legal services across the Commonwealth (Blunn and Krieger 2009: 10).

It also identified the rise of in-house legal practices as leading to variation in experience and standards and a failure to recognise the wider interests of the Commonwealth:

> Indeed there is evidence of agencies withholding information and advice from other agencies, regardless of any wider Commonwealth interest, where they perceive sharing it may not be in the peculiar interest of the agency (Blunn and Krieger 2009: 35).

One of its recommendations also echoed the disadvantages identified by the Beale Report. Blunn and Krieger recommended the introduction of measures to 'reinforce and assist agencies to meet their obligation to ensure that the Solicitor-General and/or the Attorney-General, as appropriate, are informed in a timely manner of potentially significant emerging issues' (Blunn and Krieger 2009: Recommendation 12, 15).

In contrast to the Beale Report, however, the Blunn and Krieger Report did find that the AGS was generally more sensitive to wider Commonwealth issues and was seen as more likely to ensure compliance with the model litigant principles, even at the chagrin of individual agencies (Blunn and Krieger 2009: 37).

---

18 See similar arguments that have been made in relation to the advantages of in-house counsel over the engagement of external legal providers more generally, in Le Mire 2011: 24–5; De Mott 2005: 955.

Government Response

The government has responded to the Blunn Krieger Report, but only with respect to its recommendations on the most efficient and effective means of delivering legal services. The government has subsequently commissioned a further report on the question of optimising value for money in the area of government legal services: *Learning from Experience: Purchasing Legal Services* (Gruen 2011). The Gruen Report appears to have treated the question from an entirely economic perspective; it even drew parallels between the difficulties encountered in the purchase of government legal services and those encountered in the purchase of information and communication technology (Gruen 2011: iv).

A major platform of the Commonwealth reform, and one of the key recommendations of the Blunn Krieger and Gruen Reports, has been creation of the Legal Services Multi-use List. This is a list of private law firms that by 1 June 2013 all Australian government agencies will have to use when procuring legal services from the private sector unless they have received an exemption from the Attorney-General (*Legal Services Directions 2005* (Cth): Appendix F, cl 3). The objects of the list are to (Australian Government Attorney-General's Department 2012: 5):

a. reduce barriers to entry into the market for Commonwealth legal work;
b. gather and disseminate information on the performance of Service Providers in the provision of Legal Services to Agencies; and
c. support Agencies in their ongoing function as informed purchasers of Legal Services.

To be included in the Legal Services Multi-use List, a private firm must prove that its personnel are regulated by a professional body and that it has appropriate insurance; and provide list rates and fee arrangements and written referee reports. In addition to these threshold requirements, the firm has to demonstrate that it can 'provide quality legal services' to the Commonwealth, identify and manage conflicts of interest and meet the requirements set out in the *Legal Services Directions* (Office of Legal Services Coordination 2012(a): 10–11).

While it may appear that the reporting and dissemination of information on the performance of private legal service providers could encompass information on the performance of firms in taking account whole-of-government issues or alerting clients to possible incongruence with the Core Government Principles, this is *not* its intention. The Explanatory Statement to the *Legal Services Amendment Directions (No 1) 2012* states that the purpose of the reporting is to monitor expenditure and levels of pro bono work undertaken.

The Commonwealth has also established two new bodies: a General Counsel Working Group to address 'strategic issues facing the Commonwealth legal services market' and the Australian Government Legal Network – an organisation open to all government employees – 'to improve the quality of work undertaken by in-house legal practices and to develop the role of the informed purchaser within the Australian Government' (Office of Legal Services Coordination 2012(b)). The Network's role also includes 'improving the attractiveness of government legal practice through a range of development opportunities', mirroring one of the objectives of establishing the GLS in the UK. The introduction of the Network implements a recommendation of the Blunn Krieger Report to develop an Australian government legal service network to provide a platform for information and experience sharing as well as to operate symbolically for the professionalism of in-house legal practices (Blunn and Krieger 2009: 49). It is also akin to the recommendation in the Beale Report to create a centralised liaison group to, *inter alia,* reinforce the independence of professional advice and ensure a whole-of-government approach to legal services.

The concerns regarding the involvement of the Law Officers and the Attorney-General's Department in the development of government policy, and the ability of the Law Officers to fulfil their roles, have not been addressed directly by the Commonwealth's reforms. The Beale Report – the report most critical in this area – has not even been released by the government.[19]

Changing the Focus of Reform

As much as the trend towards decentralisation – whether through in-house legal practices or, in some jurisdictions, the outsourcing of government legal work to private firms – may be rued, it is not realistic to expect government to return to using a centralised government legal services provider.[20]

While decentralisation is likely here to stay, government needs to seriously reassess the focus of its reform of the framework for providing government legal services. While value for money is important – and of course takes on a dimension of the public interest because of the expenditure of taxpayers' funds – it is not the *raison d'être* of government and should not be the sole focus of the framework for acquiring legal services by government.

Government serves the public interest. The traditional role of the Law Officers included, in addition to their political functions as members of the ministry and their legal functions, a role in acting for and protecting the public interest. The Commonwealth government must re-evaluate the focus of its government legal services reform. It ought to set a list of objectives that includes, amongst others, ensuring quality legal advice is provided that is appropriately cognisant of

19 For my research, I have obtained a heavily redacted version through a freedom of information request.

20 In the Australian Capital Territory, government legal work was re-centralised in 2005. However, the small nature of the jurisdiction and its legal work probably makes it a poor reform comparator for jurisdictions such as the Commonwealth, New South Wales or Victoria.

whole-of-government issues and congruent with the public interest and the Core Government Principles.

There are significant benefits that private law firms can offer government. They are often better resourced, staffed by lawyers who have greater specialisation (particularly in commercial areas), and have the ability to respond more quickly when legal advice is sought urgently. In some instances, it is more appropriate for independent statutory authorities to seek the advice of private law firms where their statutory mandate will bring them into direct conflict with the government proper (for example, the Auditor-General or the Ombudsman).

However, as well as concerns about over-servicing and over-charging (value for money issues), private law firms can lack complete knowledge of the department or agency's functions and legislative responsibilities, the previous position taken and potential whole-of-government implications. There are also concerns that the overly client-centric focus of many private law firms, often exacerbated by the competitive marketplace, means that lawyers are not exercising appropriate professional independence from the demands of the client (in this case, the department or agency).

Lawyers working for in-house legal practices may have greater potential to influence the actions of the department or agency as they are involved early in the decision-making continuum and trusted by management as part of the 'team'. In-house legal practices are also able to understand better the client's objectives than external lawyers brought in for a single transaction. However, in-house lawyers are generally seen as particularly vulnerable to the pressures of the client at the price of upholding their professional ethical obligations to the court and justice. In the government context, in-house lawyers may also be unable to withstand pressure from the individual department or agency to act in *its* interests, rather than the interests of the government as a whole.

A centralised legal services provider is, in contrast to private law firms or in-house legal practices, generally seen as offering legal services to government that take into account whole-of-government issues. If used across government, centralised providers ensure consistency in the government's legal position and avoid duplication of work. It is also argued that the separation between the provider and the department or agency ensures that the necessary level of independent professionalism is maintained from the client. However, these advantages are not guaranteed. The Beale Report found that the introduction of the AGS into the competitive market in untied areas had encouraged the AGS to adopt the overly client-centric approach seen in private law firms, negating many of the perceived benefits of using a government legal service provider.

How to harness the advantages of the different providers while allaying the disadvantages to the greatest level possible? In the final part of this chapter I suggest two avenues of potential reform. The purpose of this part is not to prescribe reforms that I believe *must* be implemented. Rather, I offer suggestions for consideration as part of a larger exercise in addressing the wider issue of providing a framework for government legal services that ensures value for money and quality legal advice that also addresses whole-of-government and public interest issues. These suggestions draw on many of the existing regulatory structures and recent reforms.

Monitoring and Information Sharing Beyond Value for Money

Systems need to be put in place that do not simply ensure that departments and agencies are 'informed purchasers' and share information on value for money – but that enable them to share information about their holistic experiences with providers. I am talking here about the legal services provider's demonstrated ability to monitor whole-of-government and public interest issues. The experiences of departments and agencies in these respects needs to be shared, and these also need to be included as additional dimensions to the criteria for selection onto the government's Multi-use List.

Undoubtedly, some private law firms will be better than others at achieving this. Many of the government teams in private firms, for example, are now headed by a partner from a government legal services provider, giving them greater insight into these issues.[21] It may be worth considered whether to open membership of the Australian Government Legal Network beyond government employees to lawyers working for firms on the legal services Multi-use List. Membership and involvement in the Network may be additional criteria against which firms are assessed.

By focussing not only on value for money, this framework will encourage private firms to look beyond the immediate client to the government. By changing the nature of the competition between firms, it will also encourage the AGS to retreat from its shift towards an overly client-centred focus.

However, there is a significant hurdle to this type of information sharing. Unlike value for money, awareness and advice on whole-of-government and public interest implications is not necessarily welcomed by individual departments and agencies. Individual departments and agencies often do not appreciate being reminded that they form part of a unified Crown with obligations to the public good. The Blunn Krieger Report found, for example, that some departments and agencies 'do not appreciate being alerted to such matters if they are seen as inconsistent with a narrow agency interest' (Blunn and Krieger 2009: 37).

Therefore, this type of monitoring may be better achieved by an independent body, a body that has no interest in cheap, client-centric advice. The OLSC is an obvious option, as it is already in existence. Monitoring and evaluating the services provided by private law firms would significantly increase its workload and it would require increased staffing and funding. An alternative to using the OLSC

---

21 For example, the head of the national and Queensland Government Services practice at the major law firm Clayton Utz, Barry Dunphy, is a former Queensland Crown Solicitor and acting Solicitor-General. He has emphasised the need for private law firms to consider whole-of-government and public interest questions when dealing with public clients (Dunphy 2008).

would be to use those lawyers working in-house in the departments and agencies. However, to be able to fulfil this function, more training and emphasis on the necessary professional independence and commitment to whole-of-government objectives would be required. (The creation of the Australian Government Legal Network has made some progress towards this goal.)

Increased Reporting to the Attorney-General's Department

There are currently obligations on FMA agencies[22] to report to the Attorney-General or the OLSC for 'significant issues' under the *Legal Services Directions 2005*. These include matters where:

a. the size of the claim, the identity of the parties or the nature of the matter raises sensitive legal, political or policy issues;
b. a dispute or disagreement exists between different agencies (whether or not FMA agencies), other than matters arising under legislation which contemplates that two or more agencies may be on different sides in a case;
c. a significant level of coordination between different agencies is required;
d. a significant precedent for other agencies could be established, either on a point of law or because of its potential significance for other agencies; or
e. a dispute exists with an agency of a State or Territory government.

Identifying what matters fall within this list is not an easy task. The terms are imbued with subjectivity: when are '*sensitive* legal, political or policy issues' raised? When could a '*significant* precedent' for other agencies be established? Also, because of the information available to an agency or their level of legal knowledge or understanding of government operations, it may not be apparent to government officers when the matters exist. For example, knowledge about the scope of the legal issue and its potential to affect other agencies and departments will be required to determine whether 'a significant level of co-ordination between different agencies' is required or whether 'a significant precedent for other agencies could be established, either on a point of law or because of its potential significance for other agencies'. Note 5 of the Directions states: 'If an agency is unsure about whether an issue is a significant issue that should be reported, it should contact OLSC to discuss the issue'. However, this still requires agencies to have identified an issue that *could be* a significant issue.

All of this is not to say that matters should be, or even could be, defined with greater detail. The language used allows for flexibility in application that is necessary when determining these types of issues. Some greater clarity, however, could be achieved. The AGS has recommended that further explanation of the meaning of matters that raise 'sensitive legal, political or policy issues' be given

22 An FMA Agency is a department or other agency that must comply with the Commonwealth's *Financial Management and Accountability Act 1997* (Cth).

by using examples to illustrate the different types of issue that may be involved (Beale Report: Appendix 2, [2.2]). This recommendation holds great merit.

The matters that must be reported are currently deficient in one respect: they do not include those matters that may transgress important constitutional principles, even if they may not be strictly illegal (that is, the Core Government Principles). Thus, the current reporting requirements do not ensure the Attorney-General is informed of those matters that may raise public interest issues. This can be contrasted with the Drafting Directions of the Office of Parliamentary Counsel (OPC). These require the referral of draft legislation by the OPC to various agencies, other than the instructing agency, who have rights and responsibilities in relation to the legislation (Parliamentary Counsel 2007: Direction 4.2). The types of provisions that must be referred to the Attorney-General's portfolio are numerous, including legislation that might attempt to ouster judicial review of administrative action; discriminate against an individual or raise human rights issues under international instruments or infringe civil, political or other human rights relating to privacy or freedom of speech; affect social justice for Aboriginals, Torres Strait Islanders or South Sea Islanders; or affect relations between the Commonwealth and the States and Territories.

Even if greater clarification is achieved through providing examples, there is a need to educate better departments and agencies in identifying these questions. Because of their position within the department or agency, in-house lawyers would seem to be the appropriate officers to target for this. The Australian Government Legal Network could provide the necessary training and support. The Beale Report had recommended that a centralised liaison group be tasked with strengthening 'agency-wide knowledge and understanding of the Legal Services Directions'.

There is also a question of why the responsibility to report is the agency's responsibility, and not the lawyers' (see Legal Services Direction 3.1). This is particularly notable because the reporting requirements are intended to assist the Attorney-General in performing his or her legal services functions. In its submission to the *Organisational Audit of the Attorney-General's Department*, the AGS noted:

> AGS plays an important role in assisting its clients to notify significant matters to the OLSC. However, two matters are worthy of note: first, it is the client and not AGS which decides about reporting of significant matters; and secondly, AGS is clearly not in a position to encourage an agency to report a matter where it is not the appointed legal adviser.

One reform worth considering would be to place an obligation on lawyers to report to the OLSC and Attorney-General where they think reportable matters have arisen and have not been reported by the department or agency. Appropriate reporting by a firm (whether it be the AGS or a private law firm) could be one of the matters shared between agencies if a broader monitoring system were to be put in place (see recommendation (a)). This also raises a question of whether there could be a separate obligation placed on in-house legal services providers to report matters.

Another issue raised by the AGS in its submission to the Beale Report was the need to extend the Attorney-General's ability to give directions to agencies about the conduct of how matters are handled (Beale 2009: Appendix 2 [2.4 2.5]. Under s 55ZF of the *Judiciary Act* the Attorney-General may issue directions that apply to Commonwealth legal work being performed, or to be performed, in relation to a particular matter. While 'Commonwealth legal work' is defined broadly enough to extend to include both litigation and advisory work, a 'matter' appears to be limited to court proceedings. Under clause 4.1 of the Directions, instructions can be issued only 'about the handling of claims or the conduct of litigation'. If the reporting of matters other than litigation to the Attorney-General is intended to assist him or her fulfil the Attorney-General's legal services and public interest functions, it is important that the Attorney-General not just *know* about these matters, but also have the ability to intervene in them if necessary. The reason for empowering the Attorney-General to intervene and issue instructions in litigation but not the conduct of other matters is not clear.

Conclusion

In Australia, decentralisation of legal services is a relatively recent phenomenon. It is natural that responding to the challenges this poses to government will take time. Unfortunately, at least at the Commonwealth level, the government has been too focussed on developing a framework that ensures value for money in this new environment, at the expense of addressing the other the detriments decentralisation has brought.

References

ACT Government Solicitor. 2012. *Home* [Online]. Available at: http://www.actgs.act.gov.au [accessed: 7 January 2013].

Australian Government Attorney-General's Department. 2012. *Legal Services Multi-Use List Guidance Materials* [Online]. Available at: www.ag.gov.au/.../LSMUL%20Guidance%20Material%20Final.pdf [accessed: 7 January 2013].

Australian Government Solicitor. 2001. *Management and Organisation of Legal Services to the Federal Government of Australia.*

Australian National Audit Office. 2005. *Legal Services Arrangements in the Australian Public Service.* 20 June 2005.

Australian National Audit Office. 2006. *Legal Services Arrangements in Australian Government Agencies – Better Practice.* 10 August 2006.

Beale, R. 2009. *Organisational Audit of the Attorney-General's Department: Final Report.* Allen Consulting Group, January 2009.

Beaton Consulting. 2008. *Report on the Legal Services to Government Panel Contract.*

Blunn, A.S. and Krieger, S. 2009. *Report of the Review of Commonwealth Legal Services Procurement.*

Byers, M. and Gill, M. 1993. *Review of Legal Services to Government.* Sydney: Attorney-General's Department.

Crown Law. 2009. *In My Opinion: The History of Crown Law Queensland 1859–2009.* Brisbane: Department of Justice and Attorney-General.

Crown Solicitor's Office (SA). 2012. *About the Crown Solicitor's Office* [Online]. Available at: http://www.agd.sa.gov.au/government/about-us/department/crown-solicitors-office/about-crown-solicitors-office [accessed: 7 January 2013].

Curtis, L. and Kolts, G. 1975. The Role of the Government Lawyer in the Protection of Citizens' Rights. *Australian Law Journal.* Volume 49, 335.

De Mott, D.A. 2005. The Discrete Roles of General Counsel, *Fordham Law Review,* Volume 74, 955.

Department of Justice (NT). 2012. *Agency Legal Services* [Online]. Available at: http://www.nt.gov.au/justice/solicitor/legal/services/shtml [accessed: 7 September 2012].

Department of Justice (Victoria). 2003. *Government Legal Services: Report to the Attorney-General, 1 July 2002–30 June 2003.* November 2003.

Dodek, A. 2010. Lawyering at the Intersection of Public Law and Legal Ethics: Government Lawyers as Custodians of the Rule of Law. *Dalhousie Law Journal.* Volume 33(1), 1.

Drewry, G. 1981. Lawyers in the UK Civil Service. *Public Administration.* Volume 59, 15.

Dunphy, D. 2008. *Being a Government Lawyer: A Practitioner's Observations.* Paper presented at the Queensland Law Society Government Lawyers Conference, Brisbane, 17 April 2008.

Edwards, J.Ll.J. 1964. *The Law Officers of the Crown: A Study of the Offices of the Attorney-General and Solicitor-General of England with an Account of the Office of the Director of Public Prosecutions of England.* London: Sweet & Maxwell.

Edwards, J.Ll.J. 1984. *The Attorney General, Politics and the Public Interest.* London: Sweet & Maxwell.

Fish, P. 2013. Email from Peter Fish (Deputy Treasury Solicitor) to Gabrielle Appleby. 13 February 2013.

Glassco, J.G. 1962–63. *Royal Commission on Government Organization.* Ottawa: Queen's Printer.

Goldsmith, Lord. 2001. *Politics, Public Interest and Prosecutions: A View by the Attorney General.* Paper presented at the 13th Annual Tom Sargent Memorial Lecture, London, 20 November 2001.

Government Legal Service. *Guide to Government Legal Service Departments* [Online]. Available at: http://www.gls.gov.uk/files/Department%20Guide.pdf [accessed: 7 January 2013].

Government Legal Service and Government Procurement Service. 2013. *Legal Services Framework (RM 919) Client Guidance Document.*

Greenwood, T. 1991. Ethics and Avoidance Advice. *Law Institute Journal*. Volume 65(8), 724.

Griffith, G. 2007. The Office of Attorney General in New South Wales. *Legal History*. Volume 11, 79.

Gruen, N. 2011. *Learning from Experience: Purchasing Legal Services*. Lateral Economics, February 2011.

Hawker, G. 1978. Lawyers in Government, in *Understanding Lawyers: Perspectives on the Legal Profession in Australia*, edited by R. Tomasic. Sydney: Law Foundation of New South Wales/Allen & Unwin, 373.

Hutchinson, A.C. 2008. In the Public Interest: The Responsibilities and Rights of Government Lawyers. *Osgoode Hall Law Journal*. Volume 46, 105.

Le Mire, S. 2011. Testing Times: In-House Counsel and Independence. *Legal Ethics*. Volume 14(1), 21.

Logan, B., Wicks, D., Skehill, S. 1997. *Report of the Review of the Attorney-General's Legal Practice*. Canberra: Australian Government Publishing Service.

McGrath, J. 1998. Principles for Sharing Law Officer Power: The Role of the New Zealand Solicitor-General. *New Zealand Universities Law Review*. Volume 18, 195.

Meiklejohn, C. 2001. *100 Years: Achieving a Just and Secure Society: Attorney-General's Department 1901–2001*. Canberra: Union Offset Printers.

New South Wales Government. 1993. *Government Response to the Recommendations of the Review of Legal Services to Government*. Office of Public Management, Cabinet Office, Treasury and Attorney General's Department.

Office of Legal Services Coordination. 2012(a). *Important Information and Guidance for Applicants* [Online]. Available at: http://www.ag.gov.au/LegalSystem/LegalServicesCoordination/Documents/Conditions%20for%20participation%20and%20guidance%20material%20for%20applicants.doc [accessed: 7 January 2013].

Office of Legal Services Coordination. 2012(b). *Connecting Government Lawyers* [Online]. Available at: http://www.ag.gov.au/LegalSystem/LegalServicesCoordination/Pages/ConnectingGovernmentlawyers.aspx [accessed: 7 January 2013].

Office of Legal Services Coordination. 2013. *Legal Services Directions 2005: Compliance Framework* [Online]. Available at: http://www.ag.gov.au/LegalSystem/LegalServicesCoordination/Documents/OLSC%20-%20Compliance%20Framework.PDF [accessed: 20 August 2013].

Omergee, Y. 1997. Is there an Independent Government Lawyer in the House? *International Legal Practitioner*. Volume 22(3), 102.

Parliamentary Counsel. 2007. *Drafting Direction* [Online]. Available at: http://www.opc.gov.au/about/draft_directions.htm [accessed: 7 January 2013].

Rosen, R.E. 2001. Problem-Setting and Serving the Organizational Client: Legal Diagnosis and Professional Independence. *University of Miami Law Review*. Volume 56, 179.

Rule of Law Institute of Australia. 2012. *The Model Litigant Rules: Key Facts and Cases* [Online]. Available at: http://www.ruleoflaw.org.au/wp-content/uploads/2012/08/Reports-and-Pres-8-11-Model-Litigant-Rules-Key-Facts-and-Cases.pdf [accessed: 7 January 2013].

Selway, B. 1999. The Duties of Lawyers Acting for Government. *Public Law Review*. Volume 10, 114.

Selway, B. 2002. The Different Role of an Australian Attorney-General. *Public Law Review*. Volume 13, 263.

Sexton, M. and Maher, L.W. 1982. *The Legal Mystique: The Role of Lawyers in Australian Society*. London: Angus & Robertson.

Shawcross, H. 1953. The Office of the Attorney General. *Parliamentary Affairs*. Volume 7, 380.

Tait, J. 1997. The Public Lawyer, Service to the Client and the Rule of Law. *The Commonwealth Lawyer*. Volume 23(1–2), 542.

Treasury Solicitor. *Our History* [Online]. Available at: http://www.tsol.gov.uk/about_us/our_history.htm [accessed: 7 January 2013].

PART III
Comparative Perspectives

Chapter 8
The Role of Solicitor-General in Contemporary New Zealand

David Collins

Introduction

The role of Solicitor-General for New Zealand has evolved into arguably the most fascinating and challenging position that any lawyer in New Zealand can enjoy. As this chapter will demonstrate, the role of Solicitor-General in New Zealand can be divided into five distinct functions: Chief Executive of the Crown Law Office; principal counsel for the Crown; principal legal adviser to the Crown; supervisor of the prosecution of indictable crime; and constitutional/Law Officer functions.

It will be immediately apparent that the role of Solicitor-General in New Zealand is broader than the role of Solicitor-General in the Commonwealth, States and Territories of Australia. It is also quite different from the role of Solicitor-General of England and Wales, the United States, or the role of Solicitor-General in Canada prior to that office disappearing from the Canadian government's lexicon in 2005.

This chapter is written at a time when many changes are in store for the future roles of the Solicitor-General and the Crown Law Office following the appointment of Michael Heron as Solicitor-General in August 2012 (see generally Cochrane and Dean 2012). Accordingly, this chapter necessarily focusses on the history of the role of Solicitor-General and the Crown Law Office and contains little comment on possible future changes for the roles of the Solicitor-General and the Crown Law Office. This chapter is divided into three parts. The first part briefly examines the history of the Crown Law Office and the role of the Solicitor-General in New Zealand. It will be seen that the role of Solicitor-General in New Zealand is inextricably linked to the development of the Crown Law Office. The second part of this chapter looks at the current roles of the Solicitor-General in New Zealand. The final part of this chapter examines the advantages to the way in which the roles of Solicitor-General and the Crown Law Office have evolved in New Zealand.

Historical Origins

It is generally acknowledged that the first Solicitor-General was Richard Fowler (Edwards 1964: 27). He was appointed 'King's Solicitor' in 1461 in relation to all 'matters, pleas, suits and quarrels affecting us within our realm of England'. By 1515 the title Solicitor-General (*solicitator generallis domini regis*) had been conferred upon John Fort (Bellot 1909: 410). From these times the Solicitor-General was looked upon as being the junior of the two principal Law Officers of the Crown; and, at the same time, appointment as Solicitor-General was regarded as the stepping-stone for advancement to the role of Attorney-General (Edwards 1964: 29).

In New Zealand, Walter Reid is rightly regarded as the first non-political Solicitor-General. He was, however, not the first to be honoured with the title of 'Solicitor-General for New Zealand'. That distinction belongs to the enigmatic John Hyde Harris. In the *New Zealand Parliamentary Record 1840–1949* (Scholefield 1950: 33) it is noted that from 26 October 1867 to 13 May 1868 Harris was both a member of the Executive Council and Solicitor-General in Premier Edward Stafford's ministry. Harris appears to have had a remarkable life. In a brief biography in *An Encyclopaedia of New Zealand* (McLintock 1966: 913) it is recorded that Harris was appointed a judge of the District Court in 1858 until that office was abolished in 1862. The following year he became Superintendent of the Otago Province. It is said that Harris incurred the wrath of the public of Dunedin when, in 1865, he dissolved the Dunedin Town Council. At the same time he managed to incur personal debts of £28,000 through speculating on the gold boom in Central Otago. After resigning as Superintendent of Otago he joined Stafford's ministry and served as Mayor of Dunedin while simultaneously holding office as Solicitor-General for New Zealand.

Harris' short six-month stint as Solicitor-General came to an end 13 months before the conclusion of Stafford's ministry in June 1869. Throughout his term Stafford did not have the services of an Attorney-General within his Cabinet. (Previous administrations had Attorneys-General in Cabinet: see, for example, Frederick Whitaker, who served as Attorney-General on six separate occasions during the nineteenth century, and Henry Sewell, Attorney-General on three occasions during Premier Frederick Weld's ministry.) The reason for the absence of an Attorney-General from Cabinet at this time could be found in the *Attorney-General's Act 1866* (NZ), which provided in section V that the Attorney-General had to be a barrister and solicitor of the Supreme Court and that no Attorney-General 'was capable of being a member of the Executive Council or of either House of the General Assembly'. It was during this time that James Prendergast served as a non-political Attorney-General. He was appointed Attorney-General in March 1867 and resigned from that office on 31 March 1875 when he became New Zealand's third Chief Justice.

It was during Prendergast's term as Attorney-General that the Crown Law Office was established. This occurred in 1873 when the Judicial Branch of the Colonial Secretary's Office was divided into two new and independent Departments of State, the Department of Justice and the Crown Law Office (Cornford 1964: 423). The Crown Law Office at this time had two employees that we know of in addition to Prendergast as Attorney-General: Walter Reid, the Assistant Law Officer, who had held that position since 1871 and Hudson Williamson, who remained with the

Crown Law Office until 1881 when he took up the position of Crown Solicitor in Auckland (Cornford 1964: 424).

When Prendergast became Chief Justice in 1875, Reid was appointed Solicitor-General and head of the Crown Law Office, by which time the Crown Law Office had acquired a 14-year-old clerk (Alexander Gray, later Sir Alexander Gray KC), thereby swelling its ranks to three.

Reid's appointment as Solicitor-General was not universally applauded. As an article in the *Otago Daily Times* (1878: 3) published after Reid's appointment recorded:

> Possibly no one else is more surprised at the series of accidents which placed him in his present position than Mr Reid himself. Certainly neither his ability as a lawyer nor his skills at the Bar would ever have raised him to it ... The appointment was one which the profession could scarcely approve of ...

Notwithstanding this inauspicious reception, Reid served as Solicitor-General for 25 years – by far the longest serving of this country's 16 Solicitors-General.

It is worth noting that the *Attorney-General's Act* was amended in 1876 to permit: 'the restoration of the office of Attorney-General to its proper position as a legitimate prize for lawyers who enter into political life' (Barton 1878: 36), thereby reinstating the office of Attorney-General to a ministerial position.[1] Also, in November 1876 the fledgling Crown Law Office moved into new premises on the first floor of the Government Building, now the gracious home of Victoria University's Law Faculty in Wellington. It was to remain in that building for 87 years.

Notwithstanding the existence of the Crown Law Office, prior to 1910 there was no central organisation for the control of the Crown's legal business. Every government department was, in this respect, autonomous, instructing and paying without supervision barristers and solicitors in private practice. In 1910, the year John Salmond was appointed as Solicitor-General, the legal business of the government was centralised into the Crown Law Office, and most departments were required to have their legal work done either by that office or by district Crown Solicitors with the approval of the Crown Law Office (Cornford 1964: 424). It was also in 1910 that the Law Drafting Office was absorbed for administrative purposes into the Crown Law Office, where it remained throughout Salmond's term as Solicitor-General. (The Law Drafting Office was established as an Office of Parliament in 1920 by the *Statutes Drafting and Compilation Act 1920* (NZ) and then acquired its own premises in Parliament House.)

As this brief summary illustrates, the origins of the Crown Law Office can be traced to a time of uncertainty about the role of the Solicitor-General and Attorney-General in New Zealand's constitutional framework. Similarly, the

---

1 The *Attorney-General's Act* was consolidated into the *Civil List Act 1908* (NZ) and then repealed by the *Civil List Act 1920* (NZ). The 1920 Act listed the Attorney-General as a Minister of the Crown.

role of the Crown Law Office evolved from an office, which in many respects was akin to a modern-day Attorney-General's Department, into an independent government department with ultimate responsibility for the management of much of the government's legal business.

The appointment of Richard Wild as New Zealand's ninth Solicitor-General in 1957 heralded a series of changes to the way in which the government's legal services were delivered.

These changes became most apparent when 'The Cabinet Rules for the Conduct of Crown Legal Business' were published in the *New Zealand Gazette* on 17 July 1958 (SR 1958/105). Those Rules replaced 'The Cabinet Rules for the Conduct of Business Referred to the Law Officers of the Crown' of 1932. The key parts of the 1958 Rules provided that:

> 8. No Crown Solicitor or Solicitor in private practice is to be instructed or employed by any government department without reference to the Solicitor-General, and all matters so referred are to be dealt with as he may direct.
>
> 9. No Solicitor who is an officer of the Public Service shall act in any proceeding in any Court or before any Tribunal on behalf of the Crown or any government department or officer of the Crown, unless under a general or specific authority of the Solicitor-General.
>
> 10. No appeal from any Court is to be instituted or defended until the matter has been referred to the Solicitor-General, and any proposal to appeal is to be so referred promptly.
>
> 11. The foregoing Rules apply to legal opinions, to conveyancing matters, and to litigation both civil and criminal. They do not, however, apply to the following:
>
> - ordinary criminal prosecutions in the Supreme Court;
> - preliminary investigations before Justices and the conduct of inquests in which the Police Department wishes to obtain legal assistance from a District Crown Solicitor;
> - the normal conveyancing work of the State Advances Corporation, the Department of Lands and Survey, the Mines Department, the Government Life Insurance Department, the Ministry of Works, and the Maori Affairs Department;
> - the legal work of the Public Trustee and Maori Trustee;

- the legal work of the Railways Department (except common law damages claims) and insurance claims against the State Fire and Accident Insurance Office (other than those in which that office is acting as agent for a department);

- instructions in connection with the penal provisions of the Bankruptcy Act 1908 given to a District Crown Solicitor by an Official Assignee under the authority of the Department of Justice.

Under Wild's stewardship, the Crown Law Office became the undisputed focal point for almost all government legal work. In 1966 Wild (by now Sir Richard Wild) was appointed Chief Justice of New Zealand.

In 1988 New Zealand's public sector underwent significant change. The *State Sector Act 1988* (NZ) was the catalyst for the establishment of a range of very independent government departments and agencies. A consequence of these changes was that the Crown Law Office's vice-like grip on the government's legal services loosened a little. The then Solicitor-General, John McGrath, revised the 'Cabinet Rules for the Conduct of Crown Legal Business' in 1993.

The new Cabinet Directions endeavoured to strike a balance between ensuring the Crown received legal advice and representation of the highest possible standard while at the same time ensuring the Crown Law Office no longer enjoyed the virtual monopoly that had previously existed in relation to government legal services. The 1993 Directions divide Crown legal services into two categories.

Category 1 legal work must be referred by government departments[2] to the Solicitor-General and be dealt with 'either within or outside the Crown Law Office as the Solicitor-General directs' (at para 5). Category 1 legal services are defined in the following way:

> a. Representation or advice in relation to actual or imminent litigation to which the Government or agency is or may become a party.
>
> b. Legal services involving questions of the lawfulness of the exercise of government power.
>
> c. Constitutional questions including Treaty of Waitangi issues.
>
> d. Issues relating to the enforcement of the criminal law.
>
> e. Legal issues relating to the protection of the revenue.

2 As defined in s 2 of the *State Sector Act 1988*, including New Zealand Police and any agency of the government subject to ministerial control.

All other legal services are referred to as 'Category 2' legal work. Legal services that fall within Category 2 need not be referred to the Crown Law Office, but with the proviso that 'the Solicitor-General may intervene at any stage in a particular case to require that the legal services concerned be provided as the Solicitor-General directs' pursuant to paragraph 5 of the 1993 Directions. Where any question or dispute arises as to the category into which a request for legal services falls, it shall be resolved by the Solicitor-General. Where a department seeks legal services from lawyers in private practice in relation to Category 2 work, it is the duty of the Chief Executive of the department to ensure that the lawyers engaged are free of conflicts of interest, have an appropriate level of expertise for the work they are asked to undertake and are adequately supervised by the department.

The Current Roles of the Solicitor-General for New Zealand

It is against this background that the current roles of the Solicitor-General can be conveniently considered under the following five headings: Chief Executive of the Crown Law Office; principal counsel for the Crown; principal legal adviser to the Crown; supervisor of the prosecution of indictable crime; and constitutional/Law Officer functions.

Each of these functions will be described very briefly. Those interested in a more detailed description of the roles of the Solicitor-General are encouraged to read McGrath (1998).

Chief Executive of the Crown Law Office

Section 44(2)(a) of the *State Sector Act* provides that the Solicitor-General is the Chief Executive of the Crown Law Office. However, unlike other Chief Executives, the Solicitor-General is appointed by royal prerogative and not under the *State Sector Act*. Consequently, the warrant appointing the Solicitor-General provides that the appointee holds office at Her Majesty's 'pleasure and will'.

While the Solicitor-General is not accountable under the *State Sector Act*, he or she has the responsibilities of a Chief Executive under that Act, including ensuring the Crown Law Office complies with the *Public Finance Act 1989* (NZ).

The Crown Law Office has been a separate department of the State since 1873. The office's independence is essential if it is to continue to provide the free and frank advice that Ministers and departments require without there being even the perception of constraint by way of managerial control from a larger department. The independence of the Crown Law Office also goes some way to explaining why it has continued to attract lawyers of the highest calibre to its ranks.

At the time of drafting this chapter the Crown Law Office had 106 lawyers and 92 support staff. The day-to-day management of the office is overseen by a Deputy Chief Executive and a Practice Manager who are also members of the Crown Law Management Board. The Management Board assists the Solicitor-General in the overall management of the Crown Law Office. The Management Board comprises the Solicitor-General, Deputy Chief Executive, Practice Manager and the three Deputy Solicitors-General. The Crown Law Office is divided into three broad practice groups. Each group is headed by one of the three Deputy Solicitors-General. Deputy Solicitors-General have delegated to them the powers of the Solicitor-General pursuant to s 9C of the *Constitution Act 1986* (NZ). Lawyers in the Crown Law Office are members of one of eight teams, each of which is headed by a senior Crown Counsel with managerial responsibility for the lawyers in their team. Notwithstanding the division of the Crown Law Office into eight teams, lawyers are encouraged to work laterally and ensure that issues are dealt with on a whole of Crown approach.

Principal Counsel for the Crown

One of the most pleasurable aspects of the role of Solicitor-General is the privilege of being the Crown's leading counsel in key cases involving the Crown.

As noted by McGrath (1998: 205):

> [T]he Solicitor-General is appointed from the ranks of experienced barristers of the profession, and is either working in private practice or in the Crown Law Office at the time of appointment. The person appointed is thus an experienced legal advocate and adviser.

At a practical level, the volume of litigation facing the Crown means that the Solicitor-General has to be very selective when determining what cases he will personally conduct. The establishment of the Supreme Court in 2004 has meant that the Crown Law Office must now manage a far greater final appellate court workload than when New Zealand's final appeals were to the Privy Council. By far the greatest increase in the appellate workload has been in relation to criminal appeals. The Supreme Court now hears in one year as many criminal appeals as the Privy Council heard from New Zealand from 1840 to 2004. This increased access to justice has had a significant impact on the Solicitor-General's advocacy workload, but it is also a source of one of the most professionally rewarding aspects of the role.[3]

Principal Legal Adviser to the Crown

The Solicitor-General is the government's principal legal adviser. The Solicitor-General is, of course, not the government's only legal adviser. Ministers, including the Prime Minister, take legal advice from a range of sources, including from

3 Since the Supreme Court was established in 2004 it has dealt with 319 criminal leave applications and heard 52 substantive criminal appeals. The Privy Council, by comparison, heard a total of 12 substantive criminal appeals between 1851 and 2009.

within their own departments. The Solicitor-General, however, is, subject to the Attorney-General, the final arbiter of conflicting views of the law within government (McGrath 1998: 206), and for this reason Ministers and Chief Executives do not hesitate to seek the views of the Solicitor-General, quite literally at any time. Often, the advice sought is informal and not recorded and is designed to assist busy Ministers and Chief Executives in reaching their own independent conclusions on an issue of concern.

When Ministers and departments seek formal advice, the Crown Law Office prepares an opinion either directly for the Attorney-General (in the case of advice that is provided for Ministers) or for the department concerned. All legal advice provided to Ministers or government agencies attracts legal professional privilege. That advice can only be released, and privilege in it waived, with the consent of the Attorney-General (Cabinet Office Circular CO (05)5).

The role of Crown Law Office opinions is to provide perceptive, objective, practical and authoritative statements of the law that apply to issues arising in the course of government.

The requirement for objectivity means that Crown Law Office opinions should reflect the particular need for Ministers and departments to have advice from lawyers who are seen to be detached from the immediate pressures on policy makers and administrators. The Solicitor-General's duty to give independent advice in this way is of considerable constitutional importance. Crown Law Office opinions must also address issues in a practical way.

Crown Law Office opinions will often have implications for government departments other than those directly seeking the opinion. It is the Crown Law Office's responsibility to see that, regardless of who might be the principal requestor, the perspectives of others whom the advice may affect is obtained. Recipients should be all those who have a legitimate governmental interest in the problem raised. As Marie Shroff (2007), the Secretary for Cabinet from 1987 to 2003, has said:

> From my point of view as Cabinet Secretary I saw many occasions when the Prime Minister, Attorney-General or Cabinet Secretary was obliged to call in Crown Law where legal advice was absent, patchy, self-interested or otherwise questionable.

Departments who attempt to circumvent obtaining advice from the Crown Law Office risk undermining their credibility and ultimately increasing their costs if they obtain legal opinions that lack the authority and public interest perspective offered by Crown Law's advice.

Supervisor of the Prosecutions of Indictable Crime

By convention, in New Zealand, it is the Solicitor-General rather than the Attorney-General who ultimately supervises the prosecution of indictable crimes following committal. The police and prosecuting agencies have the discretion to bring charges, subject to specific statutory exceptions, but following committal, the responsibility for the conduct of criminal proceedings rests with Crown Solicitors, as agents of the Solicitor-General. The convention which has developed in New Zealand, and which has resulted in the Attorney-General playing virtually no role in the prosecution of criminal cases, ensures there is no perception of political influence being brought to bear when decisions are made in relation to prosecutions.

The Solicitor-General, or his delegated deputy, oversees the Attorney-General's decisions to stay prosecutions. The power to stay prosecutions is found in s 378 of the *Crimes Act 1961* (NZ) and s 77A of the *Summary Proceedings Act 1957* (NZ). It is from these statutory powers that the ability to provide immunity is derived, whereby the Crown promises to stay any future prosecution in defined circumstances. The most significant case in New Zealand's recent history in which the Attorney-General took responsibility for a stay of prosecution concerned the aftermath of the *Rainbow Warrior* case. In 1991, following the arrest in Switzerland of a French citizen wanted in respect of the 1985 bombing of the Rainbow Warrior in Auckland Harbour, the Attorney-General stayed all outstanding charges against the person who had been arrested in Switzerland and other French nationals who had avoided arrest. The decision was made by the Attorney-General because such a decision could only be made in the context of international obligations and on broad national interest considerations, including the future of New Zealand's trade with Europe (McGrath 1998: 209–10).

The Solicitor-General, or his delegated deputy, is also directly involved in all criminal appeals brought against conviction and/or sentence in the Court of Appeal. Section 390 of the *Crimes Act* requires the appearance of the Solicitor-General (or his representative) in the Court of Appeal in all such cases. Similarly, decisions to appeal sentences by the Crown on the grounds of undue leniency or application of wrong principles (pursuant to s 383 of the *Crimes Act*) are made either by the Solicitor-General or delegated to a Deputy Solicitor-General.[4]

Constitutional/Law Officer Functions

The Solicitor-General discharges a number of important miscellaneous constitutional and Law Officer functions, three of which should be mentioned at this juncture.

4 The Solicitor-General also plays a role in deciding whether or not to issue proceedings for contempt of court. Requests to issue contempt proceedings arise quite regularly. However, the discretion to bring contempt proceedings is executed cautiously and sparingly as such decisions invariably involve balancing the right of freedom of expression and the right to a fair trial. (See, for example, *Gisborne Herald v Solicitor-General* [1995] 3 NZLR 563 (CA): 564.)

First, the Solicitor-General plays a co-ordinating role in relation to the appointment of Queen's Counsel. Candidates for silk are required to forward their applications to the Solicitor-General, who provides an interface between the Attorney-General, the Chief Justice and the profession during the appointment process.

Secondly, the Solicitor-General liaises between the Attorney-General and the Chief Justice on a variety of issues, including the appointment of senior judges, except when the Solicitor-General is a candidate for appointment.

Finally, the Solicitor-General provides advice directly to the Governor-General on a variety of constitutional and legal issues, particularly during the formation of a government following a general election. By convention, the Solicitor-General gives precedence to the Governor-General and does not seek the Attorney-General's permission to advise the Governor-General.

There are approximately 70 statutory duties conferred on the Attorney-General and Solicitor-General. The duties and powers conferred on the Attorney-General can be exercised by the Solicitor-General pursuant to s 9A of the *Constitution Act 1982* (NZ), but, interestingly, the converse does not apply. The statutory duties and powers specifically conferred on the Solicitor-General do not appear to be able to be exercised by the Attorney-General.

The powers and duties conferred on the Law Officers cover a myriad functions. These include authorising prosecutions, such as prosecutions under the *International Crimes and International Criminal Court Act 2000* (NZ) and the *Terrorism Suppression Act 2002* (NZ); being the protector of charities under the *Charities Act 2005* (NZ); and serving on various bodies such as the High Court Rules Committee.

Advantages to the Way the Roles of Solicitor-General and the Crown Law Office have Evolved in New Zealand

There are three preliminary observations that should be made as a prelude to this part of the chapter.

The first is that the Crown can only have one view of the law. Ministers, Chief Executives and others in government who are dependent upon legal advice need to receive just one explanation of the law. That explanation must, of course, be authoritative. It must be right. This contrasts with policy advice. Ministers and other senior decision-makers within government often relish competing policy viewpoints. Competing policy advice assists Ministers and other senior decision-makers in shaping and influencing the ultimate policy outcome. Ministers and senior decision-makers cannot, however, influence and shape explanations as to what the law is, in order to achieve their objectives.

Secondly, like Australia, the growth and compartmentalisation of government in New Zealand has resulted in the creation of a number of large government legal departments. There are currently 756 lawyers in government in New Zealand, employed by 37 departments and government agencies. The cost of providing this service is very considerable. In the year ending 30 June 2009 the cost of legal services to central government in New Zealand was $181 million (NZD). Approximately half of this sum was spent on external providers.

Thirdly, the creation of a large number of autonomous government departments since 1988, many with their own significant legal departments, has increased the risk of government lawyers providing competing advice to decision-makers, and in circumstances where it is difficult to assess the quality of that advice. However, notwithstanding these potential risks, the position in New Zealand does not appear to have reverted to the dire state which John Salmond encountered when he became Solicitor-General in 1910. When he took office, government legal departments appeared to be acting entirely autonomously with little or no regard to the Crown Law Office.

Compared to the way the role of Solicitor-General has evolved in England and Wales, Canada, the United States, Australia and New Zealand, the current roles of the office in New Zealand suits the needs of New Zealand. In particular, one of the great strengths of the office of Solicitor-General in New Zealand is the way it is inextricably bound to the Crown Law Office. The Australian position which has seen the creation of clear lines of separation between the roles of Solicitors-General, Crown/Government Solicitors and Directors of Public Prosecutions would, if adopted in New Zealand, weaken rather than strengthen the constitutional importance of the Crown Law Office and the Office of Solicitor-General in New Zealand. The reasons for this view can be briefly stated.

There is considerable advantage in having the Solicitor-General actively supervise and oversee the advice and representation that the Crown Law Office provides. By actively participating in the day-to-day business of the Crown Law Office, the Solicitor-General is able to minimise the Crown's litigation risk. When he was Solicitor-General, the writer endeavoured to ensure that the Crown's trial and lower court litigation was managed in a way that did not compromise the Crown's position if the case should proceed to the Court of Appeal or Supreme Court. If the Solicitor-General were not part of the Crown Law Office and received instructions to appear for the Crown, only say at appellate level, there is a risk that the opportunity for strategic planning of litigation would be diminished.

By heading the Crown Law Office the Solicitor-General is also able to identify those cases that require his or her immediate attention. While there is no doubt that a conscientious Crown Solicitor or head of the Crown Law Office would work constructively with an independent Solicitor-General, the risks of a breakdown in communication do not exist if the Solicitor-General has direct control over the cases being managed within the office.

The Crown Law Office has a unique advantage in having the Solicitor-General as its head. All staff in the office know they can enlist the assistance of the Solicitor-General at a moment's notice to assist in the management of a file or in the office's relationship with a government department. Removing the Solicitor-General from the Crown Law Office risks undermining the office to the point where it would be almost indistinguishable from the legal sections of regular government departments.

It is the writer's view that the Solicitor-General and Crown Law Office should continue their roles as the principal lawyers who both advise and represent the Crown in litigation. Experience has shown there is considerable advantage to one organisation providing both a whole-of-government approach to the advice they give Ministers and key decision-makers and who take a finely tuned public interest approach to the way that litigation is conducted in the name of the Crown. This approach works well in the New Zealand context in which there is a fused profession and where, as a consequence, highly qualified lawyers in the Crown Law Office provide both advice to and representation services for the Crown.

For similar reasons, there is considerable merit in the current New Zealand system whereby the Solicitor-General provides oversight to the prosecution of indictable crime and brings public interest considerations to the forefront of his mind when making decisions about staying prosecutions, granting immunities or authorising the bringing of prosecutions. Those decisions are best made by those who do not have a direct interest in the investigation or prosecution of particular cases.

There are, however, ways in which the New Zealand system can and should be improved. The creation of legal teams within autonomous government departments and agencies creates those risks referred to previously. New Zealand does need to take steps to ensure greater cohesion between lawyers in government departments and the Crown Law Office. Lawyers in government departments need to recognise their constitutional responsibilities to the Law Officers of the Crown and to appreciate the roles and functions of the Law Officers. This need will to a large extent be addressed through the creation of New Zealand's Government Legal Service, which is loosely modelled on the Government Legal Service managed under the auspices of the Treasury Solicitor in London. The New Zealand Government Legal Service is in the process of being established. Once created, the New Zealand Government Legal Service will:

- be available to assist Chief Executives with the recruitment and appointment of lawyers in government departments;
- assist in the training and development of lawyers in government departments;
- assist in the rationalisation of legal information services and law libraries within government departments; and
- provide a focal point for co-ordinating the way in which lawyers in government respond to issues that are common to other departments.

Conclusion

The evolution of the role of Solicitor-General can be traced from a period in our colonial government when considerable uncertainty existed about the roles of the Attorney-General and Solicitor-General of New Zealand. Since 1875 the role of Solicitor-General has developed in a way that is unique to New Zealand and reflects that country's small size and comparatively flexible constitutional and political structures. It also reflects New Zealand's fused legal profession.

The role of Solicitor-General is undoubtedly very challenging. It is, however, manageable provided the Solicitor-General has appropriate levels of high-calibre support. Fortunately, New Zealand Solicitors-General have always been supported by some of New Zealand's finest lawyers who have foregone the financial rewards of private practice in order to play significant roles as advisers to, and representatives of, the Crown in New Zealand.

References

Barton, G.B. 1878. *The New Zealand Jurist*. Volume 3, Part I. Dunedin: J Wilkie & Co.

Bellot, H. 1909. The Origin of the Attorney-General. *Law Quarterly Review*. Volume 25, 400.

Cochrane, D. and Dean, M. 2012. *A Review of the Role and Functions of the Solicitor-General and the Crown Law Office* [Online]. Available at: http://www.crownlaw.govt.nz/uploads/review_2012.pdf [accessed: 29 November 2012].

Cornford, P. 1964. Crown Law Office: Early History. *New Zealand Law Journal*. 423.

Edwards, J.Ll.J. 1964. *The Law Officers of the Crown: A Study of the Offices of the Attorney-General and Solicitor-General of England with an Account of the Office of the Director of Public Prosecutions of England*. London: Sweet & Maxwell.

McGrath, J. 1998. Principles for Sharing Law Officer Power: The Role of the New Zealand Solicitor-General. *New Zealand Universities Law Review*. Volume 18, 197.

McLintock, A.H. (ed.) 1966. *An Encyclopaedia of New Zealand*. Wellington: Government Printer.

Otago Daily Times. 1878. The Civil Service. *Otago Daily Times*, 30 March 1878, 3.

Scholefield, G. 1950. *New Zealand Parliamentary Record: 1840–1949*. Wellington: Government Print.

Shroff, M. 2007. *The Worldly Task: Legal Advice in a Central Government Setting*. Paper to the conference From Professing to Advising to Judging: A Conference in Honour of Sir Kenneth Keith, Wellington, 23–4 August 2007.

Chapter 9
The Law Officers of the Crown and the Rule of Law in the United Kingdom

Klearchos A. Kyriakides[1]

Introduction

In 2011, Lord Phillips of Worth Matravers, the then President of the Supreme Court of the United Kingdom, observed that the rule of law is 'the bedrock of a democratic society' and 'the only basis upon which individuals, private corporations, public bodies and the executive can order their lives and activities' (Phillips 2011).

It follows that if the rule of law is to have any integrity in a democratic society, everyone must be expected to obey the law; everyone must be subject to the jurisdiction of an independent court; and everyone must have the means to enforce their rights or defend their freedoms. No less importantly, everyone must be entitled to confidential legal advice from appropriately qualified legal advisers.

Be that as it may, neither democracy nor the rule of law can function properly in the absence of a workable constitutional framework and a phalanx of guardians. In view of the organic and convoluted constitutional arrangements prevailing in the United Kingdom in the twenty-first century, this phalanx includes Ministers and parliamentarians, together with judges and other members of the legal profession – including those within the Government Legal Service (GLS) and the Office of the Parliamentary Counsel (OPC). In so far as the Government of the United Kingdom ('the Government') is concerned, perhaps the lynchpins of the rule of law are the lawyers who are collectively known as the Law Officers of the Crown ('the Law Officers').

---

1 The author hereby records his sincere gratitude to the following: Mr John Mylonas, barrister-at-law, for inspiring him to take an active interest in the office of Attorney General; and Karen Clark, Senior Lecturer in the School of Law of the University of Hertfordshire, for her comments on an early draft of this chapter.

In recent decades, the significance of the Law Officers has unquestionably grown on account of various developments, including but not limited to: the elevated status of public international law since 1945; the remarkable growth of judicial review since a landmark case decided in 1947 (*Associated Provincial Picture Houses Ltd v Wednesbury Corporation* [1947] 2 All ER 680); the introduction of the *European Communities Act 1972* (UK), coupled with the subsequent accession of the United Kingdom to what is now known as the European Union; the enhanced status of human rights thanks to the *Human Rights Act 1998* (UK); the establishment of devolved administrations in Scotland, Wales and Northern Ireland pursuant to legislation enacted in 1998;[2] and the proliferation of overseas military expeditions in recent years, notably those of the 'post 9/11 era' relating to Afghanistan and Iraq. These developments have combined to increase the complexity of the law, to underline the importance of ministerial compliance with the law, to enhance the role of the court as a check on the executive branch of government and to reinforce the role of the Law Officers as guardians of the rule of law.

Who are the Law Officers?

This ostensibly straightforward question does not elicit a correspondingly straightforward answer. This is partly because the United Kingdom does not possess a single codified 'written' constitution that lists the key officeholders in the three branches of government and defines the scope of their powers. Even so, one may deduce by perusing relevant primary sources that, at the time of writing, there are four Law Officers, who serve in both the executive and legislative branches of government. These are:

- The Attorney General for England and Wales ('the Attorney General');
- The Solicitor General for England and Wales ('the Solicitor General');
- The Advocate General for Scotland; and
- The Advocate General for Northern Ireland (a post that is held *ex officio* by the Attorney General).

Acting under the royal prerogative, the Queen formally appoints each of the Law Officers, albeit on the recommendation of the Prime Minister. Put another way, the Law Officers are not appointed in accordance with the selection process relating to lawyers within the GLS.

Needless to say, the two most prominent Law Officers are the Attorney General and the Solicitor General ('the principal Law Officers'). Indeed, their offices are among the oldest in the Government.

2 The relevant legislation includes the *Scotland Act 1998* (UK), *Northern Ireland Act 1998* (UK), *Government of Wales Act 1998* (UK) and *Government of Wales Act 2006* (UK).

The office of Attorney General may be traced back to the thirteenth century when the sovereign required an attorney to represent him in court.[3] The title 'Attorney General' was assumed in 1461. Then, in 1673, following the English Civil War, the office was substantively modernised. Today, the Attorney General is the chief Law Officer, whose functions require him[4] to act as *inter alia*: the chief legal adviser to the Crown; a Minister accountable to the legislature of which he is a member; the guardian of the public interest; and the titular head of the Bar.

As for the office of Solicitor General, its origins lie in the post of the King's Solicitor. In 1515, the latter office was reconstituted as *Solicitator Generallis domini Regis* and judicially described as *secundarius attornatus* (Edwards 1964: 3, 29). Today, the Solicitor General is, in effect, the deputy of the Attorney General. In July 2010, the role of the former was helpfully summarised by the then Solicitor General, Edward Garnier (2010):

> [The] Solicitor General is still essentially the Attorney's deputy but since the Law Officers Act of 1997 any function of the Attorney General may be exercised by the Solicitor General, so in law at least we are equals, and indeed we share much of the work that falls to be done in the name of the Attorney General. So when I talk of the functions of the Attorney General I mean my own too.

It may be noted from the above that the Solicitor General is widely regarded as being 'essentially' the deputy of the Attorney General. This would appear to be correct, even though the *Law Officers Act 1997* (UK) does not expressly refer to the Solicitor General as the 'deputy' of his colleague.[5]

It would be remiss not to provide a rudimentary introduction to the other two Law Officers in the Government. The Advocate General for Scotland and the Advocate General for Northern Ireland serve in the executive as well as the legislative branches of the United Kingdom, while exercising various functions in their respective areas of jurisdiction subject to the devolution arrangements in place there. However, the Advocate General for Scotland and the Advocate General for Northern Ireland are clearly distinct from the Lord Advocate of

3 On the origins and history of the Law Officers, see *inter alia* Keeton 1949; Edwards 1964; Jones 1969.

4 In this chapter, for the sake of convenience, the Attorney General and the other Law Officers are referred to in the masculine. However, the post of Attorney General has been held by a woman, Baroness Scotland of Asthal (from 2007 until 2010). By the same token, the post of Solicitor General has been held by two women: Harriet Harman (from 2001 until 2005) and Vera Baird (from 2007 until 2010).

5 Mummery LJ has expressly referred to the Solicitor General as the 'deputy' of the Attorney General in the context of the *Law Officers Act 1944* (UK), which preceded the *Law Officers Act 1997*: 'I see no reason to doubt that the Solicitor General was acting in place of the Attorney General within the scope of the authority that he has, as his deputy, under Section 1 of the Law Officers' Act 1944': *Attorney General v Oakes* [2001] EWCA Civ 1297: [39].

Scotland, the Solicitor General for Scotland and the Attorney General for Northern Ireland, the latter three of whom serve as independent Law Officers within the devolved administrations in Scotland and Northern Ireland respectively.

There is at least one noteworthy difference between the Advocate General for Scotland and the Advocate General for Northern Ireland. On the one hand, as already noted, the office of Advocate General for Northern Ireland is held *ex officio* by the Attorney General for England and Wales. On the other hand, the Advocate General for Scotland is a senior figure in his own right with his own offices in Edinburgh and London. From 2010 until the time of writing, the post of Advocate General has been held by Lord Wallace of Tankerness, who is a member of the Scottish Bar, a Minister in the Government and a Liberal Democrat peer in the House of Lords. By the same token, the Attorney General for England and Wales is clearly distinct from the Counsel General for Wales, the latter of which is the independent Law Officer of the devolved government of Wales.

In short, therefore, devolution has muddied the constitutional and legal waters, all the more so in view of the pro-independence movement in Scotland and the Agreement – concluded in Edinburgh on 15 October 2012 between the United Kingdom Government and the Scottish Government – on a referendum on independence for Scotland (The Scottish Government 2012).

In his classic book published in 1964, *The Law Officers of the Crown*, J.Ll.J. Edwards notes that, from time to time, the Lord Chancellor is cited as a Law Officer of the Crown. Edwards regards such references as 'pardonable' if made in the context of the availability of the Lord Chancellor as a source of legal advice to the Prime Minister and Cabinet (Edwards 1964: 2).[6] Edwards, of course, was writing in an age when the Lord Chancellor served in all three branches of government in the United Kingdom – as a Minister in the Cabinet, as a member of the House of Lords in its legislative capacity, as a judge in the Appellate Committee of that House and as the head of the judiciary.

In 2006, in accordance with the *Constitutional Reform Act 2005* (UK) and its aim of procuring a clearer separation of powers, the Lord Chancellor *inter alia* handed over to the Lord Chief Justice of England and Wales his role as head of the judiciary. At the same time, the Lord Chancellor surrendered his status as a judge. Then, in 2007, the Lord Chancellor assumed the new post of Secretary of State for Justice, while retaining his reformed ancient office as Lord Chancellor.

As intended, the reforms have generally procured a clearer separation of powers between the judiciary and the other two branches of government. However, a side-effect has been to clip the legal wings of the Lord Chancellor by extricating him from the judiciary, by ending his role as the most senior judge and by virtually extinguishing his status as an Olympian legal personality within the Cabinet. The first three holders of the reformed office of Lord Chancellor and the connected new office of Secretary of State for Justice were barristers by profession: Lord

6 On the same page, Edwards also reminds us that there was once a Law Officer known as The King's Advocate General; the office has expired.

Falconer of Thoroton; Jack Straw; and Kenneth Clarke. Nevertheless, the fourth incumbent, Chris Grayling, who was appointed in September 2012, is neither a member of the legal profession nor even a law graduate. Time will tell as to the effect this may have upon the dynamics of the Lord Chancellor's relationship with the principal Law Officers.

In the meantime, it would now be incorrect and improper to describe the Lord Chancellor as a Law Officer of the Crown. By the same token, it is no longer appropriate or feasible for a Prime Minister to follow the precedent established by Anthony Eden prior to the Suez Crisis of 1956 when he obtained alternative – and more convenient – legal advice from the Lord Chancellor (Marston 1988). In any event, the non-statutory *Ministerial Code* now confirms that it is the function of the Law Officers (i.e. not the Lord Chancellor) to tender legal advice: 'The Law Officers must be consulted in good time before the Government is committed to critical decisions involving legal considerations' (Cabinet Office 2010: para 2.10). Tellingly, the *Ministerial Code* makes no reference to the Lord Chancellor as a provider of legal advice.

Thus, it may be said that the reforms to the office of Lord Chancellor have elevated still further the legal significance of the Attorney General and his deputy, the Solicitor General, particularly as the chief legal advisers to the Crown and as the senior lawyers within the Government.

The Unique Status of the Principal Law Officers

The principal Law Officers operate at the heart of the United Kingdom's democratic arrangements, constitutional structure and legal system. More particularly, the principal Law Officers have been described by a recent holder of the office of Solicitor General as lying 'at the interface between politics and the law' and as being '*sui generis*: not quite like other lawyers; not quite like other politicians; [and] not quite like other ministers' (Harman 2001). For these reasons, an inevitable paradox arises.

On the one hand, given the sensitive nature of their duties and the confidentiality enveloping their day-to-day work, the principal Law Officers tend to operate discreetly. They rarely enter the public consciousness or stray into the glare of publicity, except to announce a key decision, to account to Parliament, to give a public lecture or to otherwise fulfil a public engagement. This, however, is not to understate the significance of their work. In the vivid description of Garnier (2010), as stated during his tenure as the Solicitor General:

> The life of the Law Officers, although circumscribed by limitations that a real politician would not tolerate, brings one to the very centre of power even if those at the centre do not realise it. It is not the dry and fusty world of the Dickensian lawyer's office, still less the Office of Circumlocution. Of course the public only see the capital ships, dressed fore and aft, steaming full steam ahead on the

> high seas, occasionally firing their guns, but below the surface and silently, and known only to a few in the law and in Whitehall, are the two submarines, HM Attorney and Solicitor. When we go on manoeuvres we do so to have an effect as the Iraq War story perhaps unfortunately reveals but there are happier examples of activities carried out in confidence for Governments of both colours where the advice and restraining hand of the Law Officers has been both sensible and well received. When we surface it is usually to resign (or not), to apply to the courts in a contempt case, or to complain of an unduly lenient sentence. But so much of our time is not spent just saying 'No', but 'Have you thought about doing it this way?' which is what all good lawyers should do for their clients.

The above factors, in addition to the duty of confidentiality they owe to the Crown, help to explain why the principal Law Officers rarely generate headlines.

On the other hand, due to the very nature of their functions, the principal Law Officers may sometimes be pitchforked into the forefront of public attention, particularly during a diplomatic, economic, military or political crisis: the involvement of the Attorney General in the 'Zinoviev letter' affair of 1924 provides a classic historic example,[7] as does the arms-to-Iraq scandal of the 1990s.[8] Furthermore, the decisions of the principal Law Officers have the capacity to arouse intense controversy in Parliament, coupled with accusations that their thinking has been motivated by party-political considerations or loyalty to the Prime Minister, rather than by strict legal criteria or obedience to the law. Such allegations were indeed bandied around, for instance, at the time of the US-led invasion of Iraq in 2003 and the BAE Systems affair of 2006. In such exceptional circumstances, the spotlight is inevitably thrown onto the unique status of the principal Law Officers at the juncture between law and politics; and, as night follows day, questions are then raised as to whether this extraordinary state of affairs ought to continue.

This is what occurred after the two aforementioned episodes of the 2000s. Indeed, following the appointment of Gordon Brown as Prime Minister in 2007, with Mr Brown eager to make his mark in his new role and memories of these episodes fresh in his memory, the Government went as far as to publish a consultation paper ('the 2007 Consultation Paper') (Scotland 2007) and to institute an accompanying consultation exercise. At issue was whether or not the office of the Attorney General was ripe for reform. In the event, the ancient office emerged largely unscathed from this process and no substantive changes were introduced. However, this does not mean that no reforms will be introduced in the future; as the fate of the ancient office of Lord Chancellor demonstrates, no office is set in stone.

---

7 The episode is recalled in the memoirs of the Attorney General of the day, Sir Patrick Hastings: Hastings 1948.

8 This affair was the subject of an inquiry chaired by Sir Richard Scott (later Lord Scott of Foscote). See: Scott 1995–96.

The Functions of the Attorney General

In the absence of a 'written' British constitution and bearing in mind the limited scope of the *Law Officers Act 1997* and other relevant legislation, it is difficult to identify all of the functions which may be performed by the principal Law Officers and, more particularly, by the Attorney General. Nevertheless, it is possible to tease out from an array of sources a reasonably comprehensive list of the core functions which have arisen as a result of legislation, the common law, constitutional conventions, customs or practices.

In March 2012, Dominic Grieve, the Attorney General, disclosed that his historic office performs 'more than 40 separate functions' (Grieve 2012a); an Annex within the 2007 Consultation Paper presented to Parliament by Mr Grieve's predecessor specifically identified 42 functions (Scotland 2007: Annex A).

Of the 40 or so acknowledged functions of the Attorney General, four stand out as being of pre-eminent importance. These relate to his roles as: the chief legal adviser to the Crown; a Minister who has responsibility for superintending the prosecuting departments and for answering to Parliament; the non-political guardian of the public interest; and the titular head of the Bar. Each of these functions is outlined below.

The Attorney General as Legal Adviser

Of the many functions performed by the Attorney General, perhaps the most vital – and certainly the most arduous – is the advisory function. In the 2007 Consultation Paper, the then Attorney General, Baroness Scotland (2007: 2), described this particular function in the following terms:

> As the Attorney General is the Chief Law Officer of the Crown (in the wider sense, i.e. the Government and, on some issues, Parliament and the Queen), the Attorney General is currently the Crown's principal legal adviser …

Accordingly, there is more to the advisory function than initially meets the eye. This becomes clear from an Annex appended to the 2007 Consultation Paper, which explains that the advisory function of the Attorney General has several strands: acting as 'Legal adviser to the Sovereign (as Her Majesty's Attorney General)'; tendering 'Legal advice to the Crown on peerage cases'; acting as 'Chief legal adviser to the Government'; providing 'Advice to Ministers involved in legal proceedings in their official capacity'; engaging in 'Consultation with Ministers in legal proceedings in their personal capacity (in circumstances defined in the Ministerial Code)'; and giving 'Advice to Parliament on certain issues, including the conduct and discipline of Members, matters of privilege and procedure, and the meaning and effect of proposed legislation'. In other words, the Attorney

General may have one client, namely the Crown, but the Crown has more than one manifestation.

In addition, the functions of the Attorney General require him to engage in advocacy by, for instance, intervening 'in legal proceedings to assert the rights of the Parliament' and acting as an 'Advocate for the Crown in important court cases'. This latter duty was most famously performed by Hartley Shawcross at the Nuremberg War Crimes Tribunal (Shawcross 1995).

Perhaps most crucially of all, the advisory function of the Attorney General is regarded as embracing an intertwined pair of consequential duties. One requires the Attorney General to ensure that his legal advice is not simply received by the appropriate persons in the Government but, where appropriate, is integrated into the policy-making, decision-making and legislative processes. The second duty requires the Attorney General to ensure that the Government operates within the law, especially in circumstances where he has tendered legal advice or is aware of a breach, or possible breach, of the law. In the revealing words of Oliver Heald (2012), who was appointed Solicitor General in September 2012:

> [T]he core function of the Attorney General was and is to make sure that Government, that Ministers, act lawfully, in accordance with the rule of law. ... I think the role of the Attorney General as the Government's Chief Legal Adviser was neatly summed up by the former Attorney General, Lord Mayhew of Twysden, who said, 'The Attorney General has a duty to ensure that the Queen's ministers who act in her name, or purport to act in her name, do act lawfully because it is his duty to help to secure the rule of law, the principal requirement of which is that the Government itself acts lawfully'.

Needless to say, the above is an extraordinarily onerous duty.

Without doubt, the most controversial recent episode involving the advisory function – and consequential duties – of the Attorney General arose prior to and following the US-led invasion of Iraq in March 2003.[9] The chain of events is long and complex, but for the purposes of this chapter they may be stated simply as follows.

On 17 March 2003, on the eve of a US-led armed attack against Iraq in which the Armed Forces of the United Kingdom were due to fight and possibly die, Hansard published a succinct one-page Written Answer relating to the legality of the proposed course of action. Therein, Lord Goldsmith of Allerton, the then Attorney General, unreservedly asserted that in the light of UN Security Council Resolution 1441 and various other factors 'the authority to use force [against Iraq] under Resolution 678 [of 1990] has revived and so continues today' (Hansard HL Debs 17 March 2003: WA2–3).

9 The author of this chapter hereby declares an interest. In 2003, he opposed the military action against Iraq. Indeed, the author participated in the 'anti-war rally' which took place in Hyde Park, London, on 15 February 2003.

The publication of the Written Answer formed the essential backdrop to a lengthy House of Commons debate that took place on the following day. The debate hinged on a resolution moved by the then Prime Minister, Tony Blair. This resolution *inter alia* noted the opinion of the Attorney General and also agreed with the Government that 'all means necessary' should be used 'to ensure the disarmament of Iraq's weapons of mass destruction' (Hansard HC Debs 18 March 2003: columns 760–911). At the end of the debate, a majority of MPs – including the front bench of the Official Opposition but excluding the front bench of the Liberal Democrats – endorsed the resolution moved by the Prime Minister.

In the recollection of William Cash (Hansard HC Debs 9 March 2004: columns 1435–6), the Conservative Shadow Attorney General at the time of the debate on 18 March 2003 (and a solicitor by profession):

> The question that was asked most often [in the run up to the debate] was whether the war was legal. ... [T]he submission of the Attorney-General's opinion in summary form had an enormous influence on the debate.

The US-led invasion may have toppled the regime of Saddam Hussein, but it triggered a bloody insurgency against the occupying forces. They, in turn, failed to unearth any Iraqi weapons of mass destruction, as Blair subsequently conceded.[10] More to the point, a leak from within Whitehall during the General Election campaign of 2005 and a decision of the Information Commissioner brought to light a secret (but now declassified) 13-page opinion dated 7 March 2003, which was prepared by the Attorney General for the Prime Minister.

Whereas the published Written Answer of 17 March 2003 was couched in categorical terms, the secret opinion dated 7 March 2003 was nuanced and hedged with reservations, including the observation that 'the language of resolution 1441 leaves the position unclear' (Goldsmith 2003a).

All of this provoked a fierce and protracted political uproar. The Attorney General stood accused of allowing himself to be unduly influenced by the Prime Minister (or others) between 7 and 17 March 2003. In relation to his Written Answer of 17 March 2003, the Attorney General also stood accused of misinterpreting international law.[11]

---

10 When he appeared before the Liaison Committee of Parliament in July 2004, Prime Minister Blair said the following (Hansard HC Debs 6 July 2004: answer by Mr Blair in response to Question 236 posed by Sir George Young MP): 'what I have to accept is that I was very, very confident we would find them [i.e. weapons of mass destruction]; I was very confident, even when I spoke to you this time last year, that the Iraq Survey Group would find them because all the intelligence and evidence we had was that these weapons of mass destruction existed. I have to accept that we have not found them and that we may not find them'.

11 As regards the relevant points of international law, see *inter alia* Bingham 2010: 110–29; Weller 2010.

Lord Goldsmith has robustly rejected the allegations levelled against him which are, in part, the subject of the Iraq Inquiry chaired by John Chilcot.[12]

The Iraqi imbroglio not only drew attention to the critical role of the Attorney General in the Government, but it also raised some intriguing hypothetical questions. Let us take just four examples. What should the Prime Minister, or any other Minister, do if confronted with legal advice from the Attorney General which warns that a proposed course of action – such as the use of military force – would be illegal?[13] Which steps should the Attorney General take, short of resigning, if his legal advice is overlooked, or if he is encouraged by Ministers to alter his advice? To what extent does the Attorney General owe a duty to Parliament, as distinct from a duty to the Government? In which circumstances, if any, should his confidential legal advice be disclosed to Parliament? This chapter is not the place to explore these questions in any detail. It suffices to say that opinions differ as to what the answer to each question should be.[14]

The Attorney General as Minister of the Crown

Apart from acting as a legal adviser, the Attorney General is a salaried Minister who is accountable to Parliament, of which he is a member.[15] As such, the Attorney General is the ministerial head of the Attorney General's Office and a member of the Privy Council. By contrast, the Attorney General is not normally a full member of the Cabinet. From time to time, however, he may be invited to attend Cabinet meetings, especially on occasions when legal, constitutional or legislative matters are under discussion. Furthermore, the Attorney General may be invited to attend or become a member of one or more of the critically important committees of the Cabinet, where so much of the real work of government is carried out.

12 At the time of writing, the report of the Iraq Inquiry is still awaited. In the meantime, the oral and written evidence of Lord Goldsmith may be obtained from the website of the Iraq Inquiry at http://www.iraqinquiry.org.uk.

13 In the words of Alex Salmond of the Scottish National Party (and, since 2007, the First Minister of Scotland) (Hansard HC Debs 9 March 2004: column 1448): 'If the advice of the present Attorney-General had been not that war was legal, but that it was not justified and not legal, what would have been the Government's response? Would it have been to change their course of action or [change] their Attorney-General?'

14 Some of these questions are explored in Kyriakides 2003.

15 Throughout most of the twentieth century, the principal Law Officers were invariably members of the House of Commons in accordance with a constitutional convention. Members of the House of Lords were appointed as Law Officers when Tony Blair (1997–2007) and Gordon Brown (2007–10) served as Prime Minister. These were Lord Falconer of Thoroton QC (Solicitor General, 1997–98), the late Lord Williams of Mostyn QC (Attorney General, 1999–2001), Lord Goldsmith of Allerton QC (Attorney General, 2001–07) and Baroness Scotland of Asthal QC (2007–10).

As a Minister, the Attorney General has his own department – the Attorney General's Office – which helps him perform his advisory, ministerial and public interest functions. At the same time, the Attorney General oversees the functions of the Treasury Solicitor, including his role as the head of the GLS; indeed, the Treasury Solicitor is accountable to the Attorney General. Furthermore, the Attorney General has co-responsibility – together with the Home Secretary, the Secretary of State for Justice and, ultimately, the Prime Minister – for the criminal justice policy of the Government.

No less importantly, the Attorney General is responsible for 'superintending' the public bodies under his wing, namely the Crown Prosecution Service (CPS); the Serious Fraud Office (SFO); the Revenue and Customs Prosecutions Office; the Army, Royal Navy and Royal Air Force prosecuting authorities; the CPS Inspectorate; and – in tandem with the Home Secretary and Secretary of State for Justice – the Office of Criminal Justice Reform (Scotland 2007: para 1.11, 5).

The concept of 'superintendence' is rather curious, yet it repeatedly crops up in official publications. What does it mean? According to the 2007 Consultation Paper (Scotland 2007: para 1.22, 7):

> It could thus be said that that the concept of superintendence encompasses, broadly: answering for the prosecuting authorities in Parliament; responsibility for the overall policies of those authorities, including prosecution policy in general; responsibility for the overall 'effective and efficient administration' of those authorities, including matters of resources; a right for the Attorney General to be consulted and informed about difficult, sensitive and high-profile cases; but not responsibility for every individual prosecution decision, or for the day-to-day running of the organisation.

It goes without saying that the Attorney General may find himself ensnared in controversy on account of any decision taken by one of the public bodies under his ministerial remit or any dealings he may have with them.

A graphic recent illustration is provided by the BAE Systems affair. This was provoked by a decision of the director of the SFO to discontinue a criminal investigation into 'allegations of corruption' against a leading arms manufacturer involved in the Al Yamamah programme with Saudi Arabia. In turn, that decision provoked a political uproar which required the then Attorney General, Lord Goldsmith, to give an explanation to Parliament, as required by the doctrine of ministerial responsibility, on 14 December 2006. He supported the decision and, in so doing, explained that, in this particular case, it was 'necessary to balance the strong public interest in the rule of law and in prosecuting crime, including international corruption' against 'national security and intelligence, given the particular relationships that there are between this country and Saudi Arabia in relation to that' (Hansard HL Debs 14 December 2006: columns 1712–17 at 1716–17). The decision of the director of the SFO also provoked a judicial review, which was initially successful but subsequently reversed

(*R (on the application of Corner House Research and Others) v Director of the Serious Fraud Office* [2008] UKHL 60).

The Attorney General as Guardian of the Public Interest

The Attorney General holds a third key function – as independent guardian of the public interest. To quote from the 2007 Consultation Paper (Scotland 2007: para 1.11, 5), the Attorney General is:

> Guardian of the public interest, in particular in certain kinds of legal proceedings – such as decisions on the bringing or termination of criminal prosecutions, charity matters, and the appointment of 'advocates to the court' to act as neutral advisers to the court in litigation and 'special advocates' to represent the interests of parties in certain national security cases.

At first glance, the role of the Attorney General in support of the public interest seems sensible enough. Indeed, it is often exercised in circumstances that arouse little or no controversy. Sometimes, however, the actions of the Attorney General in this arena can provoke allegations that he is acting in the interests of the Government, rather than in the public interest. This famously occurred in the late 1980s after Peter Wright had written a book in Australia, named *Spycatcher* (Wright and Greengrass 1987), about his experiences as a British intelligence officer in MI5. In response, the Attorney General, purportedly acting in the public interest, sought court orders in Australia, New Zealand, Hong Kong and England 'to enforce the duty of confidentiality owing to the Crown'.[16]

Evidently enough, the public interest functions of the Attorney General, as outlined above, encompass both duties and discretionary powers. This subtle distinction was highlighted by the seminal case of *Gouriet v Union of Post Office Workers* [1977] 3 All ER 70. The case arose after the Attorney General, Sam Silkin, refused to give his consent (fiat) to the issue of proceedings – in a so-called relator action – to enforce the law against the Union of Post Office Workers. Some of the union's members had decided to engage in a boycott of communications between England and Wales and South Africa. At the time, the latter practised apartheid. This was abhorred as a matter of policy by the Labour administration led by Prime Minister James Callaghan and backed by the trade unions.

In view of the politically charged circumstances of the case, the decision of the Attorney General aroused controversy on the basis that it was allegedly motivated by political, rather than legal, considerations. A judicial review ensued. The case

16 The history of the litigation is outlined in *Attorney General v Guardian Newspapers Ltd* (No 2) [1990] 1 AC 109. See the Written Answers by Patrick Mayhew, the Attorney General, at Hansard HC Debs 11 July 1988: column 15; Hansard HC Debs 11 January 1988: column 6.

eventually reached the Appellate Committee of the House of Lords, which decided that the decision of Silkin, the Attorney General, was not unlawful. On the facts of the case in *Gouriet*, Lord Wilberforce (and three of his fellow Law Lords) agreed there was 'good cause' for the Attorney General to reach the decision that he did.

Even so, the *Gouriet* case demonstrated that, from time to time, the Attorney General must not only tread carefully when exercising his public interest functions; he must additionally ensure that he is wearing the appropriate 'hat' at the appropriate time, that is, as guardian of the public interest and not as a Minister, not as a legal adviser of the Crown and certainly not as a member of the party which commands the confidence of a majority of MPs.

In the case of *Gouriet*, Lord Wilberforce drew attention to the guiding principles which the Attorney General must follow, as originally articulated in the House of Commons on 29 January 1951 by the then holder of the office, Hartley Shawcross. According to Shawcross:

> It has never been the rule in this country – I hope it never will be – that suspected criminal offences must automatically be the subject of prosecution. …
>
> I think the true doctrine is that it is the duty of an Attorney-General, in deciding whether or not to authorise the prosecution, to acquaint himself with all the relevant facts, including, for instance, the effect which the prosecution, successful or unsuccessful as the case may be, would have upon public morale and order, and with any other considerations affecting public policy.
>
> In order so to inform himself, he may, although I do not think he is obliged to, consult with any of his colleagues in the Government; and indeed, as Lord Simon once said, he would in some cases be a fool if he did not. On the other hand, the assistance of his colleagues is confined to informing him of particular considerations which might affect his own decision, and does not consist, and must not consist, in telling him what that decision ought to be. The responsibility for the eventual decision rests with the Attorney-General, and he is not to be put, and is not put, under pressure by his colleagues in the matter. (Hansard HC Debs 29 January 1951: columns 683–4)

As soon as the above statement was delivered, it attracted support from the Opposition Front Bench and, more particularly, from Lionel Heald, the then Conservative Shadow Attorney General (who succeeded Mr Shawcross as Attorney General later in the same year). Mr Heald described the statement as 'one which will commend itself to the House … and commends itself very much to those who, like myself, have the privilege of belonging to the same great profession as he [Mr Shawcross] does' (Hansard HC Debs 29 January 1951: column 688).

More to the point, the Shawcross statement not only influenced the thinking of Lord Wilberforce in *Gouriet* but also the thinking of other judges in subsequent cases. Examples include Lord Bingham (see, for instance, *R (Corner House*

Research & Others) v The Serious Fraud Office [2008] UKHL 60) and Lord Judge, the Lord Chief Justice from 2008 until 2013, who in 2009 described the Shawcross statement as having been 'supported by Attorneys General ever since [1951]' (*R (on the application of Purdy) v Director of Public Prosecutions & Ors* [2009] EWCA Civ 92).

It follows that the functions of the Attorney General as guardian of the public interest are distinguishable from his separate functions within the executive branch of government as a legal adviser and as a Minister of the Crown. This is the inescapable conclusion one may draw from two cases which reached the Appellate Committee of the House of Lords.

In one of these, dating back to 1974, Lord Diplock referred to the Attorney General in terms which confirm that, in certain circumstances when acting in the public interest, he must shake off his cloak as a member of the executive branch of government:

> He is the appropriate public officer to represent the public interest in the administration of justice. In doing so he acts in constitutional theory on behalf of the Crown, as do Her Majesty's judges themselves; but he acts on behalf of the Crown as 'the fountain of justice' and not in the exercise of its executive functions (*Attorney General v Times Newspapers* [1974] AC 273: 311).

The other case is more recent, for it dates back to 2004 (*R v H and C* [2004] UKHL 3). This case focused on whether or not it was fair for the Attorney General, acting in the public interest, to appoint Special Counsel on behalf of defendants in certain criminal cases. In the Appellate Committee of the House of Lords, five Law Lords, presided by Lord Bingham of Cornhill, concluded that the appointment process was fair. In so doing, the Law Lords shed fresh light on the public interest functions of the Attorney General and the necessity for him, when exercising these functions, to operate outside the framework of the executive branch of government:

> It is very well-established that when exercising a range of functions the Attorney General acts not as a minister of the Crown (although he is of course such) and not as the public officer with overall responsibility for the conduct of prosecutions, but as an independent, unpartisan guardian of the public interest in the administration of justice: see *Halsbury's Laws of England*, 4th ed (1995), vol 44(1), para 1344; Edwards, *The Law Officers of the Crown*, 1964, pp ix, 286, 301–302. It is in that capacity alone that he approves the list of counsel judged suitable to act as special advocates or, now, special counsel, as when, at the invitation of a court, he appoints an *amicus curiae*. Counsel roundly acknowledged the complete integrity shown by successive holders of the office in exercising this role, and no plausible alternative procedure was suggested. It would perhaps allay any conceivable ground of doubt, however ill-founded, if the Attorney General were to seek external approval of his list of eligible advocates by an appropriate professional body or bodies, but such approval is

> not in current circumstances essential to the acceptability of the procedure (*R v H and C* [2004] UKHL 3: [46]).

All of which highlights one of the central themes of this chapter. In view of the functions exercised by the Attorney General, it is of the utmost importance that the holder of the office should be a professional person of integrity who is dedicated to the rule of law and is in possession of the requisite intellectual strength to grapple with the complexities associated with an historic office nestling at the crossroads between politics, the public interest, the administration of justice and the law.

The Attorney General and the Separation of Powers

It is obvious from the preceding analysis that the office of Attorney General is manifestly difficult to reconcile with the separation of powers doctrine. To illustrate this point still further, one may refer to the extraordinary events of 16 October 2012 when the Attorney General exercised his statutory power to issue a certificate and accompanying statement of reasons under the *Freedom of Information Act 2000* (UK) and the *Environmental Information Regulations 2004* (UK) (Grieve 2012b). This certificate, also known as an 'executive override', vetoed an earlier judgment of the Upper Tribunal made on 18 September 2012, which had authorised the publication of certain correspondence between the Prince of Wales and Ministers in seven Whitehall departments (*Evans v Information Commissioner and Seven Government Departments* [2012] UKUT 313 (AAC)). In other words, the Attorney General intervened in the judicial process and effectively negated a judicial decision. Not surprisingly, perhaps, this outcome provoked a judicial review. In July 2013, the High Court dismissed the claim and thereby upheld the legality of the Attorney General's decision. Even so, Lord Judge, the then Lord Chief Justice, grasped the opportunity to comment upon the exceptional state of affairs generated by the *Freedom of Information Act*:

> The possibility that a minister of the Crown may lawfully override the decision of a superior court of record involves what appears to be a constitutional aberration. The problem is inherent in the statutory override or veto vested in ministers and the Attorney General by s.53 of the Freedom of Information Act ... It is an understatement to describe the situation as unusual. Indeed the researches of counsel suggest that it is a unique situation and that similar statutory arrangements cannot be found elsewhere in this jurisdiction. ... It is fundamental to the constitutional separation of powers, the independence of the judiciary, and the rule of law itself that, although judicial decisions may be reversed by legislation (but very rarely with retrospective effect) ministers are bound by and cannot override judicial decisions: in our constitution that power is vested in Parliament. If ever the Government or any minister in the Cabinet could, without more, but in particular because of dissatisfaction with a

> judicial decision, not merely ignore it, but nullify it, the elementary entitlement of the citizen to *effective* recourse to independent courts would be extinguished (*R (Evans) v HM Attorney General* [2013] EWHC 1960 (Admin): [2], [9] and [12]).

Lord Judge reconciled the 'executive override' established by the *Freedom of Information Act* with the separation of powers by clarifying that 'the ministerial override will be ineffective unless reasonable grounds for its exercise are identified … laid before Parliament for scrutiny and, if appropriate, [for] parliamentary action. … More important, perhaps, is that the override decision of the minister is not final. The exercise of the override is itself subject to judicial scrutiny'.

The convoluted constitutional arrangements described by Lord Judge bring to mind the memorable observation of another judge, Lord Mustill, in a different context. Lord Mustill depicted the United Kingdom as having a 'peculiarly British concept of the separation of powers' (*R v Home Secretary, ex parte Fire Brigades Union* [1955] AC 513: 567).

Checks and Balances

All of which underlines that the Attorney General is subject to constitutional checks and balances. As indicated above, his decisions – and those of the bodies he superintends – may be amenable to judicial review in the courts.[17] Besides, the Attorney General is accountable to Parliament, of which he is a member, for the exercise of his functions and the decisions of the bodies he superintends. Indeed, such accountability is widely regarded as a virtue of the constitutional arrangements of the United Kingdom and as part of the rationale for maintaining the current 'multi-hatted' status of the Attorney General.

The primary argument in favour of the *status quo* was eloquently expressed by the late Lord Lyell of Markyate, a former Attorney General,[18] in February 2007, following the controversy sparked by the BAE Systems affair and the accompanying calls for the office of Attorney General to be reformed:

> A great strength of our constitution is that it is pyramidal in shape and that in the end, everything can be held to account in Parliament. That obviously does not apply to judgments that the Law Lords reach in their wisdom – until Parliament changes the law, that stands; but the question of the prosecuting authorities and the way that they are superintended by the Attorney-General … most certainly should involve parliamentary accountability. … My fundamental point is, as I

17 This is not the place to explore this convoluted topic which has been subject of scholarly inquiry by others. See, for instance, Mba 2010.

18 The late Lord Lyell served as Solicitor General from 1987 until 1992 and as Attorney General from 1992 until 1997.

> say, that these matters can and should be answered in Parliament. The notion that you should pass the role of the Attorney-General off to some public official, be it the individual directors – the director of the Serious Fraud Office or the Director of Public Prosecutions – or some other public official, does not fit with our parliamentary system. It would reduce our accountability and the strength of our democracy, and we should resist that (Hansard HL Debs 1 February 2007: columns 343–5).

Be that as it may, the Attorney General is shielded from parliamentary scrutiny in at least two material respects.

First, in view of the confidential nature of his advisory functions and the principles of the lawyer–client relationship, a significant constitutional convention has arisen. Under this convention, the legal advice of the Attorney General may not be disclosed to Parliament, save in exceptional circumstances. The convention also encompasses the principle that Parliament is not even entitled to know whether or not the Attorney General has given legal advice in relation to a particular matter. The convention has now been supplemented by s 35 of the *Freedom of Information Act 2000* and by the non-statutory *Ministerial Code*.[19]

Secondly, even though select committees – such as the Justice Select Committee – may question the Attorney General from time to time, the Attorney General is not scrutinised by a designated Select Committee of the House of Commons specifically tasked with overseeing his work and holding him and the Attorney General's Office to account. By contrast, the Secretary of State for Justice (i.e. the Lord Chancellor) is accountable to the Justice Select Committee and other Cabinet Ministers are held to account in a similar way; even the Prime Minister is accountable to a designated parliamentary committee, namely the Liaison Committee of the House of Commons. This lacuna was recognised by the 2007 Consultation Paper (Scotland 2007: para 1.36, 10):

> Although no Select Committee is currently dedicated specifically to scrutinising the work of the Attorney General's Office, Attorneys General have regularly appeared before Committees of both Houses. In the case of a particular prosecution decision involving sensitive questions of intelligence and national security, the former Attorney General, Lord Goldsmith, appeared before the Intelligence and Security Committee to explain the context of the decision and the national security issues.

There is no good reason why the Attorney General should not be held to account by a designated committee of Parliament. The fact that the Attorney General is not a full member of the Cabinet is not a sufficiently good excuse. In view of the significance of his work, it is surely high time that Parliament gave serious

19 The convention is considered in *HM Treasury v The Information Commissioner* [2009] EWHC 1811 (Admin); Kyriakides 2003; Stern 2012.

consideration to the establishment of such a committee. If the House of Commons does not wish – or does not have among its members the necessary expertise – to establish and maintain such a committee, perhaps the House of Lords may assume this responsibility. Such a committee could resemble the House of Lords Constitution Committee which was founded in 2001 to investigate broad constitutional issues and to examine all Public Bills for any constitutional implications. If established, such a committee would result in more regular, consistent and focused scrutiny of the Attorney General, while simultaneously enhancing his democratic accountability and elevating his status in the parliamentary as well as the public consciousness.

The Attorney General and the Legal Profession

In addition to his various functions outlined above, the Attorney General has certain duties or roles within the legal profession. In addition to being a Queen's Counsel and a member of the Bar Council, the Attorney General is the titular *ex officio* head of the Bar. The present incumbent, Dominic Grieve, also remains listed as a member of his chambers, Temple Garden Chambers, and he serves as a Bencher of his Inn, Middle Temple. All of which no doubt reminds Mr Grieve that he remains a practising barrister and, thus, a full member of the legal profession.

Interestingly enough, two recent holders of the office of Solicitor General – Harriet Harman (who was in the post from 2001 until 2005) and Mike O'Brien (who was the Solicitor General from 2005 until 2007) – were appointed from the ranks of solicitors, although, upon their appointment, they were conferred with the title of Queen's Counsel. Ironically, they became the first two solicitors to hold the office of Solicitor General since the establishment of the Law Society of England and Wales in 1825. The elevation of Harman and O'Brien reflected the enhanced status of solicitors, who, in recent years, have been eligible to become Solicitor-Advocates, Queen's Counsel and judges.[20]

Harman was also the first woman to become a Law Officer; following in her footsteps as Law Officers have been Baroness Scotland and Vera Baird (the Attorney General and Solicitor General from 2007 until 2010, respectively). All of which demonstrates that even the ancient offices held by the principal Law Officers are capable of reflecting changes in the legal profession and the society of which that honourable profession forms an integral part.

20 Indeed, in 2009, Lord Collins of Mapesbury became the first solicitor to become a Lord of Appeal in Ordinary and, thereafter, a founding Justice of the Supreme Court; he had previously been one of the first two solicitors to become a Queen's Counsel and the first solicitor to be appointed to the High Court (Chancery Division).

Conclusions

As already noted, the consultation exercise triggered by the 2007 Consultation Paper did not spawn any noticeable changes to the office of Attorney General. As such, the persuasive arguments advanced by the advocates of reform largely came to nothing. The prevailing view is that expressed by Oliver Heald (2012), the Solicitor General at the time of writing:

> The current arrangement, as awkward as it may look on paper, like so many of the eccentricities in our constitution, works because it puts at the heart of Government an independent lawyer who is trusted by those he advises because he is one of them.

Even so, the tensions inherent in the offices held by the principal Law Officers remain in place.

Interestingly enough, in *A Guide to Ethical Issues for Government Lawyers* (Law Society of New South Wales 2010: 10) ('the Guide'), the Law Society of New South Wales reminds government lawyers to bear in mind that:

> Government, like anyone else, needs honest, competent legal advice and legal officers should give the best they can, according to their individual knowledge and experience.

The Guide, incidentally, includes a comment, born no doubt from bitter experience, from an unnamed government lawyer:

> There are imperatives and I think that we are aware of them and we do our best to comply but the problems arise where the legal advice doesn't accord with what they [the client agency] want, and my view is that we give the legal advice and they can accept or reject it (Law Society of New South Wales 2010: 10).

The Guide goes on to cite the Australian High Court case of *Waterford v Commonwealth* (1987) 163 CLR 54 (at 70) in which Brennan J stated that legal officers should be:

> competent, in order that the legal advice be sound and the conduct of the litigation be efficient; [and] independent, in order that the personal loyalties, duties or interests of the adviser should not influence the legal advice which he gives or the fairness of his conduct of the litigation on behalf of his client.

The above observations ought to be taken into account by every newly appointed Attorney General and, indeed, every newly appointed in-house lawyer. After all, the attributes of a good Attorney General are the same as those of any good lawyer, namely integrity, independence of mind and intellectual strength, coupled with moral courage, political awareness and a mind-set focused on helping clients to achieve their objectives in a lawful – and ethical – manner.

In practice, this means that if the Prime Minister or any other Minister is bent on breaking the law – be it domestic law or international law – the Attorney General must not blithely stand aside. He must do all that he reasonably can to impede the Minister concerned and prevent the unlawful course of action. The rule of law demands no less, even if this has an adverse effect on the ministerial career prospects of the Attorney General or the reputation of the party of which he may be a member.

One can do little better than quote from Lord Goldsmith, in a confidential (but now declassified) memo of 3 February 2003 which he sent, in his capacity as the then Attorney General, to Jack Straw, the then Foreign Secretary (Goldsmith 2003b) and a fellow lawyer:

> It is important for the Government that its lawyers give advice which they honestly consider to be correct: that is what they are there for. I regularly see Government lawyers at all levels and I make a practice of emphasising to them that they should give the advice which they believe in, not the advice which they think others want to hear. To do otherwise would undermine their function as a legal adviser in giving independent, objective and impartial advice. This is not to say, of course, that lawyers should not be positive and constructive in helping the Government achieve its policy objectives through lawful means and [be] open-minded in considering other points of view. But if a Government legal adviser genuinely believes that a course of action would be unlawful, then it is his or her right and duty to say so. I support this right regardless of whether I agree with the substance of the advice which has been given.[21]

What overarches all of the attributes that ought to be possessed by a government legal adviser is an unequivocal commitment to the rule of law. In the words of Baroness Scotland (Scotland 2009): 'The Attorney's functions are varied and miscellaneous. But the fundamental coherent principle governing and directing them is the rule of law'. That principle, it is submitted, ought to govern and direct the functions of all lawyers, be they working within or outside government. For that to happen, however, all lawyers must be steeped in the values associated with the rule of law and all must possess the integrity necessary to wrestle the complexities associated with the law and the world we inhabit. In turn, that places an onerous duty on those of us who are privileged to teach law. After all, it is the teachers of law who, in common with others, play a central part in sculpting the mind-set of the lawyers of tomorrow.

---

21 Lord Goldsmith ventured some similar thoughts in Parliament in December 2005 although he added that the Attorney General 'should be prepared to give unwelcome advice and to stand firm where that is called for'. After all, 'legal advice is not a matter for collective responsibility'. Hansard HL Debs 5 December 2005: columns 1401–2.

References

Bingham, T. 2010. *The Rule of Law*. London: Penguin.

Cabinet Office. 2010. *Ministerial Code*. London.

Edwards, J.Ll.J. 1964. *The Law Officers of the Crown: A Study of the offices of Attorney-General and Solicitor-General of England with an Account of the Office of the Director of Public Prosecutions of England.* London: Sweet & Maxwell.

Garnier, E. 2010. *Speech to the Constitutional and Administrative Law Bar Association.* 17 July [Online]. Available at: www.attorneygeneral.gov.uk/NewsCentre/Speeches/Pages/SolicitorGeneralspeechtotheALBAsummerconference.aspx [accessed: 12 September 2012].

Goldsmith, Lord. 2003a. *Iraq Resolution 1441*. 7 March 2003 [Online]. Available at: http://http://webarchive.nationalarchives.gov.uk and http://www.cabinetoffice.gov.uk/media/cabinetoffice/corp/assets/foi/disclosure_stmnt.pdf [accessed: 24 October 2012].

Goldsmith, Lord. 2003b. *Memo from the Attorney General to the Foreign Secretary*. 3 January 2003 [Online]. Available at: http://www.iraqinquiry.org.uk/media/43514/doc_2010_01_26_11_04_38_615.pdf [accessed: 28 October 2012].

Grieve, D. 2012a. The Role of UK Law as a Model for Combating Human Trafficking and Slavery. Speech delivered to the City Law School. London, 13 March 2012 [Online]. Available at: http://www.attorneygeneral.gov.uk/NewsCentre/Speeches/Pages/AttorneyGeneralspechatCityUniversityonhumantrafficking.aspx [accessed: 17 July 2012].

Grieve, D. 2012b. Attorney General vetoes release of Prince of Wales' correspondence. Press Release. 16 October 2012 [Online]. Available at: http://www.attorneygeneral.gov.uk/NewsCentre/Pages/AttorneyGeneralvetoesreleaseofPrinceofWalescorrespondence.aspx [accessed: 28 October 2012].

Hansard. 29 January 1951. *House of Commons Debates*.

Hansard. 11 January 1988. *House of Commons Debates*.

Hansard. 11 July 1988. *House of Commons Debates*.

Hansard. 17 March 2003. *House of Lords Debates*.

Hansard. 18 March 2003. *House of Commons Debates*.

Hansard. 9 March 2004. *House of Commons Debates*.

Hansard. 6 July 2004. *Liaison Committee Minutes of Evidence*.

Hansard. 5 December 2005. *House of Lords Debates*.

Hansard. 14 December 2006. *House of Lords Debates*.

Hansard. 1 February 2007. *House of Lords Debates*.

Harman H. 2001.*The Law Officers: Where Law and Politics Meet*. Paper to the Society for Advanced Legal Studies Annual Dinner. Middle Temple, London,

7 November 2001. Transcript published in *Amicus Curae*. 2001. Volume 38, 25–6.

Hastings, P. 1948. *The Autobiography of Sir Patrick Hastings*. London: Heinemann.

Heald, O. 2012. *The Role of the Law Officers*. Speech to Kent Law School. 18 October 2012 [Online]. Available at: http://www.attorneygeneral.gov.uk/NewsCentre/Speeches/Pages/SolicitorGeneraltheroleofthelawofficers.aspx [accessed: 28 October 2012].

Jones, E. 1969. The Office of Attorney-General. *Cambridge Law Journal*. Volume 27(1), 43–53.

Keeton, G.W. 1949. *A Liberal Attorney-General: Being the Life of Lord Robson of Jesmond (1852–1918) with an Account of the Office of Attorney-General*. London: James Nisbet & Co.

Kyriakides, K.A. 2003. The Advisory Functions of the Attorney General. *Hertfordshire Law Journal*. Volume 1(1), 73–94 [Online]. Available at: https://uhra.herts.ac.uk/dspace/bitstream/2299/2514/1/902833.pdf [accessed: 28 October 2012].

Law Society of New South Wales. 2010. *A Guide to Ethical Issues for Government Lawyers*. Second edition [Online]. Available at: http://www.lawsociety.com.au/idc/groups/public/documents/internetcontent/008727.pdf [accessed: 28 October 2012].

Marston, G. 1988. Armed Intervention in the 1956 Suez Canal Crisis: The Legal Advice Tendered to the British Government. *International and Comparative Law Quarterly*. Volume 37(4), 773–817.

Mba, O. 2010. Review of the Prosecutorial Powers of the Attorney-General in England and Wales and Nigeria: An Imperative of the Rule of Law. *Oxford University Comparative Law Forum* Volume 2 [Online]. Available at: http://ssrn.com/abstract=2056290 or http://dx.doi.org/10.2139/ssrn.2056290 [accessed: 10 August 2012].

Phillips, Lord of Worth Matravers. 2011. *Judicial Independence and Accountability: A View from the Supreme Court*. Paper to the UCL Constitution Unit. 8 February 2011 [Online]. Available at: http://www.supremecourt.gov.uk/docs/speech_110208.pdf [accessed: 12 September 2012].

Scotland, Baroness. 2007. *The Governance of Britain: A Consultation on the Role of the Attorney General*. London: The Stationery Office.

Scotland, Baroness. 2009. *The Rule of Law*. Lecture delivered at the Law Society of Scotland Conference, 8 May 2009 [Online]. Available at: http://www.attorneygeneral.gov.uk/NewsCentre/Speeches/Pages/SolicitorGeneraltheroleofthelawofficers.aspx [accessed: 28 October 2012].

Scott, R. 1995–96. *Report of the Inquiry into the Export of Defence Equipment and Dual-Use Goods to Iraq and Related Prosecutions. HC 115*. London: HMSO.

Shawcross, H. 1995. *Life Sentence: The Memoirs of Hartley Shawcross*. London: Constable.

Stern, R. 2012. *The Law Officers' Convention*. Unpublished LLB thesis, University of Hertfordshire.

The Scottish Government. 2012. *Agreement between the United Kingdom Government and the Scottish Government on a Referendum on Independence for Scotland* [Online]. Available at: http://www.scotland.gov.uk/About/Government/concordats/Referendum-on-independence [accessed: 28 October 2012].

UK Parliament, *Open Parliament Licence* [Online]. Available at: http://www.parliament.uk/site-information/copyright/open-parliament-licence [accessed: 11 September 2011].

Weller, M. 2010. *Iraq and the Use of Force in International Law*. Oxford: Oxford University Press.

Wright, P. and Greengrass, P. 1987. *Spycatcher*. Richmond, Victoria: Heinemann.

Chapter 10

The Advisory Function of the Attorney General in the United States

Harold H. Bruff[1]

The role of the Attorney General of the United States in providing legal advice to the President is broadly similar to that of the Solicitors-General of the Australian Commonwealth and the States in advising their governments. Both nations drew on British precedent in forming their own governments, and the continuing adherence of both to the rule of law certainly demands a law-advising function. Yet the principal structural difference in the governments of the two nations has created important differences between them in how the advising function operates.

The United States Constitution mandates the separation of powers between the legislature and the executive; Australia's combines them in a parliamentary system that produces responsible government. This chapter explores the development of the American model to allow comparison with the Australian one. As in so many other ways, the similarities and differences between our two nations should provide intellectual stimulation for citizens of both and should nourish the bonds of mutual affection.

The constitutional and statutory arrangements that create the United States Attorney General and the Commonwealth Solicitor-General are roughly similar. Article II of the United States Constitution vests the 'executive power' in the President and charges him or her to 'take care that the laws be faithfully executed'. The Attorney General is a statutory officer charged with representing the United States in court and giving legal advice to the President and executive departments. The President nominates the Attorney General subject to confirmation by the Senate. Attorneys General serve indefinite terms at the pleasure of the President. When party control of the White House changes, the Attorney General departs along with the President.

Under s 64 of the Australian Constitution, the Governor-General appoints Ministers. The Attorney-General is a Minister, traditionally a member of the Cabinet, and must be a Member of Parliament. The Second Law Officer, the Solicitor-General, inhabits a statutory office that in modern times is non-political. He or she is appointed by the Governor-General for a term of up to seven years and

---

1 I thank Dr Gabrielle Appleby and Adam Webster of the University of Adelaide Law School for their gracious help in the preparation of this chapter.

is charged with conducting litigation for the government and giving legal advice on questions referred by the Attorney-General (*Law Officers Act 1964* (Cth)).

These rudimentary attributes of the American and Australian governments reveal two differences in the structural nature of the advising function. First, when the Commonwealth Solicitor-General reports to the Attorney-General, he or she is advising an executive officer who is also part of the legislative branch of government. The American Attorney General reports to the President and advises only the executive branch. Second, Australia has depoliticised the advising function of the Solicitor-General in pursuit of the detachment from politics that is essential to preservation of the rule of law. In contrast, the United States Attorney General is a political appointee who must balance the competing demands of law and politics. In the remainder of this chapter, as I describe the evolution of the advising function of this officer, the effects of these two differences from Australia will be apparent.

In the United States, all three branches constantly interpret the Constitution and statutes as they perform their daily tasks. When Congress passes a Bill and sends it to the President for his signature or veto, it is impliedly asserting the Bill's constitutionality. When the President decides to sign or veto the Bill, he makes an independent determination of its constitutionality, meaning and desirability. Subsequently, as executive agencies administer statutes, they do so in light of legal advice about both the statutes and the Constitution. The federal courts routinely decide questions of constitutional and statutory interpretation, and when they do so in a particular case, their opinions bind the other branches. But the courts encounter only a fraction of the legal issues that the government considers, leaving the two political branches to make final determinations of many questions. Therefore, the function of providing legal advice to the executive branch lies near the heart of both the operation and the legitimacy of the United States government.

Ever since 1789, the first year of the Constitution's operation, the President's official legal adviser has been the Attorney General.[2] Modern Americans think of the Attorney General as a central figure in the executive branch, one closely tied to the President as the nation's chief legal officer. Surprisingly, the creation of the office was attended with enough ambiguity that it could have evolved quite differently than it has. Before long, though, some decisions by George Washington placed the Attorney General at the President's side, there to remain.

Although the office of Attorney General is mentioned nowhere in the Constitution or in the records of the Constitutional Convention, it had both colonial and British antecedents. The First Congress, in which many framers of the Constitution sat, performed the task of creating the new federal government. Within months, the *Judiciary Act* of 1789, after organising and empowering the federal courts, created the Attorney General (ch. 20, § 35, 1 Stat. 73, 92–3).[3] From

2 For a good history of the office of Attorney General, see Baker 1992.

3 'And there shall be appointed a meet person, learned in the law, to act as attorney general for the United States, … whose duty it shall be to prosecute and conduct all suits

then until now, the Attorney General has been required to conduct litigation for the United States in federal court and to 'give his advice and opinion upon questions of law when required by the President of the United States' (28 U.S.C. § 511) or by the heads of the executive departments.[4]

Notwithstanding this impressive statutory charge, early Attorneys General were part-time officers, with no staff of their own and little prestige. It was not even clear whether they were exclusively executive officers or legal officers for the entire government, who would report in one way or another to all three branches. The statutory duty to conduct federal litigation created a relationship with the courts, but one that was naturally constrained by the nature of the adversary process. Early Attorneys General also appeared to feel some direct responsibility to Congress. They routinely responded to requests for legal advice from members of Congress, although the statutes did not require them to do so. That practice stopped in the 1820s in the administration of President James Monroe and has never resumed, thus clarifying the Attorney General's reporting responsibilities (Wirt 1820 in Powell 1999: 12–13).[5]

In American separation of powers law, two fundamental ways to determine which branch an officer serves are to identify who appoints and who can remove the officer (Bruff 2006). The *Judiciary Act* did not say who would appoint the Attorney General, and a draft of the Bill that became the Act would have assigned appointment authority to the Supreme Court. This provision was deleted for reasons that are lost to history, leaving the identity of the appointing authority unspecified in the Act. If the courts had retained the authority to appoint the Attorney General, it is very unlikely that this officer would ever have become an intimate legal adviser to Presidents.

Modern conceptions of separation of powers define the principal functions of the Attorney General as executive activities in the constitutional sense. Therefore, an officer who performs those functions must be appointed by the President, with confirmation by the Senate.[6] This conclusion results from a process of elimination.

---

in the Supreme Court in which the United States shall be concerned, and to give his advice and opinion upon all questions of law when required by the President of the United States, or when requested by the heads of any of the departments, touching any matters that may concern their departments … .'

4 28 U.S.C. § 512 provides: 'The head of an executive department may require the opinion of the Attorney General on questions of law arising in the administration of his department'.

5 Attorneys General do routinely testify before congressional committees, explaining their view of the law as they have presented it to their clients in the executive branch. Congress employs its own lawyers to advise it directly.

6 The Appointments Clause of the Constitution, art. II, §2, provides that the President 'shall nominate, and by and with the advice and consent of the senate, shall appoint ambassadors, other public ministers and consuls, judges of the supreme court, and all other officers of the United States, whose appointments are not herein otherwise provided for, and which shall be established by law. But the Congress may by law vest the appointment

Congress may not appoint those who execute the laws, as Attorneys General do when they decide what litigation to pursue and how federal law should be interpreted by executive officers. Nor may the courts appoint 'principal' officers with responsibilities as broad as those of the Attorney General (*Morrison v Olson* (1988) 487 U.S. 654). That leaves the President, as now seems obvious to most observers (although much that seems obvious now did not seem so at the founding).

It does seem clear that the First Congress did not envision the Attorney General as an instrument of the President's will, as the Secretaries of State and War were to be. In 1789, no such clear subordination to the President attended the formation of departments, such as the Treasury, that were not related to the President's independent constitutional authority relating to foreign affairs and war. The Attorney General seemed an afterthought, tucked in at the end of the *Judiciary Act* and lacking any department to run. (The Department of Justice would not be created until 1870, in the aftermath of the Civil War.) The brief statutory provision in the *Judiciary Act* neither instructed the Attorney General to take orders from the President nor addressed the removal issue. Did Congress intend that legal advice to the President and the heads of departments be provided from outside the direct executive chain of command, to foster its objectivity? We cannot know. Over time, this question has become obscured as the Attorney General has developed a direct relationship with the President. That process began – haltingly – in the Washington administration.

As the first President, George Washington was acutely aware that his actions would form enduring precedents about the conduct of his office. Happily for our nation's history, his judgment and administrative instincts were exceptionally sound. He soon asserted the power to appoint the Attorney General by nominating Edmund Randolph to the office; the Senate acquiesced by confirming him. Ever since, the Attorney General has been treated as a principal executive officer to be nominated and confirmed in accordance with Article II of the Constitution.

For the first Attorney General, Washington had selected his personal attorney, who had been advising him without fee. The two men had been close ever since Randolph was on Washington's staff during the Revolutionary War. The selection of Randolph began a practice that has continued to the present: Presidents ordinarily choose Attorneys General from among their close personal and political supporters, obtaining the benefits of loyalty at the cost of bypassing the legal *éminences grises* who are always available. This practice has tended to increase the likelihood that Presidents will rely on the advice of their Attorneys General and to diminish the likelihood that the advice will be dispassionate. (Especially in the wake of scandal, though, nomination of someone known for his or her independence may be necessary.)

An immediate question was whether the Attorney General would be the President's exclusive legal adviser. Within the first administration, Randolph was

of such inferior officers, as they think proper, in the president alone, in the courts of law, or in the heads of departments'.

outshone by the two brightest stars, Alexander Hamilton and Thomas Jefferson. In Washington's first term, the concept of a Cabinet to provide group advice to the President was just forming. Attorney General Randolph did not attend these meetings until 1792: he was not only below the salt but out of the room. For routine issues, Washington usually dealt directly with the head of each department on subjects relating to it, asking the views of the secretary and then deciding. Hence, Randolph could expect legal issues to flow to him, and usually they did. Because Washington was 'not a man of quick, intuitive judgments', his 'invariable practice' was to ask the opinions of those he trusted (Miller 1960: 58–9).

On issues of great importance, Washington, like most of his successors, was prepared to seek the best advice he could get without worrying about departmental protocol, for the *Judiciary Act* did not obligate the President to ask the Attorney General's advice; it just told the latter to provide it if requested. This fact has led to an enduring delicacy in relationships between Presidents and their Attorneys General. The Cabinet is never short of able and aggressive lawyers who head other departments and who are quite ready to provide legal analysis supporting presidential initiatives if the Attorney General should resist. The resulting pressure on the Attorney General to be supportive is a constant in American government.

The two greatest legal issues of the Washington administration, the constitutionality of a national bank and of a proclamation of neutrality in the war between Britain and France, illustrate the competition for advice-giving. For both, the President outlined the issues to his Cabinet and patiently elicited and considered the competing arguments. Then Washington decided each of the controversies in favour of Hamilton's position (and in line with his own natural inclinations), neither excluding nor relying on Randolph (White 1948: 33).[7]

These early episodes established two fundamental attributes of legal decision-making within the executive branch. First, the President – not the Attorney General – is the 'interpreter in chief'. This power flows from the President's constitutional duty faithfully to execute the laws. Presidents have always treated this responsibility as personal to them. They may rely on advice from others, but the constitutional and political accountability remains in their hands. Second, the Attorney General has never enjoyed a monopoly on providing legal advice to the President. Not surprisingly, Attorneys General sometimes claim such a monopoly – usually when it appears that the President is listening to someone else.

Thomas Jefferson's presidency established another fundamental attribute of legal decision-making within the executive branch: the principle of 'departmentalism', that each branch is free to interpret the law within its own assigned responsibilities. The issue arose in the early nineteenth century, in the wake of America's 'quasi-war' with France. An armed French ship, the *Schooner Peggy*, was captured by an American privateer and claimed as a prize under a federal statute that awarded part of the value of such a ship to the captors. During the litigation to condemn

7 White stated that Washington 'consulted Hamilton and Jefferson on constitutional issues as regularly as he did the Attorney General'.

the ship and distribute the award, a treaty settled outstanding differences between the United States and France. The Secretary of State asked Attorney General Levi Lincoln whether the treaty required restoration of the ship to its owners. While litigation of this question was pending in the Supreme Court, Lincoln advised the Secretary of State that the capture had become final before the effective date of the treaty (1802a: 114).

A few days later, the Court in *United States v Schooner Peggy* (1801) 5 U.S. (1 Cranch) 103 ruled to the contrary. Lincoln promptly wrote another opinion to the Secretary (1802b: 119). He began by making it clear that he disagreed with the Court's legal reasoning. Conceding that the Court's decision was binding in the particular case, Lincoln denied it any broader effect, declaring that in other cases executive officers must obey 'their own convictions of the meaning of the laws and constitution of the United States, and their oaths to support them'. President Jefferson emphatically agreed with this principle of independent interpretation.[8] So have his successors, as we shall see.

When Jefferson's protégé James Monroe later became President, he nominated an Attorney General who transformed the office. William Wirt was a distinguished Supreme Court advocate who served for 12 years beginning in 1817, the longest tenure to date. Upon his arrival, Wirt was astonished to discover that the office had no system of records whatever (White 1951: 336–8). How could he know whether any opinion he might give was consistent with what his predecessors had said? Wirt promptly set up an opinion book and a letter book, and Attorneys General have had a continuous body of precedent to draw on ever since. Wirt understood that whether or not one regards precedent within the executive as normatively binding in the way that judges respect the precedents of their own and other courts, consistency is a virtue. Moreover, past executive advisers may have found wise answers to problems. Once records were kept, it was natural to treat them as precedents having at least some binding effect. Now the Attorney General headed a (small) bureaucracy and was no longer an essentially private lawyer for the executive, one who might care little for what predecessors in that role had done.

Andrew Jackson's presidency brought departmentalism to new prominence when he vetoed a Bill to reauthorise the Bank of the United States. Congress had

---

8 In a letter to Abigail Adams (11 September 1804) Jefferson wrote: 'You seem to think it devolved on the judges to decide on the validity of the sedition law. But nothing in the Constitution has given them a right to decide for the Executive, more than to the Executive to decide for them. Both magistracies are equally independent in the sphere of action assigned to them. The judges, believing the law constitutional, had a right to pass a sentence of fine or imprisonment; because that power was placed in their hands by the Constitution. But the Executive, believing the law to be unconstitutional, was bound to remit the execution of it; because that power has been confided to him by the Constitution. That instrument meant that its co-ordinate branches should be checks on each other. But the opinion which gives to the judges the right to decide what laws are constitutional, and what not, not only for themselves in their own sphere of action, but for the Legislature & executive also, in their spheres, would make the judiciary a despotic branch' (1904: 310).

repeatedly asserted the constitutionality of the Bank by passing Bills to authorise it. Presidents including Washington had agreed by signing the Bills; the Supreme Court had upheld it in a landmark decision in *McCulloch v Maryland* (1819) 17 U.S. (4 Wheat) 316. None of this mattered to the always-wilful Jackson, who thought the Bank was not within the legislative powers of Congress. His veto message has become a famous declaration of presidential independence:

> The Congress, the Executive, and the Court must each for itself be guided by its own opinion of the Constitution. Each public officer who takes an oath to support the Constitution swears that he will support it as he understands it, and not as it is understood by others. It is as much the duty of the House of Representatives, of the Senate, and of the President to decide upon the constitutionality of any bill or resolution which may be presented to them for passage or approval as it is for the supreme judges when it may be brought before them for judicial decision. The opinion of the judges has no more authority over Congress than the opinion of Congress has over the judges, and on that point the President is independent of both (Richardson 1897: 1139).

President Jackson then decided to exterminate the Bank by removing federal deposits from it (Remini 1967). His Attorney General, Roger Taney, supported the legality of this step under the applicable statute; the Treasury Secretary, William Duane, disagreed. Jackson removed Duane, replaced him with Taney, and effected the removal. Taney's position regarding the legal issue was plausible, as was Jackson's endorsement of it. Taney eventually received a reward for his loyalty by becoming Chief Justice of the Supreme Court. Throughout the Bank controversy, Jackson had made his own legal decisions, seeking support as needed from his Attorney General.

The most spectacular examples of a President's willingness to make his own legal determinations, without relying on the Attorney General for more than a legal brief to offer as after-the-fact justification, occurred when Abraham Lincoln suspended the writ of habeas corpus and freed the slaves during the Civil War. It may have mattered that Lincoln himself was a superb lawyer with complete confidence in his judgments. Yet, as we have seen, Presidents without legal training (such as Washington and Jackson) had been ready to decide legal issues on their own responsibility.

Early in the Civil War, Confederate forces threatened to cut off rail access to the national capital. Lincoln suspended habeas corpus along the rail lines into Washington and later more widely. Article I, § 9 of the Constitution provides that the writ may not be suspended except in cases of invasion or rebellion, but does not say who suspends it. The suspension provision is, however, located in the same Article where the powers of Congress reside. Lincoln's Attorney General, Edward Bates, responded to the President's request for a legal opinion with an answer that did not encourage presidential suspension (Rehnquist 1998). Lincoln decided to go ahead anyway, and Bates wrote another opinion supporting the action once it had occurred. Lincoln subsequently sought and received congressional ratification for the suspension, placing it on a (somewhat) sounder legal footing.

The Emancipation Proclamation was Lincoln's own decision, made without consulting the Cabinet or the Attorney General but with their support once he announced that he would issue it. Lincoln viewed the Proclamation as a constitutional military order that was necessary to suppress the rebellion (hence, it did not apply to areas not under Confederate control) (Guelzo 2004). The Proclamation worked – it did undermine the Southern war effort, and it began the slaves' long march toward freedom. Today, its iconic stature lies somewhere on the boundary between law and morality. Lincoln knew that subordinate legal advisers could not answer the deepest questions about its justification. The President would answer for that, to the nation and to history.

It was not until the administration of Franklin D. Roosevelt that the complement of legal advisers to the President neared completion. During his long tenure as President, 'FDR' transformed the executive branch and the presidency, bringing them fully into the modern age (Neustadt 1990). Instead of the small cadre of direct advisers that had formerly sufficed for Presidents, there would henceforth be an 'institutional presidency' that has grown ever since. These bureaucratic developments have somewhat altered the nature of the President's relationships with his legal advisers.

By Roosevelt's time, the Attorney General had become the head of a major and complex executive department. Since 1870, the Attorney General has headed the Department of Justice and has gradually acquired various major administrative responsibilities, for example to investigate crimes (the Federal Bureau of Investigation, FBI) and to administer the federal prisons.[9] Within this complex bureaucracy, the original functions of litigating and advising have found homes. Hence, the functions of the United States Attorney General eventually evolved to become similar to those of the Commonwealth Attorney-General in Australia.

The original duty of the Attorney General to conduct litigation for the United States in the Supreme Court grew into a general supervisory responsibility for most government litigation in all of the federal courts. One of the Attorney General's principal subordinates, the Solicitor General, supervises a professional staff that conducts this part of the department's duties. Because the Office of the Solicitor General controls litigation for the Cabinet departments, the Department of Justice has substantial power to mould federal constitutional and statutory law by deciding what cases to bring and what arguments to make. (Some of the independent regulatory commissions are not subject to this authority.)

The Solicitor General is formally a political appointee, nominated by the President and confirmed by the Senate. Nonetheless, the Solicitor's close relationship with the Supreme Court, stemming from his or her managerial responsibility for federal litigation, has created a tradition of substantial informal

---

9 The Department of Justice was created by the *Act of June 2, 1870*, ch. 150, 16 Stat. 162.

independence within the Department for the Solicitor, who is sometimes called the 'tenth justice' (Caplan 1987).

In the twentieth century, the need became apparent to delegate routine advice-giving to subordinate officers within the Department of Justice. In 1933, Congress created what is now the Office of Legal Counsel (OLC), headed by an Assistant Attorney General, to write most formal opinions to the President and other executive officers (Kmiec 1993: 337). The Assistant is a political appointee, nominated by the President, confirmed by the Senate and aided by a set of political and (at times) career deputies and a staff of line attorneys that brings the full complement of the office to about 20 lawyers. As the home of some very able career lawyers and the repository of extensive records of advice given over the years, the office has a strong institutional memory.

Career attorneys in the OLC are especially apt to see themselves as protectors of the long-term interests of the executive branch, whatever the desires of its temporary leaders (Merrill 1998: 83). The political appointees in the OLC may encounter a challenge from the line attorneys when unusual claims of executive power emerge from the White House. For example, President Richard Nixon's political advisers urged him to make sweeping claims of constitutional power to 'impound' federal funds (that is, to refuse to spend them), whether or not Congress had mandated the expenditures. After the OLC refused to accede to this untenable position, Nixon fired Assistant Attorney General Roger Cramton and found a successor who would support his claims (Cramton 1990: 165). (Nevertheless, the department's career attorneys continued a policy of quiet resistance by leaving these arguments out of briefs they filed.) The OLC lost the battle and won the war. Nixon's impoundment claims collapsed, along with his presidency, and have hardly been heard from since.

The modern Attorney General has a primary competitor for primacy in providing legal advice to the President. Since World War II, the office of White House Counsel has existed as part of the President's immediate staff, within steps of the Oval Office (Rabkin 1993: 63). Franklin Roosevelt created the position in his characteristic organisational style of proliferating advisers with overlapping portfolios, allowing him to dominate them all. Not all of his successors have possessed his bureaucratic skills, but all of them have inherited the structural competition between legal advisers. The opportunity for an aggressive Counsel to displace the Attorney General is always present, although the Counsel has never enjoyed formal primacy.

Compared to the Attorney General, the Counsel exists in the shadows. He or she is appointed by the President without confirmation by the Senate, is traditionally immune from compelled congressional testimony, has no statutory duties, maintains few records and has a staff of about a dozen lawyers that changes completely with each new administration. The existence of this 'in-house' lawyer's office reduces the President's dependence on the Attorney General and, as FDR surely intended, renders the President more independent from both of his primary lawyers, since he can play them off against each other.

A gifted Attorney General can guide even a headstrong President toward acceptable legal conclusions. Robert Jackson was FDR's Attorney General in the stormy period prior to World War II (and later an eminent Supreme Court Justice). A story from Jackson's memoir illustrates his method of nudging the President toward a correct legal outcome. Jackson reported that President Roosevelt 'did not require [his subordinates] to do things that in their opinions they ought not to do'. An example was a 1938 request of the German government, after the burning of the airship *Hindenburg*, for helium (which is not flammable). The statute 'was very clear. The approval of the Secretary of the Interior was indispensable to any exportation of helium. I so advised the President'. Yet Interior Secretary Harold Ickes was adamantly opposed to any export to the Nazis, while the State Department favoured it. FDR put Jackson on the spot:

> [T]he President turned to me and said, 'Now what can I do about this?' The situation was rather tense … . I said, 'Well, Mr. President, I don't see that you can do anything about helium unless you do something about your Secretary of Interior first. As long as you have such a stubborn one, I don't see how you can transfer helium under the statute'. The President laughed heartily, as did all the rest, but that ended the matter – the President would not give a preemptory order to his Secretary that went against the latter's judgment.

Jackson had prevailed; no helium was sent (Jackson 2003: 116–17).

In a more prominent episode during the dark days of 1940, Jackson worked closely with his President in formulating an opinion supporting the exchange of some aged American destroyers for British bases in the Western Hemisphere. A series of neutrality statutes enacted by Congress made the legality of the plan suspect. For some technical reasons, Jackson was not willing to approve a sale or gift of the destroyers but concluded that their exchange for defence facilities would not contravene the statutes. He and the President collaborated on an Attorney General opinion that would be released as the public explanation for the deal. The exchange was successful, both in the limited sense that it was consummated and in the broader sense that it was one of the steps that induced Congress and American public opinion to abandon isolationism and begin steps toward full support of the Allies.

At times, a creative search for alternative ways to meet a President's desires cannot yield success, and it becomes the Attorney General's unhappy task to tell a President that a proposed action is simply illegal. An incident in the aftermath of the terror attacks of September 11, 2001, reveals the resultant tensions (Bruff 2009: ch 9). As the 'war on terror' began, the administration of George W. Bush stepped up electronic surveillance in a desperate attempt to discover and foil new terror attacks. Presidents since FDR had claimed constitutional authority to conduct such surveillance. After some notorious abuses of this power during the Vietnam War, Congress had enacted a statute providing for the issuance of secret warrants to authorise the surveillance. Finding the statutory process too cumbersome for the rapidly unfolding events of the terror war, the Bush administration decided to initiate a secret surveillance programme that bypassed the statute. Administration lawyers initially approved the programme on an emergency basis, subject to frequent reapproval.

As time went by, concern about the legality of the programme grew within the Justice Department. When one of the periodic reapprovals loomed, Attorney General John Ashcroft and his staff concluded that it was no longer possible to certify the programme. At this sensitive juncture, the Attorney General fell seriously ill and repaired to the hospital, having temporarily delegated his powers to his principal deputy, James Comey. It fell to Comey to confront the President directly about the legality of the programme. President Bush told Comey, 'I decide what the law is for the executive branch'. Comey responded, 'That's absolutely true, sir, you do. But I decide what the Justice Department can certify to and can't certify to, and despite my absolute best efforts, I simply cannot in the circumstances' (Bruff 2009: 154). Both men were correctly describing their proper roles. In the event, the President retreated and authorised the Justice Department to do what it thought was right.

President Bush's confrontation with Deputy Attorney General Comey and the President's eventual acquiescence in the department's legal advice were both prompted by information that if the programme continued against that advice, the department's entire top echelon would resign in protest. No President would lightly invite comparison to President Nixon's infamous 'Saturday Night Massacre' in 1973, in which both the Attorney General and his deputy resigned rather than execute Nixon's command to dismiss Watergate Special Prosecutor Archibald Cox, who had been promised independence in his investigations.

In such cases, threats to resign over a matter of principle carry great power because if carried out they bring internal government disputes into the light of day. President Bush had little practical alternative but to yield to his legal advisers because his refusal to do so would very likely have revealed the existence of the secret surveillance programme. This fact shows that a threat to resign, although an adviser's last buttress for the weight of his or her legal opinion, risks giving the adviser *too much* power over the principal. President Bush was correct in asserting that he was 'the decider' in this instance, but the combined judgment of his senior legal advisers effectively drove his decision. Resignations on principle are rare in the American government. As in this episode, the threat of them should be reserved for occasions that merit confrontation.

Australian observers have noted the similarity of the Nixon resignations to the 1975 resignation of Commonwealth Attorney-General Robert Ellicott in a controversy over his independence in taking legal action (Edwards 1984). These two similar historical episodes confirm that any legal adviser must reserve the option of resigning to protect the independence of his or her judgment. In the United States, the Attorney General enjoys no structural insulation from the President to avert reliance on the ultimate option of resignation. In Australia, a Commonwealth Attorney-General can rely on advice from the non-political Solicitor-General as a way to reduce conflict within the ministry. In this way, Australia may feature a substantially greater degree of insulation for legal advice than does the United States.

Because the United States Attorney General is a political appointee who serves at the pleasure of the President and is often a presidential confidante, it may appear that nothing ensures an appropriate degree of independence in this office. Such a view ignores the complexity of the historical record that I have outlined. It also ignores two potentially powerful constraints on Attorneys General: the ethical responsibilities that all counsellors share and the obligation of the oath to defend the Constitution that all executive branch lawyers take. Before exploring them, we should consider the powerful incentives to provide complaisant advice that they must counteract.

Lawyers for a branch of government are immersed in a longstanding legal tradition of shared views about their branch's powers and perquisites. The body of precedents that their predecessors have generated is known to them and is self-perpetuating because no one wants to waive or undermine traditional institutional arguments. (Any concession of authority is soon punished by the other branch or by the courts, which will cite it as an embarrassing precedent the next time the underlying issue arises.) In addition, career advancement within a branch is more likely for those who strongly champion its interests. Finally, there is never an absence of competing views from the other branch and private parties, which to the government lawyer usually seem to be skewed by interest and clearly erroneous on the merits.

The presence of these competing arguments usually spurs compensatory aggressiveness in interpretation and argument (although at times they force a retreat from extreme positions). Hence, government lawyers are far more likely to display an excess of zeal than a lack of it on behalf of their branch. The substantive legal positions they take are systematically skewed toward the institutional position of the branch they inhabit, whether or not the lawyers have the self-awareness to know that.

The President's Cabinet, as we have seen, often contains competitors for the President's ear when legal issues arise. There is no formal mechanism to reconcile the clash of views. The President hears the various opinions (or those he cares to consider) and decides among them. He usually feels quite free to pick and choose, as history has demonstrated, instead of simply deferring to whatever the Attorney General says. The Cabinet has never served as a real deliberative body that would thrash out proposed decisions for the President to review. Instead, the Cabinet began as a staff entity, a sounding board to provide advice on major issues that were occupying the President's mind. As the Cabinet grew over the years, its size hampered group discussion and debate. In modern times, it often serves largely ceremonial functions. Of course, the President can always call on its members singly or in smaller groups.

The game of influencing the President is played without rules. The insights of game theory are useful in analysing this unstructured contest. For example, since the Cabinet is composed of a group of people who share devotion to the

President and who usually serve for a period of years, an incentive to cooperate flows from the knowledge that the help of colleagues may be needed on future issues. Ambition often casts aside cooperation, however. The President always has desirable nominations in his gift – to other Cabinet posts, to the Supreme Court. Hence, it is very likely that pleasing the President will be the order of the day: 'Personalities change when the President is present, and frequently even strong [people] make recommendations on the basis of what they believe the President wishes to hear' (Kennedy 1969: 11).

In the rough and tumble of the Cabinet, the Attorney General may be uniquely vulnerable due to the presence of other lawyers who may regard themselves as having equal or superior legal skills. Also, a single legal issue can have multiple policy applications, triggering pressure from several secretaries. But the Attorney General has several weapons for fighting back. One is the duty of providing legal advice to the other departments, which they are expected to follow. (As in Australia, it is normal to consult with the affected department and its attorneys before rendering advice (Edwards 1984).) Another is the Justice Department's control of litigation involving the other departments, which enforces the advising role. History shows, though, that what matters the most is the character and capacity of the Attorney General. A strong one is rarely ignored; a weak one is rarely influential. Robert Jackson was strong enough to disagree both with his colleagues and (carefully) with his President; others have proved less effective.

The Watergate scandal of the 1970s inflicted a serious injury on the Justice Department, as two Attorneys General were convicted of serious crimes. In the aftermath, there were even proposals to make the Department independent of direct presidential supervision. To defuse suspicion, President Gerald Ford nominated the eminent outsider Edward Levi to be Attorney General, and President Jimmy Carter followed with former judge Griffin Bell, both of whom kept a substantial distance from White House staff and sometimes even from the President (Rabkin 1993: 78–80). Watergate memories dimmed, though, and since the Reagan administration, the President and his Attorney General have usually had a close relationship, with the exception of President Clinton's estrangement from Janet Reno. A single presidency can feature the entire spectrum of independence in the Attorney General. George W. Bush chose a stranger who pleased his political base (John Ashcroft), an insider whose loyalty was uncontested (Alberto Gonzales) and finally a distinguished outsider who might repair a tarnished Justice Department (Michael Mukasey). President Barack Obama chose an Attorney General with a fine record as a prosecutor, Eric Holder, instead of a close associate.

Congress has made clear that it values independent legal judgment in the Justice Department. Ever since Watergate, Congress has used confirmation hearings for a new Attorney General or a head of the OLC to obtain promises from the nominees of independent legal judgment. For example, Ronald Reagan's Attorney General, Edwin Meese, when asked whether he could reconcile his duties to the President with those to the people, said that he had 'no doubt whatsoever as to my ability to exercise independent judgment' in situations of potential conflict

(Senate Committee on the Judiciary 1984). Thus, there is institutional pressure from Congress that buttresses the Attorney General's independence.

A government attorney is governed by the ethics rules of the state Bar to which he or she belongs. Because the states usually codify the American Bar Association's *Model Rules of Professional Conduct*, the rules are essentially the same for everyone. The rules require attorneys engaged in the counselling function to 'exercise independent professional judgment and render candid advice' (2007: Rule 2.1). All new lawyers have had some ethics instruction. American law schools reacted to Watergate by making professional responsibility courses mandatory for all students. State Bar examinations also contain an ethics test. There is no excuse for ignorance.

Searching for ethical boundaries, some analysts ask, 'Who is a government lawyer's client?' The client, once identified, would be owed the duty of the attorney's loyalty. Does a Justice Department attorney advising the White House on a matter of presidential authority represent the United States, the President, the presidency, the Department of Justice or the people? One can construct arguments for any of these candidates (Lawry 1978: 61). In Australia, by contrast, where the Crown is the client, the potential for this confusion diminishes (Selway 1999: 114).

Alas, the American people know little about their Constitution and cannot readily transmit instructions to their Attorney General (Bennett 2011: 101–6). Therefore, the standard claim by Attorneys General that they represent the people is incoherent as a guideline. Perhaps, then, reference to the people is shorthand for the proposition that ultimate fidelity is owed to the law. For example, Griffin Bell said that '[t]he people are your client. At the same time, the President is your client. But if there's a conflict, the people prevail' (Baker 1992: 153–4). He then explained that this meant that he would refuse an illegal request from the White House and, if pressed, would resign.

A competing argument is that government attorneys solely represent the executive branch and the President as its head (Miller 1987: 1293). In his 1971 confirmation hearing for the Supreme Court, William Rehnquist asserted this position to Senator Edward Kennedy:

> *Kennedy*: I thought that your client was the public as well.
>
> *Rehnquist*: My client, in my position as the assistant attorney general for the Office of Legal Counsel, is the attorney general and the president.
>
> *Kennedy*: Where does that put the rest of the Constitution?
>
> *Rehnquist*: Well, that puts the rest of the Constitution in the position of having someone advising them as to what his interpretation of the Constitution is (Senate Committee on the Judiciary 1971).

This debate fairly promises to be endless. Perhaps it makes more sense to focus on the lawyer's attitude toward the client, who is at least nominally the President or other official who requests the advice. Robert Jackson did not claim a neutral stance. He would give the President 'the benefit of a *reasonable doubt* as to the law' [emphasis added] (Gerhart 1958: 221–2).[10] Jackson's position assumed some distance between lawyer and client. His central insight was that 'the value of legal counsel is in the *detachment* of the adviser from the advised' (Jackson 2003: 60). This seems to have it right. Independent judgment is a professional's usual core responsibility to a client. The judgment can be sympathetic, and should be; but, as we have seen, the incentives and culture within the executive branch certainly ensure that much. The problem is to preserve the right degree of independence.

Since political advisers will reliably be advocates, only the lawyers are likely to intrude the voices of the other two branches, to which the politicians are naturally hostile. (That is why they do not like the lawyers very much.) Part of independent judgment is advice about consequences and alternatives. The overlap with policy can deter giving needed advice because good lawyers fear exceeding their proper role. It should not do so, however, because the politicians too often do not give balanced assessments of these matters. In particular, long-run consequences need to be pressed in ways that the election cycle will ignore. And knowledge of the traditions of the executive branch and access to the past opinions of its advisers provides a store of bottled knowledge.

At the moment of taking office, each President takes an oath, one that is prescribed in terms by the Constitution, to 'preserve, protect, and defend the Constitution' (Art. II, § 1, cl. 8).[11] Each of the President's lawyers, upon entering the federal service, also pledges to defend the Constitution (5 U.S.C. § 3331).[12] What does the oath add to the general ethical obligations that all lawyers already have? One obvious answer is that it invokes a particular legal text, the Constitution, and requires the lawyer to abide by its commands.[13]

Perhaps the oath means somewhat different things to the President and to subordinate officers. In Theodore Roosevelt's phrase (1988: 388), the President is our nation's ultimate 'steward of the people'.[14] This might mean, as 'TR' seemed

10 Jackson also said that the Attorney General has a dual position, lawyer for the President and 'laying down the law for the government as a judge might. I don't think he is quite as free to advocate an untenable position because it happens to be his client's position as he would be if he were in private practice. He has a responsibility to others than the President. He is the legal officer of the United States' (Marcus 1977: 187).

11 The full oath is: 'I do solemnly swear (or affirm) that I will faithfully execute the Office of President of the United States, and will to the best of my ability, preserve, protect and defend the Constitution of the United States'.

12 This statute implements the command of Art. VI, cl. 3 of the Constitution that 'all executive … Officers … of the United States … shall be bound by Oath or Affirmation, to support this Constitution'.

13 For reflections on the meaning of oath-taking, see Levinson 1988: ch. 4.

14 The full quote is: '[I insisted] upon the theory that the executive power was limited only by specific restrictions and prohibitions appearing in the Constitution or imposed by the Congress under its Constitutional powers. My view was that every executive officer

to say, only that a President can take action not clearly forbidden when the nation seems to need it. But it could also mean what Lincoln once argued – that there is a higher obligation still, to preserve the nation even at the cost of constitutional violation.[15] The President's lawyers, who are not themselves constitutional officers, surely have more modest obligations – and powers. Their oath should be understood to confine their advice to the parameters of actions allowed by the Constitution. If the President chooses to invoke a higher law, that is a matter for his own conscience, and his continuation in office will be at stake.

For the President's lawyers, the oath provides, at minimum, a justification for attempts to hold the executive to law in the face of expedient pressures to deviate from it. In other words, no one should have to ask why the lawyers care about the rule of law and why they feel obligated to enforce it. More important, the oath serves as a daily reminder to those who take it, that they must defend the Constitution even when it is not easy to do so. The oath contains no escape clauses; the obligation is unqualified. The fact that the oath is to defend a written document no doubt adds to its force. In the United States, as in Australia, the Constitution confirms that the ultimate obligation of the executive's legal advisers is to the rule of law, upon which our societies so greatly depend.

References

American Bar Association. 2007. *Model Rules of Professional Conduct*. Chicago: American Bar Association.

Baker, N.V. 1992. *Conflicting Loyalties: Law and Politics in the Attorney General's Office, 1789–1990*. Lawrence: University Press of Kansas.

Bennett, D. 2011. Constitutional Litigation and the Commonwealth, in *Critical Reflections on Australian Public Policy*, edited by J. Wanna. Canberra: ANU E Press, 101–6.

Bruff, H.H. 2006. *Balance of Forces: Separation of Powers Law in the Administrative State*. Durham: Carolina Academic Press.

Bruff, H.H. 2009. *Bad Advice: Bush's Lawyers in the War on Terror*. Lawrence: University Press of Kansas.

Caplan, L. 1987. *The Tenth Justice: The Solicitor General and the Rule of Law*. New York: Vintage Books.

… was a steward of the people bound actively and affirmatively to do all he could for the people, and not to content himself with the negative merit of keeping his talents undamaged in a napkin … . My belief was that it was not only his right but his duty to do anything that the needs of the Nation demanded unless such action was forbidden by the Constitution or by the laws … I did not usurp power, but I did greatly broaden the use of executive power'.

15 Justifying his controversial suspension of the writ of habeas corpus, Lincoln asked, 'Are all the laws, *but one*, to go unexecuted, and the government itself go to pieces, lest that one be violated?' (Bruff 2009: 28–9).

Cramton, R.C. 1990. On the Steadfastness and Courage of Government Lawyers. *John Marshall Law* Review. Volume 23, 165.

Edwards, J.Ll.J. 1984. *The Attorney General, Politics and the Public Interest.* London: Sweet & Maxwell.

Gerhart E.C. 1958. *America's Advocate: Robert H. Jackson.* Indianapolis: Bobbs-Merrill.

Guelzo, A.C. 2004. *Lincoln's Emancipation Proclamation.* New York: Simon & Schuster.

Jackson, R.H. 2003. *That Man: An Insider's Portrait of Franklin D. Roosevelt*, edited by J.Q. Barrett. New York: Oxford University Press.

Jefferson, T. 1904. Letter to Mrs. John Adams, September 11, 1804, in *Works of Thomas Jefferson*, edited by P.L. Ford. New York: G.P. Putnam's Sons, 310.

Kennedy, R.F. 1969. *Thirteen Days: A Memoir of the Cuban Missile Crisis.* New York: W.W. Norton.

Kmiec, D.W. 1993. OLC's Opinion Writing Function: The Legal Adhesive for a Unitary Executive. *Cardozo Law Review.* Volume 15, 337.

Lawry, R.P. 1978. Who is the Client of the Federal Government Lawyer? An Analysis of the Wrong Question? *Federal Bar Journal.* Volume 47, 61.

Levinson, S. 1988. *Constitutional Faith.* Princeton, NJ: Princeton University Press.

Lincoln, L. 1802a. *Restoration under Treaty with France* [17 June 1802] 1 Op. Att'y Gen. 114.

Lincoln, L. 1802b. *Restoration under Treaty with France* [25 June 1802] 1 Op. Att'y Gen. 119.

Marcus, M. 1977. *Truman and the Steel Seizure Case.* New York: Columbia University Press.

Merrill, T.W. 1998. High-level, 'Tenured' Lawyers. *Law and Contemporary Problems.* Volume 61, 83.

Miller, G.P. 1987. Government Lawyers' Ethics in a System of Checks and Balances. *University of Chicago Law Review.* Volume 54, 1293.

Miller, J.C. 1960. *The Federalist Era, 1789–1801.* New York: Harper & Row.

Neustadt, R.E. 1990. *Presidential Power and the Modern Presidents: The Politics of Leadership from Roosevelt to Reagan.* New York: Free Press.

Rabkin, J. 1993. At the President's Side: The Role of the White House Counsel in Constitutional Policy. *Law and Contemporary Problems.* Volume 56, 63.

Rehnquist, W.H. 1998. *All the Laws but One: Civil Liberties in Wartime.* New York: Vintage.

Remini, R.V. 1967. *Andrew Jackson and the Bank War: A Study in the Growth of Presidential Power.* New York: W.W. Norton.

Richardson, J.D. 1897. *Messages and Papers of the Presidents.* New York: Bureau of National Literature.

Roosevelt, T.R. 1988. *An Autobiography.* New York: Da Capo.

Selway, B. 1999. The Duties of Lawyers Acting for Government. *Public Law Review.* Volume 10, 114.

Senate Committee on the Judiciary. 1971. *Hearings on the Nomination of William H. Rehnquist and Lewis F. Powell, Jr., to be Associate Justices of the Supreme Court*, 92nd Cong., 1st Sess. 48.

Senate Committee on the Judiciary. 1984. *Nomination of Edwin Meese III*, 98th Cong., 2nd Sess. 122.

White L.D. 1948. *The Federalists: A Study in Administrative History*. New York: Macmillan.

White, L.D. 1951. *The Jeffersonians: A Study in Administrative History, 1801–1829*. New York: Macmillan.

Wirt, W. 1820. Duties of the Attorney General, 1 Op. Att'y Gen. 335, in *The Constitution and the Attorneys General*, edited by H.J. Powell. 1999. Durham, NC: Carolina Academic Press, 12–13.

Chapter 11
Solicitors General in the United States

H.W. Perry, Jr

> I used to have a luncheon frequently with my staff, and I would tell them, we must remember that we are not judges, but advocates. But there are some things we will not advocate.
>
> Former Solicitor General of the United States (personal interview with author)[1]

> The Solicitor General is not a neutral, he is an advocate; but an advocate for a client whose business is not merely to prevail in the instant case. My client's chief business is not to achieve victory, but to establish justice.
>
> Simon E. Sobeloff, Solicitor General of the United States, 1954–56 (Waxman 2011)

> He is responsible neither to the man who appointed him nor to his immediate superior in the hierarchy of administration. The total responsibility is his, and his guide is only the ethic of his own profession framed in the ambiance of his experience and judgment.
>
> Francis Biddle, Solicitor General of the United States, 1940–41 (Biddle 1962: 97)

These quotations from former Solicitors General of the United States seem rather lofty, but on a quick reading they would not raise too many eyebrows. Upon reflection, however, they raise serious questions and perhaps some objections. The Solicitor General is a special sort of advocate; but what kind of things will the Solicitor General refuse to advocate? How are we to think about an advocate using the courts whose primary interest may not be to prevail in a particular case? Is it proper for the Solicitor General of the United States, a presidential appointee and a subordinate to the Attorney General in the Department of Justice, to consider himself not responsible to his superiors or the President? These questions in response to the above quotations beget another question. Who is the client? The President? The Congress? The laws of the United States? Answering that question is not always easy. All of these questions raise interesting normative and empirical issues about the role of the Solicitor General of the United States, an office that is in many ways unique.

---

1 I have interviewed several former US Solicitors General along with many other high-ranking attorneys in the Office of the Solicitor General as well as in the Department of Justice generally for a larger project on the Justice Department (in progress). A condition for most of the interviews was a promise of anonymity.

While there are debates in the United States about the appropriate role for the Office of the Solicitor General, there is little debate about the importance and prestige of the job. Justice Thurgood Marshall said that being Solicitor General was 'the best job I've ever had, bar none!' (Caplan 1987: 261). Former Solicitor General Rex Lee recalled:

> When I heard that I was being considered, I was very much hoping that I would be picked because that is, very simply ... one of the creamiest, ... no, it is probably the creamiest lawyering job in the country (Salokar 1992: 33).

Most Americans, however, probably have never heard of the Solicitor General, or if they have, they do not have a clear idea about what he or she does. To the extent that citizens know anything about government lawyers, it would be that there is an Attorney General, who is the nation's top legal officer and the public face of government lawyers. They would probably assume that the Attorney General is the person who governs the nation's litigating strategy and argues in the Supreme Court. They would be incorrect. Those tasks belong to the Solicitor General. Among lawyers, though, especially appellate lawyers, the position of Solicitor General is well known and regarded as the top lawyering job in the United States. Throughout much of our history, but certainly in modern times, the Solicitor General and the lawyers in the Office of the Solicitor General (OSG) have been among the very best appellate lawyers in the nation. The position of Solicitor General was not created until 81 years after the creation of the Attorney General. Much of what the modern Solicitor General does, however, is what the position of Attorney General was created to do. Therefore, to understand how the position of Solicitor General came about, as well as the reasons why it functions as it currently does, one must understand the history of the Attorney General and the Department of Justice.

Brief History of US Government Lawyers

There has been an Attorney General of the United States since 1789, but the Department of Justice was not created until 1870. The history of the government's legal representation mirrors the growth and growing pains of a nation, and that history helps explain, or at least makes more comprehensible, many of the present-day arrangements. Only a brief part of the story can be recounted here, but it is in large part a story of endless attempts to centralise power in the face of continual opposition. Interwoven into this story are questions of who the Attorney General (and later the Department of Justice and the Solicitor General) represents, and can and should the legal and the political be separated?

The Attorney General

The legislation that created the position of Attorney General was 'An Act to establish the Judicial Courts of the United States' – the famous *Judiciary Act* of 1789. This was not an obvious place to create the position of Attorney General, an executive officer. The *Judiciary Act* was a broad, sweeping piece of legislation. It determined the size of the Supreme Court, and it also outlined some of the Court's jurisdiction. Most importantly, it created the federal judiciary.[2] The *Judiciary Act* fashioned a system of 13 federal districts and provided each district with a federal court, a federal district attorney and a federal marshal.[3] It created three circuit courts of appeals, and it established the jurisdiction for the new federal courts. And, it created the office of Attorney General. Other executive offices came about in Acts creating executive departments, for example, the Department of State was to be headed by the Secretary of State, and the Treasury Department headed by the Treasury Secretary. The Attorney General, however, came without a department. There was ambivalence about what type of officer this was to be. On the Senate's second day of business, 7 April 1789, it created a committee to bring in a Bill for organising the judiciary of the United States. In the committee's report to the Senate, the Attorney General was to be appointed by the Supreme Court, and the federal district attorneys were to be appointed by their respective federal district courts (Hightower 1974: 411). This would have made the Attorney General an 'inferior officer' responsible primarily to the appointing body, the Supreme Court, rather than the President. Somewhere between the draft Bill proposed to the Senate and the one passed by the Senate and sent to the House of Representatives, the appointment language changed. The final version read:

2 The Constitution created the US Supreme Court, but it left to Congress the decision of whether or not to create a federal judiciary. In the constitutional debates, some had argued against a federal judiciary, claiming that state courts could handle federal questions because state judges were required to swear an oath to uphold the Constitution and the laws of the United States. Indeed, to this day, most federal questions (for example, interpretation of the Constitution and federal laws) can be decided in either State courts or federal courts, but the ultimate judicial authority over both systems is the US Supreme Court. See, *Martin v Hunters Lessee* 14 U.S. 304 (1816). If Congress wanted to, it could abolish the entire federal judiciary except for the US Supreme Court. Nevertheless, at the time that the Constitution was adopted, most assumed that a federal judiciary would, in fact, be created by Congress and the first major act by Congress was the *Judiciary Act*.

3 In the US, 'national' institutions (as opposed to State institutions) are often referred to as 'federal': for example, the national government is usually called the federal government. This sometimes leads to confusion. In the eighteenth century, those in favour of the creation of a federal government were referred to as 'federalists' and those opposed were the 'anti-federalists'. After the adoption of the Constitution, the Federalist Party came to represent those who favoured greater power for the national government as opposed to the States. Today, however, members of 'the Federalist Society' are those who favour increased authority being returned to the States, with a diminished role for the federal government.

> And there shall also be appointed a meet person, learned in the law, to act as attorney-general for the United States, who shall be sworn or affirmed to a faithful execution of his office; whose duty it shall be to prosecute and conduct all suits in the Supreme Court in which the United States shall be concerned, and to give his advice and opinion upon questions of law when required by the President of the United States, or when requested by the heads of any of the departments, touching any matters that may concern their departments, and shall receive such compensation for his services as shall by law be provided.

The appointment of the district attorneys (now called US attorneys) also changed from appointment by the federal district courts to appointment by the President. Since the legislation did not vest the appointments either in the President or in courts or department heads, it was assumed that the appointees were to be appointed by the President and confirmed by the Senate (Hightower 1974: 412). Some argue that the fact that the Attorney General was created by the *Judiciary Act* serves as a justification for a de-politicised Justice Department. That view has not prevailed in terms of ultimate accountability to the President, but there is a notion that a Department of Justice must be removed to some degree from politics in a way that differs from other executive departments.

In the beginning, the Attorney General was simply a lawyer retained by the government to render legal advice and conduct certain cases on its behalf. The primary role for the Attorney General was to appear in US Supreme Court cases; district attorneys handled district court cases. The Attorney General was given little salary and was expected to have a private practice. However, even with the first Attorney General, the role began to expand. Attorney General Edmund Randolph was a personal friend of President Washington, and there was a great deal of consultation between the two on legal matters. There also was the 'early emergence of issues involving questions of constitutional law' that fell to the Attorney General (Hightower 1974: 413). Nevertheless, it was a long time before the office became a particularly desirable appointment. John Marshall (later 'The Great Chief Justice' of *Marbury v Madison* fame) was asked to become the third Attorney General in 1795, but he turned it down because 'he could not afford to abandon his private law practice' (Easby-Smith 1904: 7).

Initially, the Attorney General's offices were wherever the incumbent's private practice was located. On 5 January 1814, Congress asked the House Judiciary Committee to look into the possibility of bringing the Attorney General to Washington, but the Bill failed. William Pinckney resigned when President James Madison insisted that he reside permanently in Washington (Easby-Smith 1904: 9). When Madison chose an Attorney General in 1814, he chose one likely to stay in Washington. Madison noted, 'The removal of this office [to Washington] has more than doubled its entire business under this head' (Hightower 1974: 415). Madison's practice of nominating those who would stay in Washington was followed by subsequent Presidents (Cummings and McFarland 1937: 78). Even after the move to Washington, the Attorney General bore most of his own expenses.

Location and salary were not the only problems. Attorney General William Wirt of Virginia (1817–29) wrote that:

> Finding on my appointment, this day, no book, documents, or papers of any kind to inform me of what has been done by anyone of my predecessors, since the establishment of the Federal Government, and feeling very strongly the inconvenience, both to the nation and myself, from this omission, I have determined to remedy it, so far as depends on myself, and to keep a regular record of every official opinion which I shall give while I hold this office, for the use of my successor (Easby-Smith 1904: 10).

Finally, by a Congressional Act of 20 April 1818, the Attorney General got one clerk. And in 1822, by administrative arrangement, the Attorney General got an office on the floor of the War Department building, his first official quarters (Hightower 1974: 415).

Struggle for Centralisation

Much of the historical story involves struggles over centralisation. On 26 December 1791, Attorney General Randolph wrote to President Washington that while he was frequently presented with requests from the heads of various departments, 'the want of a fixed relation between the attorneys of the districts and the attorney general, has rendered it impossible for me to take charge of matters on which I was not authorised to give instructions'. He argued that the Attorney General needed greater control over the work of the district attorneys and recommended an arrangement 'in which the harmony of the two jurisdictions may be hazarded' (Hightower 1974: 414). Washington put the proposal before Congress without endorsing it, and it was not enacted. As the nation grew, there was an increasing problem with debt collection, and President Andrew Jackson sought unsuccessfully to create a 'law department'. Still, Congress kept adding duties to the office. In his first annual message to Congress, President James Polk (1845–49) urged the creation of a Law Department with the Attorney General at its head, as well as 'placing him on the same footing with the heads of the other executive departments' (Easby-Smith 1904: 12–13). Again, the proposal went nowhere. In 1853, the Attorney General's salary was increased and he was now supposedly the chief legal officer of the United States, but he still had no control over the district attorneys. Control of these individuals was dispersed to various officers in other departments, especially to the Secretary of the Treasury (Hightower 1974: 417).

The Civil War, however, brought chaos to the government's legal forces. James Hightower (1974: 417), a chronicler of the history of the Justice Department, argues:

> No more than three or four months were necessary to bring glaringly to the public attention the incongruity of having district attorneys work individually, and at times divergently, without direction from a centralized head.

In response to this crisis, Congress passed a Bill on 2 August 1861 which charged the Attorney General 'with the general superintendence and direction of the attorneys and marshals of all the districts in the United States' (12 U.S. stat 285). However, four days later President Lincoln signed an explanatory Act (12 U.S. Stat 327) that declared that the duties of the Solicitor of the Treasury remained the same. As Hightower (1974: 417) puts it, 'Thus, the attorney general had explicit control over the district attorneys, and the Solicitor of the Treasury had explicit control over the district attorneys'. Moreover, Congress responded to the rush of litigation during the war by creating more and more independent legal officers. Hightower (1974: 417) writes:

> At the close of the Civil War, the federal court dockets seemed hopelessly overloaded. The district attorneys were receiving instructions from diverse legal officers, and there was no consistency in legal opinions.

By late 1867, three different Congressional committees were considering means 'for more direct co-ordination and control of litigation and legal advice in the government' (Hightower 1974: 417). A Bill proposing the creation of a Department of Justice was enacted and signed on 22 June 1870 by President Grant. Even with the creation of the department, however, centralised authority was soon undercut. Congress enacted the 'Revised Statutes' 'in which all of the old statutes giving duties and authority to the various [non-Justice Department] solicitors were reenacted simultaneously with the Department of Justice Act' (Key 1938: 185), which added renewed credibility to the claims of the departmental solicitors outside the Justice Department.

Much of the work to consolidate authority in the hands of the Attorney General occurred through the Supreme Court's intervention. In an 1866 case *The Gray Jacket* (72 U.S. (5 Wall.) 342, 370), the Court held that 'where the United States is represented by the Attorney General or his representative, no counsel could be heard in opposition on behalf of another Department of the Government' (Key 1938: 185). This holding was expanded in the *Confiscation Cases* (74 U.S. (7 Wall.) 454 (1868)), in which the Court established the Attorney General's 'control over and power to dismiss any action brought in the name of or for the behalf of the United States' (Key 1938: 185). The most important decision in this line of cases was *United States v San Jacinto Tin Co.* (125 U.S. 273 (1888)). Here 'the plenary power of the Attorney General over all litigation of the Government was conclusively recognized' (Key 1938: 186). The reasoning the Court used was that since the Attorney General, as defined by the common law tradition, had final say over all government litigation, this must be true by analogy for the American Attorney General (Key 1938: 186). Statutes could, however, place a specific duty elsewhere. The Attorney General was also successful in arguing that his opinions were legally binding upon administrative officers of the government (*Smith v Jackson* 246 U.S. 388 (1918)) (Key 1938: 188).

Although the Attorney General had a critical ally in the Supreme Court, the fact that some of the departmental solicitors had statutory powers significantly hindered centralisation of authority. Congress had to be persuaded to remedy this problem since it was responsible for the statutes establishing departmental solicitors. The story is one of repeated cycles of centralisation – caused by a crisis – to decentralisation as Congress gave power to others. The entry of the United States into World War I prompted the creation of a number of new agencies and bureaus, all interested in conducting their own litigation. President Woodrow Wilson sought to resolve the confusion. The *Overman Act* (40 Stat. 556 (1918)) gave him power to consolidate the work of the various executive departments. Wilson issued an executive order requiring that all law officers of the United States exercise their authority under the auspices of the Justice Department and that the opinions of the Attorney General would be binding on executive departments and agencies (Key 1938: 190). The *Overman Act*, however, expired six months after the Armistice. Thereafter, the departmental solicitors once again assumed control over their own litigation (Key 1938: 190–91). Congress aided this process of decentralisation by enabling the attorneys of the Interstate Commerce Commission to appear in 'any case in court' related to their objectives (Key 1938: 191). Congress then proceeded to give litigating authority to numerous other departments and agencies.

Again, it took a crisis, The Great Depression, to bring about centralisation. In the 'Economy Act' 47 Stat. 413 (1932), Congress gave the President the power to make changes in executive departments to bring about greater efficiency. President Franklin Roosevelt issued an executive order (#6166) 'that transferred to the Department of Justice the function of handling all litigation and the exclusive right of supervision of the United States Attorneys and Marshalls' (Key 1938: 198). As with so many things in modern American politics, the Roosevelt administration transformed the location of power. Power moved dramatically toward the executive branch with the creation of the modern administrative state.

The Solicitor General

Having walked through the general history of the Justice Department, it remains to be asked how the position of Solicitor General came about. Prior to the creation of the Department of Justice, the Attorney General increasingly needed to retain outside counsel to help him. He was particularly burdened by having to prepare arguments for the Supreme Court. In 1867, Attorney General Henry Stanbery recommended to the Senate Judiciary Committee the creation of a Solicitor General. The Joint Committee on Retrenchment, a committee looking for ways to save the government money, picked up his recommendation (Fahy 1942: 20). The Bill's sponsor, Congressman Thomas Jenckes (1870: 3035) argued:

> We propose to have a man with such learning, ability and experience, that he can be sent to New Orleans or to New York or into any court wherever the Government has any interest in litigation, and there present the case of the United States as it should be presented.

With the creation of the Justice Department came the creation of the Solicitor General. The statute called for 'an officer learned in the law to assist the attorney general in the performance of his duties, to be called the solicitor general'. Interestingly, when the office of Attorney General was created in 1789, the Attorney General was required to be 'learned in the law', but after the creation of the Solicitor General, that requirement was later removed for the Attorney General (Fahy 1942: 20). Subsequent Attorneys General all happen to have been 'learned in the law', though some were obviously not very good students. Such is not the case for Solicitors General. Almost without exception they have been top-flight lawyers. The current statutory language is virtually the same as the original language authorising the position. From the very beginning, the primary responsibility of the Solicitor General has been to handle governmental litigation, but historically he also had administrative and other responsibilities. In 1953, the position of Deputy Attorney General was created (28 U.S.C.A.: s 504), which alleviated most of the Solicitor General's administrative duties,[4] and in 1977, the position of Associate Attorney General was created (28 U.S.C.A.: s 504a).[5]

4 'The Deputy Attorney General advises and assists the Attorney General in formulating and implementing Departmental policies and programs and in providing overall supervision and direction to all organizational units of the Department. The Deputy Attorney General is authorized to exercise all the power and authority of the Attorney General, except where such power or authority is prohibited by law from delegation or has been delegated to another official. In the absence of the Attorney General, the Deputy Attorney General acts as the Attorney General' (United States Department of Justice 2012b).

5 'The Office of the Associate Attorney General advises and assists the Attorney General and the Deputy Attorney General in formulating and implementing Departmental policies and programs pertaining to a broad range of civil justice, federal and local law enforcement, and public safety matters. The Office oversees the following DOJ components: Antitrust Division, Civil Division, Civil Rights Division, Environment and Natural Resources Division, Tax Division, Office of Justice Programs, Community Oriented Policing Services (COPS), Community Relations Service, Office of Dispute Resolution, Office on Violence Against Women, Office of Information Policy, Executive Office for U.S. Trustees, and the Foreign Claims Settlement Commission' (United States Department of Justice 2012a).

The Office of the US Solicitor General Today[6]

The modern Solicitor General is best known for arguing on behalf of the government in the US Supreme Court. His responsibilities, however, are significantly broader. As one Solicitor General told me, he has four primary responsibilities.[7] First, the Solicitor General is the government's lawyer in the Supreme Court; that is, the Solicitor General represents the United States and its officers and agencies before the Court. This involves the duties of any lawyer before the Supreme Court, such as preparing briefs and conducting oral arguments. It also means that the Solicitor General mediates interdepartmental disputes that arise over matters of legal policy. It is the Solicitor General who decides what the position of the United States shall be, which may at times be in conflict with the desires of many people, including other departments, divisions of the Justice Department, US attorneys and, at times, even the President. Rarely, the Solicitor General may authorise another party outside the OSG to present arguments. Second, the Solicitor General or the OSG decides which cases the government will appeal whenever it loses in any court at any level – federal or state, trial or appellate. This includes, of course, deciding which cases to petition for certiorari in the US Supreme Court. The Solicitor General also decides when actively to oppose review. Third, the Solicitor General must give authorisation before the United States – or one of its offices or agencies – files an amicus curiae brief in any appellate court. This involves writing the briefs when the United States is an interested party or (rarely) authorising others in the government to do so. Even if the Solicitor General chooses not to file an amicus brief in the Supreme Court, with some frequency the Supreme Court issues an order 'calling for the views of the Solicitor General' (CVSG). Depending upon the stage of litigation, an amicus brief is prepared on whether or not the Court should take the case or, if review is granted, on the merits of the case. Fourth, the Solicitor General must authorise any petition for an *en banc* rehearing in a United States Circuit Court of Appeals. All of these powers come to the Solicitor General

6 Throughout the chapter, I often use the phrases 'Solicitor General' and 'Office of the Solicitor General' interchangeably. Obviously, the actual Solicitor General is the head of the office and has ultimate authority. The office, however, has one Principal Deputy Solicitor General and three Deputy Solicitors General with responsibilities over substantive areas. These Deputy Solicitors General, in turn, have legal staff under them. Deputy Solicitors General often argue in the Supreme Court, but would be referred to as 'the Solicitor General'. Likewise, the Office of the Solicitor General is often referred to as 'the Solicitor General'. As such, at times I am referring to the actual Solicitor General and at times I mean anyone from the OSG. If it is important to differentiate, I do so. When I use the term OSG, I am generally trying to stress that it is the group of lawyers who have served in that office over many years and under many individual Solicitors General.

7 What follows in the text is from notes given to me for remarks prepared for a speech by former Solicitor General Erwin N. Griswold and information gleaned by interviews. Another source for information comes from an unpublished PhD dissertation (Brigman 1966), as reported in Salokar 1992.

either by explicit statutory authorisation or by delegation to the Solicitor General by the Attorney General.

Oral argument in the Supreme Court is certainly the most glamorous function of the office, but what precedes that 30 minutes or less in the limelight is where the government's legal policy is really made. As a result, the Solicitor General – an éminence *grise* to the public and to many in government – is one of the most influential figures in the Department of Justice, and indeed the entire government. Thanks to the Department of Justice's triumph in the long historical struggle for centralisation of legal authority, the Department of Justice has become one of the most powerful executive departments. It is in the league of the Departments of State, Defense, and Treasury. And within the Department of Justice, the authority over the appellate process has been centralised and ceded to the OSG. As a general matter, the Attorney General and even the President defer to his or her judgment on litigation matters. As shall be discussed later, even the Supreme Court defers to the OSG in important ways. The deference given to the Solicitor General throughout the government is not complete, but it is extraordinary. Today, centralisation of authority of the appellate function in the Office of the Solicitor General is not questioned. That does not mean it is not resented; and, as with any bureaucracy, there are attempts at end-runs. It is not hard to understand why. When a US attorney takes a case to court, he or she is usually interested in winning the particular case, not in shaping doctrine (Perry, Jr 1998). If the government loses, the US attorney who tried the case usually wants to appeal. So, too, the clients. If an agency, governmental official or governmental entity is involved in a case and loses, naturally they want to appeal. The perspective of the Solicitor General, however, especially in the Supreme Court, is different. The desire is not necessarily to win but to protect 'the government'. The government, however, has many voices. The US attorney for New York, the Antitrust Division of the Department of Justice, the Department of Labor, the Congress, the President and a postal worker are all the government. But the government's overall interests and its long-term interests are not necessarily those of any one component. Though there are times when it is tenable to have different parts of the government take different positions in court, the government is expected by courts to speak with one voice and to say what the government's interests are, particularly in appellate courts.

The Solicitor General's power and authority comes not only from delegation and bureaucratic hierarchy. Being the quintessential 'repeat player' (Galanter 1974; McGuire 1995) brings with it many advantages, ranging from experience to perspective. Few attorneys will ever get a chance to argue before the justices of the Supreme Court. There are very few private attorneys who have appeared before the Supreme Court more than once. For those who have, they cannot come close to the number of appearances before the Court when compared to the lawyers in the OSG. The Solicitor General and senior attorneys in the OSG do it all the time. The Solicitor General is even given an office at the Court. Obviously, such experience matters. The perspective of the OSG also enhances its authority and provides numerous advantages. As a repeat player, the OSG can take a long-range interest in serving its client. Rather than winning a particular battle, they care about winning wars. The OSG has the perspective that what is of prime importance is making sure that policies, or principles or doctrines that emerge are best suited to the government's broader or long-term interest. They are free to pick and choose the cases that are most likely to accomplish that. Any particular case might not be the best vehicle to bring about the desired ends. As a repeat player, the OSG need not worry too much about pursuing a particular case or winning a case at all costs. This luxury ultimately advantages the office and, in turn, increases deference and power. In the long run, such a perspective usually benefits the component parts of the government as well, though at times they do not see it that way.

Being a repeat player is not the sole explanation for why has the OSG has come to receive so much respect and deference. The simplest explanation is that they have earned it. How? Answering that question is a bit more complicated, but the first response is that they win; they win a lot. Their extraordinary success is verification of the quality of their excellent legal skills and their good judgment. Willingness to trust the OSG and to defer to it comes not only from winning, however. The Solicitor General and those lawyers in the OSG represent what is best in an excellent lawyer. They are honest and shoot straight. They tell their clients things they do not want to hear, and they admit things to the court they would prefer not to. In the long run, such honesty results in trust. Any good lawyer is honest with his or her client. The attorney is not there to tell the client what he or she wants to hear; the attorney is there to give his or her best professional judgment. That is especially hard to do, however, when the client is one's superior – especially the President of the United States. Even Presidents, however, come to realise that they are best served when their lawyer gives them the unvarnished truth, and even Presidents need to rely on the expertise of the lawyers for good legal advice.[8] The lawyers in the OSG are among the best appellate lawyers in the nation, and that fact is well known even by the President. The quality and prestige of the OSG has become legendary and precedes any new Attorney General or President. Though the Solicitor General is a political appointment, he or she is chosen for lawyering expertise – not for fealty to a political agenda. Taking the advice of one's lawyer, no matter how painful, is usually a wise thing to do when the lawyers are this good, and even Presidents and Attorneys General realise it.

---

8 There is an office of White House Counsel within the White House. He or she is the day-to-day lawyer for the President and the administration and serves as a conduit to the Justice Department. The White House Counsel is not the lawyer for the President on personal matters; that would be handled by a private attorney. The position of White House Counsel has at times become a bit controversial and has raised some interesting questions with regard to attorney–client privilege.

Getting a Case before the US Supreme Court

When thinking about litigation in the Supreme Court, the first thing that the Solicitor General has to do is get the case accepted. With a few exceptions, the Supreme Court has complete discretion about which cases it hears. Most cases come before the Supreme Court by a writ of certiorari; in common parlance 'cert.' is granted or denied. Over 9,000 cases a year seek review, and certiorari is granted in only about 1–3 per cent of those cases. However, when the Solicitor General petitions for certiorari, cases are granted at rates varying from 70 to 90 per cent. No other litigant even comes close. The high acceptance rate can partially be explained by the fact that the Supreme Court is only interested in hearing important cases. When the government is involved, that tends to make a case more important than most (Perry, Jr 1991). But importance alone cannot explain the high grant rate. As already noted, the quality of work coming from the Solicitor General's staff is excellent, not only because of high-calibre attorneys, but also because they are repeat players who understand how to write a good petition. They spend their careers drafting petitions for the Supreme Court. Few private counsel have such experience. The primary reason that explains the high acceptance rate, however, is that the Solicitor General provides a screening function (Perry, Jr 1991: 131). The Solicitor General petitions very few of the cases lost by the government. He or she sends up only the best and most important cases, and the Supreme Court has come to trust the Solicitor General in this regard. By showing so much restraint, when the Solicitor General does choose to weigh in and say that the Court ought to take a case, the justices listen very carefully. The case screening process for 9,000 cases every year is so burdensome for the nine justices and their approximately 37 law clerks[9] that they have come to rely a great deal on the OSG. Such reliance would not occur, however, if they could not trust the OSG. The OSG knows what the Court wants, and they take their responsibility of serving the Court very seriously. Many former law clerks told me essentially the same thing that is said in the following quotations:

> I also felt that the Court looked at the Solicitor General as fulfilling part of their own screening function. They saw him as an officer of the Court doing some of the screening himself. I believe that they saw him as a bit of an extension of themselves in some ways.

> He in fact had screened for good cases and he was very careful not to squander his reputation with the Court by bringing bad cases.

9 Each justice can hire up to four clerks, with the Chief Justice up to five. The clerks usually clerk only for one year and are usually only a couple of years out of law school, often having clerked one year for a circuit judge. They are not professional clerks.

Justices told me the same thing. As one put it: '[The Solicitor General does not try] to get us to take things that don't require our attention relative to other things that do. They are very careful in their screening and they exercise a veto' (Perry, Jr 1991: 132). The Solicitor General is known for being scrupulous in representing the facts of the case and what is at issue both in the petition for certiorari and in arguing the merits. As one clerk put it, 'The Court looks at the Solicitor General as more than just a litigant. They know he won't bamboozle them' (Perry, Jr 1991: 131). In the long run, having such trust ultimately redounds to the OSG's benefit.

The S.G.'s Advantages

Not to take anything away from the extraordinary talent and success of the OSG, it is helpful to realise that there are numerous advantages in having the government as a client. I have already suggested that, in terms of getting into court, when the government is involved it enhances the importance of the case. Screening cases not only helps have a more successful cert. grant rate, but it also sets up an advantage for winning on the merits. The Solicitor General has the luxury of picking the best cases with the greatest likelihood of winning. More importantly, the Solicitor General can pick a case that is most likely to shape doctrine in the way the government wants. The government is freer than other litigants to confess error. Confessing error is seen as a noble gesture, and it builds trust. It is potentially dangerous for a private attorney to confess error. It can suggest anything from incompetence to intentional misrepresentation. When the Solicitor General confesses error, it can infuriate the US attorney or other Department of Justice lawyers who argued and won the case below. It can even anger the judge who decided it. Former US Solicitor General and later appeals court judge Wade McCree made this point when he quoted famed appeals court judge Learned Hand: 'It is bad enough to have the Supreme Court reverse you, but I will be damned if I will be reversed by some solicitor general' (McCree 1981: 343). In addition to building trust, confessing error can be used strategically. Judge Simon Sobeloff, who previously had been Solicitor General, commented: 'When I was solicitor general, I thought that confessing error was the noblest function of the office. Now that I am circuit judge, I know it is the lowest trick one lawyer can play on another' (McCree 1981: 343). Confessing error is rarely used as a strategic tactic because to do so would cause it to lose its effectiveness. Nevertheless, the greater freedom to confess error as compared to others points out another advantage of representing the government that redounds to the Solicitor General's benefit. A major advantage for the Solicitor General is that the government has extraordinary resources at its disposal. Resources can help the government win, but the government can withstand losses that no private client could. Resources, of course, can also facilitate the ability to contribute amicus briefs, which enhance the office's power. For a party to have the Solicitor General come in on his or her side is an incredible advantage. On the other hand, to have the Solicitor General come in against one's case is an incredible disadvantage. To be able to pick and choose the way the OSG does allows it to be on the side of winners more often than most. In addition to all of the advantages that have been discussed, there are others. The bottom line is that success breeds success.

Politics and the Solicitor General

The story told thus far is one of the deference to the Solicitor General with a lack of political interference, and the Solicitor General and the OSG are seen as great lawyers, not politicos. To my knowledge, no scholar would disagree with these statements as a general description. Solicitor General Erwin Griswold, the former Dean of the Harvard Law School, demonstrates the relative lack of politics. Although Solicitors General usually step down when their President leaves office, Griswold served both Presidents Lyndon Johnson and Richard Nixon. The Presidents shared a legacy of Vietnam, but their domestic presidencies could hardly have been more different. High-ranking attorneys in the OSG often have long careers in the office, serving several administrations. Though deference to the Solicitor General is the rule, there are times when the OSG does not get its way. The President at times will insist that a position be argued, but according to one former Solicitor General it is rare (Days 2001). The Attorney General often plays the role of keeping an overactive White House at bay. One Solicitor General related the following story to me:

> I remember one time I had a phone call and … it was [the President's chief assistant – a very powerful person in that administration] and he said that the President wants so and so and such and such, and I got rather huffy on the phone and said any instructions like that should come to me through my boss the Attorney General. [The Attorney General] was always very straight with me and I had always had access to his office. When I told him about it, he said 'I'll take care of it' and that was the last time I ever heard from them.

One must be careful when thinking about the nature of 'political' influence. It would be inappropriate for the President to be unable to push for a legal position so long as it was justifiable. After all, he was elected by the people to pursue a vision. Reasonable people can disagree on what constitutes equal protection of the law or disagree about the meaning of a precedent. Why else do we have 5–4 decisions among the justices themselves? When the nation elected Barack Obama as opposed to Mitt Romney, one should expect that policies and beliefs about what the Constitution means would differ. All Solicitors General have an example of when they disagreed with a President or the Attorney General and were overruled, but in most instances they see that as perfectly proper. After all, as a presidential appointee, it is likely that the Solicitor General will share the President's general beliefs and philosophy, and disagreements are likely to be more about prudential choices rather than basic philosophies.

There is one moment in time, however, when it appeared as if the independence of the Solicitor General was being threatened. For a time during the administration of Ronald Reagan, Solicitor General Charles Fried came under strong and unusual criticism. In today's ideologically polarised climate in America, at least in terms of elected officials, the era of Ronald Reagan seems almost tame. At the time, however, Ronald Reagan was the poster boy for ideology-driven conservatism. As controversies arose, especially about positions taken by the Justice Department, the Solicitor General came under public scrutiny. The *New York Times* reported:

> The Solicitor General's Office, an elite corps of lawyers who represent the Government in the Supreme Court, has usually been viewed as a place where law takes precedence over politics. But in the Reagan Administration, it has become a focus of intense political debate. Critics say the Administration has politicized the office by aggressively urging the Court to bring the law into step with the Administration's policies and to repudiate the Court's own precedents.
>
> Former Solicitors General Archibald Cox, Erwin N. Griswold and Wade H. McCree ... have expressed more muted concern that the Administration's assertive posture may have damaged the special stature of the office. Mr. Fried rejects such criticisms as 'nonsense'. He said ... that most of the critics were so hostile to the Administration's views that 'they can't bear to even have them stated (Taylor, Jr 1986).

Appearing in the American Bar Association *Journal*:

> The recent departure of top legal talent from the Office of the Solicitor General was sparked partly by dissatisfaction with the way the new solicitor general, Charles Fried, has reportedly 'politicized' the office to further the Reagan administration's conservative agenda (Blodgett 1986).

The controversy is most famously chronicled in a book entitled *The Tenth Justice: The Solicitor General and the Rule of Law*. The author argued: 'One of the great misdeeds of the Reagan administration was to diminish the institution [the Solicitor General] that, to lawyers at the highest reaches of the profession, once stood for the nations commitment to the rule of law' (Caplan 1987: 277).

There were debates then, and they continue today about how politicised the OSG was under Charles Fried. It is certainly true that the Reagan administration had an aggressive Department of Justice that sought to upend much of the prevailing law on contentious issues – especially affirmative action. Reagan appointed a committed ideologue, William Bradford Reynolds, as the Assistant Attorney General for Civil Rights who frequently locked horns with Solicitor General Rex Lee, Fried's predecessor. There is no doubt that during this time there were some high-profile battles within the Justice Department. Charles Fried, however, was and is no shrinking violet. Whether he was unduly pressured by others or if the policies that he pursued were his own is unclear. In any event, things eventually seemed to return to normal, and the office today seems to have returned to its long traditional role.

Ruminations

As suggested in the opening paragraph of this chapter, there are many normative and empirical questions surrounding the working of the office. This cannot be the venue to discuss them fully, but I shall raise some of the questions. Many of them have to do with the separation of powers in the American system. Who should be the client when there is a disagreement between the President and Congress? Or a related question is, to whom is the Solicitor General responsible when the President disagrees with a law and wishes not to enforce it? No one doubts that the Solicitor General and Attorney General serve at the pleasure of the President, but the task of the Solicitor General is to defend the United States. If a duly passed law of the United States is being attacked and the President prefers not to defend it, what is the proper role for the Solicitor General? The problem is made worse when a current Congress supports the law.[10] Another separation of powers question arises about the closeness of the OSG to the Supreme Court. In interviews that I have conducted in the OSG, it often seemed as if some of the lawyers felt more fidelity to the Court than to the President. Of course any good lawyer seeks to have a good relationship with the judges before whom he or she appears, but the relationship between the Solicitor General and the Supreme Court seemed unusually close. Particularly for the high-ranking and long-serving lawyers in the OSG, Presidents come and go but the justices tend to be the same. Another concern arises because of the legalisation of the American polity. This is, of course, nothing new. Tocqueville famously claimed that sooner or later all political questions turn into legal ones in the United States. That said, few can doubt the growth in the importance of the US Supreme Court to American public policy. One need only look at the presidential election of 2000 or the recent health care ruling for evidence. At least since the advent of legal realism we have realised that law and politics are not neatly separable, but the line has become much more blurred. As Supreme Court cases decide more of our politics, it raises all sorts of questions about how the Solicitor General uses the extraordinary powers of his or her office, particularly in light of the fact that he or she is seen as being relatively

10 As this book goes to press, there is an interesting example before the US Supreme Court. The *Defense of Marriage Act* passed by Congress and signed by President Clinton said that for purposes of the federal government marriage is defined as being between a man and a woman. So even if a State recognised same-sex marriages or unions, the federal government did not for purposes such as federal taxes. The Obama administration has agreed to enforce the law, but it has refused to defend it before the Supreme Court. House Republicans are seeking to defend the law in Court. One of the major issues before the Supreme Court is whether or not they have standing. For a brief discussion of standing in the US see Perry, Jr 2010.

apolitical. In many contexts, insulation from political pressure is desirable. The flip-side is that powerful figures with little political accountability raise other democratic issues. In sum, this out-of-the-limelight office is one that deserves greater attention by scholars. The importance of such scholarship can only grow in light of new developments to which we now turn.

The Rise of State Solicitors General[11]

When I was conducting interviews years ago for a different project, one complaint heard with some frequency from justices and law clerks was how awful the lawyers were who represented States in the US Supreme Court. State Attorneys General, so I was told, were not good appellate lawyers. The low quality seemed to be a particular frustration for the justices who were trying to reinvigorate federalism and State power, but the assessment was widespread among personnel at the Court. Most State Attorneys General are elected, and many of my informants said that State Attorneys General were in their positions because they were good politicians, not because they were great lawyers – certainly not first-rate appellate lawyers. A successful political career was usually their goal. When a case made it to the US Supreme Court, however, the State Attorney General could not resist arguing the case, especially if it were a relatively important case. It is a rare opportunity and a thrill for any lawyer to argue before the US Supreme Court, and it is also good politics for a politician. Depending upon the case, the attentive public may reach beyond his or her State (think abortion), which can help a politician aspiring to higher office. From the perspective of the justices, however, the 30 minutes of fame for the State Attorney General was very frustrating. The lack of good appellate lawyering not only hampered oral argument, but also the briefs were often of poor quality. Another problem was that frequently the case was not the best vehicle to clarify or advance the law. Justices and their clerks usually try to screen for the 'bad vehicle' problem in the certiorari process, but often the weakness of a case is not realised until it is fully briefed and argued.

Relatively recently, States began creating State Solicitors General. It is natural to think that the States are simply trying to recreate the US Solicitor General model in the States. As with many things, however, copying the federal model at the State level is complicated even when that is the intent. Many things at the State level share a name and aspects of a federal entity but in reality work very differently. Slightly over half of the States have created a Solicitor General or something that resembles it. The current number is around 33, depending on how one counts (Symposium Transcript 2010 (Schweitzer); Miller 2010). Some states have created a Solicitor General and then abolished the position. It is not

11 I am currently involved in a research project about State Solicitors General. I have interviewed several people who are or have been the State Solicitor General, as well as lawyers who work in the State Office of the Solicitor General (SOSG).

even clear how many States currently have someone who should be considered a Solicitor General (Symposium Transcript 2010 (Schweitzer)). Some States have someone called Solicitor General, who is not an appellate specialist; and many others have someone who effectively plays the role of a Solicitor General, but is not called that. Some are called 'appellate chief' or have another title (Layton 2001: 533; Miller 2010). As the Solicitor General of Missouri, James Layton, said: 'You know, what is a state solicitor, well it isn't based on title, and I can assure you that from personal experience, because I currently have the third title that I've had in my nearly fifteen years' (Symposium Transcript 2010 (Layton): 635). In some States, the Solicitor General is a statutorily created position; but in most States, it is a creation of the Attorney General, and that immediately makes the federal analogy problematic (Perry, Jr 2010).

To date, there has been little scholarship about State Solicitors General.[12] The reason for the growth in State Solicitors General is not clear. One scholar attempted to explain the growth looking at various factors ranging from demographics to the nature of the dockets (Miller 2010). One likely factor is the increased importance given to appellate advocacy in the US generally (Roberts, Jr. 2005; Lazarus 2008).[13] Some States began to realise that in order to be more effective, they needed better appellate lawyering. This was certainly true for argument before the US Supreme Court and federal appellate courts, but it was increasingly true within their own appellate courts. In my interviews with State Solicitors General, many pointed to the role played by the National Association of Attorneys General (NAAG). In an effort to improve advocacy, this association created 'The Supreme Court Project', which has come to play a very important support role for State Solicitors General and Attorneys General. It often arranges high-level moot courts for State counsel who are going to argue in the Supreme Court, and it helps facilitate joint efforts among States. The head of the project, Dan Schweitzer, has encouraged the development of State Solicitors General. The Missouri Solicitor General (Symposium Transcript 2010 (Layton): 638) explained NAAG's importance as follows:

> I don't want to say that it was NAAG itself that ... gets credit for it [the growth of State Solicitors General], but it is instrumental in its happening ... [With the creation of the Supreme Court Project] NAAG created an entity within the organization that was dedicated to improving the quality of advocacy by the

---

12 I have only found one article by a political scientist (Miller 2010), one journal article by a State Solicitor General (Layton 2001), a few columns by respected legal journalists (for example Coyle 2008: 1; Mauro 2003: 8) and a symposium issue dedicated to appellate lawyering at the University of Texas School of Law (Symposium Transcript 2010) at which the role of the Texas Office of the Solicitor General was prominently featured.

13 The American Academy of Appellate Lawyers was founded in 1990. The American Bar Association established its Council of Appellate lawyers in 2000. The Texas Bar did not have an appellate section until 1987 (Ho 2009: 473).

> states in the United States Supreme Court. So for the first time, NAAG had some place within its organization that was worried about appellate practice. … Also, in the 1980s the conferences of the chief deputies were developed. [He then goes on to recount several meetings and several policy entrepreneurs who pushed for the idea of states adopting the Solicitor General model.]

There has been movement toward State Solicitors General, but many different models have developed in the States. They range from ones that exercise little control to offices that approach the US model. In some States, the State Solicitor General, like the US Solicitor General, has the authority to approve or reject any appeal. In other States, the role is only advisory (Layton 2001: 544). Only 19 State Solicitors General supervise all appeals (Miller 2010). Also, unlike the federal level, in most States there is a distinction between authority regarding civil and criminal cases. At the federal level, US attorneys are part of the Department of Justice and they handle both civil and criminal cases. The Department of Justice has a Criminal Division that sits alongside all the other Divisions. At the State level, criminal prosecution usually resides with elected district attorneys who are not under the State Attorney General, and many State Solicitors General have limited authority in the criminal realm.

One State very consciously modelled its Solicitor General on the US model. It has also been the most successful State office, at least in terms of garnering praise from those who care about better appellate advocacy. It is the State Office of the Solicitor General (SOSG) of Texas. The office has won numerous awards from NAAG and is often used as an example to other States when creating or changing their offices. In fact, its quality has even been recognised by the US Supreme Court. To date, it is the only State office where the US Supreme Court has 'CVSG'd', or called for the views of the (State) Solicitor General comparable to what it does with the US Solicitor General. One way in which the Texas OSG is similar to the US OSG is the quality of lawyers that it is able to attract. The attorneys are of very high calibre. Five have clerked for justices on the US Supreme Court. Others have clerked on the US Circuit Courts of Appeals, the Texas Supreme Court and other courts both State and federal. Several have been partners in prestigious law firms. Lawyers leave the office to go to some of the nation's most prestigious law firms (Ho 2009: 476). There was a time when lawyers in the Attorney General's office were dedicated public servants, but they were rarely thought of as being on the 'fast track'. To be a member of the OSG in Texas now is seen as prestigious in and of itself, and it also can be a ticket to major law firms or other positions of prestige. Although Texas is an outlier, some States are moving in this direction. If this trend continues, it suggests a whole new arena that will shape not only State appellate advocacy, but it will also have effects on the private Bar as well.

Even when States seek to emulate the US model, there are important differences. The first and foremost is authority. The US Solicitor General is an office created by statute, and while the Solicitor General is subordinate to the Attorney General, the Solicitor General is a presidential appointee. As discussed above, the OSG has come to have a great deal of independence and formal and informal sources of power and authority. It has existed for 142 years, and it has had a long time to demonstrate to Presidents and Attorneys General that it is in their interest to allow the Solicitor General to be very independent. Recall that another important source of its power and independence is the high regard with which it is held by the justices of the US Supreme Court. State Solicitors General have a very different source of power and authority. They usually exist and serve at the pleasure of the State Attorney General. Unlike most US Attorneys General, State Attorneys General are often politicians seeking higher office. State Attorneys General can marginalise State Solicitors General easily, and it may be in the political interest of some to do so. The political situation is even more complex. State Attorneys General are usually elected officials and may be political rivals of the Governor. Indeed, they may not be from the same political party. Relationships within the executive branch can be quite complicated, and the relationship with the State legislature is often more complicated than what occurs in Washington, DC.

One comparison among States and with the federal government is particularly hard to assess. One important source of power for the US OSG is undoubtedly its 'winning ways'. The success rate is empirically documented and long-running. It is actually very difficult to tell how well the State Solicitors General are doing. There is no easy way to collect such data, and even offices as advanced and sophisticated as the Texas OSG do not keep such records. Even more important, however, is not the win/loss rate but whether better advocacy really matters much in terms of 'output'. No doubt judges appreciate better advocacy, but the effects on the quality of legal opinions or the effects on public policy are quite hard to measure. For example, there is much evidence to demonstrate how the US Solicitor General's briefs and oral argument shape Supreme Court opinions. There is little evidence gathered at the State level, and such data would be harder to gather. Normative questions arise as well. For all the benefits, would it really be a good thing for SOSGs to become as powerful at the State level as the US Solicitor General is at the federal level, especially given the fact that State judiciaries do not have the resources and often not the intellectual power that exists at the US Supreme Court or the federal appeals courts? The normative questions surrounding 'who is the client' are difficult enough at the federal level. At the State level, they are far more complex with non-unitary executives and more elected officials, often including elected judges and justices. In sum, much study is needed of State Solicitors General, but efforts at generalising will be difficult and there is a danger that understandings about the US Solicitor General could easily distort analysis of these State institutions.

If comparing Solicitors General within the context of the United States is difficult, how much more so is it to compare across continents? Comparative research is always fraught with dangers of superficial comparison. Nevertheless, as the chapters in this book attest, some things about Solicitors General seem to transcend time and political systems. I am struck by how many similarities I see among all the different situations described in this book. The role of the

Solicitor General is a testament to the importance of the rule of law in political systems; and, ironically, it is a testament to the importance of understanding the intersections of law and politics.

References

Biddle, F. 1962. *In Brief Authority*. New York: Doubleday.

Blodgett, N. 1986. Solicitor General: Has Office been Politicized? *American Bar Association Journal*. Volume 72(5), 20.

Brigman, W.E. 1966. *The Office of the Solicitor General of the United States*, PhD dissertation: University of North Carolina.

Caplan, L. 1987. *The Tenth Justice: The Solicitor General and the Rule of Law*. New York: Knopf.

Coyle, M. 2008. Justices Listen to a Key Voice: State Solicitors General Get More Time in High Court. *National Law Journal*. 7 April 2008.

Cummings, H.S. and McFarland, C. 1937. *Federal Justice: Chapters in the History of Justice and the Federal Executive*. New York: Macmillan.

Days, D.S. 2001. When the President Says 'No': A Few Thoughts on Executive Power and the Tradition of Solicitor General Independence. *Journal of Appellate Practice and Procedure*. Volume 3, 509.

Easby-Smith, J.S. 1904. *The Department of Justice: Its History and Functions*. Washington, DC: Lowdermilk.

Fahy, C. 1942. The Office of the Solicitor General. *American Bar Association Journal*. Volume 28(20), 22.

Galanter, M. 1974. Why the 'Haves' Come Out Ahead: Speculations on the Limits of Legal Change. *Law and Society Review*. Volume 9(1), 95.

Hightower, J. 1974. From Attornatus to the Department of Justice: An Historical Perspective reprinted in US Congress, Senate Committee on the Judiciary, Subcommittee on the Separation of Powers, *Removing Politics from the Administration of Justice*, 93rd Cong., 2nd Sess.

Ho, J.C. 2009. *Role of Appellate Lawyers at the Solicitor General's Office*. Austin: Advanced Civil Appellate Practice Course, Texas Bar CLE.

Jenckes, T.A. 1870. *Congressional Globe*, 41st Cong., 2nd Sess.

Key, S. 1938. The Legal Work of the Federal Government. *Virginia Law Review*. Volume 25, 165.

Layton, J.R. 2001. The Evolving Role of the State Solicitor: Toward the Federal Model? *Journal of Appellate Practice and Process*. Volume 3(2), 533.

Lazarus, R.J. 2008. Advocacy Matters Before and Within the U.S. Supreme Court: Transforming the Court by Transforming the Bar. *Georgetown Law Journal*. Volume 96, 1487.

Mauro, T. 2003. Stating their Case. *Legal Times*. 11 August 2003, 1.

McCree, W. 1981. The Solicitor General and his Client. *Washington University Law Quarterly*. Volume 59, 337.

McGuire, K.T. 1995. Repeat Players in the Supreme Court: The Role of Experienced Lawyers in Litigation Success. *Journal of Politics*. Volume 57(1), 187–96.

Miller, B. 2010. Describing the State Solicitors General. *Judicature*. Volume 93, 238–46.

Perry, Jr, H.W. 1991. *Deciding to Decide: Agenda Setting in the U.S. Supreme Court*. Cambridge: Harvard University Press.

Perry, Jr, H.W. 1998. United States Attorneys – Whom Shall They Serve? *Law and Contemporary Problems*. Volume 61, 129.

Perry, Jr, H.W. 2010. Access to Justice: Procedure, Polity and Politics. *Bond Law Review*. Volume 22(3), 192.

Roberts, Jr, J.G. 2005. Oral Advocacy and the Re-emergence of a Supreme Court Bar. *Journal of Supreme Court History*. Volume 30(68).

Salokar, R.M. 1992. *The Solicitor General: The Politics of Law*. Philadelphia: Temple University Press.

Symposium Transcript. 2010. The Rise of Appellate Litigators and State Solicitors General. *Review of Litigation*. Volume 29, 545–727.

Taylor, Jr, S. 1986. Solicitor General's Office; Tasting the Salty Air of Politics and Criticism. *New York Times*, 18 July 1986.

United States Department of Justice. 2012a. *About the Office* [Online: General Information, Office of the Associate Attorney General]. Available at: http://www.justice.gov/asg/about-oaag.html.

United States Department of Justice. 2012b. *About the Office* [Online: General Information, Office of the Deputy Attorney General]. Available at: http://www.justice.gov/dag/about-odag.html.

Waxman, S. 2011. *'Presenting the Case of the United States as It Should Be': The Solicitor General in Historical Context* [Online, 18 July 2011]. Available at: http://www.justice.gov/osg/aboutosg/historic-context.html.

Chapter 12

Government Lawyers and the Elusive Concept of Public Interest: A Canadian Perspective

M. Deborah MacNair[1]

Introduction

The Attorney General, as the chief Law Officer of the Crown, has been the rallying point historically for government lawyers in Canada as it is this public official who is the guardian of the public interest, who upholds the rule of law (Edwards 1984: 360) and who is the titular head of the legal profession.[2] The office of the Solicitor General no longer exists in Canada, replaced in 2004 by the Minister of Public Safety. Nevertheless, the Minister of Public Safety remains responsible for overseeing criminal law enforcement, corrections, emergency preparedness, crime prevention and national security, so the two Ministers oversee the administration of justice as sentinels at the national level (Public Safety Canada 2013).

There is an Attorney General at both the federal and provincial levels of government for criminal and civil matters,[3] and recognition for this office is found in the Constitution (R.S.C. 1985, App. II, No. 5: ss 9, 11, 34, 63) and in provincial legislation (*Krieger v Law Society of Alberta* [2002] 3 S.C.R. 372). As the Attorney General is also the Minister of Justice, this duality in mandate has had a lasting impact on how government lawyers understand the notion of public interest and apply it when carrying out their responsibilities.

The purpose of this chapter is to examine the notion of public interest for government lawyers in the Canadian context in relation to the role of the Attorney General. It is argued, in line with what others have suggested (Tait 1997: 542; Collins 2010), that it is not necessary to define the concept of public interest

1 The views in this chapter are those of the author and are not to be attributed to the federal Department of Justice. An earlier version was presented at the Australasian Law Teachers Association conference in Auckland, New Zealand, July 2010.

2 The Attorney General of Canada, Solicitor General of Canada and provincial Attorneys General are benchers of the law society by virtue of their office in some provinces: see, for example, *Law Society Act*, R.S.O. 1990, c. L.8: s 12.

3 See, for example, *Ministry of the Attorney General Act*, R.S.O. 1990, c. M.1 and the *Department of Justice Act*, R.S.C. 1985, c. J-2 (Department of Justice Act).

or to create an elaborate standard for government lawyers. It is the historical, inspirational and timeless role of the Attorney General (Stenning 1986: 72–87) that demonstrates what values are important for lawyers in the government practice of law and enables them to fulfil their professional duties credibly and responsibly (Collins 2010).

This chapter is organised in the following manner: first, it provides a brief background to the regulation of legal professionals in Canada and the position of public sector lawyers, followed by an introduction to the role of the Attorney General in civil and criminal matters and how this is relevant to understanding the public interest standard for public sector lawyers. The chapter then provides an overview of recent case law that has considered the applicable regulatory framework for lawyers in the public sector. Next, the chapter offers a glimpse into the future for government lawyers and how they grapple with the notion of public interest, before offering some concluding remarks.

Background: Private and Government Practitioners

Private and government practitioners have co-existed as two legal solitudes in Canada without much debate or reflection. The legal profession has survived on the basis of autonomy and self-regulation (*Canada (Attorney General) v Law Society of B.C.* [1982] 2 S.C.R. 307: 335–6 (Estey J)) and with a shared and equal mandate by both groups to serve the public interest. There is a body of case law on legal ethics and national and local law society codes of professional conduct that prescribe rules of conduct on a range of subjects from integrity, client relations and confidentiality to conflicts of interest. Law societies have exclusive jurisdiction to assert and enforce standards for qualification, admission and discipline.

The previously secret nature of government practice has changed partly as a result of the release of the 'Torture Memos' in the United States. The role of the American government lawyer has been thrust into the spotlight in light of the revelations surrounding the release of a number of legal opinions prepared by the Office of Legal Counsel using debatable legal reasoning to authorise the use of torture. The public interest role of American government attorneys has been debated openly by academics, and various published documents record the importance of this obligation (see, for example, the *Restatement of the Law, The Law Governing Lawyers* (American Law Institute 2000), Preamble to the *Model Rules of Professional Conduct* (American Bar Association 2007)[4] and the *Model Rules of Professional Conduct for Federal Lawyers* (Federal Bar Association 1990)).

Canadian government practitioners have unexpectedly been drawn into the debate as well (Querijero 2010: 241). However, the situation is different for government practitioners in Canada, where the employment relationship with

4 See at 3: 'The Federal lawyer should also promote public service'.

the Crown has been more nuanced and subtle by reference to the historical role in Britain of the Attorney General (Edwards 1984: 360). Canadian public sector lawyers may have felt uncomfortable at times with the mainstream legal profession and how it was structured and regulated, but there has not been any pressing need to discuss it publicly so there has been very little academic literature on point.[5] Despite the lack of discussion, there is a general sense that public sector lawyers owe a different, and perhaps more taxing, obligation to the public interest. John Tait (1997: 542), former Deputy Minister for the federal Department of Justice, aptly described the role of government lawyers as follows:

> Public service lawyers have some duties that are unique to them and others they share with all lawyers. They share with other lawyers a basic responsibility to interpret the law, advise on the law and sometimes take actions relating to legal matters.
>
> But a number of duties unique to government lawyers are: (1) Public service lawyers are guardians of the rule of law as it applies within government in a parliamentary democracy; (2) they have an important relationship to their own Minister in a system of responsible government; and (3) they have a constant focus on the public interest. Integral to these roles are a special focus on values of integrity, objectivity, loyalty, fairness and reasonableness.

The concept of public interest is not readily defined, and law society codes of professional conduct do not make any distinctions for private and government lawyers about how to interpret and apply it (Dodek 2010: 1). David Collins, the former Solicitor-General for New Zealand, takes a pragmatic view towards the role of government lawyers in advancing the public interest. He believes that, rather than further debating the definition of public interest, it is important instead to focus on how the government's obligation to advance the public interest shapes how government lawyers carry out their responsibilities (Collins 2010). In addition, this is supported by adherence to good ethical practices, following government guidelines and codes, strong legal education and skills development and good institutional practice standards (Collins 2010). Tait (1997: 544) describes the government lawyer's role as ensuring 'that policy and program development is lawful, ethical, and respectful of due process, the Constitution and the values that underpin it'. This chapter builds from this premise, evaluating the obligations of the Attorney General for Canada to the public interest and how these assist in defining and shaping the government lawyer's duties in their practical application.

5 This has been encouraged by the little case law on point. In *Everingham v Ontario* (1991) 84 D.L.R. (4th) 354, for example, the court concluded government lawyers do not have a higher ethical duty than other lawyers.

The Attorney-General and the Main Elements of Public Interest

The attributes of public interest relevant to the government lawyer in the Canadian context can be drawn from the democratic framework in which the Attorney General carries out his responsibilities. I have summarised the position elsewhere as follows:

> Historically, the role of the Attorney General encapsulates the concept of serving the public interest and this is accomplished largely on the premise that the office is independent. It is not clear if the Attorneys General must carry out their functions in a practice manner or as the symbolic defender of the public good but it is accepted that the responsibility as guardian of the public interest must take precedence. As the representative of the state it is the Attorneys General, at both federal and provincial levels of government, who superintend litigation for or against the Crown, on the civil side, and who prosecute criminal matters. Equally as important, some would argue, is the legal advisory role to public service institutions to ensure their actions are in accordance with the law. It is the Attorney General in England who historically has assumed other roles in the same vein as the 'protector of the state' where there is an obligation to act in the public interest: as *amicus curiae*, as *parens patriae*, by providing a fiat in relator actions and by giving consent to private prosecutions (MacNair 2006: 184–5).

A key element of the Attorney General's role, in contrast to other Ministers in government, is independence. This has been interpreted to mean non-partisanship so that the Attorney General is free from undue influence in making his decisions, and therefore it has many facets. The Attorney General is a member of Cabinet, and is accountable to Parliament, but by convention has reserved the right to remain free from political influence in making decisions about criminal prosecutions. This is a statement from Lord Shawcross in Britain, which was given official recognition in 1978 in the Canadian Parliament (Sterling and Mackay 2003: 169). This approach has always been viewed as an essential element of the public interest in democracy for all government lawyers as public servants for both civil and criminal matters, but it is applied differently in civil matters.[6] The principle can be challenging for government practitioners to translate into the daily practice of law. For Crown prosecutors it means exercising the discretion to prosecute impartially without bias or irrelevant considerations entering into their decision-making process. In the case of civil litigators, the conduct of litigation should be principled and based on the interpretation of case authority in a consistent manner, but there is support

6 Participation in political activities is prescribed for federal lawyers in Part VII of the *Public Service Employment Act*, S.C. 2003, c. 22: ss 12, 13. Paragraph 4(a) of the *Department of Justice Act* provides that the Minister of Justice has a responsibility to 'see that the administration of public affairs is in accordance with the law'.

for the theory that civil litigators do not have to be impartial in their advocacy.[7] The independence of the Attorney General is less inhibited, and arguably more difficult to maintain, in civil matters; but, nevertheless, it is based on an overriding duty to government and society rather than an allegiance to one political party. It is accepted that the discussion in Cabinet on civil matters can be more consultative in order to ensure that the full range of considerations on a public policy matter, legislation or civil litigation matter are noted.

The Attorney General is expected to uphold the rule of law and administer justice equally to all citizens. As the Attorney General is the public official who is most closely aligned with the public trust, it is by his independent actions principally as chief Law Officer of the Crown in initiating a criminal prosecution, providing legal advice, in the conduct of civil litigation, preparing legislation or advancing public policy that the notion of the public interest has been given substantive content. Consequently, and by tradition, legal advice and decision-making by government lawyers must be impartial, principled and balanced (Sterling and Mackay 2009: 891). The role of the criminal prosecutor is not to obtain a conviction but to respect the justness of the case (*R v Boucher* [1955] S.C.R. 16); the role of the Attorney General in civil matters is less constrained because the government lawyer is setting out the government's position on a matter. According to Tait (1997: 544), the public interest role of the government solicitor (that is, lawyers providing legal advice to government) can be reduced to the following three perspectives:

> His or her role is to advise, first on the Constitution and the law, which is one representation of the public interest; second, on the ethical matters deriving from the duties of Ministers and public servants, which are often of a fiduciary nature; and third, on the policy wisdom or public interest from a government lawyer's perspective (not just his personal views) and not in a way that fails to respect the client department's mandate and expertise.

A third element of the public interest is the Attorney General's association with the rule of law in upholding the supremacy of the law, the preservation of orderliness in the justice system and the requirement for legal authority for the exercise of a public power. While this concept is not always easy to define, it is reflected at the federal level in the Attorney General's obligation in the federal *Department of Justice Act* to uphold the law and to ensure that public officials act in accordance with the law. Consequently, government lawyers must assess and interpret the law fairly and objectively without jumping to conclusions or straining the interpretation of the law to make things easier or to please the government client.

However, other theories have been advanced. Adam Dodek argues that government lawyers are different from other lawyers because of their role to

7 *New Brunswick v Rothmans Inc.* [2009] NBQB 198; appealed on other grounds [2009] NBJ No. 293 (NBCA).

uphold the rule of law. Consequently, he further argues that government lawyers have a higher ethical duty than private practitioners because they exercise public power and act as custodians of the rule of law (Dodek 2010: 18–31).

Arguably, this theory does not conform to the current role of government lawyers in practice. Government lawyers do not exercise the power to make decisions, as government administrative action is delegated to public officials. Further, Dodek's theory is unsupported in the reported case law. The courts still maintain the traditional view that government policy and legislation adequately provide for public interest considerations and that no additional rights can be implied as a public interest override. The Supreme Court of Canada recently ruled, in a landmark decision overturning the Ontario Court of Appeal, that when the Ontario legislature decided not to provide for a public interest override for solicitor–client privilege for government legal advice in its access to information legislation, the court was not prepared to interfere (*Ontario (Public Safety and Security) v Criminal Lawyers' Association* [2010] 1 S.C.R. 815). In that case, there had been allegations of police misconduct and subsequently the Ontario Provincial Police had investigated and prepared a report. The Criminal Lawyers' Association made a request under the provincial access legislation for disclosure of the investigation records composed of a police report, two documents and legal advice. The court disagreed that the solicitor–client records should be disclosed on the basis that disclosure would be in the public interest. This approach by the courts would suggest that they are not yet ready to impose a higher duty on government lawyers by ordering disclosure of legal advice in support of a seemingly laudable public purpose, in this case lost evidence by the police that was disclosed to the defence two and a half years after the trial.

There have been similar calls in other jurisdictions to make more government-protected information available to the public, including solicitor–client information, on the basis of democratic rights by citizens to know what is going on in government (Dodek 2010).[8] The results have been different from what occurred in Canada. In the United States, for example, the Court of Appeals for the District of Columbia Circuit decided that attorney–client privilege did not apply to conversations between Deputy White House Counsel Bruce Lindsey and then President Bill Clinton that were relevant to a grand jury investigation about possible federal crimes by government officials (*In re Lindsey* (1998) 158 F.3d 1263 in Berenson 2000: 795).

As noted above, some of the legal documentation associated with the 'Torture Memos' has been released publicly, including the legal advice that became the subject of investigation subsequently.[9] There have been similar disclosures of legal advice in the United Kingdom during the Chilcot Inquiry from government

8 See also, American Constitution Society for Law and Policy 2006: 1345; Hutchinson 2008: 105.

9 The report has not yet been listed on the website for the Office of Professional Responsibility.

lawyers involved in giving advice to the Prime Minister about the decision to enter the war with Iraq (Iraq Inquiry 2010). Peter Goldsmith, the Attorney General for England and Wales during the invasion of Iraq, indicated publicly that he changed his mind about the legal position on the necessity of having a further United Nations Security Council Resolution to ensure that any invasion of Iraq was legal. Michael Wood, the Foreign Office legal adviser at the time the events occurred, indicated during the same inquiry that his legal advice was ignored. Deputy legal adviser to the British Foreign Office Elizabeth Wilmshurst resigned in protest in March 2003, a few days before the invasion in Iraq, as a result of the legal position taken by the Attorney General. A copy of her resignation letter was released to the BBC as a result of a request under the *Freedom of Information Act* (UK) (2000: c. 36; BBC News 2005). She took the position that the war with Iraq was not legal without a further United Nations Resolution. In summary, Canadian law currently recognises no general overriding public interest in the disclosure of legal advice provided to government by its legal advisers similar to what occurred in Britain and the United States.

Members of the public and the legal profession frequently identify the concept of the public interest with the role of criminal prosecutors. While there has not been much academic discussion on the point, Allan Hutchinson (2008: 115) argues that the differences between criminal prosecutors and private lawyers are more significant than the differences between prosecutors and other government lawyers because, in the case of the latter group, it is the public interest that binds them together:

> While they do not fulfill exactly the same roles or assume exactly the same obligations, government lawyers and prosecution lawyers both share a common duty to advance the public interest as a direct and explicit undertaking.

In practice, the local administration of the justice system in Canada is left largely to the provincial Attorneys General in each of the 10 provinces. There are significant exceptions to this constitutional division of powers. The prosecution of criminal offences under all federal statutes in the Yukon Territory, the Northwest Territories or Nunavut; the appointment of federal judges; the development of criminal law policy, including the *Criminal Code* (R.S.C. 1985, c. C-46.); and the prosecution of federal drug offences, tax evasions and war crimes are left to the federal Attorney General. The Attorney General presides over the federal Department of Justice and the Public Prosecution Service of Canada (*Director of Public Prosecutions Act*, S.C. 2006, c. 9, s. 121). The Public Prosecution Service of Canada, formerly known as the Federal Prosecution Service, was hived off from the federal Department of Justice in December 2006 as a separate government department for the prosecution of federal criminal offences.

According to the *Federal Prosecution Service Deskbook* (Federal Prosecution Service 2000), the Crown prosecutor must follow a two-step process in deciding whether a prosecution is merited. The prosecutor must first consider whether in light of all the evidence there is a reasonable prospect for conviction. The next step is to consider the facts and circumstances of each case and determine if it is in the public interest to undertake a prosecution. The Public Prosecution Service of Canada has developed a detailed set of 18 public interest criteria to assist Crown prosecutors with their decision-making, including the seriousness of the offence, bringing the system of justice into disrepute, whether the offence is of considerable public concern and the availability of alternatives to the prosecution (Federal Prosecution Service 2000: V-15-4–V-15-6). There is also a list of 'irrelevant criteria' that must not affect the Crown prosecutor's judgment in a negative way (Federal Prosecution Service 2000: V-15-7). In other words, this approach serves to describe clearly not only what is *in* the public interest but also what is *not* in the public interest.

The *Federal Prosecution Service Deskbook* (2000: III-8-3), now adopted by the Public Prosecution Service of Canada, contains the following reminder for counsel:

> Individual prosecutors are also subject to a form of public accountability through their membership in provincial law societies. Another form of public accountability occurs through judicial review of a prosecutor's actions, for example through the abuse of process doctrine, or judicial control of actions which may prejudice fair trial interests, such as inflammatory jury addresses. Accountability is also enhanced because of the availability to the public of the Federal Prosecution Service Deskbook, since the public is able to assess the actions of Crown counsel against the standards set out in the policies. Finally, recognition of the importance of public accountability imposes a duty on Crown counsel in certain circumstances to communicate the reasons for certain decisions to the public through the media.

In summary, the Attorney-General's traditional obligations to the public interest affect the role in its criminal and civil manifestations, although the latter is less understood in practice.

Recent Case Law

Interestingly, there is very little jurisprudence on the application of the public interest standard to government counsel. As noted earlier, *Krieger v Law Society of Alberta* did, however, reach the Supreme Court of Canada in 2002 from the province of Alberta. There were 11 interveners in the case, including the federal Attorney General of Canada, the Federation of Law Societies and the Criminal Trial Lawyers' Association. The central issue was the authority of a law society to regulate the ethical conduct of a government lawyer. For its part, the Law Society of Alberta claimed that it had jurisdiction to impose professional standards on any Alberta lawyer, including those employed by the provincial government. In reply, the Crown prosecutor and his employer, the Attorney General of Alberta, argued that the Law Society of Alberta did not have jurisdiction to review the conduct of a Crown prosecutor acting honestly and in good faith, as it was an accepted constitutional principle that Attorneys General must act independently and without regard to partisan concerns.

The facts of the case are straightforward. A provincial Crown prosecutor, Mr Krieger, declined to follow the established rules of disclosure and, when the provincial Attorney General's department investigated the Attorney General's office, concluded that Krieger had in fact made an error in judgment. Krieger was disciplined – a letter of reprimand was placed on his file and he was removed from the case. The lawyer who had complained about Krieger was advised of this outcome. The Attorney General's office also put a new guideline in place, which required Crown prosecutors to consult with the chief Crown prosecutor before deciding to delay disclosure for investigative purposes, as had been the case for Krieger. Later the accused complained to the Law Society of Alberta, and, after review, the Deputy Secretary of the Law Society accepted the complaint and referred it to the Conduct Committee for advice on how to proceed.

There were two unique features of this case that bear mentioning. The Law Society's *Code of Professional Conduct* (2012) contained provisions concerning disclosure requirements, which closely followed and codified the existing case law. Secondly, the *Code of Professional Conduct* was the only code that contained a specific chapter (Chapter 12) in which the responsibilities for government counsel were described.

The Supreme Court sided with the Law Society of Alberta,[10] that subsection 92(13) of the Constitution for property and civil rights could be used to ground its jurisdiction. The Supreme Court took into consideration the fact that provincial Crown prosecutors were required to be members of the Law Society and that the disclosure of relevant evidence was a legal duty as opposed to a specific exercise of prosecutorial discretion. However, in this case the Supreme Court concluded that the conduct of the Crown prosecutor had been inappropriate and fell within the Law Society's authority to review dishonest or bad faith conduct. The Supreme Court (at [50]) was prepared to distinguish between the scope of 'prosecutorial discretion' and 'professional conduct' by drawing the following boundaries:

> There is a clear distinction between prosecutorial discretion and professional conduct. It is only the latter that can be regulated by the Law Society. The Law Society has the jurisdiction to investigate any alleged breach of its ethical standards, even those committed by Crown prosecutors in connection with their prosecutorial discretion. This is important as the interests of the Attorney General in promoting the administration of justice may differ from those of the Law Society in regulating the legal profession and maintaining public

10 A body properly constituted under the *Legal Profession Act* (S.A. 1990, c. L-9.1 (now R.S.A. 2000, c. L-8)) as enacted by the legislature of Alberta.

> confidence. The remedies available to each entity differ according to their respective function. The Attorney General's office has the ability to discipline a prosecutor for failing to meet the standards set by the Attorney General's office for prosecutors but that is a different function from the ability to discipline the same prosecutor in his or her capacity as a member of the Law Society of Alberta. It may be that in some instances the conduct required by the Attorney General to retain employment will exceed the standards of the Law Society but of necessity that conduct will never be lower than that required by the Law Society. In addition, the Attorney General, after finding that a Crown prosecutor has acted in bad faith, does not have the power to restrict a member's practice or disbar a member. An Attorney General can do nothing to prevent a Crown prosecutor from practising law in another area.

The Supreme Court stopped short of discussing in any detail what fell under the umbrella of 'ethical standards'. When asked by the intervener, the federal Attorney General of Canada, to exclude federal Crown prosecutors from the decision, the Supreme Court declined to do so and instead expressly confirmed in the decision that federal Crown prosecutors were subject to the same ethical obligations as all other lawyers and that, consequently, federal Crown prosecutors were not entitled to any special immunity.

While the preponderance of Canadian legal authority is that government lawyers do not owe a higher ethical or professional duty to members of the legal profession or the public (*Everingham v Ontario* (1991) 84 D.L.R. (4th) 354)), the perception is that they probably should because of the link to the Attorney General's role as guardian of the public interest and keeper of the rule of law. Moreover, this perspective is built on the assumption that government lawyers should owe a duty to the members of the Canadian public because they are salaried employees who advise Ministers elected by citizens to carry out the government's mandate.

The Future

There are signs that the concept of public interest is still relevant for government lawyers and that the skill of lawyering to keep pace with it is evolving under the aegis of the Attorney General for Canada and the values instilled by that office. There are values and ethics codes that prescribe the rules of engagement for employment purposes and that refer to the public interest – a public servant is expected to prefer the public interest over any private interest and to avoid inappropriate intermingling of the two interests, particularly in any financial dealings (Treasury Board of Canada Secretariat 2011).

However, some would go further than simply encouraging government lawyers to adhere to values and ethics codes (Dodek 2010: 1). There is a movement to encourage government lawyers to identify directly with the public's democratic needs in order to fulfil the requirement to act in the public interest, a theme that has surfaced in the case of American government lawyers (Hutchinson 2008). Some of the United States debate has focussed on the different models of lawyering for government lawyers and not necessarily on the standards that should apply as a guide for their ethical conduct, a theme that is described in the following excerpt:

> Alongside the dominant model, traditional conceptions of lawyers' ethics also recognize what might be called the 'public interest' model. This model, although still adopting as central the duties of loyalty, zeal and confidentiality, puts relatively greater emphasis on the duties of the lawyer to the court and to innocent third parties. Advocates of the public interest model argued that untrammeled loyalty to the client's interests risks allowing lawyers to support manifest social injustice.
>
> …
>
> The two traditional models of legal ethics run roughly parallel to the two major approaches to government lawyers' ethics. The first approach, which can usefully be called the 'agency loyalty' approach, basically follows the dominant model in that it sharply limits the realm in which the lawyer may permissibly attempt to exert influence over the client. According to this approach, the government lawyer's client is the agency that employs the lawyer, and the lawyer owes the traditional duties of loyalty, zeal, and confidentiality to the agency just as the lawyer would to a private client. The other principal approach, which will be called the 'public interest approach', has a close relationship to the public interest model of lawyering. The public interest approach to government lawyering, however, goes further than the public interest model of private lawyering because it makes serving the public interest the government lawyer's primary duty and consequently values the interests of the lawyer's agency only to the extent that those interests coincide with the public interest (Notes 2002: 1171–3).

Is it fair to argue that government lawyers should be bound by the notion of public interest, and is it meaningful to them? I believe the answer is 'yes'. As public servants, government lawyers are in tune with their public duties and how their decision-making is sometimes limited by them. For example, public servants may have the right to express their views but this right may be constrained by the duty of loyalty to the government of the day. There is a public interest in keeping this standard in place because criticism of the government of the day can undermine the system for the administration of justice by appearing to attack the officials they advise. As employees of the government department that is imbued with the historical traditions of the office of the Attorney General, government lawyers understand the importance of maintaining values, such as independence, over time. The concept of the public interest may not be as fully developed as everyone would like, but it remains an important part of the work of government lawyers and how they conceptualise their daily obligations.

However, the review of the current literature reveals that there is room for greater discussion about the delivery of civil, as opposed to criminal, legal services. The Crown prosecutor has always been singled out for special treatment in the law society codes of professional conduct, likely because of the links to the truth-seeking function of this type of lawyer. There are other less subtle differences between Crown prosecutors and other government lawyers, and the Canadian Bar Association *Code of Professional Conduct* (2009) is revealing in that regard:

> Duties of Prosecutor
>
> 9. When engaged as a prosecutor, the lawyer's prime duty is not to seek a conviction, but to present before the trial court all available credible evidence relevant to the alleged crime in order that justice may be done through a fair trial upon the merits. The prosecutor exercises a public function involving much discretion and power, and must act fairly and dispassionately. The prosecutor should not do anything that might prevent the accused from being represented by counsel or communicating with counsel and, to the extent required by law and accepted practice, should make timely disclosure to the accused or defence counsel (or to the court if the accused is not represented) of all relevant facts and known witnesses, whether tending to show guilt or innocence, or that would affect the punishment of the accused. There is a clear distinction between prosecutorial discretion and professional conduct. Only the latter can be regulated by a law society. A law society has jurisdiction to investigate any alleged breach of its ethical standards, even those committed by Crown prosecutors in connection with their prosecutorial discretion.

On the other hand, and this appears slightly out of context for government lawyers, the Guiding Principle in Chapter IX for advocates is as follows:

> 1. The advocate's duty to the client is 'fearlessly to raise every issue, advance every argument, and ask every question, however distasteful, which he thinks will help his client's case' and to endeavour 'to obtain for his client the benefit of any and every remedy and defence which is authorized by law' must always be discharged by fair and honourable means, without illegality and in a manner consistent with the lawyer's duty to treat the court with candour, fairness, courtesy and respect (Canadian Bar Association 2009).

The public interest role of government lawyers is not without its critics. Steven Berenson (2000: 790–91) aptly summarises the criticisms of those who oppose the idea of the appropriateness of a public interest standard for government counsel:

> Some critics of the public interest serving role for government attorneys argue that government attorneys cannot work to pursue the public interest because the very concept of a 'public interest' is unintelligible and cannot provide a workable guidepost for government attorneys with regard to the choices and decisions that they must make in their professional roles. Other critics argue that even if the concept of a public interest is sufficiently intelligible to provide guidance to government attorneys in their professional decision making, government attorneys should not attempt to pursue their conceptions of the public interest in their professional capacities. In the criminal context, such critics argue that efforts by prosecutors to serve the public interest rather than to do everything possible to secure convictions will tip the balance in criminal trials in favour of defendants and their attorneys, who do not operate with similar constraints. In the civil context, the critics contend that it would be anti-democratic for government attorneys to pursue their particular determination of the public interest with regard to any particular legal controversy, and that any determinations regarding how the public interest will best be served with regard to any legal controversy should be made by public officials who are more democratically accountable than government attorneys are. Finally, some critics of the public interest serving role for government attorneys argue that even if government attorneys can and should work to pursue the public interest they will not do so. Rather, this group of critics contends that government attorneys will work to advance their individual, financial, or career-related self-interests at the expense of the broader public interest.

These arguments overlook the fact that individuals are often drawn to public service because the practice of law in this context aligns with their interest of serving the common good. Even if individual lawyers cannot articulate in express terms what the concept of the public interest means to them, they will see and debate the public interest elements in the cases in which they are directly involved. As they do so, they will be guided by instruments such as statements of mission and values and codes of values and ethics. These instruments help government lawyers by describing the appropriate constraints for their conduct and decision-making, such as acting in self-interest.

Government Lawyers and Law Societies: A Good Fit?

There are two difficulties with bringing government lawyers under the umbrella of law societies. First, there is a difficulty with importing and applying law society requirements and codes of professional conduct into the world of government lawyers. The philosophical approaches and basic expectations are not necessarily compatible. In carrying out their enforcement functions, law societies concentrate on the protection of individual, private interests; codes of professional conduct are drafted to circumscribe and fortify those interests in the general context of the privately represented individual client. It is often an impossible task for government lawyers to extrapolate the meaning of rules regarding the safekeeping of confidential information or avoiding conflicts of interest when the basic premise on which the code of professional conduct is interpreted differs so dramatically in concept for the public and private Bars. While law societies seek to protect the public, there are a significant number of government lawyers who never have any direct contact with the public, and other than the obvious case of self-represented clients, government lawyers will normally be dealing with their legal representatives. Consequently, the government lawyer's notion of advancing justice for the lawful objectives of the whole of government as a Crown entity does not always square well with the private sector's lawyers' fierceness and advancement of individual client interests in the private sector world.

There are cases that illustrate the incongruity between codes of professional conduct and the operational context for government lawyers. The case of *Tiboni v Merck Frosst Canada Ltd* (2009) 97 O.R. (3d) 125 illustrates the contrast between private values and public sector obligations. The starting point for the case is Rule 6.05(5) of the Law Society of Upper Canada *Rules of Professional Conduct* (2012):

> A lawyer who has left public office shall not act for a client in connection with any matter for which the lawyer had substantial responsibility before leaving public office.

In an action brought against the pharmaceutical company Merck Frosst Canada Ltd, the plaintiffs claimed that the company had not disclosed enough information to Health Canada, the government department charged with the responsibility of approving drugs, about the risks associated with a drug called Vioxx. As this was a class proceeding, the plaintiffs were required to bring a motion to certify the proposed class. Mr Rock, a former Minister of Health Canada from 11 June 1997 to 15 February 2002, former Minister of Justice and lawyer, had subsequently joined the law firm that now represented the plaintiffs. Merck Frosst had obtained approval for the drug Vioxx under the federal *Food and Drug Regulations* when Rock was still in office. Counsel for Merck Frosst brought a motion to disqualify Rock and his law firm – Sutts, Strosberg – from acting in the matter.

The court accepted that Rock should be disqualified from further acting in the class action as Rock had held a 'substantial responsibility' within the meaning of Rule 6.05(5), even though there was uncontradicted evidence that confidentiality screens were in place between the Minister's office, his staff and those responsible for the regulatory approval of drugs at Health Canada. The court concluded that it was inappropriate for a former Minister to cross-examine officials of his former department or to take an adversarial position against Health Canada. The court (at [19]) created what it referred to as a public interest conflict rule to describe the concept of divided loyalties at play in this case:

> Even apart from any perception of divided loyalties, I believe that rule 6.05(5) reflects a policy that public confidence in the integrity of governmental institutions and the courts would suffer if the former holders of public officers [sic] were permitted to represent parties in private litigation over matters for which the officers had previously had a substantial public responsibility. This would reflect a public interest conflict in the sense used in the cases I have mentioned above and, as such, could not be waived.

While the case can be distinguished as a unique interpretation of the applicable conflict of interest rules by a well-informed plaintiff, it does nevertheless illustrate some of the problems associated with interpreting a code of professional conduct in a public interest context. As the courts had never accepted the existence of a public interest conflict before as a category of professional conflict of interest, it does confirm the extent to which the courts will go to deal with the appearance of a conflict of interest in the government context. The court seemed concerned about maintaining public confidence in the system of justice and reaching a just result on the basis of sound public policy. It had been established that Mr Rock had never in fact been privy to any confidential information about the case, but the plaintiffs were able to argue successfully that there was a perception that he did in fact have special access or influence.

As this case amply demonstrates, it is not always possible to identify with clarity, and in advance, what the public interest will require in any particular case. This should not be fatal to still using the public interest as a substantive and ethical standard to guide the conduct of government lawyers. Government lawyers are used to making judgments in cases involving unique, sensitive and complex public policy arguments and balancing a wide variety of interests that coincide and diverge. They still rely on legal precedent, and they operate within a democratic context in which constitutional and administrative law are always at the forefront of their decision-making. There are other checks and balances in the system, especially in the bureaucratic hierarchy, which also help to define the boundaries of permissible activity. There are also other safety nets. Government lawyers usually follow a code on values and ethics as a term and condition of employment; they must swear or affirm oaths of allegiance upon their appointment as public servants; they are subject to policies on the protection of government-held information; and they have duties imposed by statute for the safeguarding of government assets. These related policy and statutory requirements help to further define the public interest context for the interpretation of public service values, constraints and obligations. The connection to public service obligations is important for the government lawyer as this attachment underscores the importance of understanding the government's operational context and maintaining the public's trust while providing service to the government as a client. As an example, a values and ethics code enhances the government lawyer's appreciation of the role the public service plays within the Canadian democracy and how public servants help Ministers serve the public interest by observing the duty of loyalty and providing candid advice.

Hutchinson (2006: 191) makes the case that law schools must shoulder some of the blame for some of the institutional lacunae in the training for lawyers, which necessarily includes those lawyers acting for government:

> If there is to be some substantial progress in overcoming these obstacles, changes will be required not only in the legal profession but also in the way legal education is carried out. Law schools and the professoriate must accept their share of the blame for the profession's continuing state of affairs. One obvious place to start is the dismal performance of law schools in taking legal ethics and professional responsibility seriously ...

This concern is relevant to government lawyers as they need to be equipped to understand how to obtain instructions in an institutional client setting and, secondly, to undertake the delicate balancing of competing societal interests in carrying out their responsibilities in the public interest.

The second caution about bringing government lawyers under the jurisdiction of law societies relates to whether they are the most appropriate institution to take responsibility for the regulation of government lawyers. Often unfamiliar with the operational needs of government agencies, and the context in which legal representation and advisory services are provided, law societies may be ill-equipped to discuss the myriad challenges faced by government lawyers. Comparing and contrasting private sector and government lawyers does not do justice to either side. Government lawyers will often risk falling short of meeting objectives in codes of professional conduct because the standards are not articulated in a fashion that makes it easy to interpret and apply in their operational context. The rationale for making such comparisons is flawed because the roles of lawyer and client officials are defined differently in the government context. Secondly, complaints can be brought more easily against government lawyers for tactical or vindictive reasons and for political or improper motives, thus placing a chill on public sector lawyer representation. By using the adversarial model for private sector lawyers as the basis on which the conduct of government lawyers is to be evaluated, this approach often prevents any meaningful discussion on alleged ethical failures and good professional conduct.

There are other options to consider as alternatives to the traditional law society model for the purpose of monitoring the ethical conduct of government lawyers. One additional support is to use a public interest concept for guidance in ethical matters and to reduce the standard to a series of brief principles that are easy to interpret and apply. Government can put a framework in place to ensure that professional standards, supported by statements of mission and values and codes of professional conduct, if appropriate, are respected and that disciplinary and corrective standards are properly applied. The Minister of Justice and Attorney General of Canada have taken steps in this direction already. The federal

Department of Justice embodies the concept of the public interest in its Statement of Mission of Values:[11]

> The Mission of the Department of Justice is to:
>
> - *support the Minister of Justice in working to ensure that Canada is a just and law-abiding society with an accessible, efficient and fair system of justice;*
> - provide high-quality legal services and counsel to the government and to client departments and agencies; and
> - promote respect for rights and freedoms, the law and the Constitution.
>
> ***Values***
>
> People: *The Department's strength comes from all members of the organization, who are committed to working together on the basis of mutual trust, support and respect.*
>
> Integrity and fairness: *As public servants supporting the Minister of Justice and Attorney General, we are committed to respecting and obeying the law and upholding the highest standards of integrity and fairness.*
>
> Service: *We aim for excellence and constructive contributions in serving our Minister, the government and our clients.*
>
> *The Department is committed to delivering high quality legal advisory, litigation, and legislative and regulatory drafting services as demonstrated by timeliness, responsiveness and usefulness in accordance with established service standards.*

In the *Krieger* case mentioned earlier, the employer, which was the provincial Attorney General in that instance, took action when a provincial Crown prosecutor was disciplined for his failure to make proper disclosure to defence counsel. This step requires positive, constructive action on the part of an employer to not only impose ethical standards but to also ensure that government lawyers live up to those standards. Therefore, it is arguable that a government department is capable of managing ethical conduct and safeguarding client interests on its own terms. *Krieger* demonstrates that this is achievable as his manager took steps to investigate and follow up on defence counsel's complaint about improper disclosure.

Secondly, independent offices can be established within government to monitor and regulate professional entities and their members. This exists already in the Province of Quebec, where a professional body regulates a number of professional

11 Available at: http://www.justice.gc.ca/eng/dept-min/mandat.html.

associations (*Professional Code* S.Q. 1973: c. 26).[12] Thirdly, an office can be established within the bureaucratic hierarchy for the purpose of investigating alleged breaches of codes of professional conduct. This is the model followed in the United States Department of Justice. The Office of Professional Responsibility is an office within the United States Department of Justice that investigates complaints made against federal lawyers.[13]

The establishment of a professional ideology for government lawyers needs to begin at an earlier stage in their career and evolve over time. Andrew Francis (2005: 175–6) advocates a similar approach:

> I argue that the increasing variety of workplace arenas within which discreet ethical choices confront lawyers means that fragmentation within the legal profession is exacerbated. Such changes represent a fundamental challenge to the ability (and structural capacity of legal professional associations to exercise regulatory (and representative) authority for a diverse profession. Despite the sustained critiques of the profession's claims to hold common ethical ideals, existing professional associations continue to espouse the existence of the 'core values' of the profession, and claim 'an inherent ethical commitment' and 'deep commitment to standards' across the profession. While such 'core values' may survive at a symbolic level, their role as starting point for the formulation of detailed rules of professional conduct may become more difficult to sustain as the discrete arenas which help shape ethical norms and form the context of regulation become increasingly diverse.
>
> Professional control will still be exercised, but may now be employed by actors, firms and sectors on an individual and contingent basis alongside a reduced role for the Law Society. In such a scenario the effectiveness of a uniform detailed regulatory code implemented and policed by a single professional association (along current lines) may be called into question. Nor is it possible in discussing the dilemmas of professional legal ethics to speak of a single business context as a site of socialisation for ethical norms.

Experience has shown in recent years that if there is misconduct that affects society at large, particularly with respect to confidence in established public and private institutions, special interest entities such as securities regulators are not hesitant to step in and establish requirements for the legal profession if others, including law societies, do not do so. In the case of the passage of the United

12 There are approximately 38 different professions that come under a public system of regulation by the Office des Professions with respect to admission, training and standards of discipline and competence.

13 See the Office's website at: http://www.justice.gov/opr.

States *Sarbanes Oxley Act* of 2002[14] that resulted from the collapse of Enron and the financial scandals that ensued, the American Securities Exchange Commission imposed a rule, Rule 307, to establish minimum standards of conduct for lawyers and reporting requirements for fraud and other misconduct. The professional Bar associations and law societies reacted to these changes. The American Bar Association *Model Rules of Professional Conduct* and the Law Society of Upper Canada *Rules of Professional Conduct* in Ontario, Canada were eventually changed to include 'reporting up' requirements within organisations as a follow-up to the passage of Rule 307 (Law Society of Upper Canada 2004).

Basic Principles for Government Lawyers

There are some basic principles that assist government lawyers in understanding how to practise their craft. There is first and foremost an understanding that the lawyer is serving the state as a whole as opposed to any one individual. Consequently, the word 'client' does little to assist a government lawyer in deciding how to advance the government's legal interests.

Secondly, there is a noticeable shift in approach as to how civil litigation cases are handled. A government lawyer will normally assess if there is a reasonable argument to be made in a litigation matter and consider conceding the case if that possibility does not exist. In other words, a concession is not perceived to be a failure. While public sector litigation does allow for advocating a strong argument on behalf of the government, it is also built on the development of a consistent, coherent and principled legal position that speaks to the broad public policy needs of government. A private sector lawyer, on the other hand, will want to advance a client's interests in a more open-ended manner and then let the courts draw the boundaries around what is an acceptable result.

Thirdly, there is no ownership in a file, in an argument or in a public official. Options are assessed according to what is the best case to be put forward and not on the basis of an individual reward. Lastly, the arguments are developed after a careful weighing of all of the known interests occurs. It is also important to respect due process, the Constitution and the principle of fairness. Hutchinson (2008: 121) summarises the elements of this role in the following terms:

> Accordingly, from a democratic perspective, it can be argued that whether it is the government generally or the public interest at large that is to be served by government lawyers, there is no compelling reason why the government lawyer's view as to what to do should take precedence over the view of elected officials and/or political superiors. Of course, government lawyers have a significant contribution to make in debates within government about how to determine

---

14 Section 307 provides for the promulgation by the Securities and Exchange Commission of 'minimum standards of professional conduct for attorneys appearing in practice before the commission'.

> what the public interest demands; they often have the training, experience, and knowledge to help develop a nuanced and sophisticated approach to identifying the public interest and crafting a range of practical strategies for its realization in difficult circumstances.

As a general matter, a public interest standard can inspire government practitioners to practise law in a different manner without completely discarding those tenets of the legal profession that are basic for every private practitioner. There are overarching principles that apply to public life even though they may sometimes apply differently in a legal advisory or litigation setting. The following is not an exhaustive list for government practitioners but it does provide an indication of some possibilities for consideration:

- a recognition that the public interest is bigger than one individual and their needs and an understanding that self-interest cannot prevail over a public one;
- an acknowledgement that public confidence in the administration of justice is important;
- the importance of the rule of law to society generally, and to the legal profession, especially with respect to maintaining the integrity of the constitutional structure (executive, judiciary, legislature);
- the importance of a free and democratic society; and
- the existence of a neutral, impartial public service.

There are also some more specific indicators that help to define the boundaries of the ethical components of a public interest standard for government practitioners. As the principles for criminal law practitioners are better known, and are discussed above, the following list focusses predominantly on civil practice:

- government lawyering is a profession with specific professional obligations that involve the public interest as a major component of the work;
- with respect to civil legal advisory services, the need to promote compliance with the law and to provide a well-reasoned, impartial analysis which considers all the relevant views and which is based on facts, if a case is fact-driven, and a review of the law, including any contrary authority;
- to promote independence and seek external legal support where conflicts of interest exist or where competency is a limitation on the quality of advice;
- with respect to civil advocacy, the need to first consider if an argument is contrary to the public interest and to avoid one-sided arguments;
- with respect to criminal advocacy, to seek justice for the state in a fair proceeding, in light of any exculpatory evidence;
- the proper identification in legal work for the government of all interests and the need to understand how to balance them;
- the need to consider if technical legal arguments will defeat the overall

advancement of, or resolution of, the case;

- the need to consider if there is a reasonable argument to be made and, if not, to be prepared to concede (or offer no evidence);
- to avoid ownership in a matter, which can result in tunnel vision and single-mindedness;
- to avoid one-sided and results-driven legal advice and advocacy which undermines the effectiveness of the principles of objectivity, independence and neutrality;
- to consider moral and ethical considerations as part of providing legal services if they are relevant to providing candid and honest legal advice and will help clarify the public interest;
- to maintain good ethical conduct even when it does not make sense to others to do so and to be accountable for a failure to do so (for example, recognise and discuss conflicts of interest between public service obligations and other professional obligations, including tensions with an employer; to provide candid advice by being prepared to say 'yes' as well as 'no').

Some jurisdictions have developed guidelines that are tailored to the needs of government lawyers. This type of thoughtful insight will help to advance the understanding of government lawyers about the nature of public work and their professional obligations. One such example is the document drafted by 19 former members of the Office of Legal Counsel in the United States Department of Justice. These lawyers have developed the *Principles to Guide the Office of Legal Counsel* to provide guidance on the overall mission of the Office of Legal Counsel and the duty of government lawyers who serve there (American Constitution Society for Law and Policy 2006: 1348). This document, which outlines 10 principles, was drafted in response to the publicity surrounding the 'Torture Memos' in order to follow up on the lessons learned from the experience of working in the Office of Legal Counsel. A summary of the principles articulated in this document has been provided by Michelle Querijero (2010: 268):

> OLC [Office of Legal Counsel] provides the legal expertise necessary to ensure the lawfulness of presidential and executive branch action, including contemplated action that raises close and difficult questions of law. To fulfill this function appropriately, OLC must provide advice based on its best understanding of what the law requires. OLC should not simply provide an advocate's best defense of contemplated action that OLC is best viewed as unlawful. To do so would deprive the President and other executive branch decision makers of critical information and, worse, mislead them regarding the legality of contemplated action. OLC's tradition of principled legal analysis and adherence to the rule of law thus is constitutionally grounded and also best serves the interests of both the public and the presidency, even though OLC at times will determine that the law precludes an action that a President strongly desires to take.

Conclusion

The public interest concept highlights the need for government lawyers to look beyond the immediate needs of one interest group, one individual or organisation to the public good. The Attorney General helps to set the tone and provide the framework within which the practice of law can occur in a credible and meaningful way. The content of the public interest obligation changes over time; it is a work in progress. Vigorous debate can ensure that the nuances of the public interest standard are debated and clarified, especially what falls 'within the law' and what is considered to be 'in the government's best interests'. Awareness of the need to serve the public interest through training and express guidance encourages government lawyers to understand and debate where those boundaries fall. The differences between criminal and civil legal roles should not detract from the overall principles at stake.

A government lawyer owes ethical obligations to the government of the day as a public servant and ultimately, subject to any conflicting duties, must take into account the impact of government action on the public. As a minimum, this means that the public servant must uphold the law and respect the rule of law. The ethical components of this obligation – honesty, candour, integrity, duty of confidentiality – provide guideposts for individual conduct.

In his review of public service ethics and values, which is referred to earlier in this chapter, Tait (1997) emphasised the importance of the concept of public interest to public servants. He cautioned that importing new values into the public service and replacing old values with them would be problematic. In particular, he noted the practice of using the words 'customer' and 'client' to promote the notions of quality service and customer satisfaction, thereby encouraging a business orientation to the public service. While not dismissing this practice out of hand, he noted that these notions had to evolve, and thinking about how to use them had to mature to ensure that the notion of public service was still a prime motivator for public servants. He observed (at 548–9) as follows:

> the duties of public service lawyers are more relevant and significant than I knew. The higher duty of public service lawyers is to the law and the Constitution. Performing this duty broadly and effectively provides timely reminders to government of factors that are essential to good governance in a parliamentary democracy. At times of stress, understanding the most fundamental principles is the key to avoiding confusion and error.

In this regard, it is equally important for Canadian government lawyers to preserve the notion of the public interest as a key component in their practice and to be guided by it under the aegis of the Minister of Justice and Attorney General.

References

American Bar Association. 2007. *Model Rules of Professional Conduct*. Chicago: American Bar Association.

American Constitution Society for Law and Policy. 2006. Guidelines for the President's Legal Advisors. *Indiana Law Journal* [Online]. Volume 81, 1345. Available at: http://www.acslaw.org/files/Microsoft%20Word%20-%2011_Johnsen_OLC.pdf.

American Law Institute. 2000. *Restatement of the Law, The Law Governing Lawyers*. 3rd edition. St. Paul, MN: American Law Institute.

BBC News. 2005. Wilmshurst Resignation Letter [Online, 24 March]. Available at: http://news.bbc.co.uk/2/hi/uk_news/politics/4377605.stm [accessed: 18 February 2013].

Berenson, S. 2000. Public Lawyers, Private Values: Can, Should and Will Government Lawyers Serve the Public Interest? *Boston College Law Review*. Volume 41(4), 790–91.

Canadian Bar Association. 2009. *Code of Professional Conduct*. Ottawa: Canadian Bar Association.

Collins, D. 2010. Address at Annual Australasian Law Teachers Association Conference, University of Auckland, New Zealand, 6 July 2010.

Dodek, A. 2010. Lawyering at the Intersection of Public Law and Legal Ethics Government Lawyers as Custodians of the Rule of Law. *Dalhousie Law Journal*. Volume 33, 1.

Edwards J.Ll.J. 1984. *The Attorney General, Politics and the Public Interest*. London: Sweet & Maxwell.

Federal Bar Association. 1990. *Model Rules of Professional Conduct for Federal Lawyers*. Washington, DC: Federal Bar Association.

Federal Prosecution Service. 2000. *Federal Prosecution Service Deskbook*. Ottawa: Department of Justice.

Francis, A.M. 2005. Legal Ethics, the Marketplace and the Fragmentation of Legal Professionalism. *International Journal of the Legal Profession*. Volume 12(5), 175–6.

Hutchinson, A.C. 2006. *Legal Ethics and Professional Responsibility*. 2nd edition. Toronto: Irwin Law.

Hutchinson, A.C. 2008. 'In the Public Interest': The Responsibilities and Rights of Government Lawyers. *Osgoode Hall Law Journal*. Volume 46, 105.

Iraq Inquiry. 2010. *Evidence* [Online]. Available at: http://www.iraqinquiry.org.uk/transcripts/oralevidence-bydate/100126.aspx [accessed: 18 February 2013].

Law Society of Alberta. 2012. *Code of Professional Conduct* [Online]. Available at: http://www.lawsociety.ab.ca [accessed: 18 February 2013].

Law Society of Upper Canada. 2004. *Amendment History, Amendments to Rules 2.02 and 2.03 re: Role of Lawyers in Corporate Governance, as approved by Convocation*. Available at: http://www.lsuc.on.ca/with.aspx?id=672 [accessed: 18 February 2013].

Law Society of Upper Canada. 2012. *Rules of Professional Conduct* [Online]. Available at: http://www.lsuc.on.ca/with.aspx?id=671 [accessed: 18 February 2013].

MacNair, D. 2006. In the Name of the Public Good: 'Public Interest' as a Legal Standard. *Canadian Criminal Law Review*. Volume 10, 184–5.

Notes. 2002. Rethinking the Professional Responsibilities of Federal Agency Lawyers. *Harvard Law Review*. Volume 115, 1170.

Public Safety Canada. 2013. *What We Do* [Online]. Available at: http://www.publicsafety.gc.ca/abt/wwd/index-eng.aspx [accessed: 18 February 2013].

Querijero, M. 2010. Without Lawyers: An Ethical View of the Torture Memos. *Georgetown Journal of Legal Ethics*. Volume 23(1), 241.

Stenning, P. 1986. *Appearing for the Crown*. Cowansville, Quebec: Brown Legal Publications.

Sterling, L. and Mackay, H. 2003. Constitutional Recognition of the Role of the Attorney General in Criminal Prosecutions: Krieger v. Law Society of Alberta. *Supreme Court Law Review*. Volume 20(2d), 169.

Sterling, L. and Mackay, H. 2009. The Independence of the Attorney General in the Civil Law Sphere. *Queen's Law Journal*. Volume 34(2), 891.

Tait, J.C. 1997. The Public Service Lawyer, Service to the Client and the Rule of Law. *Commonwealth Law Bulletin*. Volume 23(1–2), 542–9.

Treasury Board of Canada Secretariat. 2011. *Values and Ethics Code for the Public Sector* [Online]. Available at: http://www.tbs-sct.gc.ca/pol/doc-eng.aspx?id=25049 [accessed: 18 February 2013].

Index

Note: hyphenation style: Australia and New Zealand: *Attorney-General/Solicitor-General*
Canada, UK and US: *Attorney General/Solicitor General*

www.ingramcontent.com/pod-product-compliance
Ingram Content Group UK Ltd.
Pitfield, Milton Keynes, MK11 3LW, UK
UKHW022014180926
475701UK00003B/351
9780367600938